FIRST EDITION

# Handwritten Notes

# ECONOMIC DEVELOPMENT AND SCIENCE & TECHNOLOGY (GS-3)

**ARIHANT PUBLICATIONS (INDIA) LIMITED**



卐 **Administrative & Production Offices**

**Regd. Office**

'Ramchhaya' 4577/15, Agarwal Road, Darya Ganj, New Delhi -110002
Tele: 011- 47630600, 43518550

卐 **Head Office**

Kalindi, TP Nagar, Meerut (UP) - 250002
Tel: 0121-7156203, 7156204

卐 **Sales & Support Offices**

Agra, Ahmedabad, Bengaluru, Bareilly, Chennai, Delhi, Guwahati, Hyderabad, Jaipur, Jhansi, Kolkata, Lucknow, Nagpur & Pune.

卐 **PRICE** ₹435.00

**PO No :** TXT-59-T064052-03-25

Published by Arihant Publications (India) Ltd.

For further information about the books published by Arihant, log on to www.arihantbooks.com or e-mail at info@arihantbooks.com

Follow us on    

# Few Words
## to the Budding UPSC Aspirants

**The UPSC Mains Exam is the most crucial stage on your path to becoming a civil servant.** But conquering it isn't a walk in the park - it's a strategic game. You need the right arsenal (effective study materials) and honed tactics (answer writing skills) to succeed. **PULSE Mains Series** equips you for every challenge, a one-stop solution for your Mains preparation.

Forget about sifting through mountains of irrelevant information. **PULSE Mains books** are meticulously organized, packed with dynamic analysis and updated with the latest developments.
These books provide only exam-relevant content and removing the cluttered content available in the market, thus bringing time-optimised notes for the students.

**Following are the salient features of Pulse Mains books:**

- **Comprehensive and Exam-oriented content** covering all relevant topics in depth.
- **Content Enrichment with the help of current examples,** data & facts, case studies and supreme court judgements.
- **Innovative exam-ready frameworks** (PESTEL, Stakeholder, Life-cycle, etc) to meet evolving answer writing demands.
- **Visually appealing presentation by incorporating** flowcharts, timelines, mindmaps, hand-drawn diagrams, tables and maps.
- **Integration of PYQs at the end of each chapter** to align the content with the recent exam trends.
- **Easy for multiple revision of the syllabus** which can help in improving the Mains score.

On behalf of MentorsHut, I would like to express our deepest gratitude to each and every student for placing your trust in Pulse Books. **Thanks to your incredible support, Pulse Books have become best-sellers!**

We are also incredibly thankful to **Arihant Publications** for partnering with us and providing the opportunity to develop the PULSE series for the UPSC Mains examination.

The creation of these masterpiece Mains books wouldn't have been possible without the tireless, combined efforts of the entire MentorsHut family, who dedicated thousands of hours to the project. Our sincere thanks go to **Shadab Ahmad, Vishal Singh, Ashutosh Bansal, Tarun Sahu, Vishal Anand** and **Avinish Kumar** for their exceptional contributions. Their creativity in content presentation, clear handwriting and unwavering support for each other were instrumental in this success.

We also want to express my **deepest gratitude to my daughter, Prisha Mangtani.** While I poured my heart into these books, I know the sacrifices this meant for you. You are truly special!

We at MentorsHut are dedicated to continuous improvement. While we believe Pulse Books represent our best effort, we recognize the possibility of human error. We welcome any suggestions for improvement to the content. Please feel free to share your thoughts at info@mentorshut.com

**Amit Mangtani**
**CA Shalini Wadhwani**
**Founder, MentorsHut**

# Let's Begin Our Journey

## Part-A Economic Development

## Edict-4: Growth and Development



## Edict-5: Mobilisation of Resources



## Part-B Science and Technology



**Note:** The book covers current developments till May 2024. Recent current developments and some peripheral issues will be given as Value Addition Material (Online). Scan the QR Code to get access of current issues.

# 5 MAJOR EDICTS
# ECONOMIC DEVELOPMENT (MAINS)

## Indian Agriculture

- Major Crops - Cropping Patterns in various parts of the country, - Different Types of Irrigation and Irrigation Systems; Storage, Transport, and Marketing of Agricultural Produce and Issues and Related Constraints; E-technology in the aid of farmers.
- Issues related to Direct and Indirect Farm Subsidies and Minimum Support Prices; Public Distribution System - Objectives, Functioning, Limitations, Revamping; Issues of Buffer Stocks and Food Security; Technology Missions; Economics of Animal-Rearing.
- Land Reforms in India.

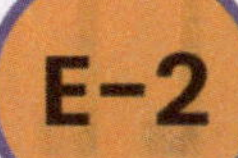


## Industrial Sector

- Food Processing and Related Industries in India- Scope and Significance, Location, Upstream, and Downstream Requirements, Supply Chain Management.
- Effects of Liberalization on the Economy, Changes in Industrial Policy, and their Effects on Industrial Growth.

E-3

## Infrastructure

- Infrastructure: Energy, Ports, Roads, Airports, Railways, etc.
- Investment Models.

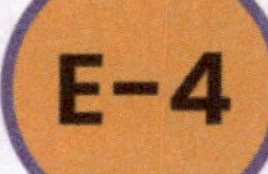


## Growth & Development

- Indian Economy and issues relating to Planning, Mobilization of Resources, Growth, Development and Employment.
- Inclusive Growth and issues arising from it.

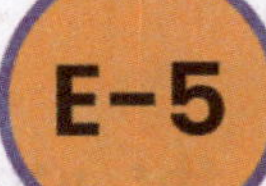


## Mobilisation of Resources

- Government Budgeting

**Edict-1:** Indian Agriculture

CHAPTER 01

# AGRICULTURE – A BIRD'S EYE VIEW

## OVERVIEW

- The share of GVA of Agriculture and Allied activities was 18.3% in 2022-23.

Allied Activities →
- Livestock Sector
- Horticulture
- Fisheries Sector
- Sericulture

- Crop sector is the major contributor to agriculture (>50%) followed by livestock, Forestry and Fishing.
- India's Horticulture production (around 351 million tonnes) in the country for 2022-23 (Rice > wheat > Coarse cereals > Pulses)

Economic Survey 2022-23

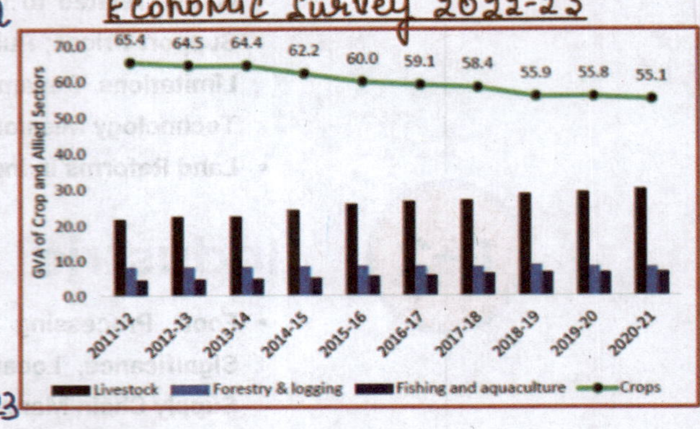


- Indian Agriculture has witnessed various revolutions since independence.

| Name of Revolution | Production | Global Ranking |
|---|---|---|
| Green Revolution | Cereal Production | 1st |
| White Revolution | Milk Production | 1st |
| Blue Revolution | Fisheries Production | 3rd (after china) |
| Gene Revolution | Cotton Production | 2nd (after China) |
| Yellow Revolution | Oilseeds Production | 4th (after US, China, Brazil) |
| Golden Revolution | Horticulture Production | 2nd (after China) |
| Sweet Revolution | Honey & related Products | 8th. |

➩ Agriculture Census: It is a statistical operation for collecting, processing and disseminating data on the structure of agriculture, covering the whole or a significant part of the country.

Findings of 10th Agricultural Census 2015-16:

1. Total number of operational landholding has increased to 146.45 million (2015-16)
2. Total operated area in country has decreased to 157.82 million ha (2015-16)
3. Highest number of operational holders belonged to UP followed by Bihar
4. Rajasthan has the highest operated area followed by Maharashtra.
5. Average size of operational landholding has declined to 1.08 ha (2015-16)
6. Percentage share of female operational landholders increased to 13.96% (2015-16)
7. Small and Marginal farmers (0-2 ha) constitutes 86% of total landholdings.

# Importance of Agriculture

Gunnar Myrdal: It is the agricultural sector that battle for long term economic development will be won or lost

M.S. Swaminathan: If agriculture goes wrong, nothing else will have a chance to go right in India

## Economic Importance

- GDP Contribution (~17%)
- Largest employer (PLFS 2022-23) ≃ 45%
- Poverty reduction
- Inclusive Growth
- Forward/Backward linkages (Dependence of other sectors on Agriculture for Raw materials & consumption)
  - Food Processing Industries (FL)
  - Seed, Fertiliser, Pesticides Industries (BL)
- Agricultural exports (Around 2% of GDP)

## Social Importance

- Food Security (GHI, 2023: 111 Rank)
- Inequality reduction (Income Rural-Urban)
- Nutritional Security (Addressing issue of hidden hunger)
- Urban Migration Reduction → Urban Slum ↓.
- Farmer's Suicide (NCRB 2021: 7% of total suicides is by farmers)

## Environmental Aspect

- Non-Judicious Sustainable use of resources

↓

- Groundwater Depletion
- Soil-Land Degradation
- Air Pollution/Water Pollution

# DECODING INDIAN AGRICULTURE

**Production Phase** → **Post-Production Phase**

**Production Phase**

- Aimed for maximising production of crops. 2 possible strategies
  - Bring more land under cultivation
  - Increasing agricultural productivity

Depends primarily on 4 major factors

1. Physical Factors: Temperature, Rainfall, Soil etc.
2. Institutional Factors: Land Size, Land Tenure etc.
3. Infrastructural Factors: Credit, Insurance, Irrigation etc
4. Technological Factors: Fertilisers, GM Crops, Farm mechanisation etc.

**Post-Production Phase**

Aimed for ensuring remunerative income to farmers against their production.

- ➡ Post-Harvest Management
- ➡ Minimum Support Prices (MSP)
- ➡ Agriculture Markets (APMC)
- ➡ Agriculture Exports.

# EVOLUTION OF AGRICULTURE POLICIES

## Pre-Independence

- British policies responsible for poor state of Indian Agriculture at the time of independence

➡ Exploitative Land Revenue Policies such as Zamindari System, Ryotwari System and Mahalwari System → High rent on the farmers → Farmer is not left with any Surplus capital → No land improvement Programs by farmers

➡ Lack of State Support or any investment on building agricultural infrastructure.

- High rents charged on farmers → losing ownership of land → Emergence of Absentee Landlordism (Rent seeking was more profitable than undertaking agriculture) → Regressive Agrarian Structure.
- Forced Commercialisation of Agriculture → Cultivation of commercial crops for sale in market (Eg- Indigo)
- Partition of India → Rice food producing areas of West Punjab and Sindh went to Pakistan.

## 1950-51 Indian Agriculture on the Eve of Independence

- Stagnant and Backward Agriculture
- Low level of production & productivity (Output per hectare is very low)
- Production is based on primitive tools and techniques (Inefficient use of fertilisers.
- Mainly dependent upon rainfall.
- Predominantly Subsistence Farming (Lack of Capitalist Farming)
- Small and Fragmented Landholdings.

## 1950-Mid 1960s

- Policies mainly focused upon Industrialisation (Nehru-Mahalanobis Strategy) rather than agriculture.
- Land Reforms were adopted - Abolition of Zamindari System, Land Tenancy legislations and Land Ceiling Laws.

## Mid 1960s State of Indian Agriculture

- India was a food importing nation; getting wheat aid under USPL-400 programme → NO Self sufficiency in food grains.
- Drought and Famine combined with Indo-China war in 1962 reoriented the focus from Industrial sector to agriculture sector.
- Late PM Lal Bahadur Shastri gave the famous slogan - 'Jai Jawan, Jai Kisan' which gave impetus to farmers & focussed on Self-Sufficiency in agriculture.
- New Agriculture Strategy (NAS) was adopted that emphasised upon Technological Modernisation & Modernisation of Technology which later resulted into Green Revolution.

## Green Revolution (Discussed ahead in Detail)

## Post 1990s

- LPG reforms led to the Service led growth (Tertiarization of Economy) and therefore credit to agricultural credit declined in Short-term.
- Even today, agriculture is facing an agrarian distress because of various structural problems (Discussed under Vicious Cycle of Indian Agriculture)

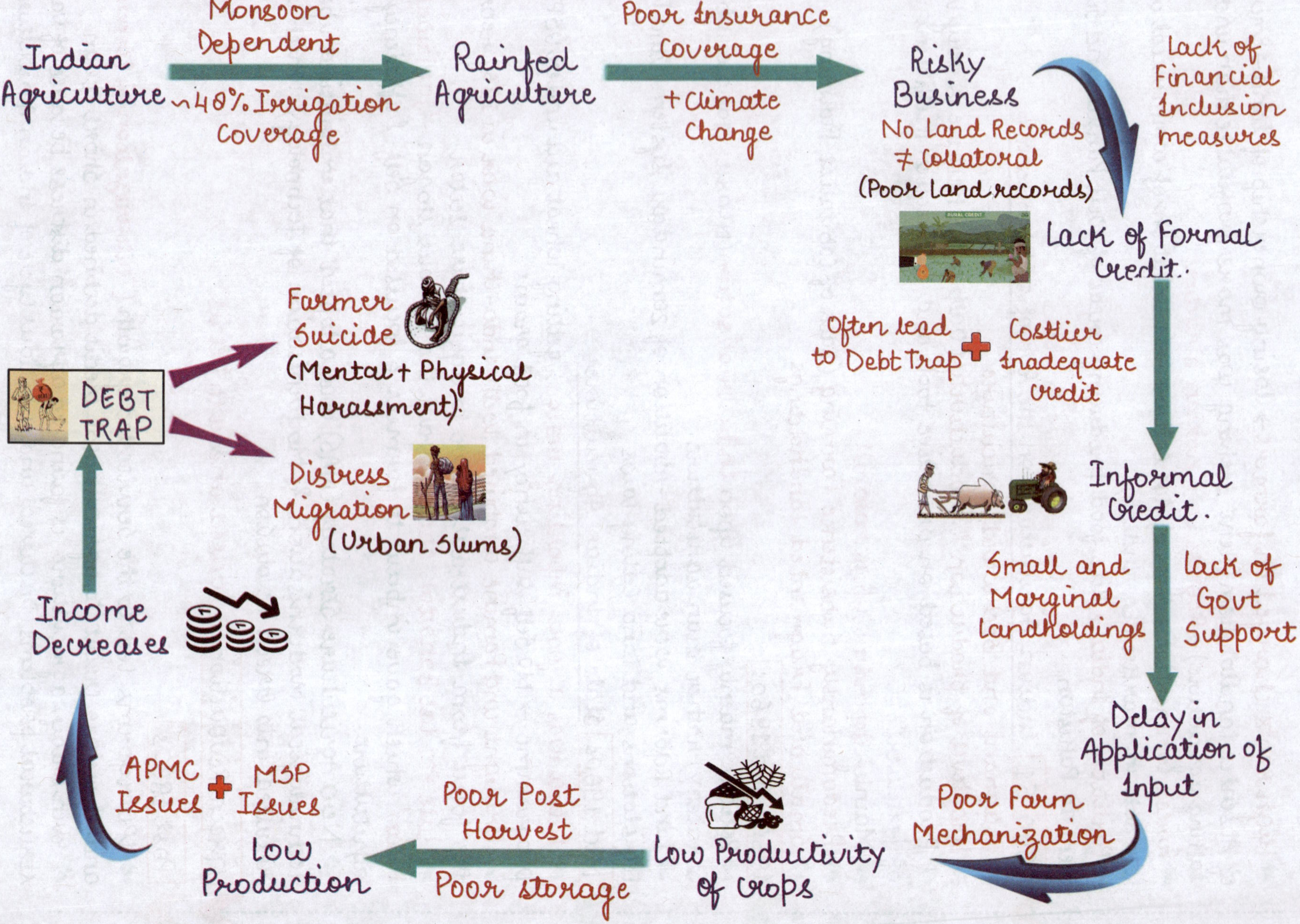
VICIOUS CYCLE OF INDIAN AGRICULTURE
Indian Agriculture
Monsoon Dependent
~40% Irrigation Coverage
Rainfed Agriculture
Poor Insurance Coverage
+ Climate Change
Risky Business
No Land Records ≠ Collatoral
(Poor Land records)
Lack of Financial Inclusion measures
Lack of Formal Credit.
Often lead to Debt Trap + Costlier Inadequate Credit
Informal Credit.
Small and Marginal Landholdings
lack of Govt Support
Delay in Application of Input
Poor Farm Mechanization
Low Productivity of Crops
Poor Post Harvest
Poor storage
Low Production
APMC Issues + MSP Issues
Income Decreases
DEBT TRAP
Farmer Suicide
(Mental + Physical Harassment).
Distress Migration
(Urban Slums)

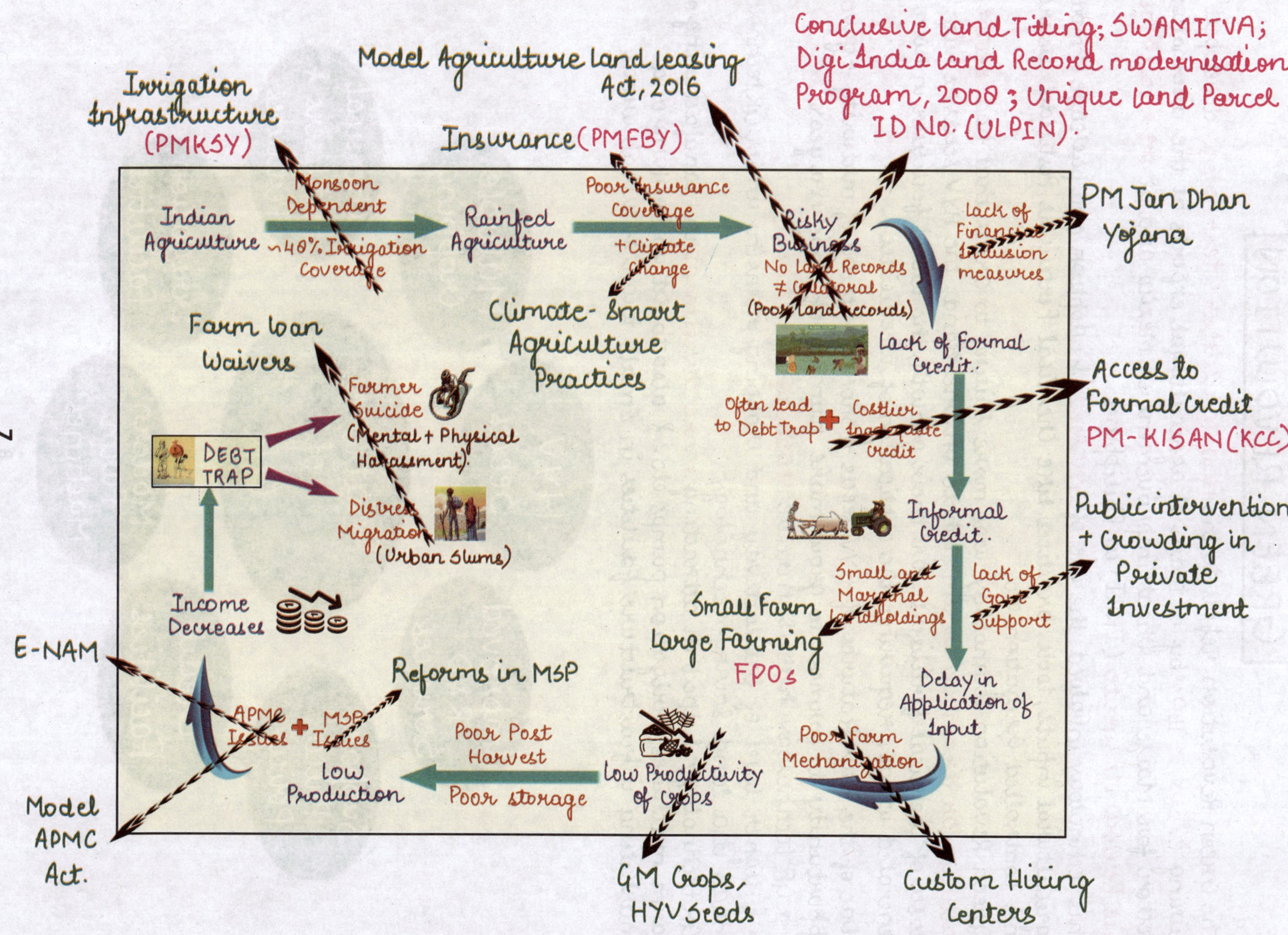
BREAKING THE VICIOUS CYCLE
Conclusive Land Titling; SWAMITVA; Digi India Land Record modernisation Program, 2008; Unique Land Parcel ID No. (ULPIN).
Model Agriculture Land leasing Act, 2016
Irrigation Infrastructure (PMKSY)
Insurance (PMFBY)
Indian Agriculture
Monsoon Dependent
~40% Irrigation Coverage
Rainfed Agriculture
Poor Insurance Coverage
+ Climate Change
Risky Business
No Land Records ≠ Collateral (Poor Land Records)
Lack of Financial Inclusion measures
PM Jan Dhan Yojana
Climate-Smart Agriculture Practices
Farm loan Waivers
Lack of Formal Credit.
Access to Formal Credit
PM-KISAN (KCC)
Often lead to Debt Trap
Costlier Inadequate credit
DEBT TRAP
Farmer Suicide (Mental + Physical Harassment).
Distress Migration (Urban Slums)
Informal Credit.
Public intervention + Crowding in Private Investment
Small and Marginal Landholdings
Lack of Govt Support
Income Decreases
Small Farm Large Farming
FPOs
E-NAM
Reforms in MSP
Delay in Application of Input
APMC Issues
MSP Issues
Poor Post Harvest
Low Production
Poor storage
Low Productivity of Crops
Poor Farm Mechanization
Model APMC Act.
GM Crops, HYV Seeds
Custom Hiring Centers

# GREEN REVOLUTION

- The Green Revolution refers to the new agriculture technology developed during 1950s - 1960s by a team of agricultural experts at the international Sector for Maize and Wheat improvement in Mexico and at International Rice Research Institute (IRRI) in Philippines.
- This technology involved the use of HYV seeds & adoption of a package of modern agricultural inputs, tools, practices like Chemical Fertilisers, Pesticides, assured and controlled irrigation etc.
- Green Revolution technology was more suiting to areas that had irrigation facilities or drainage system. While on one hand, the HYV seeds require high doses of chemical fertilisers for their growth, the use of fertiliser in turn generated weeds, requiring the application of weedicides
- One of the key features of HYV seeds → shorter period of maturity → gave opportunity to farmers to grow more number of crops in a year
    - GR technology helped increase cropping intensity.
    - Higher level of productivity and cropping intensity under GR technology made it a land saving technology
- GR technology helped in attracting more investment in manufacturing of farm machines, irrigation pumps etc. & also to set up banking and marketing infrastructure facilities in small town & rural areas.

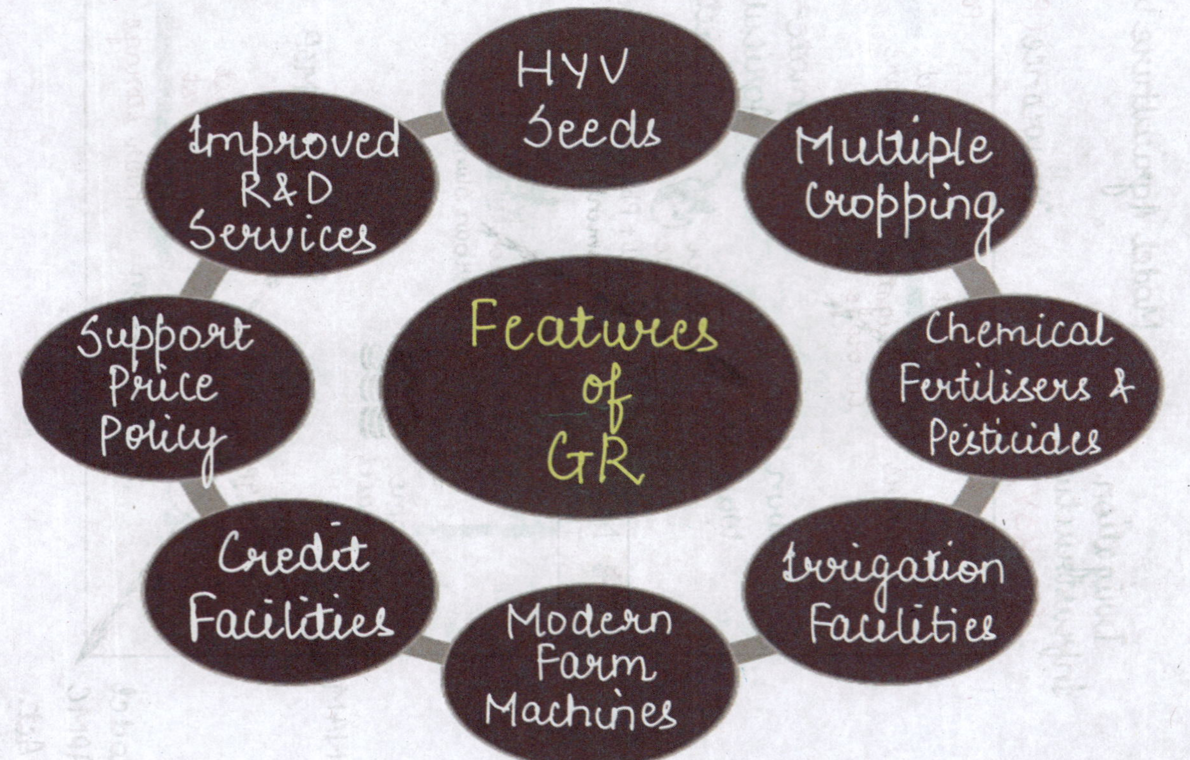

## Critical Analysis of Green Revolution

| Positives | Concerns |
|---|---|
| 1. Increasing the agriculture Production which led to Self-Sufficiency & fulfilling the goal of Food Security.<br>• India Produced 50.82 million tonnes of food grains in 1950-51 which increased to only 70 mT in 1965-66.<br>• After Green Revolution, it increased to 130 mT in 1970 & in 2022-23, India recorded highest ever food grain production of 323 million tonnes.<br>2. India became world's largest Cereal Producer.<br>3. From Food importer to Food Exporter: Nearly 3 million tonnes of food grains were imported under PL-480 schemes in very first year which kept rising & reaching more than 4.5 mT in 1963.<br>• Today India is amongst top 10 wheat exporters & played a crucial role in Russia-Ukraine war.<br>4. Increased cropping intensity & higher productivity → GR technology became a land saving technology.<br>5. Generation of Marketable Surplus → Increased Farmer's income.<br>6. Flow of public and private investment in Agriculture<br>7. Employment generation which resulted in migration of labour to GR areas<br>8. Boost to farm mechanisation & banking sector in rural areas. | 1. Input intensive Agriculture (Costlier input such as HYV seeds, chemical fertiliser etc) → unsustainable for small & marginal farmers → Increased agricultural indebtness.<br>2. Cereal Centric Agriculture → Skewed cropping pattern (rice & wheat) & neglect of coarse cereals like millets & pulses.<br>3. Achieved food security but nutritional security missing (Problem of Hidden Hunger)<br>4. Monoculture cropping pattern → Vulnerable to climate change & pest attacks<br>5. Extinction of Indigenous Varieties of crops: India lost about 1 lakh indigenous rice types during green revolution.<br>6. Inter-regional & intra-regional disparity:<br>• GR has hardly benefitted Eastern Region including Assam, WB, Odisha.<br>• GR requiring costlier inputs benefitted mainly large farmers and not small & marginal farmers.<br>7. Overuse of resources → Environmental Implications<br>• Declining Groundwater table due to predominant cultivation of water-intensive crops such as Rice.<br>• Soil degradation due to resulting monoculture.<br>• Air pollution due to stubble burning. |

Need for Evergreen Revolution was called out by late Dr M.S. Swaminathan, the Father of Green Revolution in India.

- Under the Evergreen Revolution, it is envisaged that productivity must increase, but in ways which are environmentally safe, economically viable & socially sustainable.
- The Evergreen Revolution involves the integration of ecological principles in technology development and dissemination.

Evergreen Revolution = Raising Agricultural Productivity + Agricultural Diversification + Adoption of Sustainable Practices.

# PRODUCTIVITY CHALLENGE

- India recorded the highest ever food grain production of 323 million tonnes in 2022-23 and is among the top producer of several crops such as wheat, rice, pulses, sugarcane and cotton
- It is the highest producer of milk and second highest producer of fruits and vegetables.
- Despite this, India's rice yield as reported in 2016, was 2191 kg/hectare vis-a-vis the global average of 3026 kg/hectare, while the yield of wheat was 2750 kg/ha as against the world average yield of 3289 kg/hectare.
- Although India ranks third in the production of rice, its yield is lower than Brazil, China and US The same trend is observed for pulses, where it is the second highest producer.

## Factors for Low Agricultural Yield

- **Fragmentation of land holdings:** The average size of holdings in India is very low (1.08 hectares) because of which small, scientific techniques cannot be adopted and thus makes agriculture economical
- **Dominance of small and marginal farmers:** Constitute more than 86% of total operational landholdings which prevents capitalist farmings and thus promotes subsistence type of agriculture
- **Poor land record management** also affect the access to formal credit.
- **Inadequate irrigation facilities:** Mostly dependent on rainfall (only 48% irrigation coverage) and very few farmers avail the facility of artificial irrigation
- **Inadequate and costly farm credit** costly despite the efforts of government and the RBI to extend farm credit through formal channels.
  - As per RBI Report 2019, only 40% of small & marginal farmers can access formal credit which affects their ability to purchase inputs.

- Overcrowding in agriculture: Disguised unemployment and low marginal productivity is an issue as too many people (around 45% of the workforce) are directly dependent on farming.
- Unscientific and scientific use of fertilisers and poor focus on organic agriculture leading to input cost and even poor productivity.
  - There has been a decline in soil health & thus affects agricultural productivity.
- Uneven access to modern technology in different parts of the country.
- Seeds: low speed replacement rates, low quality seeds and poor R&D in seed varieties leading to poor crop productivity.
- Pest issues: In India, the crop losses due to insect pests accounts for 15.7%
- Climate Change: leading to vulnerabilities like unusual floods & droughts, untimely rainfall etc.
- Unscientific farming practices: Ex: Growing crops without proper soil testing, over irrigation & excessive use of fertilisers etc.
- Poor financial health of framers: This constraint them from using machines like pesticides sprayers, fencing to protect crops from animals etc.

## Government measures for improving agricultural productivity

- National Mission for Sustainable Agriculture (NMSA): Aimed at promoting sustainable agriculture by climate change adaptation measures, boosting agriculture productivity especially in Rainfed areas focussing on integrated farming, soil health management & synergizing resource conservation.
- National Mission on Agricultural Extension & Technology: Mission aims to disseminate information and knowledge to farming community in local language/dialect regarding agricultural schemes.
- Kisan Credit Card Scheme: Under this, farmers are given short term loans to purchase equipment and for their other expenses also.
- PM Krishi Sinchayi Yojana: 'Har Khet ko pani'; creating sources for assured irrigation and also creative protective irrigation by harnessing rainwater at micro level through 'Jal Sanchay' & 'Jal Sinchan'
- Soil Health Card Scheme: Gives information to farmers on nutrient status of their soil along with the recommendations on appropriate dosage of nutrients to be applied for improving soil health and its fertility
- Sub-Mission on Agricultural Mechanization: It seeks to increase reach of farm mechanization to small and marginal farmers & to the regions where availability of farm power is low.
- PM Fasal Bima Yojana: It provides insurance coverage to farmers in case of destruction of crops so that farmers are encouraged to use high quality agricultural inputs

- Paramparagat Krishi Vikas Yojana (PKVY). PKVY is an initiative to promote organic farming. According to this, farmers will be encouraged to form groups or clusters and take on organic farming methods over large areas in the country.

## Measures to be taken for improving agricultural productivity

- Irrigation Facilities: Canals, tube wells should be constructed to provide better irrigation facilities for the security of crops along with promotion of micro-irrigation facilities.
- Institutional credit should be made available at reasonable cheap rates in rural areas.
  - The land mortgage banks and cooperative credit societies should be strengthened to provide loans to the cultivators.
- Supply of Quality input at proper times and at controlled prices.
- Consolidation of Holdings in the specific time period. Big areas of land which are lying waste, can be reclaimed and made fit for cultivation.
- Land Reforms: Efforts should be made to plug the loopholes in the existing land legislations so that the surplus land may be distributed among the small and marginal farmers.

**PYQs Corner**

*(Write the Answer and Get Free Evaluation)*

1 From being net food importer in 1960s, India has emerged as a net food exporter to the world. Provide reasons. [250 Words] [15 Marks] **[2023]**

Edict-1: Indian Agriculture

CHAPTER 02

# PRODUCTION FACTORS OF AGRICULTURE

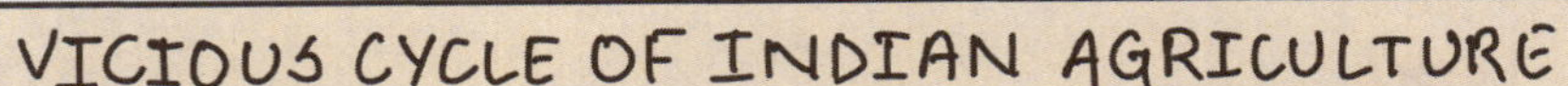


Indian Agriculture → (Monsoon Dependent; ~40% Irrigation Coverage) → Rainfed Agriculture → (Poor Insurance Coverage + Climate Change) → Risky Business

Risky Business → (Lack of Financial Inclusion measures; No Land Records ≠ Collatoral (Poor Land records)) → Lack of Formal Credit.

Lack of Formal Credit → (Often lead to Debt Trap + Costlier inadequate credit) → Informal Credit.

Informal Credit → (Small and Marginal Landholdings; Lack of Govt Support) → Delay in Application of Input

Delay in Application of Input → (Poor Farm Mechanization) → Low Productivity of Crops

Low Productivity of Crops → (Poor Post Harvest; Poor storage) → Low Production

Low Production → (APMC Issues + MSP Issues) → Income Decreases

Income Decreases → DEBT TRAP

DEBT TRAP → Farmer Suicide (Mental + Physical Harassment)

DEBT TRAP → Distress Migration (Urban Slums)

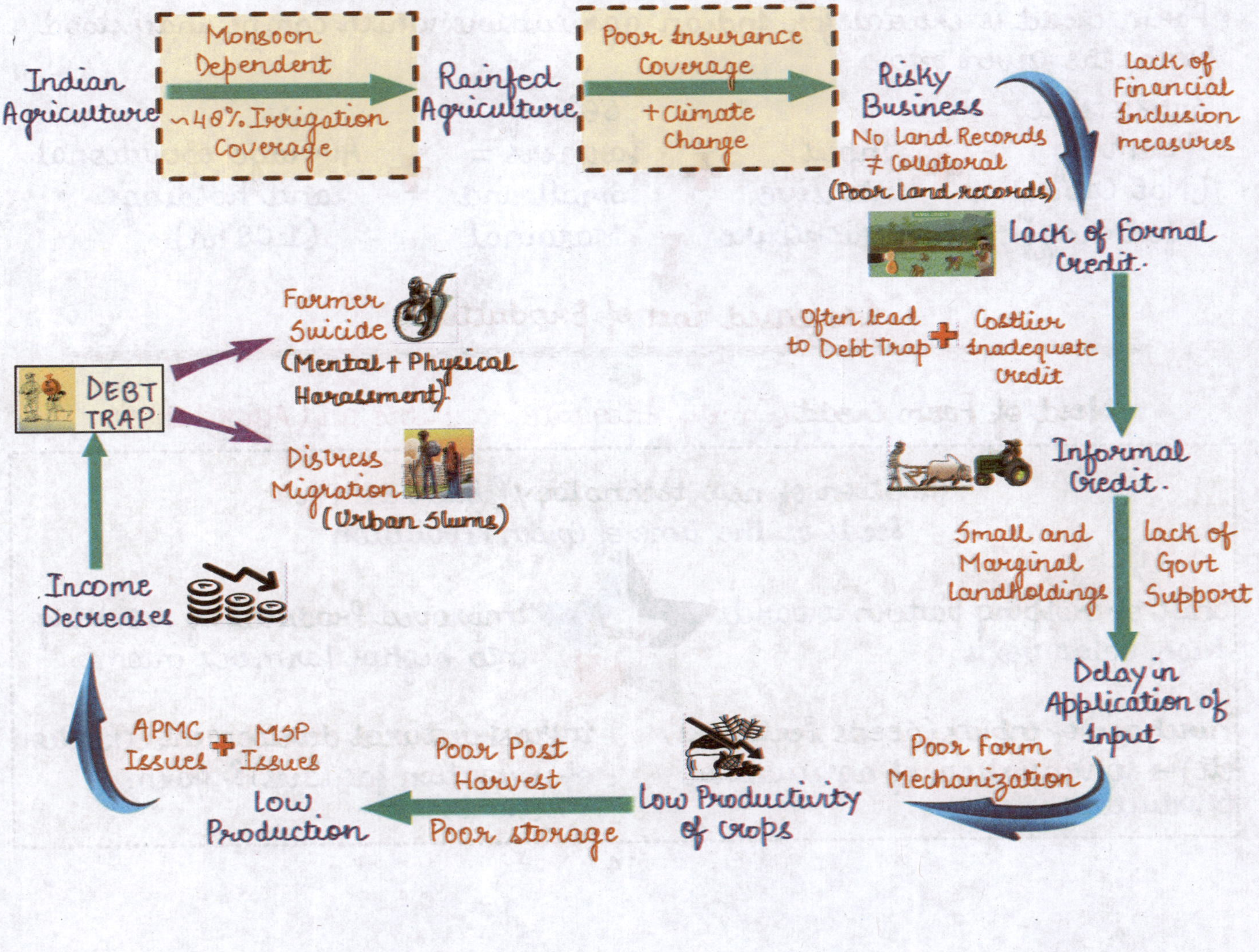

# AGRICULTURAL CREDIT

• Farm credit refers to the loans taken by farmers to meet their cultivation needs which is categorized on the basis of following criteria.

**Sources**

1. Institutional Sources = Formal credit → Timely, Adequate, Affordable, Accessible
   - Commercial banks
   - Cooperative banks
   - Regional Rural banks
   - Micro-Finance Institutions

2. Non-Institutional Sources
   - Moneylenders
   - Relatives
   - Friends/Peers

**Purpose**

- Short-Term
  - Purchase of inputs
- Long-Term
  - Farm modernisation (Adoption of Technology) → Increase in Agriculture productivity.

• Farm credit is crucial for Indian agriculture which can be understood from the given below.

Subsistence Farming (Not Capitalist farming) + Input Intensive Agriculture + 86% of farmers = Small and Marginal + Average operational land holdings (1.08 ha)

↓

Increased Cost of production

↓

**Need of Farm Credit** (Timely, Adequate, Accessible and Affordable)

**Need**

- Adoption of new technology (Such as HYV seeds at the time of Green Revolution
- Improved Productivity resulting into higher farmer's income
- Infrastructural development (Creation of irrigation facilities) & farm mechanization
- Purchase of inputs (Seeds, Fertilisers, etc) → Continuation of agricultural production.
- Shift of cropping pattern towards high value crops.

# Evolution of Farm Credit in India

| Pre-Independence Era | 1951 - 1969 | 1970 - 1990 | 1990 Onwards |
|---|---|---|---|
| • Introduction of Taccavi laws<br>• Introduction of Cooperative institutions | • Boost to the Cooperative Sector<br>• Creation of SBI & increased role of Commercial Banks | • Nationalisation of Commercial Banks<br>• Lead Bank Scheme<br>• Regional Rural Banks | • LPG reforms<br>• Narasimhan Committee<br>• Crisis in early 2000s. |

## Pre-Independence Era

- Farmers relied on the informal sources of credit i.e. moneylenders or landlords for meeting their credit requirements.
- Moneylenders plays multiple roles with respect to the farmer.

Lender → Charges high interest rate

Employer → Poor wages and Exploitative conditions

Crop Buyer → Buys the produce from the farmers at lower prices.

Results into effective high interest rate charged on farmers leading to debt trap for farmers and thus, farmer loses ownership of land.
+ Caste-Based Discrimination = Impoverishment of the peasantry.

Taccavi loans – The history of formal rural credit goes back to 1883 when the British Indian government first introduced Taccavi loans under the land improvement loans Act, 1883 and the Agriculturist loans Act, 1884.

- The Taccavi loans were very small disbursed by government during natural calamities such as famine, drought, flood & other distress conditions provided at lower rate of interest.
- The quantum of loans disbursed was inadequate and was tied up with procedures and formalities which were difficult to be fulfilled and as a result, many farmers were left uncovered under the Taccavi loans.
- Thereafter, the government looked for alternative form of organisation for solving the problem of rural credit. The Cooperative Credit Societies Act, 1904 and a more comprehensive Cooperative Societies Act, 1912 was passed and a provincial cooperative banks were established in almost all the major provinces
- Institutional Source of farm credit started.

• Another step was taken in 1935 when the RBI got established and Section 54 of RBI Act confers power on the RBI to set up an agricultural credit department. Section 17 of the act empower it to provide agricultural credit to state cooperative banks or any other banks engaged in the business of agricultural credit.

• During the period between 1935 and 1950, RBI played a central role in task of building a cooperative credit structure which generally evolved into 2 separate arms - One for short term credit & another for long term credit.

## 1951-69

Report of the All India Rural credit Survey 1954 showed that formal credit institutions provided less than 9% of rural credit & cooperatives accounted for only 5% of rural credit inspite of 50 years of existence.

- The Survey also observed that agricultural credit fell short of right quantity, did not serve the right purpose and failed to go to right people.
- The Survey observed that cooperation has failed but cooperation must succeed.
- The Survey recommended for the well defined role of commercial banks in delivering credit for agriculture in specialised areas. Towards this end, it recommended the establishment of SBI and through the extension of commercial banking facilities to rural & Semi-urban areas (SBI created in 1955).
- The Agricultural Refinance corporation was set up by RBI in 1963 to provide funds by way of refinance

## 1970-1990s Phase of Radical Expansion/Multi-Agency Approach for Rural Credit.

- In 1969 - National credit council noted that while industry accounted for a mere 15% of country's GDP, its share in commercial bank credit was nearly 67%. On the other hand, agriculture that contributed to 50% of GDP, virtually got nothing from the banks.
- Following steps were taken for rapid growth of agriculture credit:

a. Nationalisation of 14 of India's largest Scheduled Commercial banks
b. Adoption of Lead Bank scheme in 1969.
c. Priority Sector lending (PSL) requirement criteria in 1969
d. Banking licensing Policy, which require that for every new branch in already banked area, each bank should open atleast 3 in unbanked rural or Semi-Urban areas.

e. Creation of RRBs in 1976. With the establishment of RRBs, it is described as multi-agency approach of providing credit to rural areas.

f. Another major impetus to agricultural credit was provided by the establishment of NABARD(National Bank for Agricultural & Rural Development) in 1982.

**1992** Self-Help Group-Bank Linkage Programme (SBLP) aimed at harnessing the flexibility of an informal system with the strength and affordability of a formal system. The SHG-BLP model accepted informal groups as clients of banks - both deposit and credit linkage & allowed collateral-free lending to groups.

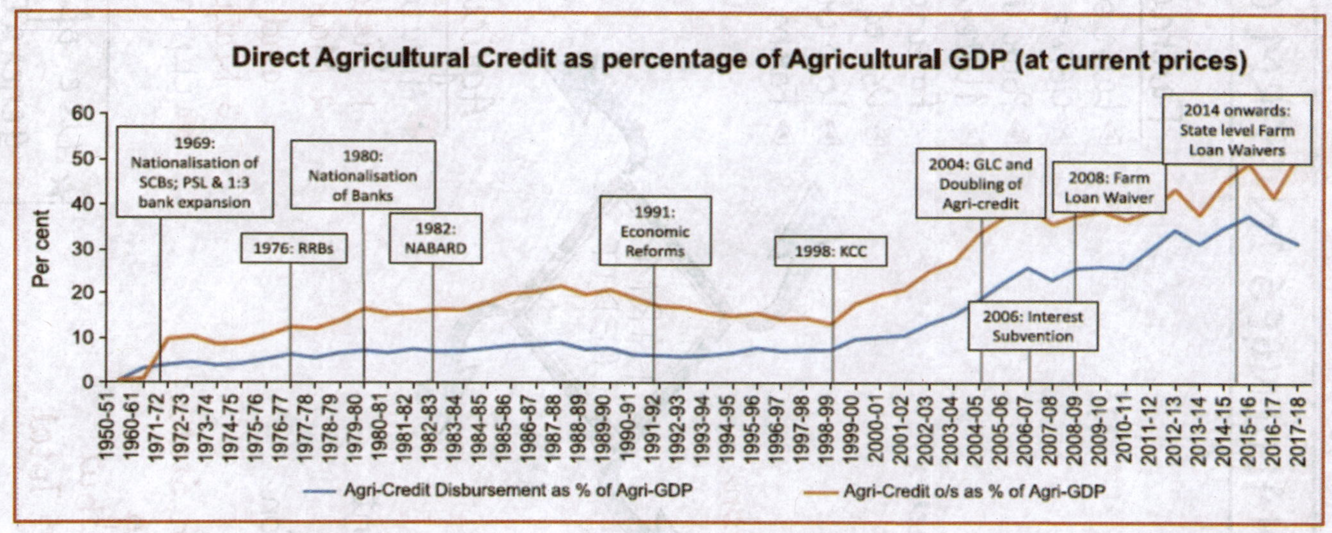


- At present, India has a multi-agency approach to the rural credit comprising of various institutions - Cooperative Banks, Commercial Banks, Regional Rural Banks & Micro-Finance Institutions (MFIs)

## Important Findings of Farm Credit

1. 72% of the credit requirement of agricultural households was met through institutional sources and 28% from non-institutional sources.
2. Scheduled Commercial Banks (70-80%) > co-operative Banks (15%) > RRBs (5%)
3. Crop loans account for almost 90% of the agricultural credit while allied sector gets only 10% of total credit.
4. Proportion of short term loans to crop-related investment credit has changed from 51:49 in year 2000 to 75:25 in the year 2018.

# ISSUES/CHALLENGES IN FARM CREDIT

## Banks/Financial Institutions

- General reluctance to give loans to Agriculture due to High Risks.
- Arrogant/rude behaviour of banking officials.
- Procedural formalities/Complexities
- Inadequate Financial Inclusion.
- High Financial Transaction cost.
- Inadequate credit
- Multiple Agencies - Poor coordination
- Problem of Cooperatives - NPAs

## Farmers

- Lack of Collateral
- 86% = Small/marginal (Lack of Capital)
- Poor insurance coverage
- Illiteracy (Both Educational and Financial.
- Use of credit for consumption
- Low credit Absorption capacity.
- Farm loan waivers (Moral Hazard)

FARM CREDIT

## GOVERNMENT

- Farm loan Waivers
- Poor Land Record Management (Inconclusive land Rights)
- Inadequate Financial Inclusion initiatives
- Regional Disparities (Southern States = More than 1/3rd outstanding Agriculture credit disbursal but account for less than 1/5th of Total Farm Households).

## Agriculture

- Agriculture faces 3 Risks -
  1. Yield Risks
  2. Market Risks (Overproduction and Underproduction)
  3. Nature Risks (Rainfall, Monsoon)
- Climate change.

★ Use of Stakeholder approach in generating dimensions of points.

# REFORM MEASURES (Green Colour)

→ Increased Sub-Targets for Small & Marginal farmers
→ Separate targets for working capital & Term-loan towards Allied activities
→ Sensitization of Banking officials
→ KCC.
→ Bank Correspondant ("Bank Saathi")

Revisiting PSL Guidelines for
→ improving credit offtake & increased allocation of RIDF to central, Eastern & NE states

**ks / Financial Institutions**

- General reluctance to give loans to Agriculture due to High Risks.
- Arrogant / rude behaviour of banking officials.
- Procedural formalities / complexities
- Inadequate Financial Inclusion.
- High Financial Transaction cost.
- Inadequate credit
- Multiple Agencies - Poor coordination
- Problem of Cooperatives - NPAs

**Farmers**

- Lack of Collateral
- 86% = Small/marginal (Lack of Capital)
- Poor insurance coverage
- Illiteracy (Both Educational and Financial).
- Use of credit for consumption
- Low credit Absorption capacity.
- Farm loan waivers (Moral Hazard)

FARM CREDIT

**OVERNMENT**

- Farm loan waivers
- Poor land Record Management (Inconclusive land Rights)
- Inadequate Financial Inclusion initiatives
- Regional Disparities (Southern States = More than 1/3rd outstanding Agriculture credit disbursal but account for less than 1/5th of Total Farm Households).

**Agriculture**

- Agriculture Faces 3 Risks -
  1. Yield Risks
  2. Market Risks (Overproduction and Underproduction)
  3. Nature Risks (Rainfall, Monsoon)
- Climate change.

→ Land leasing Framework
→ Small Farmers Large farmings
→ PMFBY
→ Financial literacy. (PMJDY)
→ Promote FPOs (women specific FPOs)
→ Cooperative Farming

→ Policy change
→ Land Record Management
- SWAMITWA
- National Digital Land Record Modernisation Scheme

→ Awareness drive for land consolidation
→ PMJDY

Budgetary Allocations [≃ 20 Lakh Cr (Budget 2023-24)]

Replace Interest Subvention scheme with DBT.

Collaboration with Agri-Tech Start-ups (Agri-preneurs)

→ Tech Driven Solution
→ Farm mechanization
→ MSP
→ Improved irrigation coverage (PMKSY)

Climate Smart Agriculture

# AGRICULTURAL INSURANCE

- Agricultural Insurance is a type of insurance that protects farmers from financial losses due to natural disasters, such as drought, floods, hail, pest infestations and diseases.
- It can also provide coverage for losses due to market fluctuations and other agricultural risks.
- It is an important part of Safety net for farmers especially in the context of climate change to deal with the impacts of extreme, uncertain and unseasonal weather patterns.

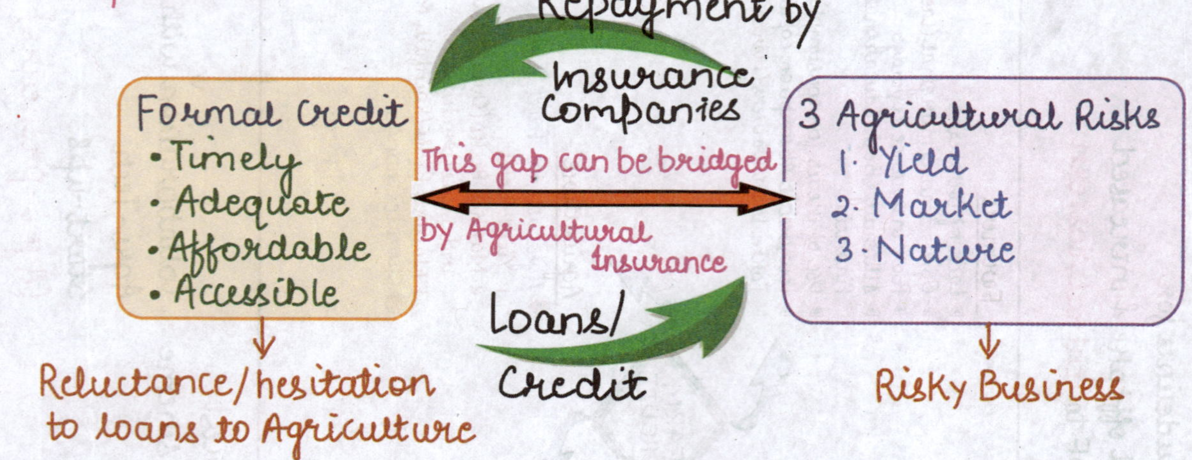


## Rationale of Crop Insurance

- Rainfed agriculture making it risky and prone to crop failure (ES: 2021-22: Around 49% of net sown area is irrigated)
- Financial support to farmers (Crop loss/damage) → reduce farmer's indebtedness.
- Encourage farmers → adopt innovative & modern agricultural practices.
- Enhancing growth & competitiveness of the agriculture sector, besides protecting farmers from production risks.
- Climate Change and crop failures: Protects the crop yield especially in the wake of climate change.
- Stability in income to ensure their continuance in farming → Acts like a tool that allows farmers to manage yield & price risks. ES 2018 estimated income losses of 15-18% (for irrigated farm) & 20-25% (for unirrigated farm) due to negative impacts of climate change
- Availing formal credit and ensuring credit worthiness of farmers
- Provide awareness to help farmers understand the effect of natural calamities and also protect their farms.

# Pradhan Mantri Fasal Bima Yojana

| | |
|---|---|
| Launch | PMFBY is the flagship agriculture insurance scheme launched in 2016 by Ministry of Agriculture which underwent revision in 2020 and referred to as PMFBY 2.0. |
| Aim | • To provide comprehensive insurance cover to farmers against failure of crops & help in stabilizing income of farmers. |
| Predecessors | • Replaced the earlier insurance schemes - National Agricultural Insurance Scheme (NAIS) launched in 1999 and modified NAIS (2010). PMFBY has more farmer friendly provisions than its predecessors.<br>• It reduced the burden of premium on farmers significantly and expanded coverage.<br>• It also promoted use of advanced technologies to estimate losses accurately & accelerate payments to farmers. |
| Coverage of farmers | • Covers loanee farmers (mandatory), non-loanee farmers (On voluntary basis), tenant farmers and sharecroppers.<br>• PMFBY 2.0 made it completely (100%) voluntary for all farmers from the Kharif Season (2020). |
| Crops Coverage | • Covers food crops, oilseed crops, commercial & horticulture crops<br>• Every state has notified crops (major crops) for the Rabi and Kharif Seasons. The premium rates differ across seasons. |
| Premium | • It fixes a uniform premium of 2% of sum insured for all Kharif crops, 1.5% for Rabi crops, & 5% for annual commercial & horticulture crops. Remaining premium burden to be borne equally by the central and state governments.<br>• Revised guidelines in 2020 cap the Centre's premium subsidy under the scheme for premium rates (30% for unirrigated areas and 25% for irrigated areas. |
| Coverage of Risks | • Cover sowing / planting risks, loss to standing crop, post harvest losses and localised calamities.<br>• State governments are given the flexibility to implement PMFBY and given them the option to select any number of additional risk covers/ features |
| Innovative Technology use | • Recommends technology use in agriculture to assess crop losses, Satellite imagery, remote sensing technology, drone etc.<br>Eg: Use of drones to estimate crop losses, mobile phone usage to reduce delays in claim settlements by uploading crop cutting data on apps/ Online. |

| | • Crop Insurance App: Provides for easy enrolment of farmers & facilitate easier reporting of crop loss within 72 hours of occurrence of any event PMFBY Portal: For integration of land records |
|---|---|
| ICE Activities | • Insurance companies are mandated to now spend 0.5% of the total premium collected on Information, Communication and Education (ICE). |

## Challenges in the PMFBY (Stakeholder Approach)

### Insurance Companies

- Delay in Settlement of insurance claims (Sometimes up to 18 months)
- Yield related disputes and rejection of claims.
- High premium charged especially in areas prone to crop failures.
- Non existence of local offices in each tehsil.
- Poor ICE (Information, Communication & Education) activities.
- Low penetration in certain clusters such as certain regions of Maharashtra
- Number of companies decreased from 19 to 11 in Kharif 2021.

### Farmers

- Poor Network Connectivity (Complexity in uploading forms and applications)
- Low Awareness about "Opting Out" from the Scheme.
- Opposition from Farm leaders (Only Insurance company's benefitting - Huge Profit)

### Government

- Revised PMFBY guidelines like centre limiting subsidy upto 30% of premium → increased fiscal burden on states → States withdraw from Scheme (Bihar, Telangana etc)
- Only 15 states have notified Grievance Redressal Committees at both state and district level
- Failure of state Government - Delayed transmission of yield data + Delay in release of their share in premium subsidy by state govt.

## Suggestions to improve the performance of PMFBY

→ Union government should consult with state governments and explore the possibility of replicating the Beed Model in the PMFBY.
- Beed Model was first experimented in Beed district of Maharashtra in 2020

→ Rationalising waivers and service delivery: Loan waiver schemes announced by state governments along with mandatory Aadhar linkage should be rationalised to enable PMFBY of greater coverage

→ Enable timely compensation to farmers.

→ Farmers must be informed before deducting farm insurance premium.

→ Robust assessment of crop loss should be done through capacity building of state governments, involvement of PRIs & farmers in loss assessment

- Incorporation of technology such as remote sensing, drones and online transmission of data.

→ Robust scheme monitoring & grievance redressal mechanism should be in place

→ Disputes related to yields should be addressed by enhancing quality of yield data and making it readily available.

→ State Governments should also be prompt in release of their share of premium subsidy.

## Working of the Beed Model

Beed Model is also called 80-110 Model and balances the interests of Insurance Companies and the Government.

| Claims exceed Premiums | Premiums exceed Claims |
| --- | --- |
| Premiums Collected: INR 100 | Premiums Collected: INR 100 |
| Claims: INR 125 | Claims: INR 60 |
| Claims Paid by Insurance Company: INR 110 | Premium Surplus: INR 40 |
| Amount Paid by the State Government: INR 15 (Bridge Amount) | Premium Surplus retained by Insurance Company: 20%*INR 40 = INR 8 |
| | Premium Surplus returned to the Government: INR 32 |

# IRRIGATION

- It is the artificial application of water to the soil or agricultural field. It is the replacement or supplementation of rainwater with another source of water.

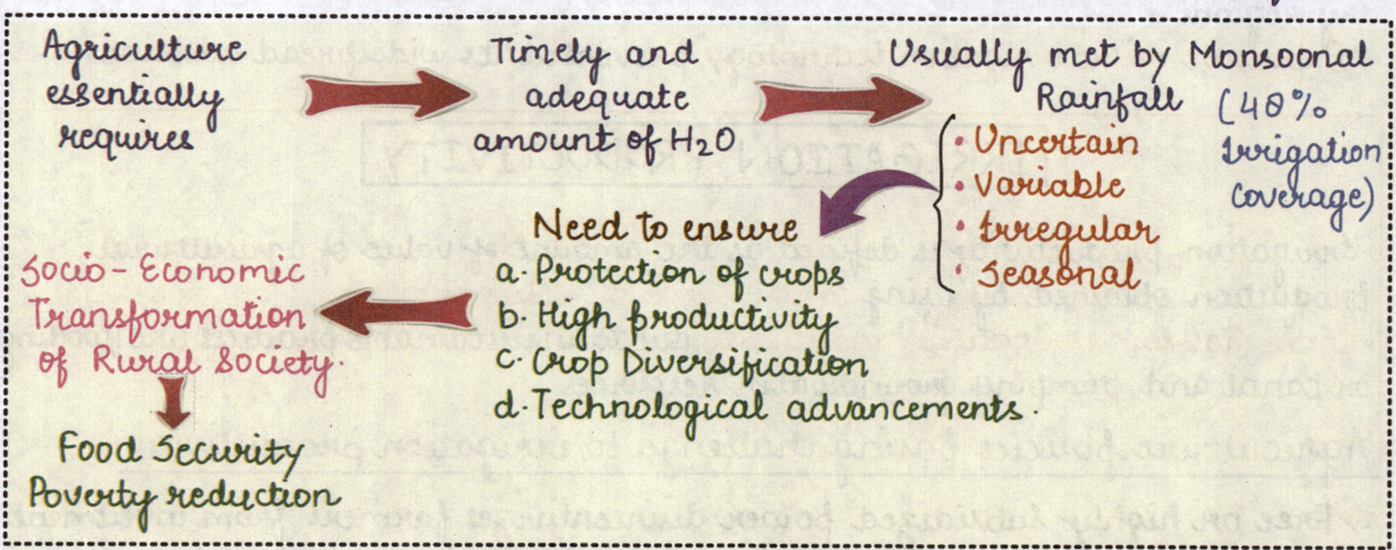


## Sources of Irrigation

**Surface Irrigation** (low water use efficiency than micro-irrigation)

→ Canal Irrigation

→ Tubewell Irrigation

→ Tank Irrigation

**Micro-Irrigation**

→ Drip Irrigation

→ Sprinkler Irrigation

## Challenges faced in the Irrigation

- **Inadequate irrigation coverage:** The share of net irrigated area accounts for about 49% of the total net sown area in the country. (Economic Survey 2021-22)
- **Delay in the completion** of major & medium irrigation sectors.

Reasons: lack of synchronization between project components, delayed tendering & contract management, issues in land acquisition etc

- **Time and cost overruns** due to delay in completion of projects.
- **Regional disparities in irrigation development** with stark gap between Northern region and North-Eastern region.
- **Underutilisation of irrigation potential.**
- **Inter-State Water disputes:** Irrigation is a state subject in India and narrow regional outlook brings inter-state rivalries over distribution of water supply.
- **Heavy dependence on ground water:** Out of net irrigated area, about 60% is irrigated through groundwater. (Economic Survey 2021-22)
- **Heavy dependence on flood irrigation** Since green revolution along with heavy subsidies to farmers has led to overexploitation of groundwater and widespread environmental damage.
- **Decline in water table** in several parts of the country, especially in western dry regions.
- **Expensive micro irrigation technology** prevented its widespread adoption.

## IRRIGATION PRODUCTIVITY

- Irrigation productivity is defined as the amount of value of agricultural production obtained by using unit volume or value of water.
- India has low irrigation productivity due to unsustainable practices like flooding or canal and pumping groundwater resources.

### Agriculture policies posing challenge to irrigation productivity

- **Free or highly subsidized power** disincentivizes farmers from investment in water conserving methods particularly in the country's northwest.
  - Leads to overextraction of groundwater & traditional flooding of fields.
- **Economies of scale and operations** don't allow farmers to adopt new irrigation methods.
  - India has a very small average landholding size of 1.08 hectares (Agri census, 2015-16) and that too is scattered over different places in small parcels
  - This makes individual ownership of irrigation machinery economically viable

- High installation cost of modern irrigation techniques doesn't allow farmers to invest in it.
- Low Income level of farmers: 86% of farmers in India are marginal & Small and earn on an average of Rs 6,426 per month (NSSO 2016 report). This hinders the huge investment needed for mechanization of irrigation.
- Credit procedure for irrigation mechanization is very cumbersome. Also the rate of interest is higher for such loans as compared to crop loans.
- Limitations of Subsidy: Modern irrigation methods like micro-sprinklers require subsidies to the extent of 40-90% of its cost but the current subsidy regime is skewed in favour of urea, Power, MSP subsidy.
- Skewed cropping pattern towards water-intensive crops such as rice & Sugarcane because of high MSP and FRP along with subsidized power even in the water-scarce region of Marathwada, Western Rajasthan etc.
- Low awareness among farmers about benefit of micro-irrigation methods.

• Government has taken various initiatives to maximise irrigation productivity in the country; such as National Water Policy (2012), National Water Mission, PMKSY, Setting up a dedicated "Micro Irrigation Fund" with NABARD etc.

## Futuristic Measures

As per the National Commission for Integrated Water Resources, irrigation sector will consume about 79% of the available water resources by 2050. This calls for focussed attention to promote improved water management practices in irrigation projects.

• The following measures could be taken to solve the challenges faced by irrigation Sector in India:

- Adoption of micro-irrigation Systems Such as Drip Irrigation or Sprinkler irrigation. (Ashok Dalwai Committee)
- Focus on Command Area Development (CAD) approach which leads to water saving, Soil health management and prevents water logging.
- Realignment of cropping patterns based on per unit of applied irrigation water productivity.
- Awareness among farmers through the use of Kisan Vigyan Kendra (KVK) & Kisan Mitra for the maintenance and operation of these new irrigation techniques
- Direct Cash transfer to farmers for irrigation machinery subsidy instead of routing it through companies.
- Small irrigation machinery/implements (individually operated) need to be promoted keeping in view the versatality of various crops, cropping patterns & agriculture operations.

➜ Needed Innovation in custom hiring service or a rental model by the institutionalization of high cost irrigation machinery to reduce cost of operation.

# MICRO-IRRIGATION

- Micro-Irrigation (MI) refers to the techniques such as drip irrigation, sprinkler, rain gun, porous pipe system etc where water is supplied directly to the crops and is considered an innovative water saving technology.
- Micro-irrigation helps to tackle growing water crisis & improving agricultural productivity

➜ In India per capita annual water availability has declined from 5177 cubic metre in 1951 to 1508 $m^3$ by 2014 & is likely to reduce further to 1465 $m^3$ by 2025

➜ As per Central Ground Water Board, around 256 out of 700 districts are either critical or over exploited.

➜ As per CAG report 2021, Groundwater extraction has increased from 58% to 63% between 2004 and 2017, which has exceeded the recharge capacity.

1. High Water use Efficiency (WUE) - It has water use of around 75-90% as compared to the traditional flood irrigation methods, which have WUE of around 35-40%.
   - WUE indicates the ratio between effective water use and actual water withdrawal. It is used to describe how effectively water is delivered to crops & to indicate amount of water wasted at plot, farm, command or system level.
2. Energy Efficiency - It can effectively save power due to less water and thereby, ensures energy consumption savings upto 30.5%.
3. Fertilizer Use Efficiency - Proper mixing of fertilizers and water, control of optimum dosage and direct application of fertilizers to the root zone results in savings of fertiliser consumption upto 20.5%.
4. Increase in Productivity - It increases the crop yield, which would also result in increasing farmer's income.
5. Reduced Irrigation life-cycle Cost.
6. Ecological Benefits: Reduction of water loss due to runoff, evaporation; Aids in soil health management and prevents water logging
7. Less labour requirement and therefore irrigation cost saving
8. Dryland Farming: It will facilitate cultivation in dryland areas, thus correcting agricultural production disparity between various regions of the country.

## Challenges

1. High Initial Cost – The initial set up cost is too high which is not feasible for over 86% of the farmers who are small and marginal.
2. Declining land Holding Size – Another impediment is that the average size of land holdings have halved since 1960s and this declining size of land holdings impact the farm income which is closely associated with the capability of the farmer to adopt expensive micro-irrigation systems.
3. Energy crisis – Power outages, voltage fluctuations and unscheduled interruptions exist across rural and Urban India, which is a major deterrent in the adoption of irrigation systems.
4. Technical Support – There is lack of technical support for maintenance & operation
5. Failure of State government for the ineffective implementation of PMKSY & underutilisation of funds.

- As a consequence, mere 4% of the gross irrigated area is under drip irrigation and 80% of this adoption is concentrated only in few states.

**Pradhan Mantri Krishi Sinchayee Yojana (PMKSY)**

- It was launched in 2015 with a vision to ensure access to some means of protective irrigation to all agricultural farms in the country, to produce 'per drop more crop', thus bringing much desired rural prosperity.
- **The major objectives of PMKSY are:**
    - to achieve convergence of investments in irrigation at the field level
    - to expand cultivable area under assured irrigation
    - to improve on-farm water use efficiency to reduce wastage of water
    - to enhance the adoption of precision-irrigation and other water-saving technologies
    - to enhance recharge of aquifers and introduce sustainable water conservation practices by exploring the feasibility of reusing treated municipal based water for peri-urban agriculture and attract greater private investment in a precision irrigation system.
- **4 Main Components of PMKSY:**
    - **Accelerated Irrigation Benefits Programme (AIBP)** aims to provide financial support for faster completion of major and medium irrigation projects.
    - **Har Khet Ko Pani (HKKP)** aims for the enhancement of physical access on the farm and the expansion of cultivable areas under assured irrigation.
    - **Watershed Development:** It focuses on the development of rainfed areas towards soil and water conservation, regeneration of groundwater, arresting runoff and promoting extension activities related to water harvesting and management.
    - **Per Drop More Crop (PDMC):** To enhance the adoption of precision-irrigation and other water-saving technologies

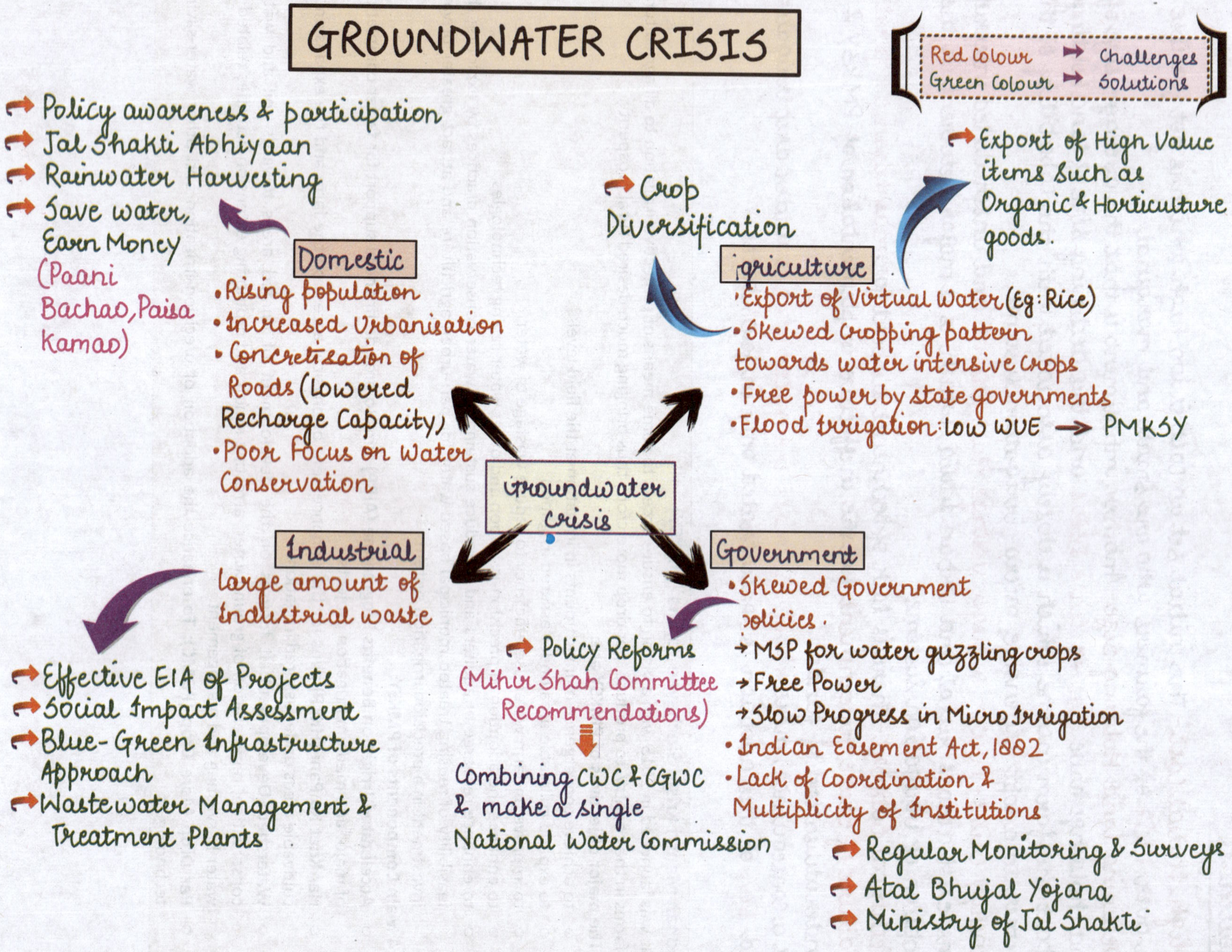

# GROUNDWATER CRISIS

Red colour → Challenges
Green colour → Solutions

Groundwater Crisis

## Domestic
- Rising population
- Increased Urbanisation
- Concretization of Roads (Lowered Recharge Capacity)
- Poor Focus on Water Conservation

Solutions:
- Policy awareness & participation
- Jal Shakti Abhiyaan
- Rainwater Harvesting
- Save water, Earn Money (Paani Bachao, Paisa Kamao)

## Agriculture
- Export of Virtual Water (Eg: Rice)
- Skewed cropping pattern towards water intensive crops
- Free power by state governments
- Flood Irrigation: Low WUE → PMKSY

Solutions:
- Crop Diversification
- Export of High Value items such as Organic & Horticulture goods.

## Industrial
large amount of industrial waste

Solutions:
- Effective EIA of Projects
- Social Impact Assessment
- Blue-Green Infrastructure Approach
- Wastewater Management & Treatment Plants

## Government
- Skewed Government policies.
  - → MSP for water guzzling crops
  - → Free Power
  - → Slow Progress in Micro Irrigation
- Indian Easement Act, 1882
- Lack of Coordination & Multiplicity of Institutions

Solutions:
- Policy Reforms (Mihir Shah Committee Recommendations) ⇓ Combining CWC & CGWC & make a single National Water Commission
- Regular Monitoring & Surveys
- Atal Bhujal Yojana
- Ministry of Jal Shakti

# FERTILISER SECTOR

- Plants require nutrients for their growth which are provided through fertilisers

| Common Fertilisers | Macro-nutrients | Micro-nutrients |
|---|---|---|
| Urea | Nitrogen (N) | Iron (Fe) |
| Diammonium phosphate | Phosphorus (P) | Boron (B) |
| Muriate of Potash (MoP) | Potassium (K) | Manganese (Mn) |
| | | and many more |

**Ideal Ratio**
N:P:K = 4:2:1

## Important Facts

- India is the 3rd largest producer of fertilisers after China and USA.
- India is 2nd largest consumer of fertilisers after China.
- India ranks 2nd in the production of nitrogenous fertilisers and 3rd in phosphatic fertilizers.
- India is the World's largest urea importer with around 8-9 million tonnes per annum mostly from China, Oman, Ukraine and Egypt.
- On an average, around 5 Million tonnes of phosphatic fertilisers are imported to India mostly from China, Morocco, Saudi Arabia, Russia & Jordan
- Potash supplies which is around 4 Million tonnes a year is fully imported from Canada, Russia, Belarus, Jordan etc

## Fertiliser Policy in India

- Excessive reliance on chemical fertilisers (Increased after Green Revolution)
- Promotion of alternative fertilisers (Organic Fertilisers, Bio-fertilisers)

- Government provides fertiliser subsidy but follows different regime for urea and non-urea based fertilisers.
  - Urea → Statutory Notified Price
  - Non-urea → Nutrient-Based Subsidy

### Statutory Notified Price

Market Price ↑ If MP ↑, subsidy ↑se because SP is fixed

Borne by the Government = Subsidy | Urea

Notified Price is the price statutorily notified at which urea is to be sold to the farmers. (This is selling price)

→ In this case, selling price to farmers is fixed while subsidy is variable

### Nutrient-Based Subsidy

Market Price ↑ If MP ↑ses, selling price ↑ses (fixed subsidy)

Non-Urea Fertilisers | Subsidy = Fixed based on the amount of nutrients in a fertiliser.

Selling Price to the Farmers

In this case, selling price to farmers is variable while subsidy is fixed.

**Nutrient Based Subsidy (NBS)**

- It is a fixed rate of subsidy decided on an annual basis & implemented since 2010 by Department of Fertilisers under Ministry of Chemicals & Fertilisers.
- Under NBS, a fixed amount of subsidy is provided for phosphatic and potassic fertilisers depending on its nutrient content (in Rs/Kg) and does not include urea-based fertilisers.
- Given on nutrients - Nitrogen, Phosphate, Potash, Sulphur.
- NBS is available for imported complex fertilisers except Ammonium Sulphate

## Distortions in the Fertilizer Sector

1. India is not Self-Sufficient ⇒ Dependent upon imports.
2. Subjected to international price volatility.
3. High Government Subsidy → Imports; Reliance on Chemical Fertilizers.
   - Fertiliser Subsidy has more than doubled in a short period of 5-6 years. For 2023-24, the Union Budget has estimated fertiliser subsidy at ₹1,75,100 Cr (from 66,468 Crore in 2017-18)
4. Different Subsidy Regime → Imbalanced use of fertilizers (Excess consumption of Urea)
5. Affecting the soil health ⇒ Decreased Productivity.
   N:P:K → 4:2:1 (Ideal)
   N:P:K → 13:5:1 (Distorted at present)
   N:P:K → 34:8:1 (Punjab)
6. Environmental Pollution → Leaching of Nitrates.
7. Violates 'One product one Price System'. Urea is subsidized only for agricultural purposes and not for industrial purposes so there is going to be black marketing that involves corruption and ultimately leakages (not going to target beneficiaries).
8. Subsidy given to the manufacturers on 'Cost plus Basis' ⇒ Discourages the manufacturers to be competitive ⇒ Discouraging domestic production ⇒ Increase in Imports.
9. So much price distortion that ultimately small and marginal farmers are not benefitted.

- The existing system of fertiliser subsidies in India has been prone to leakages, diversion and black market activities.
- According to Economic Survey 2016, the fertiliser sector is highly regulated, which causes a major distortion in the sector. The subsidy which is intended to help small farmers benefits a small proportion of them.

- 24% of the Subsidy is spent on inefficient urea producers.
- Of the remaining, 41% is diverted to non-agricultural uses & abroad and of the remaining, 24 percent is consumed by large farmers.

**Adverse Outcomes**

- Diversion to other sectors of economy
- Black-marketing to nearby countries
- Affects mostly the small farmers
- Inefficiency in fertiliser manufacturing
- High import dependency ---> International price volatility
- Imbalanced use of fertiliser – Environmental impacts
- No-Denial Policy
- High Fertiliser subsidies leading to huge fiscal burden
- Inter-state disparities in fertiliser subsidy
- Negative health impacts

**Reform measures**

- Bring urea under NBS regime
- Use of DBT instead of subsidies to fertiliser manufacturers
- Cap on the total number of subsidised fertiliser bags.
- Self-reliance in the fertiliser production
- Innovations to develop alternative fertilisers
- Promotion of organic fertilisers & bio-fertilisers

**Government Interventions**

- Soil Health Card Scheme
- DBT in Fertilisers: e-Urvarak portal
- Neem coating of Urea
- New Urea Policy, 2015
- PM-PRANAM
- Promotion of organic and zero-budget natural farming
- Liquid nano Urea
- One Nation, One Fertiliser

## PM PRANAM - PROMOTION OF ALTERNATIVE FERTILISERS

- Announced in Budget 2023-24 to reduce the use of chemical fertilisers by incentivising states to adopt alternative fertilisers.
- Encourage the balanced use of fertilisers in conjunction with bio-fertilisers and organic fertiliser which will reduce the subsidy burden on chemical fertilisers.
- There will be no separate budget for the PM-PRANAM scheme. Instead it will be financed by the savings of existing fertiliser subsidies under schemes run by the Department of Fertilisers, Ministry of Chemicals and Fertilisers.
- Centre will provide 50% of the subsidy savings to the states as a grant. Out of the grant, 70% can be used to create assets related to the technological adoption of alternative fertilisers and production units.

According to the Indian Agricultural Statistics Research Institute (IASRI), the consumption of chemical fertilizers in India increased from 13.6 million metric tons (MMT) in 2000-01 to 31.1 MMT in 2019-20, reflecting its importance in ensuring sustainable and efficient agricultural practices for the nation's development.

## PM-PRANAM can help in addressing distortion of fertilisers through following ways

- Encouraging the use of bio-fertilisers, composts and organic manures can reduce environmental pollution, promotes soil fertility and provide a healthier option for farmers and consumers.
- Reduced fiscal burden of fertiliser subsidy: Promoting organic farming & natural inputs through the PM-PRANAM Scheme will help in reducing imports and therefore less dependence on international prices.
- Improved Soil Health through practices like nutrient recycling, crop rotation, cover cropping and organic amendments, resulting in long term benefit for agriculture
- Enhancing nutrient availability and improve nutrient use efficiency, leading to optimized crop growth and yield.
- Enhanced agricultural productivity: By providing support and incentives for organic farming, the scheme can contribute to sustainable & high yield agricultural practices.
- Support Research and Developmental Efforts in the field of organic farming and natural inputs.
    - This includes developing new and improved organic fertilisers, exploring innovative farming techniques and lead to the development of customized solutions, tailored to specific agro-climatic conditions and crop requirements
- Reduced Environmental Pollution: Promotion of sustainable agricultural practices reduce the leaching of harmful chemicals into water bodies, minimizing water pollution and preserving ecological balance
    - CPCB reported that excessive nitrate levels, mainly from agricultural sources, were found in 14% of India's groundwater monitoring levels.

## ONE NATION, ONE FERTILISER

- Ministry of Chemical and Fertilisers announced the implementation of ONOF by introducing a single brand for fertilisers and logo by all the manufacturers under the Centre's fertiliser scheme known as PM Bharatiya Janurvarak Pariyojana
- The single brand name for Urea; DAP, MOP, NPK etc would be Bharat Urea, Bharat DAP, Bharat MOP, Bharat NPK etc. respectively for all fertiliser companies, State Trading Entities (STEs) and Fertiliser Marketing Entities (FMEs)
- Under ONOF, companies are allowed to display their name, brand, logo & other relevant product information only on 1/3rd of space of their bags.
- On the remaining 2/3rd space, the Bharat brand and PMBJY logo have to be shown.

➡ This ONOF scheme aims to address the distortion in the fertiliser sector through the following ways:

i. Standardisation: This will standardise fertilizer brands across nation irrespective of the company that manufactures it.

ii. Affordability: The scheme will ensure quality affordable fertilizers of Bharat brand to farmers.

iii. Single Branding: Competition among companies that push their brands get reduced with this single branding, which will ensure sufficient supply of fertilisers across the country.

iv. Reduced freight charges: A single brand name will help in reduction of freight charges due to stopping of criss-cross movement of fertilizers and thus reducing the transit time.

v. Stopping Urea Diversion for industrial purposes

# FARM MECHANISATION

- Refers to usage of Farm Equipments/Machinery at various stages that replaces Human and Animal labour.
- These machines are designed to improve productivity and efficiency in farming operations, and the industry encompasses both small-scale and large-scale farming equipments.
  - Examples – Tractors, Combine harvesters, irrigation systems, tillers, etc.
- One of the reason for such low productivity is lack of adequate mechanisation in Indian agriculture.

## INDIA

### Status

➡ Low Farm mechanization (≃40-45%) against
- USA ≃ 95%
- Brazil ≃ 75%
- China ≃ 60%

➡ Dominated by usage of Tractors (≃80%)

### Need

➡ Timeliness & precision of operation

➡ Reduced Input cost
(Fertiliser Consumption get reduced by 12.7%)
(Diesel Consumption get reduced by 22%)

➡ Increased productivity ≃ 10%

➡ Reduced work Burden

➡ Sustainable/Optimal use of Resources.

## Challenges Associated

### Demand Side

- Land Fragmentation
  Average Size = 1.08 hectare (Agriculture census 2015-16)
- Greater than 80% Small and Marginal Farmers
- Subsistence Agriculture
- No Collateral to access farm credit for purpose of Machinery
- Ownership of Tractors confined to few states especially Punjab, Haryana
- Export Tractors and import Non-Tractor farm equipment
- Lack of information to guide selection of machinery.

### Supply Side

- Poor R & D in non-Tractor farm equipments
- Little Academia-Industry collaboration
- No specific NIC code for farm equipments
- Shortage of skilled manpower
- Ease of Doing Business
- Competitive disadvantage with respect to China.

## Sub-Mission on Agricultural Mechanisation (SMAM)

- It was launched in the year 2014-15 under the National Mission on Agricultural Extension and Technology.
- Under the scheme, Government of India releases funds for Farm Mechanization like Establishment of Custom Hiring centres, Farm Machinery Bank, High-tech Hubs to different states.

### Objectives of the Scheme

- To increase the reach of farm mechanization to small and marginal farmers and also to increase the reach in regions where availability of farm power is low.
- To promote 'Custom Hiring Centres' to offset the adverse economies of scale arising due to small landholding and high cost of individual ownership.
- To create hubs for hi-tech & high-value farm equipment.
- To create awareness among stakeholders through demonstration and capacity building activities.
- To ensure performance testing and certification at designated testing centers located all over the country.

Advantages of CHC

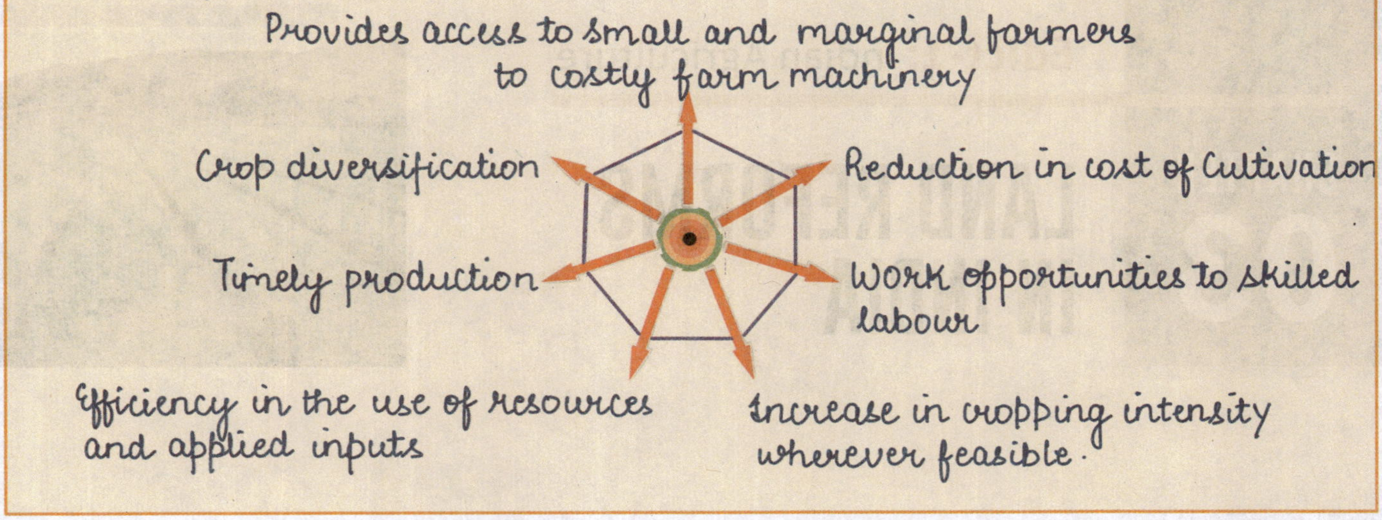

Provides access to small and marginal farmers to costly farm machinery

Reduction in cost of Cultivation

Work opportunities to skilled labour

Increase in cropping intensity wherever feasible.

Efficiency in the use of resources and applied inputs

Timely production

Crop diversification

## PYQs Corner

*(Write the Answer and Get Free Evaluation)*

1. How and to what extent would micro irrigation help in solving India's water crisis? [150 Words] [10 Marks] [2021]Suggest measures to improve water storage and irrigation system to make its judicious use under depleting scenario. [250 Words] [15 Marks] **[2020]**
2. What is water-use efficiency? Describe the role of micro-irrigation in increasing the water-use efficiency.[200 Words] [12.5 Marks] **[2016]**
3. Give the vulnerability of Indian agriculture to vagaries of nature, discuss the need for crop insurance and bring out the salient features of the Pradhan Mantri Fasal Bima Yojana (PMFBY). [200 Words] [12.5 Marks] **[2016]**
4. "In the villages itself no form of credit organization will be suitable except the cooperative society."–All India Rural Credit Survey. Discuss this statement in the background of agricultural finance in India. What constraints and challenges do financial institutions supplying agricultural finance face? How can technology be used to better reach and serve rural clients? [200 Words] [12.5 Marks] **[2014]**

**Edict-1:** Indian Agriculture

# CHAPTER 03
# LAND REFORMS IN INDIA

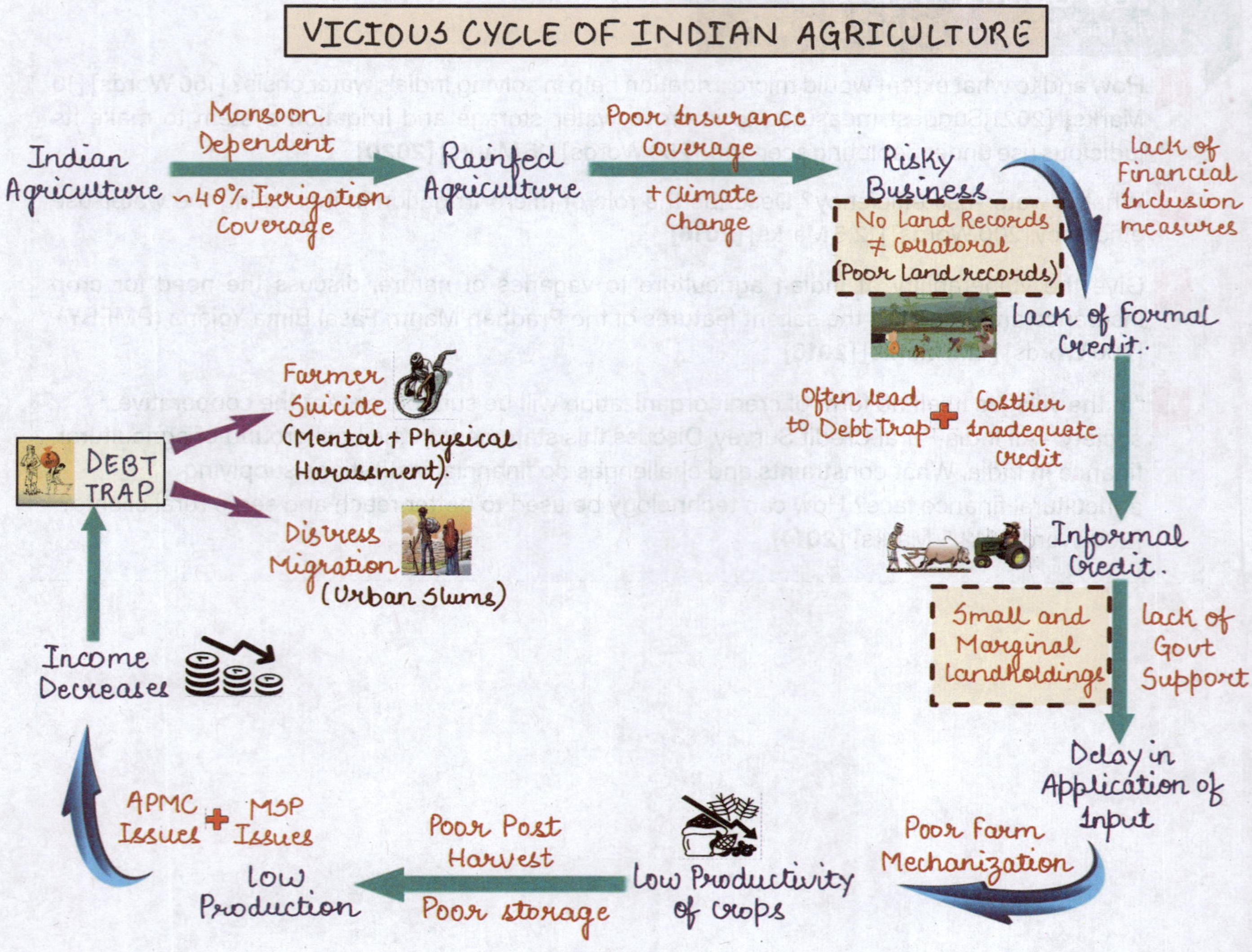

## VICIOUS CYCLE OF INDIAN AGRICULTURE

Indian Agriculture → (Monsoon Dependent; ~40% Irrigation Coverage) → Rainfed Agriculture → (Poor Insurance Coverage + Climate Change) → Risky Business

No Land Records ≠ Collatoral (Poor Land records)

Lack of Financial Inclusion measures

Lack of Formal Credit.

Often lead to Debt Trap + Costlier inadequate credit

Informal Credit.

Small and Marginal Landholdings

lack of Govt Support

Delay in Application of Input

Poor Farm Mechanization

Low Productivity of crops → (Poor Post Harvest; Poor storage) → Low Production

APMC Issues + MSP Issues

Income Decreases

DEBT TRAP

Farmer Suicide (Mental + Physical Harassment).

Distress Migration (Urban Slums)

# BRITISH LAND REVENUE POLICIES

| Criteria | Permanent Settlement | Ryotwari System | Mahalwari System |
|---|---|---|---|
| Region | • Bengal, Bihar & Orissa | • Bombay, Madras, Assam, Sindh & Coorg. | • Awadh, Punjab and Central India. |
| Features | • Revenue rates were fixed permanently & Zamindars became hereditary land-owners along with having the responsibility of collecting revenue from the peasants. | • Individual peasants were recognised as direct cultivators & paid revenue directly to British administration. | • Villages or Mahals → revenue units. Revenue was collected collectively from entire village community, with joint responsibility among villagers. |
| Aim & Impact | • Aimed to provide revenue stability but resulted in number of intermediaries between British administration & tillers, oppressive rent collection, leaving peasants vulnerable to exploitation and impoverishment. | • Aimed to establish direct control but often led to high revenue demands, causing distress and indebtedness among peasants. | • Aimed to maintain collective ownership and shared responsibility. |

## Impact of Land Revenue Policies

⇨ Impoverishment of Poverty due to burden of high revenue assessment.

⇨ Rural Indebtness- High land Revenue taxes + Monsoon failure + inability to pay taxes.

⇨ Disintegration of Village Economy: Loss of land rights + Destruction of traditional practices + Huge tax burden + Commercialisation of agriculture.

⇨ Absentee Landlordism: Increased number of intermediaries gave rise to culture of absentee landlordism.

⇨ Private Property: Permanent Settlement and Ryotwari System having provisions of ownership rights gave birth to private property in arena of farming land.

⇨ Rise of new Social classes like Zamindars, moneylenders, peasant, Tenants. These policies initiated culture of Sub-infeudation.

⇨ Famine and Poverty: Poverty coupled with food shortage led to widespread famines. 28 crore people died between 1850 and 1900.

➾ Commercialisation of Agriculture (Food crops → Cash crops)

➾ Absence of Capitalist Farming (Rent Seeking was more profitable than undertaking cultivation of agriculture)

➾ Regressive Agrarian Structure dominated by landlords, moneylenders, merchants & Colonial state.

- By 1940s, landlords controlled over 70% of land & along with moneylenders & colonial state appropriated more than half of total agricultural production.

➾ Extreme Subdivision of land into small holdings & fragmentation due to the increase in tenant farming & sharecropping or overcrowding of agriculture.

➾ Destruction of Traditional handicraft and Artisanal Industry & absence of a rapid growth of modern industry created an enormous population pressure on agriculture and an adverse land-man ratio of about 0.92 acre per capita at independence.

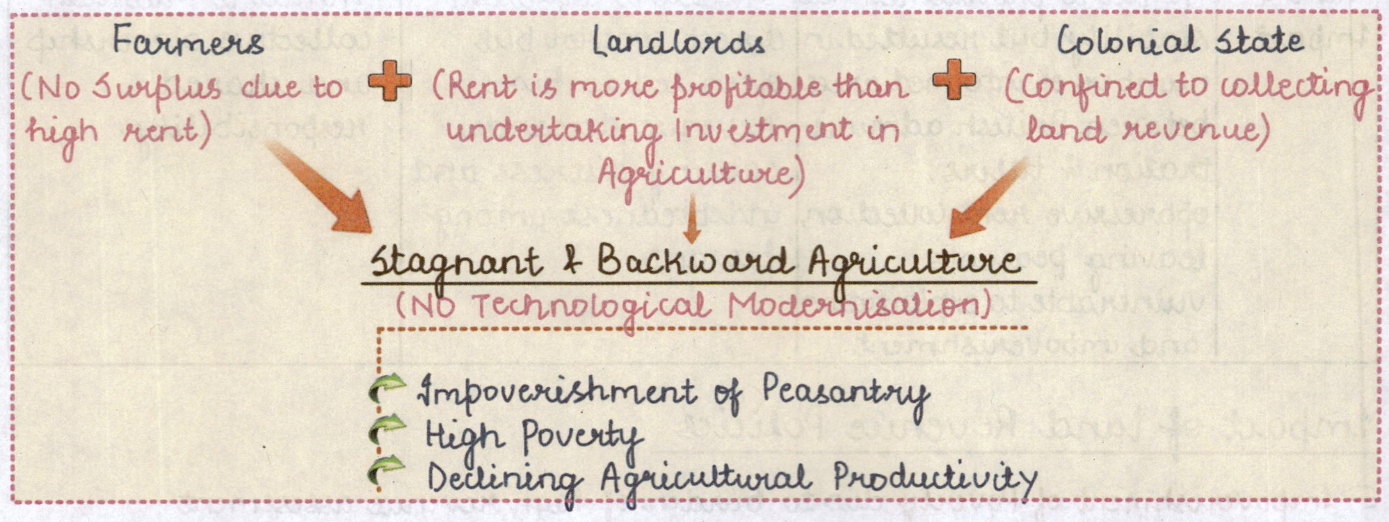


**Land Revenue System facilitating commercialisation of Indian Agriculture**

- **Revenue Demands and Cash crops**: British land revenue system imposed high exploitative revenue demands on farmers and that too in cash, compelling them to focus on cash crops for generating income.
  - Farmers had to cultivate commercial crops, such as indigo, cotton, tea & jute to meet the revenue obligations imposed by British administration.
- **Shift from Subsistence to Market Oriented Farming**: The revenue system created an economic imperative for farmers to produce surplus for sale in markets.
- **Britain's Industrial Revolution**: British administration actively encouraged the cultivation of cash crops for export to meet the demands of British industrial revolution.
  - Many commercial crops like cotton, jute, tea, ~~tobacco~~ were introduced to meet the demand in Britain.

☛ Zamindars motivated by Profits often played a crucial role in encouraging farmers to engage in commercial agriculture to maximise their own revenue collections.

Commercialisation of agriculture & differentiation within peasantry occurred on an unprecedented scale but did not mark the shift towards capitalist commodity production & the rise of the rich peasant / capitalist farmers.

- Commercialisation of agriculture in colonial India facilitated extraction of surplus from peasantry (through land revenue demand in cash) & the transfer of this surplus from India to Britain by bringing agricultural produce to export market.
- Differentiation of peasantry in India by & large did not lead to rise of rich peasant / capitalist farmer but to the creation of a rentier landlord class.

# LAND REFORMS

## Land : Scare Resource in India

INDIA
→ 10% of World's Population
→ 2.4% of World's Geographical Area → Hills, Plateaus, Plains.

Competing uses of land
→ Agriculture → Thus optimal usage of land is needed in Agriculture → Thus, the need for LAND REFORMS
→ Industrialization
→ Urbanisation
→ Environmental Conservation

- Land Reforms is a planned & institutional reorganisation of relation between the man and the land i.e. changes introduced into the system of land tenure and the farming structure.
- Land ownership was highly unequal at the time of Independence as around 70% of the lands were owned by landlords by 1940s.
  - On the other hand, over 60% of rural households either owned no land or were semi-proletarian (having marginal holdings of land).
- Regressive Agrarian Structure: there was a class of intermediaries (interested in only rent-seeking activities) who played no role in production.
  - On the other hand, the vast majority of actual cultivators were either tenants or sub tenants, without any security of tenure.

- This has impacted agricultural productivity reaching to even zero & there was a decline in per capital agricultural production by 14% between 1901 & 1941
- India's land reform Policy had the following specific goals:
- The first is to remove any impediments to increasing agricultural production that arises from the agrarian structure that has been passed down from generation to generation.
- The second goal is to eliminate all elements of exploitation & social injustice from the agrarian system.
- To provide security to the soil tiller, and to ensure quality of status and opportunity to all sections of the rural population.

## First Phase of Land Reforms

- After Independence, attempts had been made to alter the pattern of distribution of land holdings on the basis of two types of experiments, namely:
  - Land Reforms "from above" through legislation on lines broadly indicated by Central Government, enacted by state legislators, & finally implemented by the agencies of the state government.
  - Land Reforms "from below" through permission of landlords & peaceful processions by peasants as in the case of Bhoodan and Gramdan.

| | |
|---|---|
| Abolition of Zamindari System | • Ownership and land revenue related rights of zamindars were abolished.<br>• Land transferred to the superior tenants.<br>• Compensation to Zamindars and the lands for 'Personal Cultivation' exempted from the Act.<br>• First such legislation was enacted by Madras in 1940. Orissa Estate Abolition Act, 1951. |

| | |
|---|---|
| Tenancy Reforms | • Regulation of rent - Fair and reasonable rent. Maximum of 20-25% although varies state to state.<br>• Security of Tenure - Increase in productivity & promotion of social justice. Tenants not evicted without any reason. Exception of 'Personal Cultivation' for the landlord.<br>• Ownership Rights - State laws permit the tenants to acquire the land by paying fair compensation to the owners. |

| Land Ceilings | • Fixing the maximum amount of land that an individual or family can posses & Second is distribution among small farmers and landless people.<br>• Reduction of existing disparities in pattern of land-aonership.<br>• Upto 1972 - Landowner was treated as the unit of application & After 1972 - Family was treated as the basis of landholding. |
|---|---|

| Economic Rationality | Social Rationality |
|---|---|
| • Prof. C.H. Hanumatha held the view that small farmers provide more equal opportunities.<br>• They require less capital compared to the large farms<br>• He further added that small farms can be made into large farms through cooperative effort so as to have scale economies. | • It is socially unjust to allow small number of people to hold large part of land.<br>• Such condition is against the justice, equality & prosperity of the majority of the people.<br>• Ceilings on the land holdings can go a long way in raising income and bringing prosperity of the toiling masses in the country. |

## BHOODAN

- It was a socio-political movement started by Acharya Vinoba Bhave in 1951 in India.
- It aimed to persuade wealthy landowners to donate a portion of their land to landless peasants.
- The movement gained momentum when Vinoba Bhave walked from village to village requesting land owners to donate their land.
- Bhave's approach was rooted in the philosophy of non-violence & the idea that the land owners should donate their land out of compassion and empathy for the poor.

## GRAMDAN

- The next phase of Bhoodan Movement was the Gramdan movement which aimed to create self-sufficient villages by bringing about collective ownership of land.
- The Gramdan movement urged villagers to donate their land to village council which would then manage and distribute the land to the villagers

- Atleast 75% of landowners in the village should surrender landownership to the village community such land should be atleast 60% of the village land.
- 5% of the surrendered land is distributed to the landless in the village for cultivation.

All reforms undertaken in the first Phase resulted into land Fragmentation and therefore, second phase of land reforms focussed upon land consolidation and 'Economics of Scale'.

## Second Phase of Land Reforms

Land Consolidation — Cooperative Farming

Benefits of 'Economics of Scale'

Digitisation of Land Records

Updating the Land Records

## Land Consolidation

- Bringing together various small plots of land of a farmer scattered all over the village as one compact block, either through purchase or exchange of land with others.
- This can help in solving various problems arisen of land fragmentation - wastage of land, difficulties in land management & in adoption of new technology dispute over boundaries, low productivity etc.
- As much as 120 lakh hectare of land has been consolidated by the end of 4th Plan while 440 lakh hectare of land was consolidated by end of 5th FYP.

## Cooperative Farming

- Cooperative Farming involves voluntary cooperation by farmers for undertaking the farming. This involves the increase in collective bargaining power resulting into reduced input cost, high productivity & higher selling price. Thus making agriculture more profitable reducing the indebtness of farmers.
- Cooperative Farming also ensures the optimal use of land.

# DIGITISATION OF LAND RECORDS

- It was introduced with the National Record Modernisation Program in 2008 the purpose of digitization was to computerize all land records & improve transparency in land records, maintenance systems, digitized maps and surveys, update all settlement records and minimize scope of land dispute.

➡ NLRMP (National Land Record Modernisation Programme) was a centrally sponsored Scheme (CSS) which was later revamped & renamed as The Digital India Land Record Modernisation Programme (DILRMP) in 2016 as the Central Sector Scheme (CSS) with 100% funding by the Centre.

➡ Some of the features of DILRMP are:

1. A unique land parcel identification number or Bhu-Aadhar has been assigned for a land parcel which is a 14-digit alpha-numeric unique ID, based on geo-coordinates, which will serve as a Pan-India number for obtaining ownership details of a plot.

2. The records of rights have been translated in all the 22 scheduled languages mentioned in the constitution to address the problem of linguistic barriers in land governance in the country.

➡ DILRMP will transform the land Administration in the following ways:

- Improving the quality and accessibility of Land Records by digitizing and updating the textual and spatial records of land ownership & transactions, such as sale deeds, inheritance records, mortgage & lease documents, Cadastral maps etc.
- Free accessibility to the records will reduce the interface between the citizen and government functionaries, thereby reducing rent seeking and harassment.
- Reduce Litigation and Frauds: DILRMP aims to implement the conclusive land-titling system with title guarantee, which means that land records provide a conclusive proof of ownership of land and are backed by the government.
  - This helps to reduce the scope and frequency of land-related disputes & frauds, which account for a large proportion of pending court cases in India.
  - As per the study by the World Bank, nearly 66% of litigations pending in Indian courts are related with land disputes & subsequent crimes.
- Promote Development and Growth: DILRMP aims to create a conducive environment for land markets and transactions by reducing transaction costs, risks and uncertainities.
  - It also enables landowners to access credit, insurance & markets by using their land titles as collateral. This helps to attract investment, promote industrialisation, and boost growth in various sectors such as agriculture, infrastructure etc.

## Other Government steps for digitization of land records

- **Bhoomi Project (Karnataka), 2000**: It was the first project in India started by Karnataka government to digitize land records. The necessary documents like the record of crops, rights and tenancy have been made available with the help of Kiosks. This project was soon followed by Andhra Pradesh and Tamil Nadu in 2001.
- **Dhatitree**: It is the first web-based land records management system in India implemented in the state of Assam.
- **National Generic Document Registration System (NGDRS)**: NGDRS is an in-house advanced software application for the registration of land and is a big step towards national integration and leap towards 'One Nation, One Software'.
- **Integrated Land Management Information System (ILMIS)**: It aims to integrate land record database with the banks, financial institutions, circle rates, Registration offices and other sectors to provide effective and efficient service deliveries by respective offices.

The PM SWAMITVA Scheme (Survey of Villages and Mapping with Improvised Technology in Village Areas) is a government initiative launched in April 2020 in India. The Primary objective of the scheme is to provide rural property owners with legal documents, including a record of rights, which establishes their ownership of residential properties in rural areas.

Objectives of SWAMITVA Scheme.

- **Establishing Property rights**: Aims to establish and organize property rights for rural landowners.
- **Preventing land disputes**: Intends to reduce land related disputes and conflicts by providing an official record of rights to property owners.
- **Facilitating access to credit and financial services**: The issuance of property cards through PM SWAMITVA scheme enables rural property owners to use their land as collateral for accessing credit and financial services.
- **Promoting Rural Development and Planning**: Accurate information of land can be utilised for effective planning of infrastructure development, implementation of government schemes & overall rural development initiatives.
- **Encouraging Economic growth and investment**: By establishing clear property rights, the PM SWAMITVA scheme aims to encourage economic growth and investment in rural areas.
  - An estimated 7.7 million people in India are affected by conflict over 2.5 million hectares of land, threatening investment worth more than Rs 14 lakh crore.

• Digitization and mapping of rural land records: Utilises modern technology, Such as drones and other geospatial tools and aims to create a comprehensive and accurate database of rural landholdings, enhancing efficiency and transparency in land administration.

## CRITICAL ANALYSIS OF LAND REFORMS

### Relationship between Land Reforms, Agricultural Productivity and Elimination of Poverty

Land Reforms are visualised as an instrument of Social Justice as they seek to do away with exploitative relationships characterised by sharp inequalities between rich landowners and impoverished peasants with no security of tenure. In addition to bringing equity in land distribution, it also improved efficiency of the land because of the following reasons:

- Owner cultivated plots of land tend to be more productive than those under sharecropping tenancy as owners are willing to invest more in their farm.
- Abolition of Intermediaries strengthens the posing of actual cultivators that help them to enhance their social and economic stature.
  - This also increased profit margin because of direct procurement by the government.
- Increased access to land for poor landless masses by the redistribution of land ensures them an income guarantee.
- Land Consolidation: Consolidating plots makes the task of irrigation management, land improvement & personal supervision of different plots efficient and easier, thereby improving productivity
  - This also raised the prospect of Capital Farming.
- Easier access to agricultural Credit due to land ownership or land tenancy agreements which has a direct impact on agricultural productivity.
- Modernisation of Agriculture: Green Revolution was mainly successful in those states where land reforms were implemented.
- Tenancy Reforms increased bargaining power of tenants vis-a-vis land-owners by regulating aspects of the tenancy relationship, such as the crop share and the duration of the contract (Security of tenure)
- Increased agricultural growth and productivity and thus enhanced farmers' income due to land reforms is directly related to rural poverty reduction.
  - Because the majority of India's population depends upon land for their livelihood, poverty issues are also closely associated with land policy.

## Some of the Successes of land reforms can be seen from given below fact:

- 1700 lakh hectare land were taken from zamindars. Over 2 crore superior tenants benefitted and this reorganisation is carried out within the democratic framework.
- 4 Million hectares of land got mobilised as a part of people's movement.

## Challenges faced by Land Reform Policies

### 01 Issues with respect to designing of Policies

The report of the Task force on Agrarian Relations of the Planning Commission of India (1973) had the following overall assessment of land reforms in India: "the Programme of land reform adopted since independence have failed to bring about the required changes in agrarian structure." the report directly blames the political will of the state governments for this failure.

- Land is a State Subject which makes it difficult to design the land reform measures at national level and thus, there existed a variation in land reform policies among various states.
- Poor land records: lack of digitalization and incomplete land records make the determining of ownership difficult leading to obstacles in land reforms.
- Exemption for 'Personal Cultivation' was misused by the landowners.
- Land ceiling laws: In a situation where more than 70% of landholdings in India were under 5 acres, the ceiling fixed on existing holdings by the state were very high.
  - In Andhra Pradesh, it varied from 27 to 312 acres (depending on the class of land), Assam 50 acres, Kerala 15 to 37.5 acres, Punjab 30 to 60 acres etc.
- Optional nature of laws: Most of the laws granting ownership rights to tenants are not mandatory. They are rather optional & the tenants have to move the government for grant of ownership rights.
- Emergence of new agriculture technology: The new seed-cum-fertiliser technology, for its successful adoption, needs ample resources and dynamic entrepreneurship which can be fulfilled only by the large farmers.
  - Therefore, many economists have come out in favour of the abolition of ceilings on land holdings.

### 02 Issues with respect to Implementation of policies

- Land Reforms which was aimed to bring Social Justice clashed with Fundamental Right to Property leading to increased litigation in the courts. This delayed the implementation of land reforms.

- Lack of strong political will and bureaucratic political nexus preventing effective implementation of land reforms.
- Tenant, small and marginal farmers are often ignorant or lack the resources to approach the government for effective implementation of land reforms.
- Tenancy legislations: Most tenancies are oral and informal, that is they were not recorded and the tenants therefore could not benefit from legislation in their favour.
- Lack of Financial Support: Five Year Plans did not provide any funding specifically for financing land reforms.
- Undue advance publicity and delay in enactment of land reforms: This has enabled the landowners to make necessary adjustments so as to be able to evade various provisions of land reform legislations.
- Bureaucratic Corruption: Land Reforms provided a golden opportunity to the Patwari and other functionaries of the Revenue Department to make money.
- Malafide transfer of land: To escape the laws relating to land ceilings, the zamindars have indulged in large scale transfer of land to their family members or kinsmen.
  - Such malafide transactions did not make any change in operational aspect of agriculture.
- Only 4% of the land got transferred under land ceiling laws and most of the surplus land is fallow and uncultivable.

# LAND FRAGMENTATION

## 10th Agriculture Census 2015-16

Following are the findings of the census vis-a-vis land holdings in India:

- Increase in number of operational holdings which has gone up by 5.33% to 146 million in 2015-16 from 138 million in 2010-11.
- Decline in average size of operational agricultural holdings: It has declined to 1.08 hectares (ha) in 2015-16 from 1.15 ha in 2010-11.
- Rise in the percentage of female landholding farmers: Not only is there the rise in female tillers but the percentage of female operational landholders increased from 12.79% in 2010-11 to 13.87% in 2015-16.
- Increase in the number of smaller and medium level landholdings: Out of the total landholdings as much as 86.21% of India's cultivated farmland is held by small and marginal farmers with less than two hectares of land, while those with 10 hectares and more account for just 0.57%.

| REASONS | IMPACT |
|---|---|
| Government Policies (1st phase) i.e. Zamindari Abolition, Tenancy Reforms, Land ceiling (Led to reduction of Average landholdings) | Difficult access to Formal credit (RBI Report - Only 40% Small and Marginal Farmer's accessing Formal credit) |
| Inheritance Laws | Challenges in Mechanisation of Agriculture |
| Increasing pressure on Agricultural land (Demographic Pressure) (Land : Man = 0.2 ha / rural population) | Poor Technological Adoption |
| | Land Wastages (Boundary of Small land Parcels) (≃ 6% Wastage in Punjab) |
| | Litigation |
| | Land Management difficulties ↓<br>▸ Subsistence type of Farming<br>▸ Private Investment reduced<br>▸ Reduced Cultivation of High Value crops. ↓ |

Low Productivity + Climate Change

Less Profitable Agriculture and High Indebtedness

## Measures to overcome the prevalent issues

Adoption of model leasing laws by the states to enable landholders with unviable holdings in leasing out land for investment, thereby enabling greater income and employment generation in rural areas.

- Encourage Land Consolidation
- Greater access to institutional credit markets for providing suitable input to Small landholdings.
- Promotion of Co-operative Farming.
- Skilling & educating farmers along with providing high yield Variety Seeds to enhance productivity.

Encouraging Farmer Producer Organisations (FPOs) that can enhance economy of scale and bargaining power of member farmers.

## PYQs Corner

*(Write the Answer and Get Free Evaluation)*

1. State the objectives and measures of land reforms in India. Discuss how land ceiling policy on landholding can be considered as an effective reform under economic criteria. [150 Words] [10 Marks] [2023]
2. How did land reforms in some parts of the country help to improve the socio-economic conditions of marginal and small farmers. [150 Words] [10 Marks] [2021]
3. Discuss the role of land reforms in agricultural development. Identify the factors that were responsible for the success of land reforms in India. [200 Words] [12.5 Marks] [2016]
4. In the view of the declining average size of land holdings in India which has made agriculture non-viable for a majority of farmers should contract farming and land leasing be promoted in agriculture? critically evaluate the pros and cons. [200 Words] [12.5 Marks] [2015]
5. Establish relationship between land reforms, agricultural productivity and elimination of poverty in the Indian economy. Discuss the difficulties in designing and implementation of agriculture-friendly land reforms in India. [200 Words] [10 Marks] [2013]

**Edict-1:** Indian Agriculture

CHAPTER 04

# POST PRODUCTION FACTORS

## VICIOUS CYCLE OF INDIAN AGRICULTURE

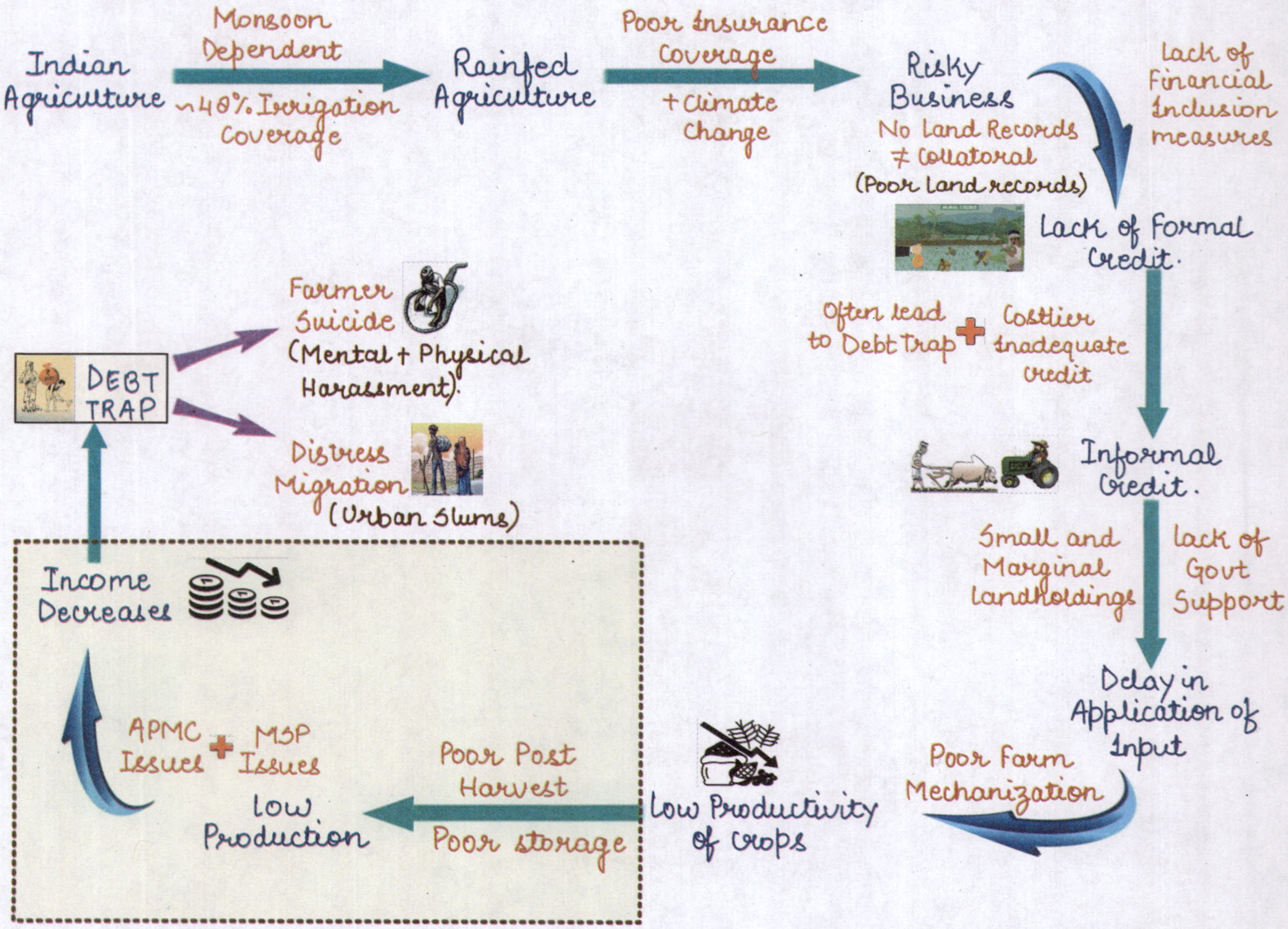

Indian Agriculture → (Monsoon Dependent; ~40% Irrigation Coverage) → Rainfed Agriculture → (Poor Insurance Coverage + Climate Change) → Risky Business

No Land Records ≠ Collatoral (Poor Land records)

Risky Business → (Lack of Financial Inclusion measures) → Lack of Formal Credit.

Lack of Formal Credit → (Often lead to Debt Trap + Costlier Inadequate credit) → Informal Credit.

Informal Credit → (Small and Marginal Landholdings; Lack of Govt Support) → Delay in Application of Input

Delay in Application of Input → (Poor Farm Mechanization) → Low Productivity of crops

Low Productivity of crops → (Poor Post Harvest; Poor storage) → Low Production

Low Production → (APMC Issues + MSP Issues) → Income Decreases

Income Decreases → DEBT TRAP

DEBT TRAP → Farmer Suicide (Mental + Physical Harassment).

DEBT TRAP → Distress Migration (Urban Slums)

# DECODING INDIAN AGRICULTURE

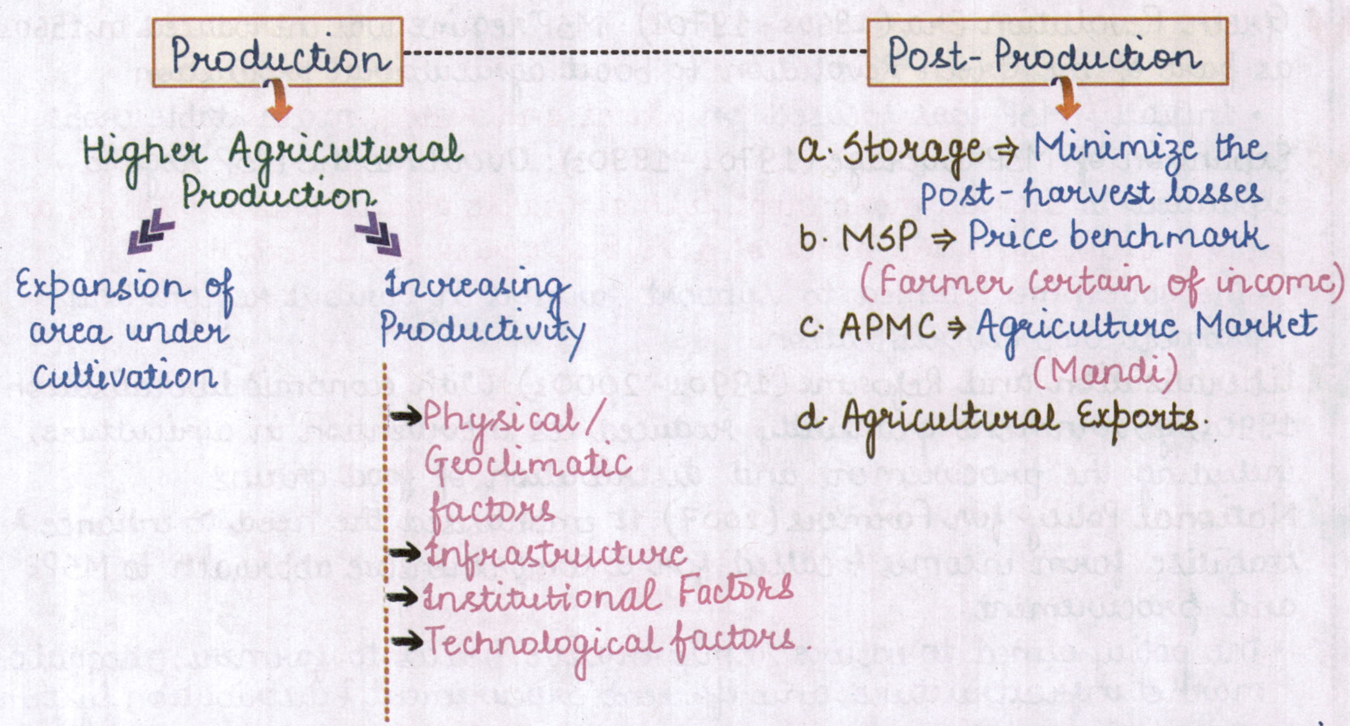


- Agriculture faces 3 types of risk which can be addressed through the following factors:

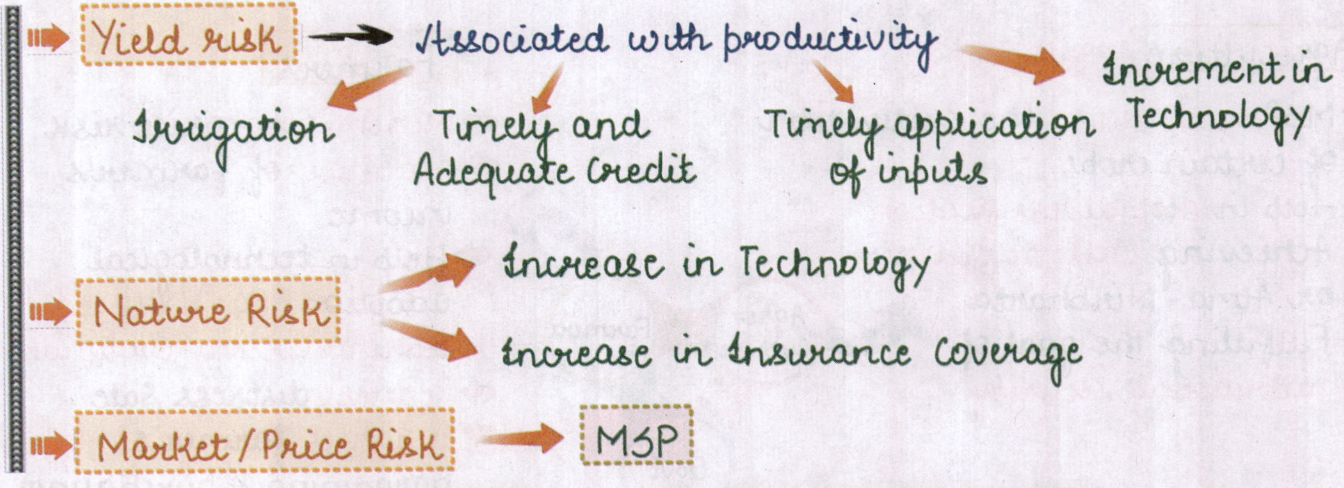


# MINIMUM SUPPORT PRICE

➪ It is the minimum price set by the government at which farmers can expect to sell their produce for the season. It is done by the farmers to insure agricultural produce against a sharp fall in the price of agricultural commodities.

## Evolution of MSP Policy

- Green Revolution Era (1960s - 1970s): MSP regime was introduced in 1960s as part of the Green Revolution to boost agricultural production
  - Initially MSP was focused on Wheat and Paddy, main staple crops.
- Expansion of MSP Coverage (1970s - 1990s): Over time the MSP regime expanded to include more crops such as coarse grains, pulses, Oilseeds and cotton, addressing the needs of a diverse agricultural sector.
  - The government aimed to support farmers in various regions and promote crop diversification.
- Liberalisation and Reforms (1990s - 2000s): With economic liberalisation in 1990s, government gradually reduced its intervention in agriculture, including the procurement and distribution of food grains.
- National Policy for Farmers (2007): It emphasised the need to enhance & stabilise farm incomes & called for a comprehensive approach to MSPs and procurement.
  - The policy aimed to ensure remunerative prices to farmers, adequate market infrastructure, and efficient procurement & distribution systems

## Rationale of MSP (Stakeholder approach)

**Agriculture**

- MSP incentivize the cultivation of certain crops
- Help in crop diversification
- Achieving Self-Sufficiency or Atma-Nirbharta
- Fulfilling the goal of nutritional security

**Farmers**

- Minimizing price risk
- Stability of farmer's income
- Help in technological adoption (Eg: HYV Seeds during Green Revolution)
- Reduces distress sale
- Enhances farmer's bargaining & purchasing power.

Agri-Culture

Farmers

Govt.

**Government**

- Achieving redistribution of Welfare Objectives
- Procurement of cereals or pulses etc for food security.

# Issues of MSP

## Government

1. Open ended procurement

a. High Fiscal burden or High Economic cost : In 2021-22 Rabi Season, government paid a total of 1.95 lakh crore to farmers as MSP for procurement of crops which was highest ever procurement of wheat & rice at MSP in a single season.

b. Storage issues (Procurement is greater than Storage Cap. leading to wastage of produce)

2. Skewed policy : Confined to four crops Sugarcane, paddy/rice, wheat, Cotton
(3/4th) (50%) (40%) (25%)
Coverage of total production

3. High food subsidies may breach WTO's aggregate Measurement of Support

## Environment

1. Facilitates cultivation of water intensive crops → Groundwater depletion, reduced soil fertility
2. Overuse of Nitrogenous fertilisers → Water Pollution

The area under cultivation of rice and wheat from time of Green Revolution till recently increased from 30 million ha to 44 million ha (50% increase) & 9 mn ha to 31 mn ha (250% increase) respectively. While that of coarse cereals declined from 37 mn ha to 25 mn ha (33% decrease)

ISSUES

## Farmers

1. Limited Coverage → Shanta Kumar Committee observed that only 6% of farmers are benefitted from MSPs. This essentially deprives small & marginal farmers who have limited access to market
2. Imbalance Regional Procurement → 80% of wheat from Punjab, Haryana, UP, MP and 30% of Paddy from West Bengal, UP, Punjab
3. Poor awareness among farmers for availing MSP benefits.
4. Increasing input cost but there is no proportionate income in MSP.
5. No MSP for agri-allied sectors
6. Calculation of MSP based on A2+FL cost which does not cover all costs of production.

## Agriculture / Economy

1. Inefficient use of Resources
2. Distorted Cropping pattern
3. Discourage crop diversification
4. Wastage of Agri-Produce (Post harvest loss)
5. Reduced Agriculture Exports
6. Higher Inflation

## Reforms Needed (Green Colour)

### ISSUES

**Government**

1. Open ended procurement
   a. High Fiscal burden or High Economic cost: In 2021-22 Rabi Season, government paid a total of 1.95 lakh crore to farmers as MSP for procurement of crops which was highest ever procurement of wheat & rice at MSP in a single season.
   b. Storage issues (Procurement is greater than Storage Cap. leading to wastage of produce)
2. Skewed policy: Confined to four crops Sugarcane, paddy/rice, wheat, Cotton
   (3/4th) (50%) (40%) (25%)
   Coverage of total production
3. High food subsidies may breach WTO's aggregate Measurement of Support

**Environment**

1. Facilitates cultivation of water intensive crops → Groundwater depletion, reduced soil fertility
2. Overuse of Nitrogenous fertilisers → Water Pollution

**Farmers**

1. Limited Coverage → Shanta Kumar Committee observed that only 6% of farmers are benefitted from MSPs. This essentially deprives small & marginal farmers who have limited access to market
2. Imbalance Regional Procurement → 80% of wheat from Punjab, Haryana, UP, MP and 30% of Paddy from West Bengal, UP, Punjab
3. Poor awareness among farmers for availing MSP benefits.
4. Increasing input cost but there is no proportionate income in MSP.
5. No MSP for agri-allied sectors
6. Calculation of MSP based on A2+FL cost which does not cover all costs of production.

**Agriculture / Economy**

1. Inefficient use of Resources
2. Distorted Cropping pattern
3. Discourage crop diversification
4. Wastage of Agri-Produce (Post harvest loss)
5. Reduced Agriculture Exports
6. Higher Inflation

### Reforms

- ✓ Capping on Procurement
- ✓ Reduced leakages (Price Deficiency Payments)
- ✓ Improved targeting of beneficiaries (JAM Trinity)
- ✓ Shift towards water Productive crops
- ✓ Encourage use of alternate fertilisers such as Biofertilisers and Organic fertilisers.
- ✓ Improve the reach of MSP.
- ✓ Increased awareness about MSP with advanced announcements
- ✓ Balanced Regional procurement with linkage with production
- ✓ Alternative Fertilisers
- ✓ C2+50% Method.
- ✓ Emphasis on Nutritional Security.
- ✓ MSP for diverse crops (Moving away from cereals)
- ✓ Focus on Millets (aka-Nutri cereals)

## Alternative approaches to improve the existing MSP regime

- Price Deficiency Payment (PDP): Both NITI Aayog and Economic Survey recommend PDP as adopted by some states; like Madhya Pradesh (Bhavantar Bhugtan Yojana), Haryana government (Bhavantar Bharapai Yojana)
- Direct Income Support which would benefit farmers in the times of agrarian distress.
- In its 'Strategy for New India @75' document, NITI Aayog suggested reforms like:
  - long term Solution lies in the creation of a competitive, stable & unified national market to enable better price discovery and a long term trade regime favourable to exports.
    - Raising MSP or prices can only be a partial solution to the problem of assuring remunerative returns to farmers.
  - Modernisation: Modernising the agriculture sector through improving irrigation facilities, marketing reforms, post harvest management & better crop insurance products.
  - Promote Contract farming.

### ENSURING REMUNERATIVE **PRICES TO FARMERS**

Cabinet approves Pradhan Mantri Annadata Aay SanraksHan Abhiyan

**PRICE SUPPORT SCHEME (PSS)**

Physical procurement of pulses, oilseeds & Copra by Centre Nodal Agencies. Central Government to bear procurement expenditure and loses due to procurement

**PRICE DEFICIENCY PAYMENT SCHEME (PDPS)**

To cover all oilseeds for which MSP is notified. Farmers to get direct payment to the difference between MSP & selling price

**PILOT OF PRIVATE PROCUREMENT & STOCKIST SCHEME (PPPS)**

Private sector participations in procurement operation to be piloted. For oilseeds, states have the option to roll out PPPS on pilot basis

# AGRICULTURAL MARKETING

- It includes all the operations involved in the movement of farm produce from the producer to the ultimate consumer
- Agriculture market falls under 'State list' (list II) of Seventh Schedule and thus agriculture market (commonly known as 'Mandis') are regulated by the states under APMC Acts (Agriculture Produce Marketing Committee)
- The scale of agricultural commodities can occur only in the Mandis through auction and this sale process is regulated through commission agents who mediate between farmers and traders.
- The whole geographical area in the state is divided & each one is declared as a market area managed by the Market Committee (MC) constituted by the state government. This has resulted into fragmentation of markets.
- Farmers are mandated to do their first sale in the APMC markets.

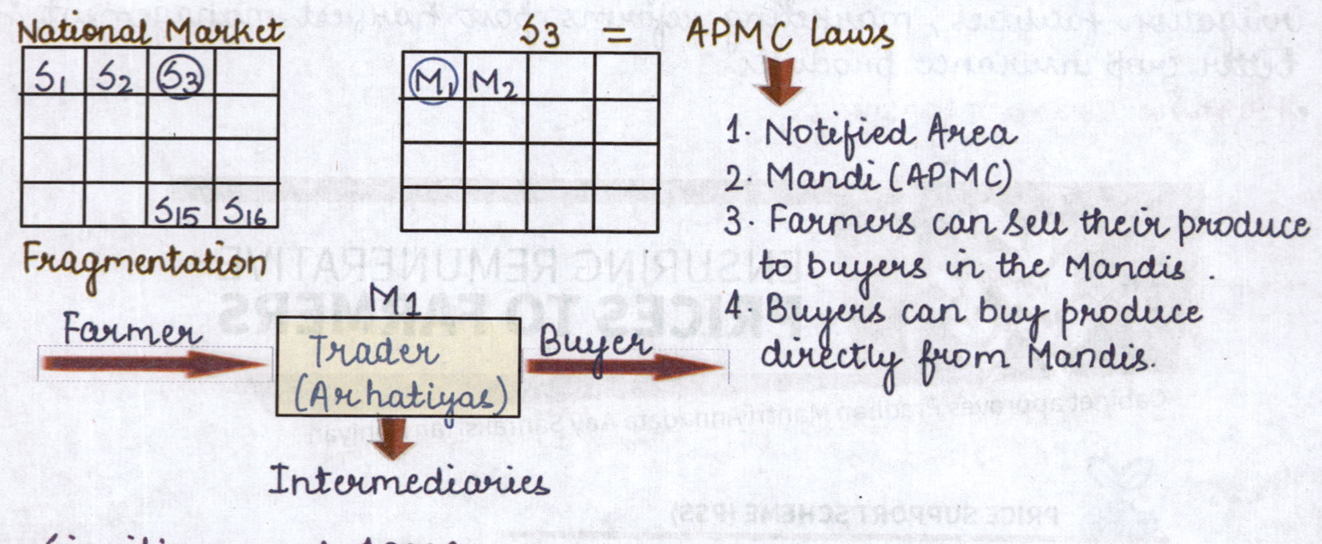


## Significance of APMCs

| Economic Significance | Social Significance |
|---|---|
| Resource optimisation and Output Management<br>Increase in Income for Farmers<br>Contribution to GDP growth<br>Growth of Agro-based industries<br>Price Signals to Farmers<br>Adoption of Technology | Employment generation<br>Higher standard of living<br>Reduced Farm Suicides. |

## Challenges in Agricultural Marketing

1. Market Fragmentation: Monopoly of APMCs in agricultural market reduces buyer Competition along with the agriculture in the state list results into fragmentation of an integrated market as it limits the geographical range of mandis, number of buyers and Sector specific buyers.

2. Inadequate number of Mandis: limit the access of agricultural markets. there were only 6630 mandis in 2019 with an average area served of 463 Sq. km. There is huge variation in the density of regulated markets varying from 118 Sq. km. in Punjab to approximately 11,000 Sq. km. in Meghalaya. [Ideal area to be served by a Mandi should be 80 Square km as per the National Commission on Agriculture].

3. Entry Barriers: licence fee in these markets are highly prohibitive & at the same time, having a requirement of physical possession of a shop is discouraging to operate as a trader.

4. There is also a requirement of separate licence for different Mandis.

5. There is high incidence of market fees and charges which works out to be about 15% of the sales produce, which is excessive

6. Cartelisation: limited number of trader in a single mandi gets to form a cartel, which deliberately restrain from higher bidding. Thereby produce is procured at manipulatave discovered price (lack of transparent price discovery) & sold at higher price to the consumers.

7. Lack of Marketing Infrastructure: Cold storage units exists in less than 1/10 of the markets & grading facilities < 1/3 of the markets.
   - There is no proper storage or warehousing facility for farmers in the villages where they can store their agricultural produce. This lack of storage facility results into almost 15-30% of wastage of agricultural produce.

8. Distress Sale: Most of the Indian farmers are very poor & thus have no capacity to wait for the better price of their produce in the absence of proper credit facilities and thereby farmers go for distress sale.

9. Conflict of Interest: APMC play dual role of regulator & market and consequently its role as regulator is undermined by vested interest in lucrative trade.

| Institutional Issues | Infrastructural Issues | Governance/Policy |
|---|---|---|
| • Highly fragmented markets --> Poor competitiveness<br>• License requirements --> High corruption<br>• Market Fees/Charges<br>• Cartelisation<br>• Asymmetry in Price information | • Inadequate marketing infrastructure --> Lack of cold storage facilities + Perishable Goods & long-distance ---> Distress sale<br>• Lack of grading and standardization<br>• Huge wastage of fruits and vegetables | • Conflict of Interest<br>• Monopoly of APMCs<br>• Limited private investment in marketing infrastructure<br>• Insufficient markets and huge regional variation |

# E-NAM

- National Agriculture Market (NAM) is envisaged as a pan-India electronic trading portal which seeks to network the existing APMCs to create a unified national market (One Nation, One Market) for agricultural commodities.
- Aim: To create a national network of physical mandis which can be accessed online.
    - It seeks to leverage the physical infrastructure of the mandis through an online trading portal, enabling buyers situated even outside the state to participate in trading at the local level.
- Need: Overcoming challenges posed by present agri-marketing namely - fragmentation of state into multiple market areas each administered by separate APMC, multiple levy of mandi fees, requirement for multiple licence for trading in different APMCs, licensing barriers leading to conditions of monopoly, poor quality of infrastructure and low use of technology, opaque process for price discovery, high level of market charges, movement controls etc.

## Salient features of e-NAM

➡ Online trading: It does away with the need for consumers to be physically present in Mandis (Market places) and allows them to trade from anywhere using computer or mobile device.

- This has resulted into transparent sale transactions & price discovery in regulated markets, Kisan Mandis etc. According to official data, e-NAM has cut transaction time from 8-10 hours to 30 minutes resulting into speedier and efficient trading

➡ Single Market: It gives farmers access to multiple markets and consumers outside of their area giving them more market prospects.

➩ **Reduction of Intermediaries**: E-NAM also eliminates intermediaries and many layers of middle men, which according to official data is around 2 to 3 in number (reduction of Intermediaries), resulting into higher income of farmers.

➩ **Liberal licensing of traders or Buyers** and commission agents by state authorities without any pre-condition of physical presence in the market yard.

➩ One license for traders is valid across all market in the state.

➩ **Quality Testing and Grading**: The platform offers agricultural commodities, quality testing & grading Services. This ensures that buyers obtain high quality goods & motivates farmers to improve product quality.

- There are also provision of soil testing laboratories near the mandis to facilitate visiting farmers to access this facility in the mandi itself.

➩ **Single Point levy of Market Fees**, that is, on the 1st wholesale purchase from the farmer.

➩ **Data Driven Decision making**: Commodity prices, arrivals and trading patterns are all generated by e-NAM, which can assist farmers, traders and policy makers in making decisions about production planning, market strategy and policy interventions.

Model Agricultural Produce and Livestock Marketing (Promotion and Facilitation Act), 2017.

- The new model law seeks to establish a regulated wholesale agri-market at a distance of every 80 km. To enable this, it has been proposed to issue licenses to new private players and traders who wish to set up a wholesale market. Even private market yards, warehouses & cold storages will be allowed to act as regulated markets.
- Unlike the current System, now only by paying unified single fees, farmer/trader will be able to transact in all such regulated agri-markets within the state. There will be no separate fees for individual markets
- It caps market fee (including developmental and other charges) at not more than 1% for fruit and vegetables, and 2% for food grain. It caps commission agents' fee at not more than two percent for non-perishable and 4% for perishables.
- Besides, it stipulates a single license for trading within the state & national level
- All regulatory powers will lie with the office of the director of agricultural marketing in the state, who will also issue licenses to traders and new private players. As of now this power lies with the mandis managed by Board of Directors.
- It also has the provision for promoting online or spot (e-national agriculture market) agriculture market platforms

| Other Reform Measures to be taken | | |
|---|---|---|
| Legislative and Institutional Measures | Infrastructural & other measures | Ashok Dalwai Committee Recommendation |
| • APMC → Encourage Farmer's organisation<br>• APMC Act → States should implement APLM Act.<br>• Number of Markets → More than 10000 mandis.<br>• Density of Markets with a radius of 5km<br>• Fruits & Vegetables outside APMC Act (X Market fees)<br>• Promotion of alternate marketing channels → Farmer market, Private market etc. | • Cold storage, banking, digital connectivity & other facilities in markets<br>• Investment in market yards<br>• Standardised Scientific assaying and grading<br>• Warehouse based trading system.<br>• Roping AgTech Startups for price discovery mechanisms. | • One India Market → Agriculture marketing under concurrent list.<br>• Greater Price Sector participation.<br>• Implement Model APLM Act.<br>• Reduce wastage → Cold chain integration.<br>• Min target of 7000 FPOs.<br>• Country need → 1000 wholesale & 20,000 rural retail markets<br>• Comprehensive guidelines to promote warehouse based Post harvest loan & eNWR based trade |

## CONTRACT FARMING

Farmers (Small and Marginal, Large Farmers, FPOs) — Pre-Harvest Agreement — Buyer (Agro-based Industries, Agri-Exporters)

Farm Produce → Buyer; Inputs / Extension Services / Formal Credit → Farmers

- Contract farming signifies an agricultural production (including livestock and poultry) based on a pre-harvest agreement between buyers (such as food processing units and exporters) & producers (farmer or farmer organisations).
- Under contract farming, farmers can be given seeds, credit, fertilizers, machinery and technical advice so that their product is tailor-made for the requirement of the companies.
- There would be no middlemen involved and farmers would get a predetermined sale price from the companies.
- The farmer does not have to make trips to the mandis nor worry about getting seeds and credit for farming operations.

- In India, contract farming is regulated under Indian Contract Act, 1872.
- In addition, the Model APMC (Agricultural Produce Market Committee) Act provides specific provisions for contract farming, like compulsory registration of contract farming sponsors and dispute settlement.
- Since agriculture is a state list subject, therefore contract farming is not uniform

### Some Cases of Contract farming in India

- The first widely acknowledged incident of contract farming in the Indian context was the entrance of Pepsi Foods Ltd. into Punjab in 1909. The company intended to specifically focus on exports of value-added processed foods.
  - The PepsiCo model of contract farming opened up new options for farmers, led to productivity increase, and introduction of modern technology for the tomato crop.
- Following the PepsiCo example, local firms such as Nijjar in Punjab and Bhilai Engineering in MP also took up a tomato contract cultivation.

## Pros and Cons of Contract Farming

| Benefits (Pros) | Challenges (Cons) |
|---|---|
| **Farmers**<br>• Reduced the fluctuating market price risk<br>• Stable and consistent demand from bulk consumers<br>• Improved access to markets.<br>• Technical assistance, management support and supply of quality inputs by the agri-business firms.<br>• Access to cheaper institutional credit<br>• Improved competitiveness of small scale farming via assured quality inputs and certain market. | **Farmers**<br>• Biased towards large farmers and exclusion of small producers.<br>• Exploitation of poor farmers; manipulative prices practiced by large buyers; highly technical contract terms and conditions.<br>• Contracting agreements are mostly informal or verbal.<br>• Dis-empowerment of farmers such as unable to grow multiple crops in land and forced to grown only one type of crop in the same land. |
| **Buyers**<br>• Un-interrupted supply of raw materials<br>• Prevented from market price fluctuations<br>• Diversified supply base & thus reduced risk involved with crop damage & loss.<br>• Reduced cost of collection. | **Buyers**<br>• Breach contract by farmers & thus reducing factory output.<br>• Not able to generate required yield as per the contract terms. |

| Other | Other |
|---|---|
| • Addressing traditional ills of marketing<br>• Reduced government burden of procurement<br>• Enhances private investment in Agriculture<br>• Enables the food processing industries to invest in warehouses and cold storage in long-term | • Promotes monoculture and thus puts a burden on the natural resources.<br>• Enhancing the disparity between small and large farmers.<br>• Negative Externalities such as decline in soil fertility, pollution etc. as the firms are interested only in profits. |

## Experience of Contract Farming in India

The Punjab and Haryana contract farming experience has been far from satisfactory with studies revealing that contract growers faced many problems like undue quality cut on produce by firms, delayed deliveries at the factory, delayed payments, low price, and pest attack on the contract crop which raised the cost of production. The firms also manipulated provisions of contracts in practice and also delayed payments up to 60 days.

## Model Contract Farming Act, 2018

- **Farmer's Protection:** The Act lays special emphasis on protecting the interest of the farmers, considering them weaker of the two parties entering into contract.
- **Contract Farming:** Contract farming to be outside the ambit of APMC act. In addition to contract farming, services contracts all along the value chain including pre-production, production and post-production have been included.
- "Registering and Agreement Recording Committee" or an "Officer" for purpose at district/block/taluka level for online registration of sponsor & recording of agreement is provided.
- **FPOs:** Promotion of Farmer Producer Organisation (FPOs)/Farmer Producer Companies (FPCs) to mobilize small and marginal farmers has been provided.
- **Protecting Farmland:** No rights, title ownership or possession to be transferred or alienated or vested in the contract farming sponsor etc. No permanent structure can be developed on farmers' land/premises.
- Contract Farming Facilitation Group (CFFG) for promoting contract farming and services at village/panchayat.
- Accessible and simple dispute settlement mechanism at the lowest level possible provided for quick disposal of disputes.

# FARMER PRODUCER ORGANISATIONS

- The Concept of FPO consist of collectivisation of producers especially small and marginal farmers so as to form an effective alliance to address many challenges of agriculture such as improved access to investment, technology, inputs, markets.
- Department of Agriculture and Cooperation has identified FPO registered under the special provisions of the companies Act, 1956 as the most appropriate institutional form around which the mobilisation of farmers is to be made for building their capacity to collectively leverage their production and marketing strength.

## Need for Farmer Producer Organisations (FPOs)

- **Structural Challenges in agriculture:** Poor market infrastructure, credit unavailability, access and knowledge about market, information asymmetry, lower bargaining power and holding capacity, higher input costs, lower yield due to fragmented buying and selling etc.
- **Failure of Cooperatives:** Due to political interference, bureaucratic control and capturing of management by poor leadership and powerful elite, cooperatives have not been as effective as expected.
- **For better price realisation and higher income:** FPOs enable member-farmers to reap benefits of economies of scale in purchasing of inputs, processing and marketing of their produce and value addition.
- **Better access to government services:** FPOs can also work as a platform to facilitate liaison with the government leading to better access to government services like PDS, MGNREGA, Scholarship and Pensions etc.

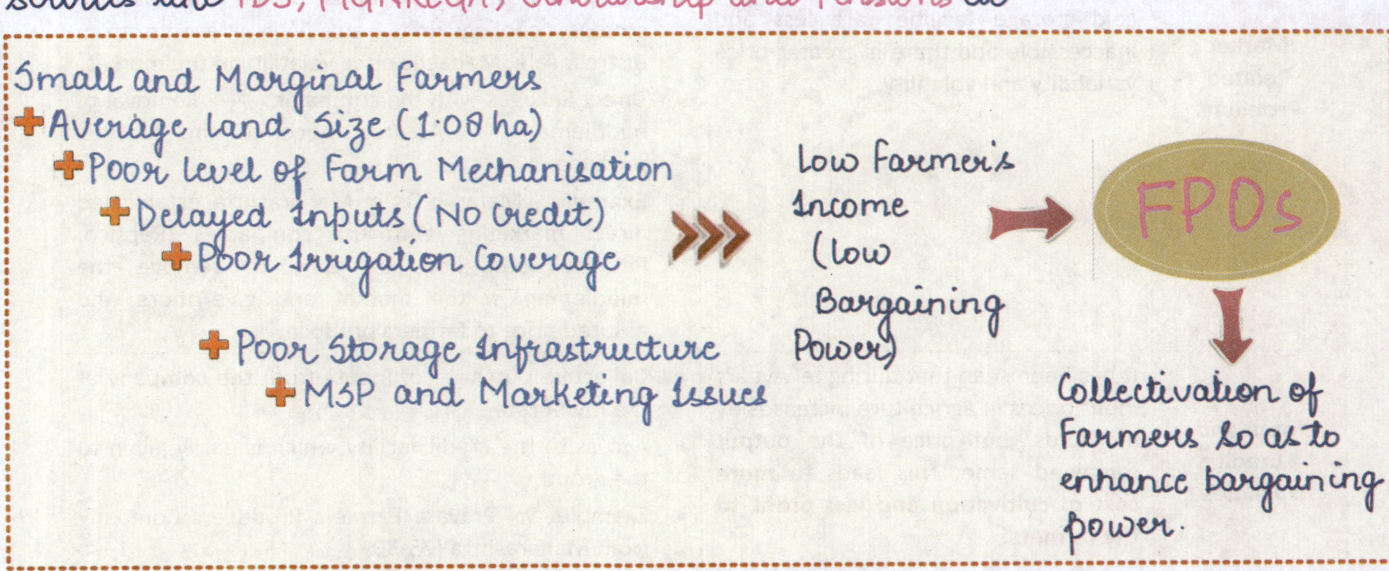

| Area | Problem | FPOs providing solution |
|---|---|---|
| **Promotion of Mechanisation in Agriculture** | **Level of farm mechanisation in India is 45-50 per cent,** of which majority contribution (60-70%) is of rice and wheat harvesting, which is less compared to other developed countries (up to 95 %). | • FPOs can play important role in making available these machineries and equipments to the members collectively by charging nominal fee from the members through custom hiring centers.<br>• **Small and marginal farmers can have access to machineries by collectively purchasing the machineries in FPO.**<br>• **Ex -** Satmile satish club, an NGO from Cooch Behar district of West Bengal. |
| **Post-Harvest Losses and Value Addition** | As per estimates of Ministry of food processing industries (2016), **post-harvest loss of India's major agricultural produce is estimated at Rs 92,651 crore**. Despite of second largest producer of fruits and vegetables, **only 2.2 per cent of fruits and vegetables are processed** (Much lower than Brazil-70 %, USA-65 %) and in case of milk, 37.7 per cent is processed. | • Can mobilise investment opportunities for establishment of processing and storage infrastructures at grassroots level which will help in reducing post-harvest losses, enhancing shelf life and better price realization for the farmers produce.<br>• **Example:** In Maharashtra, **MAHAGRAPES,** a marketing partner to grape growers cooperative had established cold storage units at each cooperative society. |
| **Extension and Research** | **Inadequate public extension system in the country.**<br>**Low participation of private sector.** | • Complement and supplement the efforts of public, private and NGOs in providing extension services to the farmers.<br>• Timely, relevant information and training services to farmers by establishing knowledge linkages.<br>• Example: Maharashtra state grape grower's association (MRDBS) |
| **Market Related Problems** | International Food Policy Research Institute (IFPRI), South Asia, observed that in **India, market surplus is relatively low, producers share in consumer rupees is low, transaction cost is high, price volatility is more**, cold storage facilities are less and inaccessible and there is greater price variability and volatility. | • By pooling out their resources, **more economy of scale can be achieved by small and marginal farmers.**<br>• Collective marketing by FPO ---> Reduction in transaction cost and more bargaining power.<br>• Boost to post-harvest infrastructure such as cold storage, cooling units, etc. ----> Prevents from distress sale. Manages price volatility in the market.<br>• Direct linkages with the companies ----> Removal of middlemen ---> Assured price to the farmers produce.<br>• **Example -** Many FPOs in Maharashtra established direct marketing with the companies (Pepsico, Patanjali etc) and are able to remove the middlemen in the market and give more and assured price to farmers produce. |
| **Input and Credit Facilities** | It has been seen that during few years input prices in agriculture increases by 4-5 folds, but price of the output remained same. This leads to **more cost of cultivation and less profit to the farmers**. | • Collective purchase of inputs from the company at the lower rate.<br>• Access to the credit facility which is easily given to the group.<br>• Example: Sai Pravara Farmers Producers Company from Maharashtra (25-30%) |

# AGRICULTURE EXPORTS

## Status of Exports

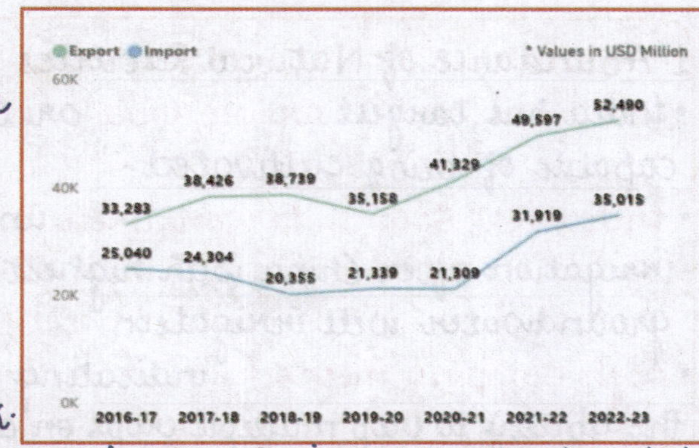


- Total agricultural export basket accounts for a little over 2.15% of world agricultural trade.
- India has remained at the lower end of the global agri-export value chain given that the majority of its exports are low value, raw or semi-processed and marketed in bulk.
- The share of India's high value and value added agri produce in its agri-export basket is less than 15% compared to 25% in US and 49% in China.

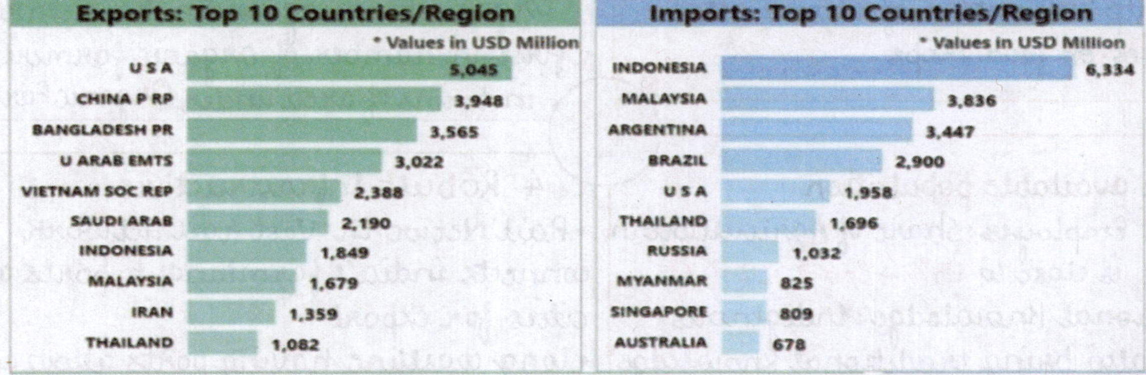


## Benefits

### Economic Benefits

- Higher Exports → Trade Surplus
- Decline in CAD → Boost foreign Reserves
- Global Integration
- Increased market penetration
- Attract private investment

### Social Benefits

- Doubling Farmer's income
- Boost to Allied Sectors.

### Tapping the potential of Indian agriculture

- High agro-climatic zones, largest arable land, leading agricultural producer, traditional knowledge, long coastline, well developed rail networks, growth of agri-tech startups etc.

## Government Initiatives

- Institutions: APEDA and MEDA
- Policies: Agricultural Export Policy, 2018, 100% FDI.
- Infrastructure Development: TIES, SAMPADA Yojana etc.
- Transport and marketing assitance for specified Agricultural Products
- Krishi UDAN 2.0
- Farmer connect Portal

## Potential for Agricultural Exports

**1. Abundance of Natural Resources**
- India has largest arable land or land capable of being cultivated.
- India has second largest area under irrigation after China with highest groundwater well irrigation.
- High cropping intensity indicating the ability to crop multiple crops on a single land.
- India has 20 types of agro-climatic zones that help cultivation of almost all varieties of food crops.

**2. High Agricultural Production**
- Dairy: Largest milk producer in the World
- Fisheries: 3rd largest fisheries production in the world.
- Horticulture: World's second largest producer of fruits and vegetables after China.
- Spices and Condiments. World's largest producer and exporter of spices in the world.
- Organic Farming: India has been ranked first in number of organic farmers & 9th in terms of area under Organic Farming

**3. Huge available population**
- Largest Employer: Share of Agriculture in Exports is close to 45% (PLFS 2022-23)
- Traditional Knowledge: Indigenous people, also bring traditional knowledge in making organic & unique varieties of crops.

**4. Robust Infrastructure**
- Rail Network: Vast rail network connects India's farmlands to ports and cities for export.
- Long coastline having ports allow agri-exports from various parts of the nation.
- Agri-Tech: India's agritech startups have been growing at 25% year on year, thus promising high returns in sector in future.

## Reason for low share of agriculture Exports

**PRODUCTIVITY CHALLENGE**
- Lower than World average Yield rate of rice (2.4 t/ha) and wheat (3.15 t/ha) lower than China, South Africa & many developed nations.
- Fragmented landholdings and small scale farming leads to poor price competitiveness due to lack of initial aggregation.
- Monsoon dependent and poor irrigation coverage.
- Poor logistics connectivity such as congestion at the ports due to high waiting periods of shipment, lack of proper road connectivity to hinterland etc.
- Environmental Factors - Declining water table, soil degradation, fertiliser overuse

| GOVT. POLICIES | |
|---|---|
| | • Adhoc and unstable foreign trading policy regime.<br>• Pro-consumer bias leads to export restrictions. Eg: Wheat export ban.<br>• Poor post harvest infrastructure such as cold storage etc leading to higher wastages<br>• Inadequate implementation of Agriculture Export policy such as low market diversification.<br>• Inadequate trade support to Exporters.<br>• High MSP to farmers. |

| INTERNATIONAL TRADE | |
|---|---|
| | • India's exports are low value, semi-processed items and the share of high value and horticulture crops is lower than global average.<br>• Sanitary and phyto sanitary issues leads to rejection of Indian agri-Exports.<br>• Disputes at the WTO.<br>• India's poor export competitiveness.<br>• High tariffs: Indian agro-products bearing high exports potential have been facing high import duties Eg: Sri-Lanka & Philippines imposed as high as 35% & 40% tariff respectively on Indian Wheat.<br>• Import quota limitation in markets like China (for wheat, corn, sugar etc) and Thailand (instant coffee, rice, pepper etc) are examples of restriction on Indian exports |

## Agricultural Export Policy, 2018

• Launched in 2018 with an aim to utilize the export potential of Indian agriculture, by means of appropriate policy instruments and make India a global power in agriculture and raise farmer's income.

Following are the objectives of policy:

• It is also towards the goal of increasing share of agricultural exports from present about USD 30 billion to over USD 60 billion.

• Getting to one of the top 10 exporting countries of agricultural products is also one of the goals of this policy.

## Elements of Agriculture Export Policy

| OPERATIONAL | |
|---|---|
| | ☛ Focus on clusters<br>☛ Promoting Value-added Exports<br>☛ Marketing and Promotion of "Brand India".<br>☛ Attract Private Investment in Production & processing<br>☛ Establishment of Strong Quality Regimen<br>☛ Research and Development<br>☛ Miscellaneous |

**STRATEGIC**

- Stable Trade Policy Regime
- Liberalising Land leasing Norms & adoption of Model Contract Farming Act by state governments in order to promote agricultural exports → Mobilise private investment leading to large scale mechanisation.
- Reforms in APMC Act & Streamlining of Mandi Fee.
- Holistic Approach to Boost Exports
- Greater involvement of State Governments in Agriculture Exports.
- Identification of a Nodal State Department / Agency for Promotion of Agriculture Export.
- Focus on Export Centric clusters for pre and post harvest management of the production as well as in upgrading supply chain.
- Inclusion of Agricultural Exports in state Export policy.
- Infrastructure and logistics to Facilitate Agricultural Exports
- Institutional mechanism at Union level, State level and Cluster level to Support Exports.

## PYQs Corner

*(Write the Answer and Get Free Evaluation)*

1. What are the main constraints in transport and marketing of agricultural produce in India? [150 Words] [10 Marks] [2020]
2. What do you mean by Minimum Support Price (MSP)? How will MSP rescue the farmers from the low-income trap? [150 Words] [10 Marks] [2018]
3. There is also a point of view that Agricultural Produce Market Committees [APMCs] set up under the State Acts have not only impeded the development of agriculture but also have been the cause of food inflation in India. Critically examine. [200 Words] [12.5 Marks] [2014]

**Edict-1:** Indian Agriculture

CHAPTER 05

# SUBSIDIES AND CROPPING PATTERN

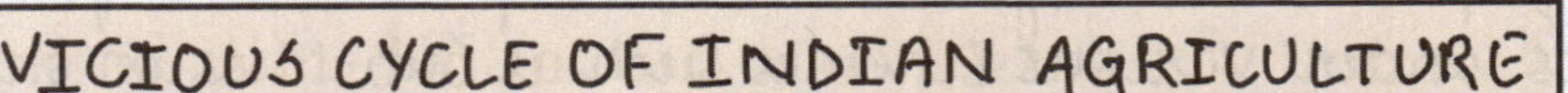


Indian Agriculture → (Monsoon Dependent; ~40% Irrigation Coverage) → Rainfed Agriculture → (Poor Insurance Coverage; + Climate Change) → Risky Business

Risky Business: No Land Records ≠ Collatoral (Poor Land records)

→ (Lack of Financial Inclusion measures) → Lack of Formal Credit.

Often lead to Debt Trap + Costlier Inadequate credit

→ Informal Credit.

→ (Small and Marginal Landholdings; Lack of Govt Support) → Delay in Application of Input

→ (Poor Farm Mechanization) → Low Productivity of crops

→ (Poor Post Harvest; Poor storage) → Low Production

→ (APMC Issues + MSP Issues) → Income Decreases

→ DEBT TRAP

DEBT TRAP → Farmer Suicide (Mental + Physical Harassment).

DEBT TRAP → Distress Migration (Urban Slums)

# AGRICULTURE SUBSIDIES

- An agricultural subsidy is a governmental financial support paid to farmers and agri-businesses to supplement their income, manage the supply of agricultural commodities and influence the cost and supply of such commodities.
- According to Economic Survey 2021, India spends about 2% of GDP on farm subsidies.

## Types of Agricultural Subsidies

- **Credit Subsidy**: Government provides credit subsidy in the form of interest subvention scheme or farm loan waivers.
- **Electricity Subsidy**: Many states throughout India provide free of cost electricity to farmers. Eg: Punjab, Andhra Pradesh, Karnataka etc.
- **Fertiliser Subsidy**: Estimated to be 1.75 lakh crore (FY 2023-24)
- **Agriculture Equipment Subsidy**: Subsidies are provided to farmers through state governments under various schemes such as Sub-Mission on Agricultural Mechanisation (SMAM), Rashtriya Krishi Vikas Yojana (RKVY) for the purchase of various agricultural equipments and machines
- **Income Support**: Government also provides income support such as PM-KISAN Scheme.
- **Minimum Support Price**: Government procure the crops from the farmers at MSP prices for food security and provides to beneficiaries under National Food Security Act (NFSA), thus bearing huge subsidy burden.
- **Other Subsidies**: Seed subsidy, Irrigation subsidy under PM Krishi Sinchai Yojana etc

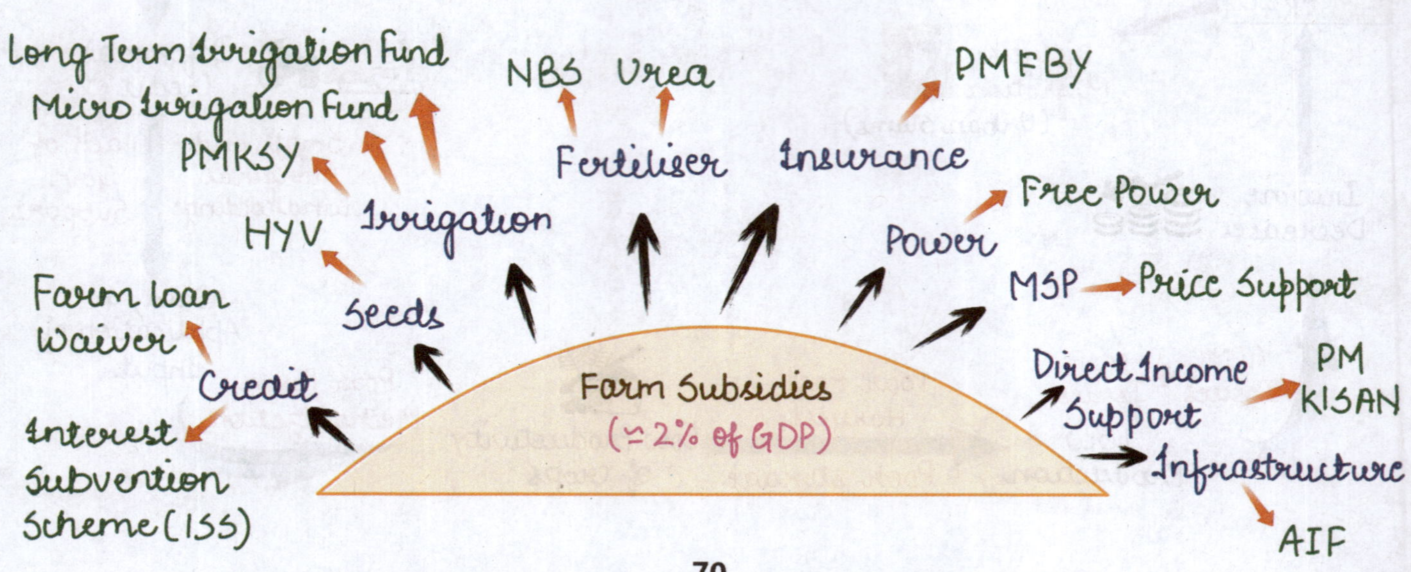

## Benefits of Agricultural Subsidies

- Assured Farmer's income and increase in purchasing power of farmers.
  - Farm Subsidies constitute around 21% of farmer's income (Ministry of Agriculture and Farmer's welfare)
- Support to small and marginal farmers (86% of the farmers are Small and Marginal.
- Economic rationale of subsidies: Incentivising the producers to increase production leading to high growth in national income & achieving desirable structure of production.

  Eg: Subsidies during Green Revolution increased the production of cereals from 50 million tonnes of food grains (food importing nation) in 1950s to more than 300 million tonnes presently (food exporting nation)
  - Recent push is being given for production of millets, oilseeds and pulses in achieving the goal of nutritional security.
- Improvement in productivity of land Such as fertiliser subsidies ensure balanced use of fertilisers, improving soil productivity.
- Improvement in human development: Improved farm incomes & food security aids in addressing issues like malnutrition, improving overall living standard.
- Crop Diversification: Incentivising 'less focused' crops that can have nutritional and environmental benefits.

  Eg: Recent push to millet (Shree Anna) production
- Adoption of technology and promotion of farm mechanization which is socially desirable but whose adoption needs huge capital and producers believe it to be risky investment.

  Eg: Green Revolution provided Support to adopt new HYV seeds & chemical fertilisers
- Increased use of technology and better infrastructure in agricultural activities lead to increased efficiency, profitability and reduce distress migration
- Creation of Capital Assets (Eg. Cold storage) through infrastructure subsidy to reduce post harvest losses of perishable agricultural produce.

  Eg: Agriculture Infrastructure Fund (AIF)
- Minimization of income inequalities i.e inter-regional and intra-regional imbalances.
- Boost to agricultural Exports.

## Distortions created by agricultural Subsidies

- Cereal Centric, Regionally Biased and Input Intensive: Neglectful towards pulses, oil Seeds and Coarse cereals → Import of these crops and food inscurity in lower strata which depend upon coarse cereals.

➡ Unsustainable fiscal burden: In 2017-18, the annual central government subsidies to farmers was of Rs 1,20,500 crores. In the same period, the annual state government subsidies are almost of an equal amount of Rs 1,15,500 crore.

- Pose a threat to sustainability to subsidies itself.

➡ Indiscriminate use of Price Subsidies: They tend to create inefficiencies since they embed incentives for fraud, diversion and waste.

➡ Regressive nature of Subsidies: Most of the subsidies go to the rich farmers and the rich states which are able to grow marketable surplus and have well developed infrastructure.

Eg: Fertiliser subsidies are generally cornered by manufacturers and rich farmers of Punjab, Haryana and Western U.P.

➡ Compromise of investment in capital infrastructure in agriculture which is responsible for increasing agricultural productivity.

- From 1976 to 2003 - Subsidies increased but public investment in agriculture declined.

➡ Inefficient and wasteful use of natural resources: Eg- Power subsidy has led to overuse of groundwater which has further resulted into dramatic fall in groundwater levels.

➡ Environmental Effects and decline in Soil Fertility: The Parliamentary Standing Committee on Agriculture observed that there is an imbalance in fertiliser use in terms of NPK as evidenced by their wider consumption ratio of (6·7):(2·4):1 in country against their desirable ratio of 4:2:1.

- Punjab & Haryana have NPK use ratio as high as (31·4):8:1 and (27·7):(6·1):1 respectively.
- This harms the soil fertility, biodiversity, & also leads to eutrophication (increased nutrients in water bodies, eventually leading to decreased oxygen concentration in them) and bio-accumulation/bio-magnification.

➡ WTO Concerns: MSP is considered trade distortionary and breaches the Aggregate Measure of Support (AMS) level limited by the WTO norms.

- Developing countries can provide subsidies which fall under Amber Box (trade-distorting subsidies) upto 10% of agricultural production in 1986-88.

## SUBSIDIES VS INVESTMENT

- The share of public sector investment in total agricultural investment was as high as 33·6% during 1960s but has come down to 15% during 2010-17 (average Rs 40,100 crore per annum.
- Corporate investment is only 3% of the total Private investment, predominantly by farm households is 82% and it holds the major share of total investment in agriculture and allied activities.

• Almost 80% of the public expenditure going to agriculture is in form of input Subsidies (fertilisers, power, irrigation) and only 20% as investment in Agriculture.

## Critical Analysis of Subsidies

### Benefits / Need

**Economic Reasons**
- Adoption of new technology.
- Increased farm productivity
- Wide number of small and marginal farmers
- Desirable structure of agricultural production
- Increase in exports
- Part of farm income (21% per hectare
- Boost to national Output

**Social Aspects**
- Addressing inter-regional & intra-regional inequalities
- Food Security (Part of redistributive policies)
- Emergence income support.

### Issues

**Economic Effects**
- Fiscal Implications
- Unsustainable short term solutions
- Market disruptions which ultimately affects poor farmers.
- Inefficient usage of resources - leakages, misutilisation, frauds.
- Does not cater to demand of consumers
- Concentration to few crops.

**Environmental Impact**
- Depletion of groundwater table
- Declining soil fertility.
- Environmental Pollution (Air, Water, etc)

**Other issues**
- Increased disparity between small, marginal & large farmers.
- Issue of Targeting: Lack of Conclusive Land Titles. Lack of Database
- Regressive nature of subsidies, Delay in payment of subsidies.

## Need for Higher Investment in Agriculture

➜ **Long term Infrastructure development**: Improve rural infrastructure such as irrigation systems, roads and storage facilities.
- This can enhance productivity, reduce post harvest losses and improve market access for farmers.

➜ **Crop Diversification**. Encourage the cultivation of perishable products, thereby exerting favourable influence on crop diversification.

➜ **Higher Returns**: Research clearly shows that marginal returns on agri-investments are 5 to 10 times higher than from agri-input subsidies.
- Every Rs 10 lakh invested on farm research potentially pulled 328 people

out of poverty.

- likewise, every Rs 1 spent on agricultural research & development increase farm GDP by Rs 11.2.

➦ Poverty Reduction: Poverty showed a marked reduction (from mid 1970s to the end of 1980s) was also a decade when investment in agriculture rose phenomenally and agriculture Sector growth was highest.

➦ Support Agricultural Research and Development leading to the adoption of new technologies, improved seeds and better farming practices.

## Government steps to improve capital formation

➡ Irrigation Infrastructure: PM Krishi Sinchayee Yojana, Long term Irrigation Fund and Micro-Irrigation Fund.

➡ Post-Harvest Infrastructure: Agri tech Infrastructure Fund (AIF)

➡ Rural Infrastructure: Rural Infrastructure Development Fund (RIDF), PM Gram Sadak Yojana.

➡ Subsidised loans and interest rate subsidies. Eg: Kisan Credit Card (KCC) and Interest Subvention Scheme (ISS)

➡ Research and Development Support to improve farming techniques, crop varieties and livestock breeds. Eg: HYP Seeds, GM Crops like BT mustard

➡ Public Private Partnerships: leverage the strength of both sectors to enhance investment, technology transfer & market linkages in the agricultural sector.

➡ Farmer's training and Capacity building. Eg: Krishi Vigyan Kendras (KVKs)

## Ways to improve Investment in Agriculture

➡ Public investment in agriculture & irrigation must increase at 14% per annum (Ashok Dalwai Committee)

➡ Each state must prioritize public expenditure on investment and subsidy that will enable higher productivity gains.

- Research shows that low per capita income states, largely lagging in agricultural growth & having dominance of small holders, will get higher payoffs from additional public investment in irrigation & in power and irrigation subsidies.

➡ Private capital can also be encouraged in certain rural projects such as in Solar power, weather stations, digital information on rainfall, soil moisture and irrigation requirements etc.

- India spends barely 0.5% of national income on R&D in agriculture, which is very low compared to about 3% in developed countries.

➡ Intensify research on yield augmenting & water conserving technologies.

➡ Investment in the backward states has greater productivity-enhancement effect than investment in the favoured regions, since the scope for productivity growth and poverty reduction in backward states are greater.

# CROPPING PATTERN

- Cropping pattern refers to the proportion of the area under different crops at a particular period of time in a unit area
  - It is yearly Sequence and spatial arrangement of sowing and fallow on a given area
- It is a dynamic concept as the pattern changes because of the influence of physical, cultural, technological and economic factors.
- The changes due to differences in irrigation facilities are mainly happening from traditional crops to the HYV crops and from cereals to commercial & cash crops.

## Factors affecting Cropping pattern of a region

- **Geo-Climatic factors**: It includes factors like nature of soil, climate, rainfall etc.
  - Rice is the most appropriate crop in areas having sufficient rainfall & suitable conditions for water logging like in West Bengal.
  - Jowar and Bajra are grown in rain-deficit areas such as Rajasthan & Gujarat
  - The fertile well drained soil of indo-Gangetic Plains is suitable for growing Wheat.
  - The Black soil in Deccan and Malwa Plateau supports Cotton cultivation.
- **Economic factors**:
  - Profitability is the most important factor. Farmers have changed their cropping pattern from traditional crops towards the cultivation of cash crops to reap the benefits of higher demand and increased purchasing power of people.
  - Prices of agricultural commodities, income of farmers, availability of agricultural inputs and marketing facilities, nature of land tenure, availability of finance etc. also determine cropping pattern.
  - Poor farmers with small landholdings prefer to grow cereals & other food grains rather than opting for cash crops.
- **Government Policies** such as price incentives (MSP/ FRP) or subsidies play a very important role in the cropping pattern.
  - There has been a shift from pulses to wheat-rice cropping pattern in certain areas.
  - National Mission on Edible Oil-Oil Palm (NMEO-OP) is launched to increase edible oil production and availability in the country.
- **Infrastructure factors** such as irrigation has helped in cultivation of rice in areas which is not naturally suitable for its cultivation.
  Eg: Punjab and Haryana gets less amount of rainfall but still able to cultivate rice.

• Good road infrastructure and cold storage facilities have boosted the production of horticulture crops.
• Encourage multiple cropping.

- **Historical factors:** Crops such as Tea, Coffee, tobacco & cashew nuts were brought to India by British and Portuguese.
- **Technological factors:** Eg- Green Revolution using HYV seeds led to record production in cereals. Gene Revolution using Bt cotton led to record production in cotton.
- **Socio-cultural factors:** It includes religion, customs, traditions etc.
  Eg: Sikh farming community discards the cultivation of tobacco in Punjab despite profitability & favourable environmental conditions suitable for tobacco cultivation.
  • Food habits also play a role - East and South India prefers rice as staple food while it is wheat in North India.

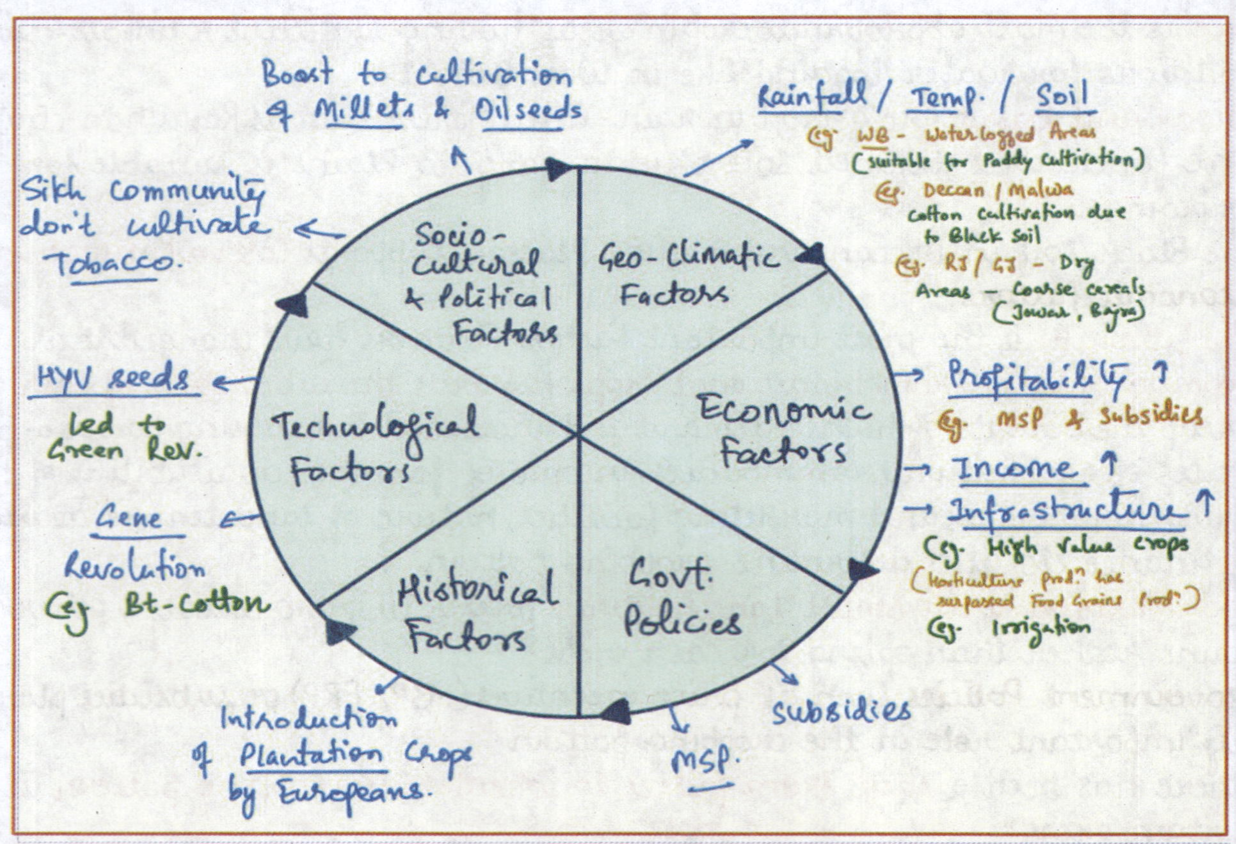


Role of Subsidies in encouraging crop diversity and changing cropping pattern according to the demands of people

- **Financial incentives for diversification:** Eg- Government of India's National Horticulture Mission provides subsidies for cultivation of fruits, vegetable, and other high-value crops, promoting crop diversification.

- Support for market driven crop choices and achieving Self-reliance: Eg- Subsidy Support provided for cultivation of pulses and Oilseeds.
- Research and Development Subsidies can promote crop diversification & the adoption of new cropping patterns
- Infrastructure Development Subsidies: Eg- Subsidies for cold storage facilities can facilitate the cultivation and marketing of perishable horticultural crops
- Risk Mitigation subsidies can encourage farmers to experiment with new crops & cropping patterns.
  - this can include subsidies for crop insurance, weather based insurance or income support during transition period.
- Collaboration with Private Sector and NGOs: Subsidies can be utilised to encourage collaboration between the public Sector, private sector and non-governmental organisations (NGOs) to promote crop diversification.

## Evolution of Cropping Pattern

**Pre-1960s — Pre-Green Revolution**

- 3/4th area under Food Crops (Due to historical and Economic factors)

**1960s-1980s — Green Revolution**

- Technological factors
- Government policies
- Economic factors

↓ Cropping pattern change

↓ Rice-wheat cropping pattern

**Economic Reforms (1991 Onwards)**

- Increase in Per capita Income
- Increase in Urbanisation
- Changed tastes & preferences
- Agriculture modernisation
- Infrastructure Development

Food Crop → Non-Food Crop

76.7% (1950) — 23% (1950)

65% (2c — 37% (2001)

(Esp. Horticulture)

- Increase in consumption of vegetable & fruits; milk, egg, fish, edible oils.
- Shift in allocation of area from food crops to non-food crops reflect a change from subsistence cropping to commercial cropping.

## Rice-Wheat Cropping Pattern

- Rice-wheat cropping system is India's most widely adopted cropping system practiced on an estimated area of around 11 million hectares.
- This system is prevalent in Indo-Gangetic Plains (IGP) and is predominant in Uttar Pradesh, Punjab, Haryana, Bihar, West Bengal, Madhya Pradesh etc.
- The Pattern in itself is so robust that three fourth of the country's annual domestic need for wheat and rice is fulfilled by a handful of states in region.

## Monoculture (Rice-Wheat)

| Reasons | Consequences |
|---|---|
| 1. Ideal geographical conditions such as water through monsoonal rainfall, cool & moist weather etc.<br>2. Green Revolution: Adoption of HYV seeds (input-responsive, short duration varieties) resulting into multiple cropping.<br>• In this pattern, rice is grown during the summer months, followed by wheat in winter months.<br>3. High MSPs for both of these crops resulting into high profitability for the farmers.<br>4. Rice and wheat are core food preferences in India.<br>5. Low land holding farmers (86% farmers are small & marginal) produce rice & wheat for own consumption.<br>6. Technological Penetration: Increased availability of machines, irrigation technology led to increased cropping area and more productivity.<br>7. Rice is top agricultural exports from India. | 1. Threat to nutritional security resulting into hidden hunger (Neglect of coarse cereals and pulses)<br>2. Overuse of chemical fertilisers & pesticides result into soil degradation and poor underground water quality.<br>3. Soil degradation → low agricultural productivity → Threat to Food Security.<br>4. High subsidy burden on government due to open-ended procurement.<br>5. Wastage of food grains as open-ended procurement of rice and wheat has exceeded the storage capacity & thus resulting in unscientific storage.<br>6. Monoculture nature of Rice-Wheat system makes it susceptible to pest & disease outbreak & vulnerable to climate change, which can lead to crop failures & reduced yields.<br>7. Ecological Effects: Groundwater crisis as rice is a water-intensive crop (Punjab and Haryana); Air Pollution due to crop residue burning (UP, Punjab & Haryana); loss of biodiversity due to excessive use of hybrid seeds and fertilisers; GHG emissions due to methane generation etc<br>8. Import dependency for crops like pulses, Oilseeds etc. |

## CROP DIVERSIFICATION

- Crop Diversification refers to the practice of cultivating a variety of crops instead of relying on a single crop.
- This can be done in various forms such as addition of new crop(s) as intercrop &/or predecessor or successor crops, changing number of crop (multi-cropping),

modified cropping system and adopting a new, integrated cropping pattern with changing agronomical practices.

- The traditional pattern of agriculture in India has wider crop diversity, and is more stable and pro-nature.
- In the Garhwal Himalayan region of India, Barahnaja is a crop diversification system for cultivating 12 crops in a year.
  - 'Barah Anaaj' literally means '12 foodgrains' and is the traditional heritage of the area

| Type of Diversification | Nature of Diversification | Potential Benefits |
|---|---|---|
| • Improved structural diversity | • Makes crops within field more structurally diverse | • Pest Suppression. |
| • Genetic diversification in monoculture | • Cultivation of mixture of varieties of same species in a monoculture | • Disease Suppression, Increased production stability |
| • Diversify field with fodder grass. | • Growing fodder grasses alongside of food/pulse/vegetable oilseeds etc. | • Pest suppression, opportunity to livestock farming. |
| • Crop rotations | • Temporal diversity through crop rotations (Sequential cropping) | • Disease Suppression, Increased production stability |
| • Polyculture | • Spatial and temporal diversity of crops (Growing two or more crop species within the field) | • Insect, pest disease suppression, climate change buffering and increased production. |
| • Agroforestry | • Growing crops & trees together (Spatial and temporal diversity) | • Pest Suppression and climate change buffering. |

## Benefits of Crop Diversification

1. Nutritional Security: The Cultivation of millets & pulses have significant benefits for the person's health & economy's health also.
2. Sustainable agricultural practices: Crop diversification promote biodiversity, reduced soil erosion, enhance soil fertility & minimize the risk of pest and disease outbreaks. Adoption of crop diversification helps in conservation of natural resources like - Introduction of legumes in the rice-wheat cropping pattern, which has the ability to fix atmospheric nitrogen and help in Sustaining soil fertility.

3. Food Security: Crop diversification strengthens food security by reducing risk associated with mono-cropping and strengthening the resilience of the agricultural system.

4. Shift from water intensive crops to water productive crops, thereby addressing water crisis.

5. Increase in farmers income: Crop Diversification allows farmers to tap into multiple markets & diversify their income sources. By growing a range of crops, farmers can take advantage of price fluctuations, market demand and value-added opportunities.

6. Self-Reliance: India meets more than 50% of its oil seed requirement through imports.

7. Climate resilient agriculture.

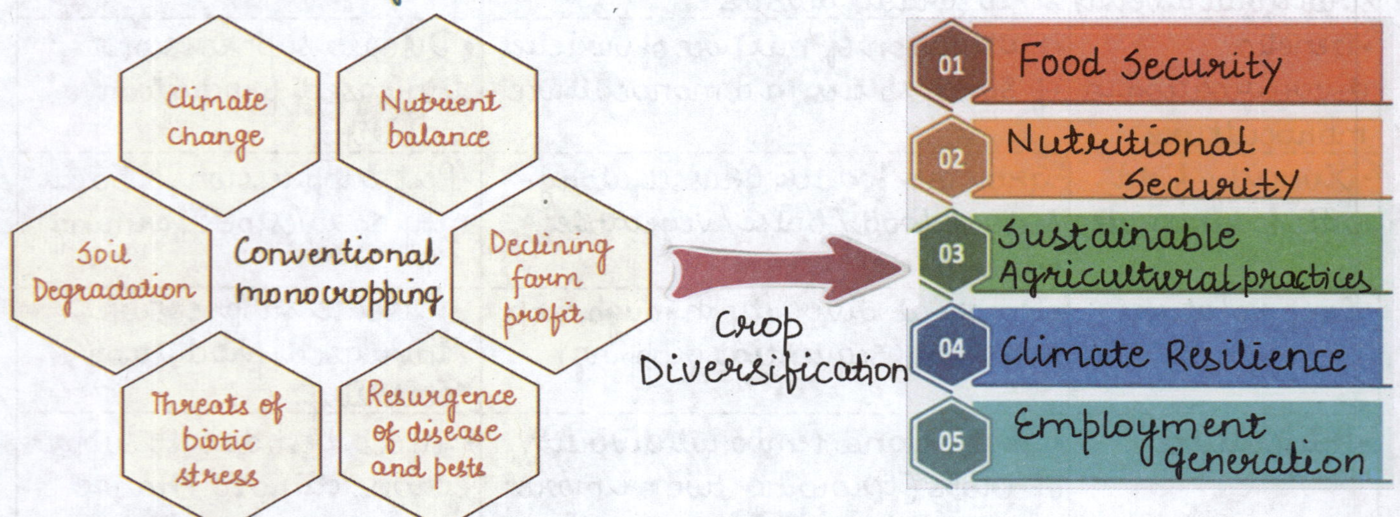


## Measures taken by government to promote crop diversification

Rashtriya Krishi Vikas Yojana (RKVY): Supports state governments in implementing various agricultural development programs, including crop diversification

National Mission on Oilseeds & Oil Palm (NMOOP): increase production of Oilseeds & Oil Palm

National Food Security Mission (NFSM): Increase production of pulses, oilseeds, and coarse cereals

Pradhan Mantri Krishi Sinchayee Yojana (PMKSY): Farmer are encouraged to diversify their crops & cultivate water intensive crops in a sustainable manner

Market Intervention Schemes: Price Support and procurement mechanisms for alternative crops which incentivize cultivation of diversified crops

# LAND PRODUCTIVITY TO WATER PRODUCTIVITY

- Water productivity is a measure of water use efficiency in agriculture measured on the basis of total water input & total crop output
- Land productivity tells us about crop produced from unit area of agricultural land
  - Green Revolution focused on increasing production and improving land productivity while water was treated as surplus unlimited resource
- India's cropping pattern highlights the rampant cultivation of water intensive crops such as sugarcane production in Maharashtra, Paddy in North-West India which are amongst water stressed regions of India.
  - Along with this, India is the largest exporter of rice which is commonly observed as export of virtual water by the Economic Survey.

## Reason behind this trend of water-intensive crop cultivation

- Government's incentivize structure that includes subsidies on water, power & fertilizer has promoted farmers to cultivate highly water intensive crops such as paddy and sugarcane
- High MSP & effective procurement mainly of water-intensive crops.
- Demand for water intensive crops: Rice is one of the most important staple food crops in India; large industrial demand for crops like cotton.
- India's agri-export basket consists mainly of those items which are water-intensive such as rice, coffee, tea & therefore putting more pressure on water resources.
- Lack of sensitization among farmers about the strain on natural resources due to water-intensive crops.

## Why is there a need to shift from 'land productivity to water productivity'

Economic Survey 2018-19 suggest a transition from land productivity to irrigation water productivity, which emphasizes on more crops per drop, improving total nutrition per drop and total food crops per drop. The need for such a shift is due to the following factors

- Water Crisis: India has only 4% of world's water resources while accounting for 18% of world's population. This causes a stark gap in demand-supply of water resources, leading to already water-stressed situation
  - Example of recent water crisis: Bengaluru (2024), Delhi (2024) etc
- Skewed balance of input & output: India's agricultural sector accounts for 87% of groundwater extraction (Ministry of Jal Shakti) for irrigation purposes, but contributes only 15% to the country's GDP
- Nutrition and Food Security: Focus on cultivation of less water intensive

crops like Millets, Bajra etc & simultaneously address the persistent malnutrition problem.

- Climate change has increased the frequency of drought in the country.
- Improving soil productivity: Overuse of water has resulted into the Salinisation of soil in states like Punjab and Haryana which has lowered the productivity.

## Futuristic Measures

- Focus on crop diversification, sustainable practices like Zero Budget Natural Farming (ZBNF), nudging farmers to use micro-irrigation techniques such as drip irrigation and micro-sprinklers.
- The focus should be on growing crops, which are climatically suitable for any region
  - In Eastern India, water intensive crops can be grown while in semi-arid regions of India like Central India, Rajasthan etc the focus should be on cultivation of less water intensive crops like millets and bajra etc.
- Use of traditional methods for water conservation (Eg-Johad) would improve alongside modern methods as fog catchers, grey water usage, water recycling etc.
- ICT can optimize optimal water use in form of Precision Agriculture etc.
- Economic Survey suggests use of optimal fertiliser dose based on soil health status, promotion of neem coated urea, promotion of micro nutrients, promotion of organic fertilisers & promotion of water soluble fertilisers.

## OILSEEDS SECTOR

INDIA → World's Largest Importer of Oilseeds
(50% of domestic requirements met by Imports)

- 62% → Palm Oil (Indonesia, Malaysia); 22% → Soyabean (Argentina, Brazil); 15% → Sunflower (Russia, Ukraine)

### Reason for Import Dependency

- Insufficient Domestic production to keep pace with the rising demand.
  - Limited availability of arable land (70% rainfed), low productivity & unfavourable agro-climatic conditions.
- Growing Demand: Driven by factors such as population growth, increasing urbanisation, higher income and changing dietary patterns
  - India is the world's second largest consumer of edible oils (Economic Survey 21-22)
- Price Competitiveness: Imported edible oils, particularly palm oil & soyabean oil, often prove to be more price competitive compared to domestically produced oils

- Challenges in the Cultivation of Palm oil:
- Climate limitations: Country's diverse agro-climatic zones limit the suitable regions for palm oil cultivation as it requires tropical or sub-tropical climates with high temperatures & abundant rainfall.
- High land requirements for large scale plantations but the suitable land is limited due to competing land uses for food crops, forests & other agricultural activities
- water guzzling crop and therefore, has high water footprint.
- Environmental concerns: Impact on deforestation, biodiversity loss, and greenhouse gas emissions.
- long gestation period of around 3-4 years
- low productivity in India as compared to other major palm oil-producing countries like Indonesia and Malaysia.

  Reason: Sub-optimal agronomic practices, limited adoption of modern technology and best practices and inadequate access to quality planting material & inputs.
- Susceptible to pests and disease outbreak → Impacting the productivity.

## NATIONAL MISSION ON EDIBLE OIL- OIL PALM (NMEO-OP)

- Objectives: It is a new centrally sponsored scheme with following objectives:
  - To harness domestic edible oil prices that are dictated by expensive palm oil imports and become self-reliant in edible oil
  - To raise the domestic production of palm oil by three times to 11 lakh MT by 2025-26.
- Features of the Scheme
  - Raising the area under oil palm cultivation to 10 lakh hectares (Additional 6.5 lakh hectares) by 2025-26 and 16.7 lakh hectares by 2029-30.
  - Oil palm farmers will be provided financial assistance and will get remuneration under a price & viability formula.

Oil palm produces 10 to 46 times more oil per hectare compared to other oilseed crops and has yield of around 4 tons oil per ha.

- Price Assurance: The viability formula is a Minimum Support Price-type mechanism and the government will fix this at 14.3% of crude Palm Oil (CPO) price which will eventually go up to 15.3%.
  - This assurance will inculcate confidence on the Indian oil palm farmers to go for increased area and thereby more production of palm oil.
- Improving the productivity of oilseeds and oil palm: To substantially increase the support of input/interventions, implementing advanced agricultural practices, promoting efficient irrigation techniques and adoption of modern technologies.

- Special emphasis of the scheme to India's North Eastern (NE) states and the Andaman & Nicobar Islands due to conducive weather conditions in the regions.

- Benefits
  - The Scheme will eventually benefit the oil palm farmers, increase capital investment, create employment generation, shall reduce import dependence and also increase the income of farmers.
  - Protect the farmers from the fluctuations of the international CPO prices and protect him from the volatility.

## MILLETS (NUTRI-CEREALS/SHREE ANNA)

- United Nations General Assembly (UNGA) declared 2023 as the International Year of Millet (IYM), a proposal sponsored by Government of India to promote these
- Millets are a highly varied group of small-seeded grasses, widely grown around the world as cereal crops/grains for fodder & human food.
- Among 1st crops to be domesticated in India with several evidences of consumption during Indus Valley civilization.
- India = Largest producer of Millets in the world.
- India, China and Nigeria are the largest producers of millets in the world, accounting for more than 55% of the global production
- Major Millets Producing States: Rajasthan, UP, Haryana, Gujarat, MP, Karnataka, Maharashtra, Tamil Nadu, Andhra Pradesh, and Telangana
- Three states; Rajasthan, UP and Haryana accounts for more than 81% share in total millet products. Rajasthan contributes half of total millet production.

### Significance of Millets

- Less Expensive and Nutritionally Superior to wheat and Rice owing to high protein, fibre, vitamins and minerals like Iron content.
- Rich in Calcium and Magnesium. Eg - Ragi is known to have highest calcium content among all food grains.
- Gluten free and have low Glycemic Index (a relative ranking of Carbohydrate in foods according to how they affect blood glucose levels) - Helps to tackle lifestyle problems & health challenges such as Obesity and Diabetes.
- Low carbon and water footprint (Rice plant needs atleast 3 times more water to grow in comparison to millets.
- Less Water Consuming and are capable of growing under drought conditions, under non-irrigated conditions even in very low rainfall regions

☛ Alignment with the SDGs: By promoting millet consumption, India Contributes to SDG 2 (Zero Hunger) and SDG 13 (Climate Action).

## Millets : an approach for sustainable agriculture and healthy World

**Food Security**
- Sustainable food source for combating hunger in changing world climate.
- Resistant to climatic stress, pests and diseases.

**Economic Security**
- Climate resilient crop.
- Sustainable income for farmers
- Low investment needed for production
- Value addition can lead to economic gains.

**Nutritional Security**
- Rich in micronutrients like calcium, zinc, iron, iodine etc.
- Rich in bioactive compounds
- Better amino acid profile.
- Address the problem of Hidden Hunger.

**Safety from diseases**
- Gluten free: a substitute for wheat in celiac diseases.
- Low GI. a good food for diabetic persons.
- Can help to combat cardiovascular diseases, anaemia, calcium deficiency etc

## Constraints in Millet production

1. Low productivity of Millets as compared to other crops.
   Eg: Pearl millet (bajra) typically yields around 1000 kg per hectare, whereas rice yields can be significantly higher (around 3000 kg per hectare).
2. Decline in the cultivable area from 35 million hectares to just 15 million hectares.
   Reason: Urbanisation, changing cropping patterns and shift towards cash crops like Cotton and Soyabean.
3. Lower Demand for Millets as compared to other competitives staples like Rice and wheat.
   - Lack of awareness about health benefits of millets, leading to low demand.
   - High cost: Millets are often priced higher than traditional cereals, making them less accesible to low-income consumers.
   - Negative perception: Millets are often associated with poverty and considered "Poor man's food" which discourages consumption as incomes rise and lifestyles change.
4. Limited processing facilities hindering value addition & market presence.

5. Short Shelf life: Millet flour may become rancid more quickly than wheat flour.

## Initiatives taken by the Indian government to promote millet production

- National Millets Mission (NMM)
- Sub-Mission on Nutri-cereals (Millets) under National Food Security Mission (NFSM)
- PLI Scheme for Food Processing Industry for Millet-based Products (PLISMBP)
- International Year of Millets (IYM) - 2023.
- Inclusion of Millets under the Poshan Abhiyan.
- MAHARSHI Initiative (Millets and Other Ancient Grains Initiative)
- Integration of millets in the PDS System.

## PYQs Corner
*(Write the Answer and Get Free Evaluation)*

1. What are the direct and indirect subsidies provided to farm sector in India? Discuss the issues raised by the World Trade Organization (WTO) in relation to agricultural subsidies. [150 Words] [10 Marks] [2023]
2. Explain the changes in cropping pattern in India in the context of changes in consumption pattern and marketing conditions. [150 Words] [10 Marks] [2023]
3. What are the present challenges before crop diversification? How do emerging technologies provide opportunity for crop diversification? [250 Words] [15 Marks] [2021]
4. What are the major factors responsible for making rice-wheat system a success? In spite of this success how has this system become bane in India? [250 Words] [15 Marks] [2020]
5. How has the emphasis on certain crops brought about changes in cropping patterns in recent past? Elaborate the emphasis on millets production and consumption. [250 Words] [15 marks][2018]
6. What are the major reasons for declining rice and wheat yield in the cropping system? How crop diversification is helpful to stabilize the yield of the crop in the system? [250 Words] [15 marks][2017]
7. How do subsidies affect the cropping pattern, crop diversity and economy of farmers? What is the significance of crop insurance, minimum support price and food processing for small and marginal farmers? [250 Words] [15 marks] [2017]
8. What are the different types of agriculture subsidies given to farmers at the national and at state levels? Critically analyse the agricultural subsidy regime with reference to the distortions created by it.[200 Words] [10 Marks] [2013]

CHAPTER 06

# ALLIED SECTORS

Farmer's Income

Moving from Farm Sector to Non-Farm Sector
- Boost to manufacturing Sector
- Labour Intensive Industries Promoted

Promotion of Food Processing industries
- Reduced Post Harvest losses
- Contract Farming
- Employment Generation.

Encouraging Allied Sectors
- Supplement Farm's Income
- More resistant to Climate change and other calamities.

Remunerative Prices against their produce
- Improved Storage Infrastructure
- Reduced Post Harvest losses
- MSP Reforms
- APMC Reforms (Alternative market channels need to be improved)
- Boosting Agri-Exports.

Increase Productivity
- Timely & Adequate Credit
- Increased Insurance Coverage
- Increased Irrigation Cover. (+ Micro-Irrigation)
- Technological Factors
- Land Reforms (Digitisation, land lease)

# AGRICULTURAL DIVERSIFICATION

## Allied Sectors

Agricultural Diversification

Crop Diversification → Promotion of Allied Sectors.

- Agricultural Diversification comprises of two set of activities:
  - 01 Crop Diversification that encourages the farmers to grow multiple varieties of crops (especially farmer should shift from low value crops to high value crops).
  - 02 Promotion of Allied Sectors: Activities which are related to agriculture
    - (a) Livestock: Raising of domesticated animals, which can be used for a variety of purposes like cow, buffalo, sheep, goat.
      Dairy Sectar, Poultry Sectar
    - (b) Fisheries
    - (c) Horticulture - Fruits/Vegetables
    - (d) Sericulture

### Need of Agriculture Diversification

**Meeting Consumer Demand**

- Rise in per capita income + Increase Urbanization ↓ Change in Dietary Preferences towards nutritious Food.
- Food Security to Nutritional Security (Hidden Hunger addressed)

**Issues in Agriculture**

- Supplement Farm Income
- Additional source of livelihood (Empowerment Generation)
- Income Diversification
- Resilience from climate change.

**Socio-Economic Benefits**

- Inclusive Growth
  - Poverty Reduction
  - Equitable Distribution of livestock
  - Promates Gender Equity
- Social Status
- Economic Security
- Helps to Boost Agriculture Exports.
- Bio-gas (Energy Security)

Agricultural Diversification is a solution to various issues of Indian Agriculture

- Migration of risks associated with mono-cropping such as pest outbreaks and weather-related disasters.
  - Example: Intercropping of legumes with cereals improving soil fertility,

enhances pest control and provides income diversification for farmers.

- Increased Income Opportunities : Crop Diversification enables farmers to tap into new markets, increase their income, and reduce dependence on a single crop.
- Soil Health Improvement by reducing the risk of nutrient depletion and erosion.
  - Example : Farmers in Punjab have successfully implemented crop rotation by incorporating legumes like pulses in their rice-wheat cropping system and reduces the need for synthetic fertilizers.
- Efficient Resource Utilization by matching crop with specific soil and climatic conditions, resulting in improved water and nutrient management.
  - Example : Cultivation of drought-tolerant crops like millets in arid regions of Rajasthan and Karnataka has enabled farmers to maximize water efficiency and adapt to water scarcity conditions.
- Enhanced Nutritional Security by increasing the availability of diverse and nutrient-rich food options.
  - Example : Millets Mission in India focuses on the cultivation and promotion of millets, which are rich in protein, fibre and micronutrients, addressing nutritional deficiencies.
- Contributes to climate resilience by reducing vulnerability to climate change impacts, such as erratic rainfall and temperature fluctuations.
  - Example : In the flood-prone areas of Assam, farmers have succesfully diversified their crops by incorporating flood-tolerant varieties of rice and vegetables, ensuring food security even during periods of flooding.
- Market Diversification catering to varied consumer preferences and reducing market risks.
  - Example : Cultivation of specialty crops like aromatic rice, exotic vegetables, or organic produce enables farmer to tap niche markets, local markets, generating higher returns.
- Promotion of sustainable farming practice, reducing the reliance on synthetic inputs and enhancing agroecosystem resilience.
  - Example : Integrated farming system incorporating crop diversification, live-stock rearing and agroforestry, have shown promising results in sustainable agricultural practices.
  - System of Rice Intensification (SRI) integrates crop diversification, reduced water usage, and organic practices, resulting in higher yields and reduced input costs.

# Livestock Sector

- As per the Economic Survey - 2021, the contribution of Livestock in total agriculture and allied sector Gross Value Added (at Constant Prices) has increased from 24.32% (2014-15) to 28.63% (2018-19).

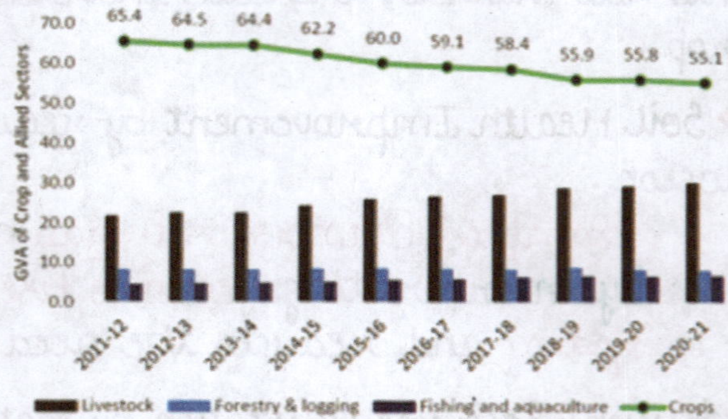


- Livestock provides livelihood to two third of rural community.
    - **India is the highest livestock owner of the world.**
- The total Livestock population is 536.76 million in the country showing an increase of 4.8% over Livestock Census 2012.
- **In 20th Livestock Census,** 35.94% - Cattle (2nd), 27.80% -Goat (2nd), 20.45% - Buffaloes (1st), 13.87% - Sheep (3rd) and 1.69% - Pigs.
- Uttar Pradesh (UP) has recorded highest livestock population in 2019 followed by Rajasthan, MP, West Bengal and Bihar.

## Challenges

- **Degradation and encroachment of grazing land**
- **Outbreak of Diseases: Food and Mouth Disease, Black Quarter Infections, etc.**
- **Yield and Productivity Issues: Largest producer of milk but yield is only about 50% of the global cattle average.**
- **Emission of GHGs: Contributes 58% of agricultural emissions.**
- **Lack of Technology advancements: Limited artificial inseminations, deficiency in quality germplasm, lack of technical manpower.**
- **Funding Issues: Only 12% of the total expenditure on agriculture and allied resulting in inadequate veterinary care,**
- **Poor extension services: Only 5.1% of farm households**
- **Poor Insurance coverage**
- **Underdeveloped and unorganised markets for livestock**
- **High presence of informal sector**
- **Lack of testing facilities for quality checking and standardisation of animal products**
- **Export Constraints: Ad-hoc export policy**

## Government Initiatives

- **Dairy Processing and Infrastructural Development Fund**
- **Animal Husbandry Infrastructure Development Fund**
- **National Livestock Mission**
- **National Animal Disease Control Programme (NADCP)**
- **National Artificial insemination Programme**
- **National Programme for Dairy Development**
- **Rashtriya Gokul Mission**
- **E-Pashu Haat Portal**
- **Pashu-Aadhar**
- **Gobar-Dhan**
- **E-Gopala App**
- **Dairy Entrepreneurship Development Scheme**
- **Geotagging of animals**

# Dairy Sector (360° Analysis)

**Government Initiatives**

- **KCC for Animal Husbandry**
- **Funds – DPIDF, AHIDF**
- **Rashtriya Gokul Mission**
- **Pashu Aadhar**
- **National Artificial Insemination Programme**
- **National Animal Disease Control Programme**

Government Initiatives

Potential of Sector

Challenges in the Dairy Sector

Operation Flood (White Revolution)

**Potential of Sector**

- **Largest bovine population in the world**
- **Milk production increased from 146.3 million tonnes (mt) in 2014-15 to 187.7 mt in 2018-19**
- **NSSO Survey (70th Round) – 23% of agricultural households = Livestock as their principle source of income.**
- **Single-largest agri-commodity in India**
- **Contributes 5% to the national economy**
- **Labour Intensive sector – 70 million people**

**Challenges in the Dairy Sector**

- **Inadequate market facilities and informal sector. Eco. Survey 2018-19 – 36% by the organised sector.**
- **Unhygienic conditions of the cattle**
- **Incidence of Diseases**
- **Low productivity ---> 7.1 kg per day as compared to 25.6 in UK, US (32.8) and Israel (38.6).**
- **Climate Change ----> Increase in temperature ---> Affecting productivity**
- **Poor coverage of livestock insurance.**
- **Infrastructural deficiencies such as cold storage facilities.**

**and many more.....**

**Operation Flood (White Revolution)**

- **Verghese Kurien – Father of Milk Revolution in India**
- **Bedrock of the revolution – Milk Producer Co-operatives**
- **Production by the masses and not by mass production**
- **Improvement in cattle breeding and adoption of new technology**
- **From milk-deficient to largest milk producer surpassing USA in 1998.**

# Poultry Sector (360° Analysis)

**Government Initiatives**

- **National Livestock Mission**
- **Cross-breeding of indigenous species with exotic stocks**
- **Meat Processing Plants**
- **Establishment of disease free zones.**
- **Increasing the number of farmers rearing buffalo under the contractual farming.**

Government Initiatives

Potential of Sector

Concerns in the Poultry Sector

Pink and Silver Revolution

**Potential of Sector**

- **Second-largest poultry market in the world.**
- **World's 3rd largest egg producer and 5th largest meat producer.**
- **Higher production rate than agricultural production.**
- **Growth Factors: Rise in per capita income, increased urbanisation and low poultry prices in India as compared to other countries.**
- **Meat products constitutes one of the largest items of export.**

**Concerns in the Poultry Sector**

- **Low productivity**
- **Quality standards of farm management**
- **Environmental Issues: High GHG emissions; Huge Energy consumption.**
- **Health Risks of various diseases**
- **Marketing and Infrastructural Support**
  - **Unorganised market**
  - **Poor infrastructure such as proper abattoirs and cold storage facilities.**
- **Lack of Government Support**
- **Low processing and value addition**
- **Disparity between states (60% production comes from the Andhra Pradesh)**
- **Avian Influenza – Low demand and less exports**
- **Shortage of human resources**
- **Increasing cost of feed (Corn and soyabean)**

## Fisheries Sector (360⁰ Analysis)

- Blue Revolution 2.0 (Neel Kranti Mission)
- Pradhan Mantri Matsya Sampada Yojana
  - National Genetic Improvement Facility for shrimp breeding
- Fisheries and Aquaculture Infrastructure Development Fund (FIDF)
- KCC for Fisheries
- Announcement of Seaweed Park in Tamil Nadu
- Development of 5 major Fishing Harbours
- Sagar Parikrama

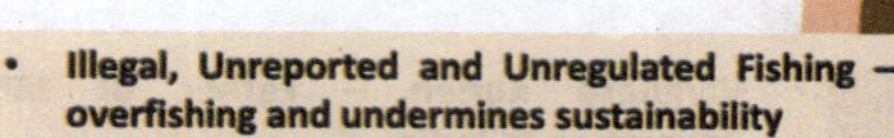

- Vast coastal area and more than 2800 species including marine, freshwater and exotic water varieties.
- World's third largest fish producer
- Marine products constitute the largest item of agriculture export. (4th in world)
- More than 1% contribution to GDP
- Lower climate impact than meat production.
- Cheap and Nutritious food.
- Growth of a subsidiary industries
- Employment to 28 million people

- Illegal, Unreported and Unregulated Fishing – overfishing and undermines sustainability
- Weak monitoring and surveillance systems
- Poor infrastructure leading to post-harvest losses (Inadequate cold-storage facilities)
- Low access to modern technology such as fish finder GPS technology.
- Climate change
- Socio-economic issues (Small-scale and artisanal farmers)
- Limited value addition and inadequate market linkages
- Limited extension services
- Inadequate price discovery mechanism
- Quality of fish products – Exports decline

- Rapid increase in the production of fish and marine product through a package program.
- Launched: During the 7th Five Year Plan (FYP) - 1985 to 1990 during which the government sponsored the Fish Farmers Development Agency
- During the 8th FYP, from 1992-97, the Intensive Marine Fisheries Program was launched in which collaboration with MNCs was encouraged.
- Adoption of the new techniques of fish breeding, rearing, marketing and export.
- From 7.5 lakh tonnes in 1950-51 to record breaking 162.48 lakh tonnes in 2021-22.

### FISHERIES AND AQUACULTURE INFRASTRUCTURE DEVELOPMENT FUND

- **Objective:** FIDF would provide concessional finance to State Governments / UTs and State entities,cooperatives, individuals and entrepreneurs etc., for taking up of the identified investment activities of fisheries development.
- **Funding Pattern:** Funds raised by Nodal Loaning Entitities, Beneficiaries Contribution and Budgetary Support from the GoI.
- **Nodal Loaning Entities (NLEs):** National Bank for Agriculture and Rural Development (NABARD), National Cooperatives Development Corporation (NCDC) and all scheduled banks are the designated NLEs in disbursal of the fund.
- **Interest rate:** Department of Fisheri es under the FIDF provides interest subvention up to 3% per annum for providing the concessional finance by the NLEs at the interest rate not lower than 5% per annum.

## Horticulture Sector (360⁰ Analysis)

- Mission for Integrated Development of Horticulture (MIDH)
- National Horticulture Mission
- Operation Greens
- Cluster Development Programme
- Schemes of Agriculture
- Schemes of Food-processing industry

- **Ranks 2nd in terms of fruits and vegetable production.**
- **Low cost-producer: Favourable agro-climatic conditions, availability of labour and low input costs.**
- **Contributes around 30% of India's GDP.**
- **Horticulture production (Cultivable area =~28 mH) surpassed the food grain production (=~140 mH)**
- **Higher productivity as compared to food grains.**
- **Growth Factors: Rising income, greater health awareness and export demands**
- **Same other benefits like other sectors.**

- **Only account for 1% share in global trade**
- **Production challenges: Small operational land-holdings, lack of irrigation and poor soil management. Pests and diseases.**
- **Limited outreach of farm insurance and farm mechanization + Lack of access to institutional credit.**
- **Increased demand and Climate Change**
- **Land lease constraints**
- **Marketing challenges: Perishable nature, Fragmented supply chains**
- **Poor logistics and inequitable cold storage & warehousing facilitiies**
- **Inadequate storage facilities**
- **Weak FPOs**

- **Period between 1991 to 2003 is known as the Golden Revolution period.**
- **Marked by increased productivity in areas of Horticulture, honey and production.**
- **Horticulture exports of India marked an increase from ₹ 6308.53 crores in 2004-2005 to ₹ 28,62861 crores in 2014-2015.**

### Mission for Integrated Development of Horticulture (MIDH)

- It is a centrally sponsored scheme, launched from 1st April 2014, for the holistic growth of the horticulture sector covering fruits, vegetables, root & tuber crops, mushrooms, spices, flowers, aromatic plants, coconut, cashew, cocoa and bamboo.
- While Government of India (GOI) contributes 60% of total outlayfor developmental programmes in all the states except the states in North East and Himalayas in which 90% contribution is from GOI. In case of Union Territories 100% fund is contributed by central government.
- MIDH has played a significant role in **increasing area and production** during the years 2014–15 to 2019–20.
- Moreover, the mission has boosted best practices to be followed in farms which have significantly improved the quality of produce and productivity of farmland.
- **The initiative of MIDH has not only resulted in India's self-sufficiency in the horticulture sector but also contributed towards achieving sustainable development goals of zero hunger, good health and wellbeing, no poverty, gender equality etc.**

### National Horticulture Mission (NHM)

National Horticulture Mission, a sub-scheme of Mission for Integrated Development of Horticulture (MIDH), is a centrally sponsored scheme launched in 2005-06 to enhance horticulture production and income support to farm households through area-based differentiated strategies.

- **Modernizing production:** NHM focuses on modernizing production through adoption of improved technologies for ensuring the quality of all horticultural crops. NHM provides support for rejuvenating senile plantations at 50% of the cost subject to a maximum ceiling of Rs. 15,000/- per ha limited to 2 ha per beneficiary.
  - Productivity of horticultural crops has increased by about 38% between 2004-05 and 2019-20 and is much higher compared to productivity of food grains (12.49 tones/ha against 2.23 tones/ha.).

- **Provision of critical inputs:** Under production and distribution of planting material, nurseries for producing planting material are established through central assistance.
- **Creation of water sources:** Under NHM, grant will be provided for creating water sources through the construction of community tanks and farm ponds with plastic lining. Example: Establishment of farm ponds at Morasar village, Rajasthan.
- **Nutrient management:** Developing facilities like disease forecasting units, biocontrol labs, plant health clinics and tissue labs will enhance the productivity of horticulture crops. **Example:** Banana tissue culture unit established at Hamalpur, Madhya Pradesh.
- **Increased efficiency:** NHM provides holistic growth through an area based differ entiated strategies and automation in harvesting which will increase the efficiency of the produce. **Example:** Kinnow cultivation in Amritsar district, Punjab
- **Increase in cultivated area:** NHM has played a significant role in increasing the area under horticulture crops. Area and production from 2014-15 to 2019-20 has increased by 9 per cent and 14 per cent respectively.
- **Training of the farmers:** The NHM provides training to farmers to adopt modem method of planting, protecting and harvesting which help in increasing the productivity of crops.
    - **Example:** Farmers were trained in grape cultivation in Karnataka under NHM.

## PYQs Corner

*(Write the Answer and Get Free Evaluation)*

1. Assess the role of National Horticulture Mission (NHM) in boosting the production, productivity and income of horticulture farms. How far has it succeeded in increasing the income of farmers? [250 Words] [15 marks] [2018]
2. Livestock rearing has a big potential for providing non-farm employment and income in rural areas. Discuss suggesting suitable measures to promote this sector in India. [200 Words] [12.5 Marks] [2015]

**Edict-1:** Indian Agriculture

CHAPTER 07

# ROLE OF TECHNOLOGY IN AGRICULTURE

## TECHNOLOGICAL INTERVENTIONS

| Farm Mechanisation | Agricultural Biotechnology | Information and Communication |
|---|---|---|
| ➡ Use of Farm machines<br>➡ Modern Agricultural practices<br>⬇<br>During 1960s | ➡ Use of GM Crops (Bt cotton)<br>(Gene Revolution)<br>➡ Animal Husbandry (Selective Breeding)<br>➡ introduction of HYV seeds | ➡ Satellite-based advisory services.<br>➡ Use of Drones<br>➡ Internet of Things<br>➡ Artificial Intelligence<br>➡ Precision Farming. |

## Why Technological Adoption?

| Indian Agriculture | ➜ Challenges | ➜ Technological Adoption |
|---|---|---|
| ⬇<br>GOALS<br>⬇<br>☛ Food Security<br>☛ Nutritional Security (Millets, Pulses)<br>☛ Self-Reliance (Oilseeds Decline)<br>☛ Farmer's Income<br>☛ Poverty Alleviation<br>☛ Stabilized Prices | ➡ Productivity Challenge<br>➡ Stagnant / Declining Cultivable area ≃ 140 mn ha<br>➡ Poorland Records<br>➡ Climate change<br>➡ Monoculture<br>➡ Rising Population & High demand for Food Security<br>➡ Competing use of land.<br>➡ Declining water table. | (Agriculture Biotech + Information Technology = Tools for Rural Problems)<br>⇩<br>➡ Decreased Rural Poverty<br>➡ Employment Generation<br>➡ increased Productivity<br>➡ Quality improvement of crops<br>➡ Better marketing opportunities<br>➡ Improved Decision making (Soil Health cards / KCC)<br>➡ Improved access to financial services.<br>➡ Productive & Competitive Market (E-NAM) |

# ROLE OF TECHNOLOGY IN AGRICULTURE

01 Improved Producitivity or Crop yield: Technology has enabled farmers to increase their yields by using advanced tools and techniques to monitor crop growth and optimise inputs such as water, fertilizers and pesticides

02 Sustainable Farming Practices: Technology can help farmers to adopt sustainable farming practices, reduce their carbon footprint and prevent soil degradation.

03 Enhaning Crop Quality: Biotechnology has made it possible to introduce certain strains into other genes of crops or animals. This boost the resistance of crops to pests and drought

04 Weather Prediction through Artificial Intelligence: Modern equipment and tools based on AI enable data gathering and tools based on AI enable data gathering and informed decision making using vital information on temperature, rainfall, soil, humidity.

- Agriculture Sensor help farmers in determining soil composition and moisture content, nutrient detection, location for precision, airflow, etc and thus allow farmers to maximize yields using minimal natural resources.

05 Supply Chain Management: With the help of data analysis, farmers can receive information about the prevailing market prices of crops, demand and supply situation and platform to buy and sell their products quickly. This greatly reduces their inventory cost, post harvest losses and transportation cost.

06 Efficient Use of Resources: Technology can provide farmers with access to information, resources and markets which help them in making informed decisions about their crops and thus improve efficiency.

- Redution of Post-harvest losses and increase harvest gains.

07 Overall, the technology helps in better price realisation along with reduced losses and improved efficiency, which in turn improve the economic status and standard of living.

## Role of Biotechnology in Agriculture

- Improved crop yield: Biotechnology can be used to develop crops that are resistant to pests and diseases, have improved nutritional value and can grow in adverse environmental conditions.
  - This can lead to increased crop yields, which can improve the incomes and food security of farmers.
  - Ex: The yield of Bt cotton has increased from 300 Kg/ha in 2022 to over 500 Kg/ha after introduction of Bt cotton in India.
- Increasing the diversity of the gene pool.
- Production of Plants that have a short maturing period, higher yield, potential to promote food production even in adverse conditions like drought, salinity.
- Develop Pest and disease-resistant crops, reducing the need for chemical pesticides and

herbicides. This can reduce the cost of farming and improve the health and safety of farmers

- GM Crop can reduce pesticide use in brinjals, known to be most pesticide-intensive vegetable

- **Efficient Use of Resources:** Biotechnology can be used to develop crops that require less water and fertilizer, reducing the cost of farming and improving the sustainability of agriculture
  - This will reduce the input costs and Indian farmers who rely on livestock for their livelihoods.
- **Climate-resilient crops:** The technology can be used to cultivate crops making it resilient to the climate change which is impacting agriculture yields.
  - Example: Water-resistant paddy can tackle incessant rains.
- **Bioremediation:** Biotechnology can be used to clean up contaminated soil and water bodies which can improve the environmental conditions and livelihoods of farmers.
- **Addressing hidden hunger:** Genetic engineering can help to improve nutritional content of crops and simultaneously enhance the nutrition intake by the farmers.
  - Example: Golden rice can help fight Vitamin A deficiency; Costa Rica's pineapple has high level of Carotenoids compounds.
- **Diversified Income:** The health and productivity of livestock and poultry can be enhanced, giving the farmers the diversified income and reduce vulnerability to market fluctuations
  - Example: Transgenic cow produce milk with a more balanced protein, which can give higher income by selling such premium products to farmers.
- **Poverty Alleviation:** The increased outputs and the remunerative price brought by using the biotechnology will help in generating a surplus income, alleviating poverty and thus reducing farmer's dependence on the banks.

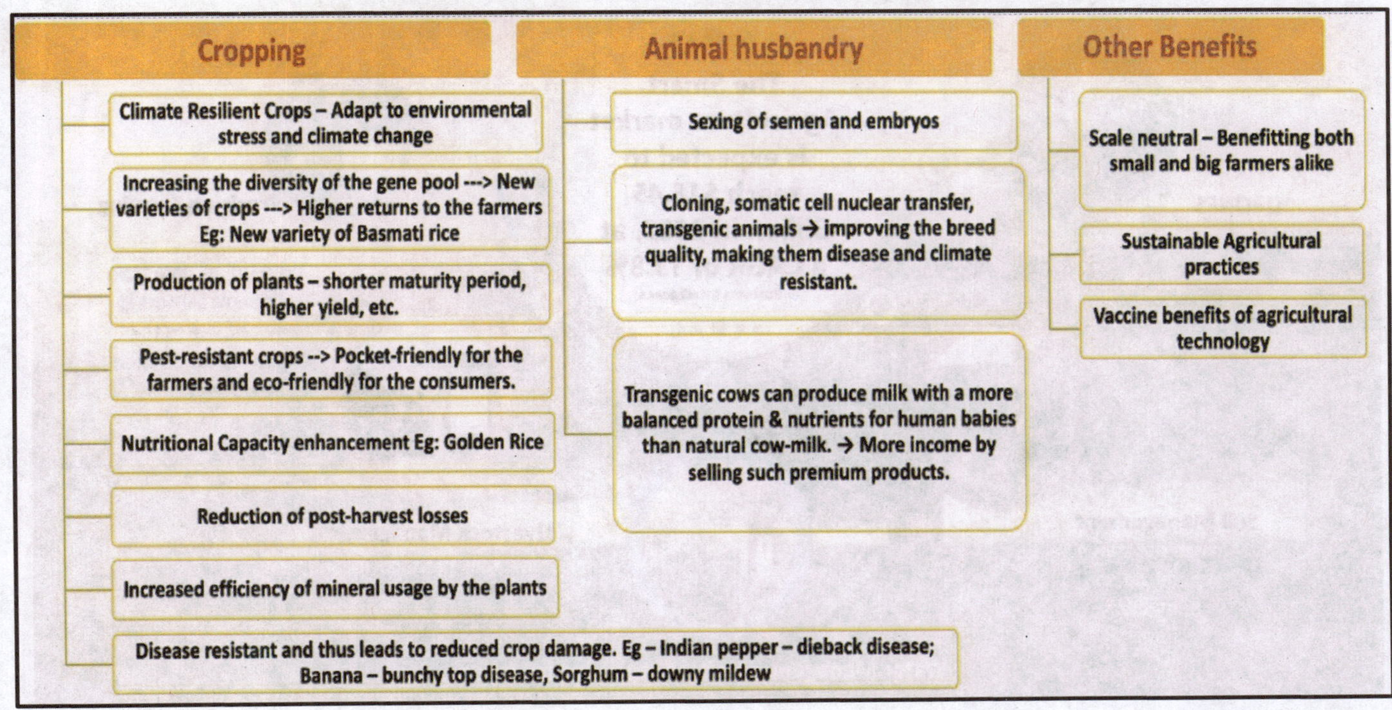

# USE OF ICT IN AGRICULTURE

## Production Phase

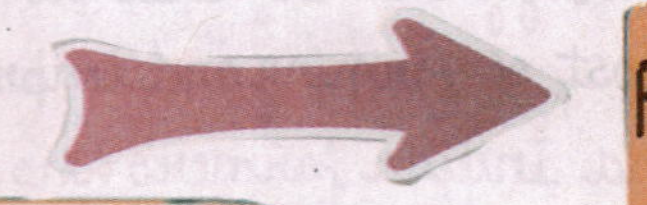

- Digital Land Records Modernisation Programme
- Credit-Kisan Credit Card (KCC)
- Adoption of GM Crops/HYV Seeds
- Direct benefit transfer (DBT) Central Agri Portal
- Extension Services: e-Choupal, Kisan Call centre, Village Resource centres, KISAN TV, Agrisnet, m-Kisan portal, Mahindra Kisan Mitra, etc.
- Agristack
- Latest technological interventions such as use of Drones, Big Data Analytics, Blockchain, Artificial Intelligence, etc.
- Precision Farming.

## Post-production Phase

- Marketing- E-NAM, AGMARKNET
- Digital Mandi
- E-Procurement of Crops
- Agricultural Commodities Markets
- Digital Agriculture Mission (2021-25)
- Sub Mission on Agricultural Mechanisation (SMAM)

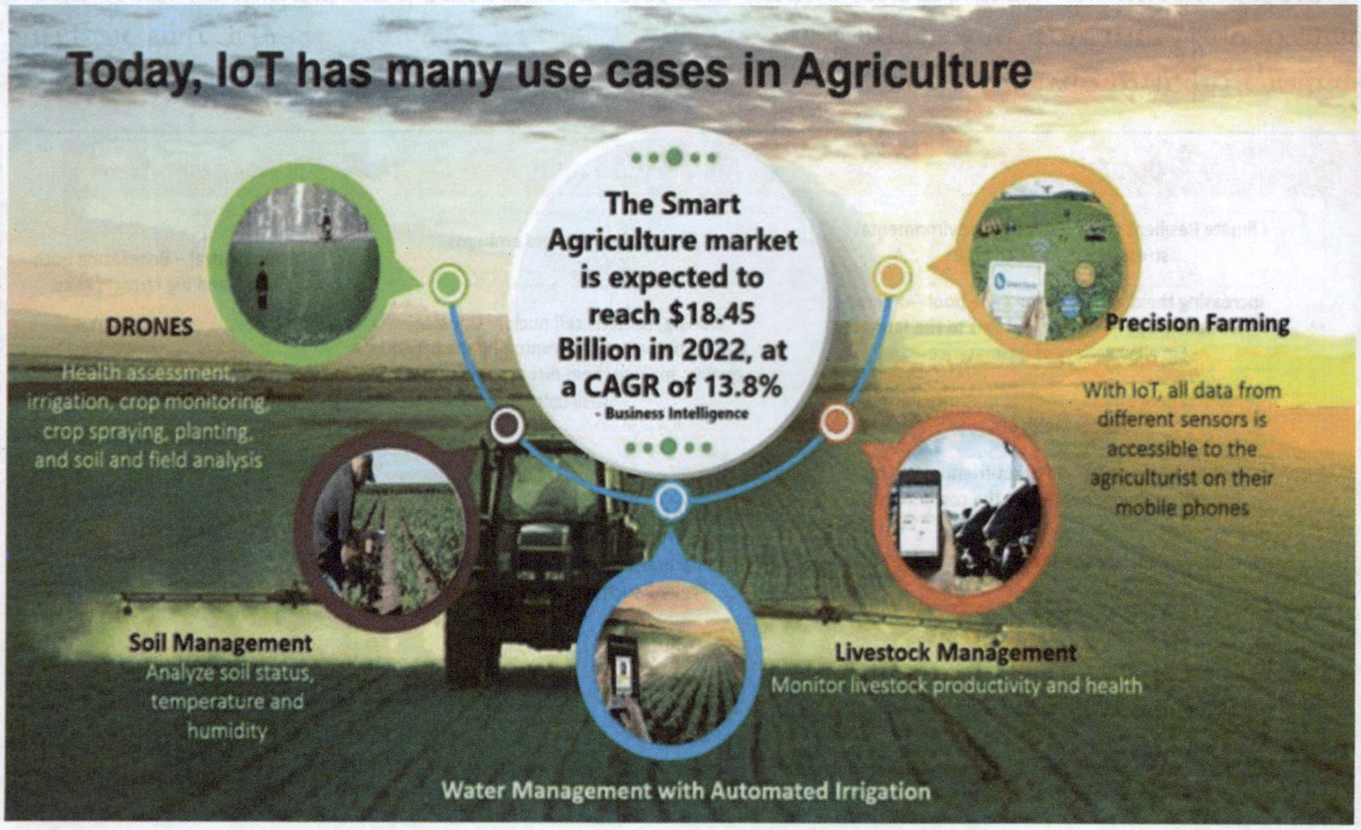

**Today, IoT has many use cases in Agriculture**

The Smart Agriculture market is expected to reach $18.45 Billion in 2022, at a CAGR of 13.8%
- Business Intelligence

**DRONES**
Health assessment, irrigation, crop monitoring, crop spraying, planting, and soil and field analysis

**Precision Farming**
With IoT, all data from different sensors is accessible to the agriculturist on their mobile phones

**Soil Management**
Analyze soil status, temperature and humidity

**Livestock Management**
Monitor livestock productivity and health

**Water Management with Automated Irrigation**

## Challenges in the adoption of Technology

### Unequal distribution of digital dividend

- 2016 World Development Report - Unequal benefits to the people. Persistence in regional disparity.

### Triple Divide

- Digital Divide, Rural Divide and Gender Divide.

### Financial Implication

- Inadequate reach of the technology due to finances.

### Limitation in the adoption of E-Technology

- Inadequate access of telecommunication infrastructure.
- Lack of access to hardware creating digital divide
- Language and Content limitation - absence of content in regional languages.
- Lack of Seamlessness: Limited expertise, existing gaps in agricultural research, poor data quality and lack of access to data, and a lack of collaboration among different stakeholders

### Increasing disparity between the large farmers and small & marginal farmers

- Drones, precision farming, etc. goes against the small & marginal farmers.
- High costs of serving small halding farmers and building their own distribution system. (86% of the farmers are small and marginal)

### Other Issues

- Agri-Techs startups are still faced with limited funding and yet to be validated business models in Indian agriculture systems.
- Subsidies Structure: The existing subsidy regime does not provide incentives and support for adopting agriculture technologies and innovations rather it prevents diversification and promotes excessive reliance on fertilisers

## PRECISION FARMING

- It is an approach where inputs are utilized in precise amounts to get increased average yields, compared to traditional cultivation techniques.
- Precision farming utilizes multitude of advanced technologies and tools to monitor several parameters and collect information related to crop growth (like soil moisture, pH etc.)

→It is referred to as 'precision' because it is focused on performing the right intervention (e.g. providing water to crops), in the right place, at the right time, responding to the specific demands of individual crops and individual areas of land with superior levels of precision.

## Technologies include a vast array of tools of hardware, software and equipment

» **Global Positioning System (GPS):** It provides an accurate positioning system necessary for field implementation of variable rate technology in agricultural input management.

» **Grid sampling:** It is a technique for segmenting fields into small units (~0.5-5 hectares) from which soil samples are used to calculate the proper application rates for crop inputs.

» **Variable-rate technology:** Consists of farm field equipment with the ability to precisely control the rate of application of crop inputs that can be varied in their application including fertilizers, irrigation, tillage, insect control etc.

» **Yield Monitors:** Crop yield measuring tools fitted on harvesting machinery are called yield monitors. The yield data monitors. The yield data helps in decision related to the requirement of targeted intervention.

» **Remote Sensors via** satellite or low-flying aircraft/drone.

» **Proximate Sensors:** Proximate sensors can be used to measure soil parameters (Nitrogen content, pH etc.) and crop properties.

» **Computer hardware and software:** Computer support is required to analyse the data gathered by other components of precision farming technology and to make it accessible in formats such as maps, graphs, charts, or reports.

## Benefits of Precision Farming

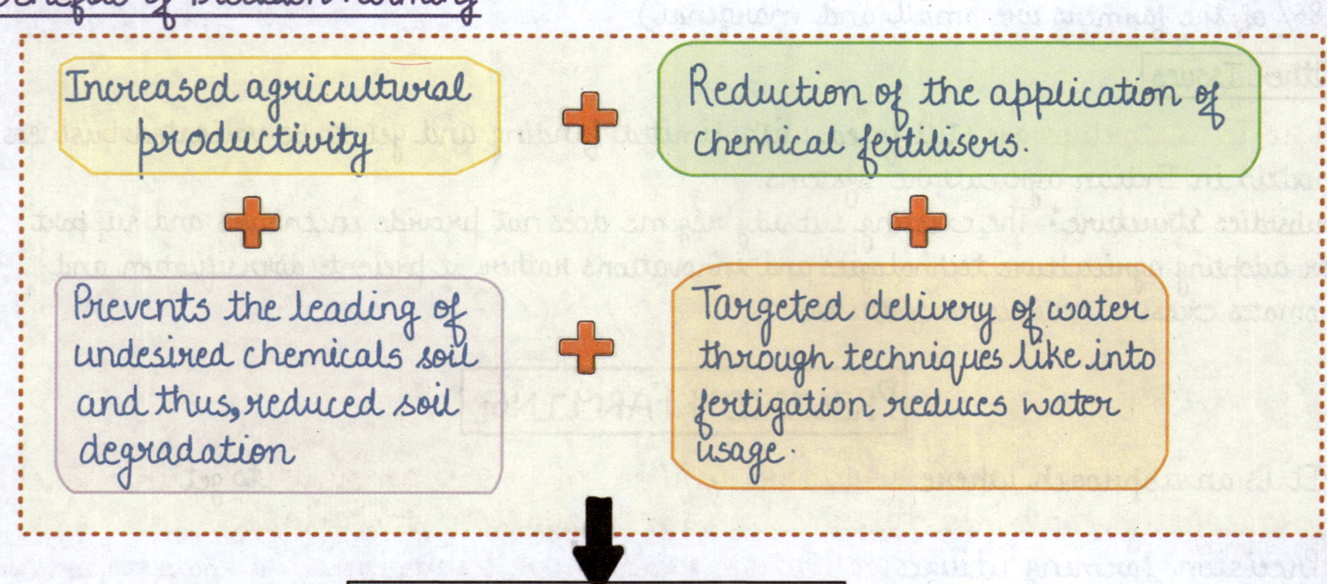


Improvement in Farmers Income

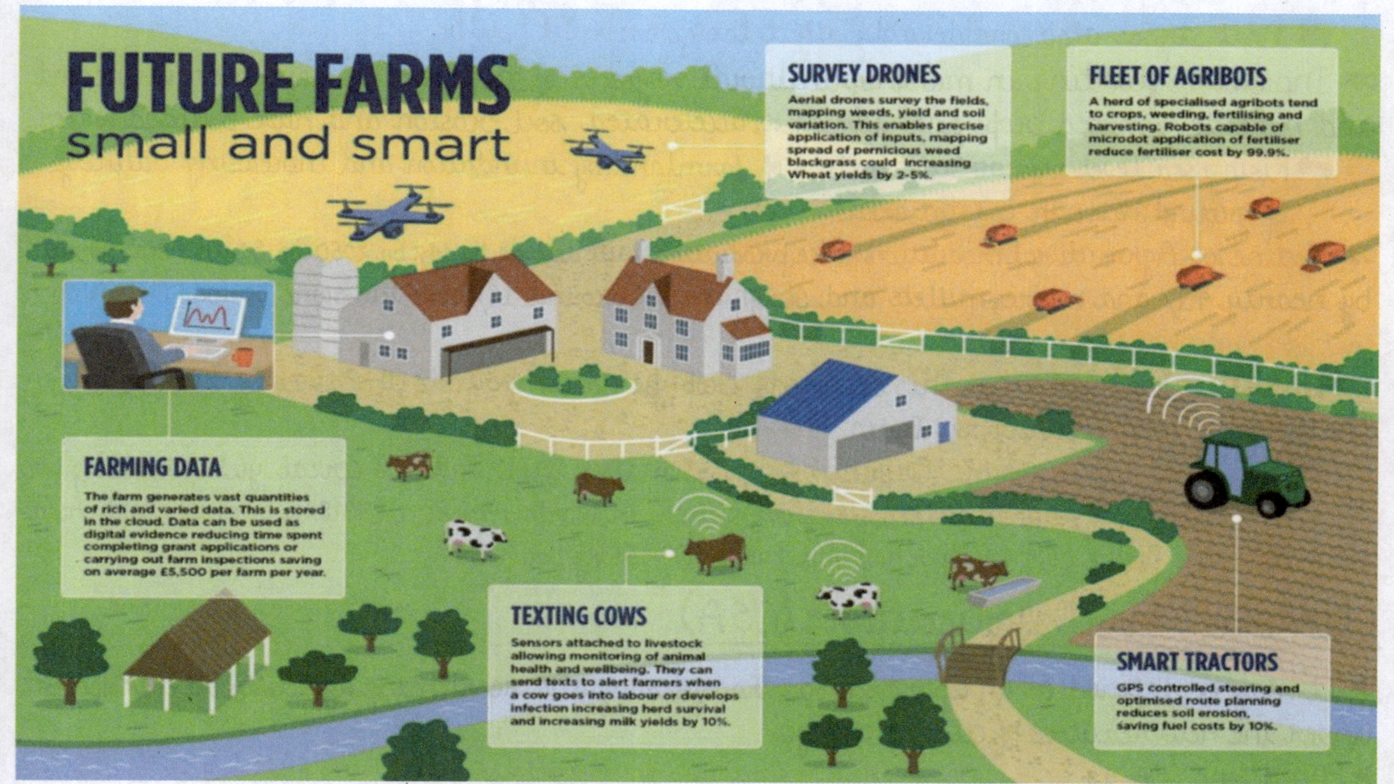


# CLIMATE SMART AGRICULTURE

## Economic Survey 2018 Observations

- It observed that climate change is taking a toll on India's agricultural productivity and farmers' incomes.
- It observed that the impact of temperature and rainfall on agriculture is felt during extreme changes- when temperatures are much higher, rainfall significantly lower and the number of "dry days" greater than normal.
- It is also noted that such impact is more adverse in unirrigated land compared with irrigated areas.
- The Surveys says that the change in agricultural productivity patterns as a result of climate change could reduce annual agricultural incomes between 15% and 18% on average between 20% and 25% particularly for unirrigated areas.
  - Since agriculture contributes 16% of India's GDP, climate change cause about 1.5% loss in GDP.

## Impact of Climate Change on Indian Agriculture

It is affecting the agriculture in the following ways:

- Extreme heat events and reductions in crop yields for every 1°F increase in the temperature (Journal of Climatology & Weather Forecasting).
  - Heatwave threaten livestock by increasing their vulnerability to disease, reducing fertility and milk production.

- Heat stress also considerably affect the commercial poultry.

- Increased flooding in many agricultural regions of the country have been witnessed and have devastated crops and livestock, accelerated soil erosion and have polluted water
  - Rising sea level may result in loss of farmland by inundation and increasing salinity of groundwater in coastal areas.
- Decline of Agricultural Production: Rice production will decline by 14% by 2050 in South Asia; wheat by nearly 49% and maize, millets and sorghum by around 19% over the same period. (International Food Policy Research Institute).
- Impact on Food Security: This declining crop yields compounds the already serious Challenge of food security in India.
  - Food and Agriculture Organization estimates that India's cereal yield (2,993 Kg per hectare) as of 2016 is drastically lower than in North America (7318 Kg per ha), East Asia and the Pacific (5,976 Kg per ha) and Europe (4,155 kg per ha).

## Climate Smart Agriculture (CSA)

- It may be defined as an approach for transforming and reorienting agricultural development under the new realities of climate change.
- FAO define CSA as "agriculture that sustainably increases productivity, enhances resilience, reduces/remove GHGs where possible, and enhances achievement of national food security and development goals".
- Climate-smart agriculture that broadly works on three parameters:
  - Sustainably increasing agricultural productivity and farmer's incomes
  - Adapting to climate change and making farming more resilient
  - Reducing greenhouse gas emission (GHG).
- Intervention by the government- National Mission for sustainable agriculture, National Initiative on Climate Resilient Agriculture (NICRA), National Adaptation fund, state action plant on climate change etc.

## Techniques used in 'Climate Smart Agriculture'

- Identifying and promoting sustainable agriculture practices and tools e.g. organic farming; Agroforestry; Use of erosion control plants.
- Controlling soil moisture by farm ponds, bunds, trenching, mulching, drip irrigation etc.
- Using inputs more efficiently and effectively to grow more from less e.g. alternate wetting and drying of paddy by letting the fields drain periodically, methane emissions from flooded rice production can be cut to half.
- The practice save water and increase profit margin of farmers.
- Increasing the productivity of milk and meat production so that fewer animals are required to produce the same amount of milk or meat, which also reduce the emission generated in producing that food.

**Edict-1:** Indian Agriculture

CHAPTER 08

# FOOD SECURITY AND PDS SYSTEM

## FOOD SECURITY

• According to Food and Agriculture Organisation (FAO), 'food security exists when all people, at all times, have physical and economic access to sufficient, safe and nutritious food to meet dietary needs and food preferences for an active and healthy life'

### Components of Food Security

1. Availability of Food means food production within the country. Emphasis upon increasing the agricultural productivity

2. Affordability implies than an individual has enough money to buy sufficient, safe and nutritious food to meet one's dietary needs

3. Stability of Food Grains by maintaining buffer stock and encouraging crop diversification.

4. Accessibility means the food is within the reach of every person through Public Distribution System

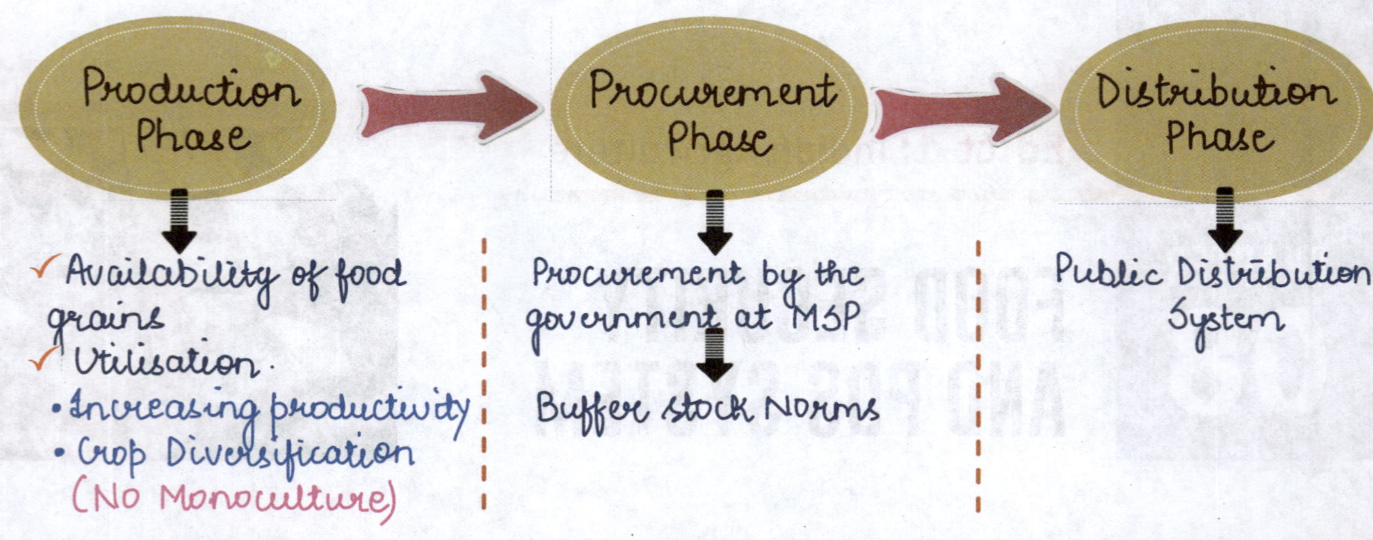


**Important Facts**

- Food Security and Malnutrition Report 2023: 74% Indians could not afford a healthy diet in 2021.
- Hunger in India: As per National Family Health Survey (NFHS)-5 (2019-21), stunting among children under five years of age reduced marginally from from 38.4% (NFHS-4) to 34.7%.
- India's rank in Global Hunger Index declined to 111 in 2023 from 107 indicating the "Serious hunger level issues.
- Regional disparity. Bihar, Uttar Pradesh and Madhya Pradesh have higher prevalence rates compared to Kerala and Tamil Nadu.

## Current Framework of Food Security in India

* Please Note: All the given below components have been discussed in detail.

- **Constitutional provision:** No explicit provision regarding right to food but fundamental right to life enshrined in Article 21 of the constitution can be interpreted to include right to live with human dignity, which may include the right to food and other basic necessities.
- **Buffer stock:** Food Corporation of India (FCI) has the prime responsibility of procuring food grains at MSP and maintain a minimum buffer stock
- **National Food Security Act, 2013 (NFSA):** It marks a paradigm shift in approach to food security from welfare to rights based approach. NFSA covers 75% of total population and 50% of the urban population.
- **Public Distribution System (PDS):** Under the PDS, presently wheat, rice, sugar and kerosene are being allocated to the state/UTs for distribution. Some states/UTs also distribute additional items of mass consumption through PDS outlets such as Pulses, edible oils, iodized salt, spices etc.

## 2 Major threats in ensuring Food Security in India

1. Monoculture. Monoculture is affecting Food Security in following ways

- Impact on Nutritional Security: Distortion of food consumption patterns and replacement of nutritious millets with polished rice and wheat has negatively affected our nutritional security.
- Reduced Soil fertility: Wheat and Paddy, unlike pulses and legumes, cannot fix nitrogen from the atmosphere.
  - Their continuous cultivation without any crop rotation leads to depletion of soil nutrients and growing dependence on chemical fertilisers and pesticides.
- Reduced climate resilience: Rice-wheat cropping sytem in Punjab constitutes about 84.6% of total area and has been profitable to farmers.
- Higher irrigation demand: Due to monoculture, top soil loses elements that could help it retain moisture.
- Increase in pest attack: Monocultures are shown to be increasing the spread of new pathogens, which led to reduce agricultural yield.

2. Climate change: Changing precipitation patterns and growing frequency & intensity of extreme weather events such as heatwaves, floods are already reducing agricultural productivity in India, posing a serious threat to food security.

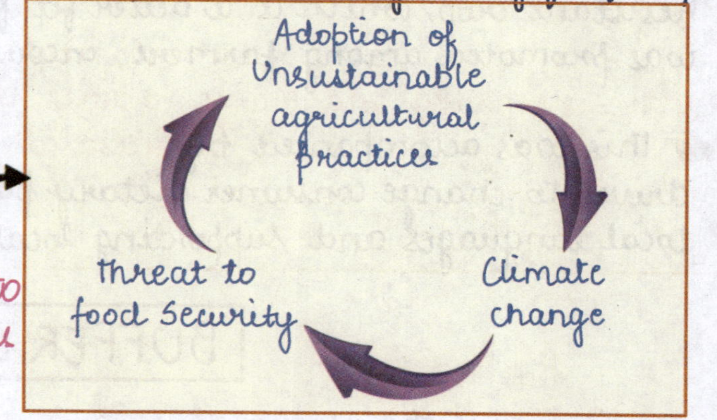


- Agriculture Sector is the second largest greenhouse gas emitter (Due to unsustainable agricultural practices such as pesticides and insecticides)

## Measures to be taken to ensure long term food security

- Promotion of Sustainable agriculture practices that preserves & improves ecosystem health and productivity while promoting social and economic well-being.
- Improvement in agricultural productivity through greater use of biotechnology, intensified watershed management, use of nano urea and access to micro-irrigation facilities and bringing crop yield gaps across the states.
- Promoting agricultural production system to match the agro-ecological resources is critical for sustainability

Eg: Promotion of dry land agriculture rather than input intensive farming in arid and semi-arid areas and promoting less water intensive crops like pulses and millets.

- Poly cultures and crop rotation can lead to reduction in the need to apply fertilizers and pesticides.
- Greater emphasis on nurturing the soils rather than plants will provide higher benefits on sustaining yields, improving ecosystem health & sequestering carbon.
- Initiatives such as Zero Budget Natural Farming, with low external input & production costs, could help restore ecosystem health and diversified livelihoods of smallholder farmers.
- Greater investments are needed in improving post production infrastructure, including storage space in rural areas and improved harvesting techniques and transportation to reduce food wastages.
- Efforts should be undertaken to shift cultural and behavioural preferences to encourage uptake and create market demand for new crops.

> - The 'Millet Mission' in India is an example. The revival of hardy, drought-resitant crop, which is a better fit for increasingly water-stressed regions, was promoted among farmers, encouraging a shift away from water-intensive paddy and maize, across states in India.
> - This was accompanied by inclusion of Millet in PDS and awareness drives to change consumer dietary patterns through millet recipe books in local languages and supporting local centres to create millet-based products

## BUFFER STOCK

- Food Buffer is the minimal amount of food grains that the central government must keep on hand at the start of every quarter to ensure adequate supplies for the PDS and other government distribution programmes.
- The concept of buffer stock was first introduced during the Fourth Five Year Plan (1969-74)
- Objectives: Buffer stock of food grains in the central Pool is maintained by the Government of India for the following objectives:
  - Meeting the prescribed minimum buffer stock norms for food security.
  - Monthly release of food grains for supply through Targeted PDS (TPDS) & other Welfare Schemes (OWS) like Mid Day Meal Scheme etc.
  - Meeting emergency situations arising out of unexpected crop failure natural disasters etc and

- Price stabilisation or market intervention to augment supply so as to help moderate the open market prices.

## Issues in the Buffer Stock Management

- Inadequate storage infrastructure and unscientific storage practices contribute to the depletion of enormous food stocks.
- Open ended procurement of food stocks further complicates the proper storage and consumption of buffer stocks.
- Existing procurement System has been highly 'leaky' with large amount of grains pilfered and diverted to open market.
- No pro-active, pre-defined, sustainable policy for residual food grains.
- Financial Implications: The buffer carrying costs, which include the cost of acquiring, storing, warehousing, stock maintenance has increased more than doubled since 2001-02.
  - This has resulted in an increase of food subsidy to more than 25 times (in nominal terms) during the last two decades.
- Issues with transportation: During transportation, lot of food is wasted due to spills and deterioration contributing to an increase in losses.
- Abuse and robbery: Ghost recipients, alcoholic beverage manufacturing facilities and illicit markets may occasionally receive the buffer stockpiles.
- Unfair trade practices: Government's purchase of food grains & maintenance of buffer stocks are seen as trade-distorting by many western industrialised nations and raises complaints in WTO.

# Futuristic Measures

- There is an urgent need to implement Shanta Kumar Committee recommendations to improve operational effectiveness in the purchase, storage and distribution of food grains.
- Clear and Open Buffer stock liquidation procedures: FCI should be given more freedom to conduct business; when needed, it should sell surplus goods on the open market or export.
- Permit the private sector to buy and store grains of food.
- Grain Outsourcing: Implementation of a negotiable warehouse receipt (NWR) system
  - Farmers can deposit their produce in these authorized warehouses under new arrangement, & bank will advance them 80% of MSP value of their produce.
- FCI should engage in full fledged grain procurement only in states with weak procurement capabilities.
- States should handle procurement in cases of conditions that are performing well like Haryana, Punjab, Andhra Pradesh, Chhattisgarh, Madhya Pradesh and Odisha.

# NATIONAL FOOD SECURITY ACT (NFSA), 2013

- NFSA was enacted in 2013 that guarantee subsidized food grains to a large section i.e. two third of total population, making it the largest food security program in the world.
- With the intention of providing food security to approximately 800 million people, the NFSA plays a crucial role in ensuring access to essential access to essential nutrition and combating hunger across the country.

## Features of NFSA

- **Entitlements** to eligible individuals and households, including subsidised food grains under the Targeted Public Distribution System (TPDS).
- **Subsidized Food Grains:** The eligible persons will be entitled to receive 5 Kgs of food grains per person per month at subsidized prices of 3/2/1 per Kg for rice/wheat/coarse grains.
    - The existing Antyodaya Anna Yojana (AAY) households, which constitute the poorest of the poor, will continue to receive 35 Kgs of foodgrains per thousand per month.
- **Diversification of the food basket** through the inclusion of other nutritious cereals (such as bajra, jowar, ragi and maize).
- **Nutritional Support:** Special emphasis on providing nutritional support to pregnant women, lactating mothers, and children through the provision of nutritious meal and take-home rations.
- **Maternity Benefit:** The NFSA includes the provision of maternity benefits, ensuring proper nutrition and support to pregnant and lactating women during the pregnancy and six months after childbirth.
- **Women Empowerment:** Eldest woman (18 year or aboe) to be the head of the household for the purpose of issuing of ration cards.
- **Establishment of Grievance Redressal Mechanism (GRM)** to address any complaints or issues related to the distribution of food grains and benefits under the NFSA.
- **Use of technology, such as Aadhar-based identification,** to ensure the proper targeting and delivery of benefits.
    - Enhance the promation of transparency and accountability in the implementation of food security programs.

## Achievement of the National Food Security Act (NFSA) in last 10 years

- Expansion of the coverage of food security program in India
- Nutritional Support to women and children through ICDS & Midday Meal
- Strengthened PDS to ensure efficient and transparent delivery of subsidized food grains.

- Digitization, Aadhar based identification, & reforms in distribution mechanisms have helped in reducing leakages & improving targeting.
  Eg: Chhattisgarh PDS.

➜ Increased awareness about food security rights among population and greater citizen participation in monitoring the implementation of the act.
- Social audits and grievance redressal mechanisms have empowered the beneficiaries to hold authorities accountable.

➜ Played a crucial role during COVID-19 pandemic by providing additional food grains and expanding coverage to support vulnerable populations affected by the lockdowns and economic disruptions.
  Eg: PM Garib Kalyan Yojana.

## Objections raised by the countries at WTO against India's NFSA

➔ Trade Distortion as it may result in excessive production of certain crops and overstocking of food grains.
- This can impact global markets by influencing supply and demand dynamics, potentially affecting prices and trade flows.

➔ Price Distortion as subsidized food grains under NFSA can lead to lower prices for domestically produced agricultural products.
- Other countries argue that this could affect their ability to export agricultural commodities to India at competitive prices.

➔ Market Access: Procurement and distribution mechanisms under NFSA such as the MSP and the PDS may create barriers to market access for foreign agricultural products.

➔ Subsidy limits: India's subsidy under NFSA generally exceeds the De-minimis level set at 10% of the value of agricultural production.
- Countries at the WTO raise concerns about the level of subsidies provided under the program although India secured a Peace clause in the Bali Ministerial Conference (2013).

## PUBLIC DISTRIBUTION SYSTEM

- It is an Indian food Security System established under the Ministry of Consumer Affairs, Food and Public Distribution.
- PDS evolved as a system of management of scarcity through distribution of food grains at affordable prices.
- PDS is operated under the joint responsibility of central and state governments
- Under the PDS, presently the commodities like wheat, rice, sugar and kerosene are being allocated to the states/UTs for distribution. Some states/UTs also

distribute additional items of mass consumption through the PDS outlets such as pulses, edible oils, iodized salt, spices etc.

## Evolution of PDS System

- **World War II** PDS system evolved during world War II as a wartime rationing measure.

- **During world War II - 1960s** PDS was dependent on import of food grains.

- **1960s - 1970s : Green Revolution** Increased production and productivity of food grains ⇒ PDS self-sufficient.

- **1972 : PDS became universal scheme ⇒ Universalised**. In 1972, PDS scheme got universalised under which the distribution of subsidized food grains has been made available to all. But till 1992, it was just General Entitlement scheme without any specific targets.

- **1992** Revamped PDS system was launched with a view to strengthen and streamline the PDS as well as improve its reach in the hilly, remote & in accessible areas where a substantial section of the underprivileged class lives.

- **1997** Targeted PDS system was launched by government which divided the beneficiaries / population into 2 Categories:

  - BPL (Below Poverty line households)
  - APL (Above the Poverty line)

- **2003** Poorest of the Poor → AAY (Antyodaya Anna Yojana) was launched which was aimed at reducing hunger amongst the poorest segments of the BPL population. It was launched for 1 crore poorest of the poor families.

- **2013** Enactment of National Food Security Act, 2013.

## Management of Food Grains

**Farmer** → Responsible for cultivation of crops. Production factors that can improve productivity have been discussed in the earlier chapters.

*Procurement at MSP*

**Centre (FCI)** → It is responsible for procurement of crops from the farmers for the following objectives:

1. Food grain distribution throughout the country
2. Maintaining a sufficient level of operational and buffer food grain stocks.

*Allocation at Central issue price.*

**State Government** → Bear the responsibility of transporting food grains from these godowns to each fair price shop (Ration shops)

*Distribution*

**Fair Price Shops (FPS)** → These are issued licenses by state governments & have the following responsibilities under scheme.

- Sale of commodities as per the entitlement of ration card holders at retail issue prices fixed by state governments.
- Maintenance of records and display of information such as the list of BPL and AAY beneficiaries, entitlement of essential commodities etc.
- Maintenance of accounts of actual distribution of essential commodities & the balance stock at the end of the month to government official and Gram Panchayat.

*Sale of grains at Central issue price*

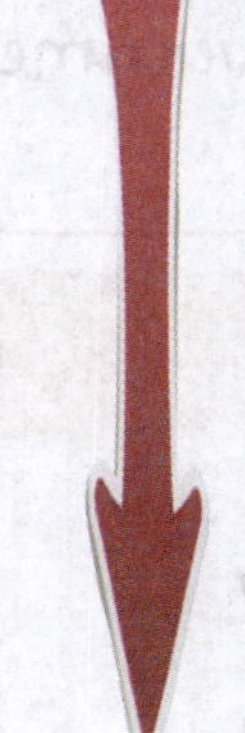

**Beneficiary**

## Issues in the PDS System

- **Identification of beneficiaries**: Prone to large inclusion and exclusion errors i.e. the misclassification of the poor as non-poor and vice-versa.
- **Leakage of food grains** during transportation to and from ration shops into open market.
- **Rising Food Subsidy**. Food Subsidy has increased over the years, having more than quadrupled from Rs 21,000 crore in 2002-03 to Rs 1.97 lakh Cr in 2023-24
- **Open-ended Procurement** i.e. all incoming grains accepted even if buffer stock is filled, creates a shortage in open market.
  - A performance audit by CAG has revealed a serious shortfall in the government's storage capacity
- **Environmental Issues**: Over emphasis on attaining self-sufficiency and a surplus in food grains, which are water-intensive has been found to be environmentally unsuitainable.
  - Procuring states such as Punjab and Haryana are under environmental stress, including rapid groundwater depletion, deteriorating soil & water conditions from overuse of fertilisers.
- **FCI inefficiency**. FCI operational inefficiencies due to poor technology, over-bureaucratization, lack of coordination with state governments lead to wastage of food grains.

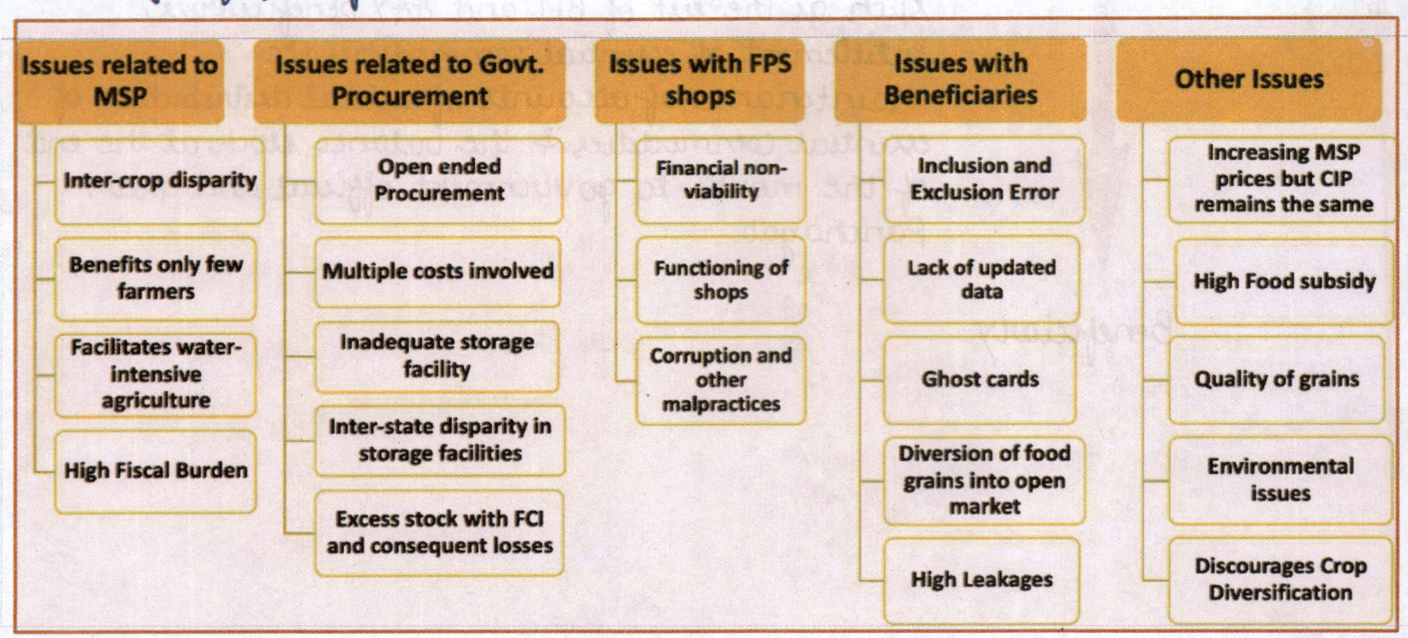

- **Low-Purchase Entitlement ratio**: lack of demand by households due to poor quality; irregularity of FPS operations in most rural areas are cited as key reasons.
- **Migrant workers**: These workers are unable to access FPS as their stay is not fixed.
- **High operational Costs**: Besides so high level of corruption & inefficiencies, the running cost of such a massive subsidy program due to high transportation and storing costs leads to significant financial burden on exchequer.

## PDS VS CASH TRANSFERS

| Mechanism | Advantages | Disadvantages |
|---|---|---|
| PDS | • Insulate beneficiaries from inflation and price valatility.<br>• Ensures entitlement is used for food grains only.<br>• Well-developed network of FPS ensures access to food grains even in remote areas. | • Low off-take of food grains from each household.<br>• High leakage and division of subsidised food grains.<br>• Adulteration of food grains.<br>• Lacks of viability of FPS due to lost margins. |
| Cash Transfer | • Cash in the hands of poor increases their choice.<br>• Cash may relieve financial constraints faced by poor, make it possible to form thrift societies and access credit.<br>• Administrative costs of cash transfer programmes may be significantly lesser than that of other schemes.<br>• Potential for making electronic transfer. | • Cash can be used to buy non-food items.<br>• May expose recipients to price volatility and inflation.<br>• There is poor access to banks and post offices in some areas. |

## REFORMS UNDERTAKEN TO IMPROVE PDS SYSTEM

Technological Reforms

One Nation, One Ration (ONOC)

1. Technological Reforms (End to End Computerization of TPDS operations)

It is an initiative by the Government of India to leverage technology for efficient management and delivery of food grains under the TPDS. Following are the features of the scheme:

- Digitization of beneficiary database and maintained in a centralised database
- Electronic Point of Sale (ePoS) Devices are provided to Fair Price Shops (FPS) to automate the process of ration distribution.
  - These devices enable real time authentication of beneficiaries using Aadhaar or other identification methods, ensuring that subsidized food grains reach the intended beneficiaries.
- Computerization of Procurement and Supply chain management processes from the allocation of food grains to states to their distribution at FPS level has improved the efficiency of supply chain management.
- Aadhar Integration to eliminate duplication or impersonation. This has significantly reduced leakages by eliminating ghost beneficiaries & reducing the scope for corruption and pilferage.
- Robust Management Information System (MIS) to capture and analyse data related to TPDS operations.
  - This helps in real-time performance monitoring, identifying gaps, & making data-driven decisions for effective implementation of the program.
- Grievance Redressal Systeme through implementation of toll-free helplines (1967/ 1800-series), online grievance registration facility.

| Type of Reforms | Benefits of reform | States Implementing Reforms |
|---|---|---|
| Digitisation of ration cards | • Allows for online entry and verification of beneficiary data<br>• Online storing of monthly entitlement of beneficiaries, number of dependants, offtake of food grains by beneficiaries from FPS, etc. | Andhra Pradesh, Chhattisgarh, Tamil Nadu, Madhya Pradesh, Gujarat, |
| Computerised allocation to FPS | • Computerises FPS allocation, declaration of stock balance, web-based truck challans, etc. | Chhattisgarh, Delhi, Madhya Pradesh, Tamil Nadu. etc. |
| Issue of smart cards in place of ration cards | • Secure electronic devices used to store beneficiary data such as name, address. biometrics.<br>• Prevents counterfeiting | Haryana, Andhra Pradesh Orissa. etc. |
| Use of GPS technology | • Use of Global Positioning System (GPS) technology to track movement of trucks carrying food grains from state depots to FPS | Chhattisgarh, Tamil Nadu |
| SMS based monitoring | • Allows monitoring by citizens so they can register their mobile numbers and send/ receive SMS alerts during dispatch and arrival of TPDS commodities | Chhattisgarh, Uttar Pradesh, Tamil Nadu |
| Use of web-based citizens' portal | • Publicises grievance redressal machinery, such as toll free number for call centres to register complaints or suggestions. | Chhattisgarh |

## Current IT Challenges in TPDS System

- Fragmented system across states and lack of integration with other ministries.
- Limited use of data analytics and other cutting edge technologies.
- Hinderances in ICT adoption due to inadequate telecommunication systems, improve device design, poor network strength and lack of IT personnel.
  - Wide inter-state variations exist in both seeding and use of e-PDS devices at Fair Price Shops.
- Technical Expertise: Training and capacity building of staff involved in TPDS operations is crucial to ensure efficient use of the computerised system.
- Identification failures because of poor quality of fingerprints and poor internet connectivity, beneficiaries tend to lose their entitlements.
- Digital Divide: Direct use of e-governance technology by citizens in India is hindered by lack of training and education as well as existing digital divide.
  - For instance, North Eastern states show their incapability in this regard due to persisting network connectivity issues.
- Financial incapacity of Fair Price Shops to make e-POS purchases, install them, and train necessary personnel to work on them.
- Resistance to change: Transitioning from traditional manual processes to a computerised system may face resistance from stakeholders who are accustomed to the old methods.
- Cybersecurity and Data Protection: With computerization, comes the need to address cybersecurity risks and protect sensitive data.
- Monitoring and evaluation: Implementing a computerized system requires effective monitoring and evaluation mechanisms to access its performance, identify bottlenecks, and make necessary improvements.

## One Nation, One Ration Card

- It is a central scheme that allows nation-wide portability of ration cards under National Food Security Act (NFSA) with biometric authentication.
- This system allows all NFSA beneficiaries, particularly migrant beneficiaries, to claim either full or part foodgrains from any Fair Price Shop (FPS) in the country through existing ration card with biometric/Aadhar authentication in a seamless manner.
- The system also allows their family members back home, if any, to claim the balance food grains on same the ration card.
- Under this plan, the distribution of highly subsidized food grains is enabled through nation-wide portability of ration card through the implementation of IT-driven system by the installation of ePoS device at FPSs, seeding of Aadhaar number of beneficiaries with their ration cards and operationalization of biometrically authenticated ePoS transactions in the State/UTs.

## CONSTRAINTS ADDRESSED BY ONE NATION ONE RATION CARD

| PROBLEM | SITUATION |
|---|---|
| 1 Beneficiary confined to a particular Fair Price Shop (FPS) | **Ration Card tagged to a particular FPS**<br>❑ Ration card holders avail entitlements from tagged FPS only<br>❑ Dependent on the whims-and-fancies of the FPS dealer |
| 2 Migrants lose access to PDS foodgrains | **Migration = Loss of Food Security**<br>❑ Migrant beneficiaries lose access to subsidised foodgrains<br>❑ Forced to purchase from open market at inflated prices<br>❑ Very purpose of 'Food Security' under NFSA is not fulfilled |
| 3 Time Consuming and Cumbersome Process | **Difficult to obtain New Ration Card**<br>❑ Cumbersome to apply new ration card in a new place<br>❑ **5-6 months** to complete formalities and process<br>❑ Dependency on various supporting documents/proofs<br>❑ Leads to duplicity of ration card/beneficiary |

**RESOLUTION**

- NO NEED TO SURRENDER & RE-APPLY NEW RATION CARD
- NO NEED TO REGISTER FOR PORTABILITY
- NO PAPER-WORK
- USE EXISTING / SAME RATION CARD NUMBER or AADHAAR
- JUST WALK-IN TO ANY FPS WITH E-POS
- AUTHENTICATE ON E-POS WITH AADHAAR BIOMETRIC
- RECEIVE PART OR FULL ENTITLEMENTS
- FAMILY MEMBERS CAN ALSO ACCESS IN NATIVE PLACE

## Obstacles in ONORC

- **Does not account for the interstate variation in PDS:** Due to historical, political and varying consumption habits, PDS across the country varies with respect to the items supplied through fair price shops to the below-poverty-line (BPL) card-holders.
  - → **Product difference:** Maharashtra supplies only wheat to the BPL families, while Andhra Pradesh provides only rice. BPL households in a few states like Himachal Pradesh and Chhattisgarh are also given pulses.
  - → **Quality difference:** In Tamil Nadu, a BPL family gets 20 kilograms of rice, while in Karnataka a BPL household receives 5 kg of rice per member.
  - → **Cost difference:** In Tamil Nadu, 20 kg rice is given free of cost while in Uttar Pradesh and Bihar, it is provided at Rs 3 per kg.
- **State specific issues:**
  - → Low Aadhar Seeding in Assam (only 36-38% against all India average of 92%) due to concern related to National Citizens register
  - → Center-State tussle has been delaying the scheme in states such as Bengal. Delhi wants to implement its own door to door ration delivery system.
  - → Chhattisgarh has its own digitized system of PDS which create issue of compatibility with ONORC system.
- **Operational challenges:** Internet penetration is still less in India for the smooth functioning of ONORC.
  - → Changes in fingerprints have also been reported both due to genetics and due to constant wear and work-related wear and tear especially in case of labourers.

- **logistics bottlenecks & Supply-demand mismatch:** ONORC can cause disruptions by creating shortage in some FPS and wastage in others.
- **Exclusion:** The scheme seeks to provide subsidized food grains, to Aadhar linked, digitalized ration cards which could lead to exclusion of many beneficiaries.
- **Reconciling and updating of migrant data** especially when members of a family migrate for few months.
- **Weak preparedness of states:** Many states are in installation of electronic Point of Sale (e POS) machines. Only 77% of FPS have installed ePOS.

## Shanta Kumar Committee Recommendations to Improve PDS System

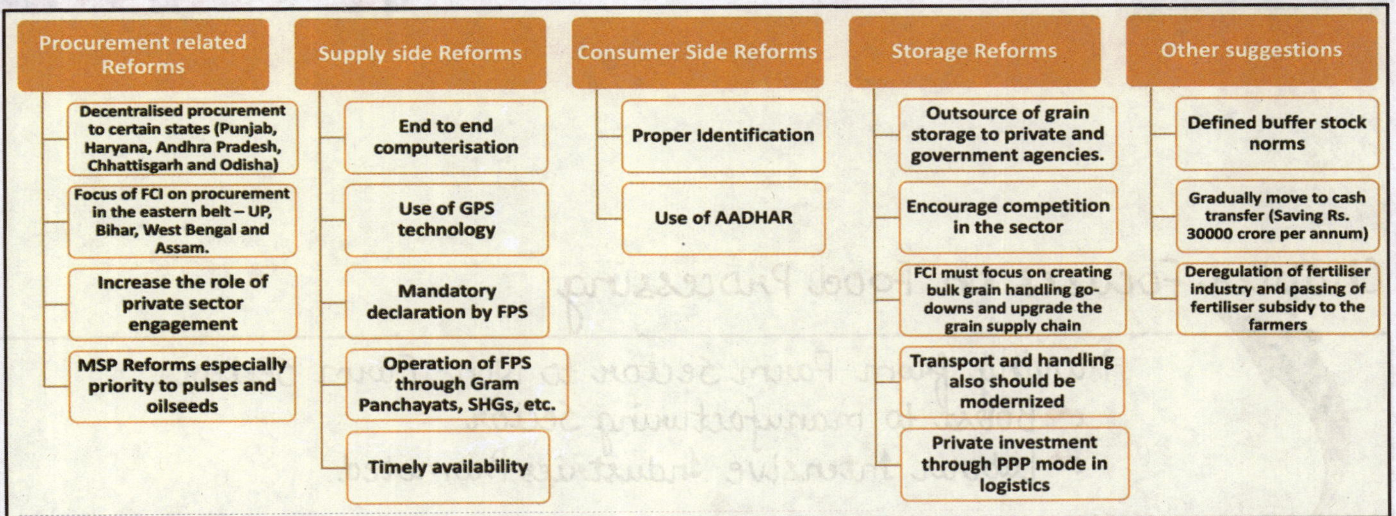


## PYQs Corner

*(Write the Answer and Get Free Evaluation)*

1. What are the major challenges of Public Distribution System (PDS) in India? How can it be made effective and transparent? [150 Words] [10 Marks] [2022]
2. What are the salient features of the National Food Security Act, 2013? How has the Food Security Bill helped in eliminating hunger and malnutrition in India? [250 Words] [15 Marks] [2021]
3. What are the reformative steps taken by the Government to make food grain distribution system more effective? [250 Words] [15 marks] [2019]

**Edict-2:** Industrial Sector

# CHAPTER 09 FOOD PROCESSING INDUSTRY

Chapter Focuses on Food Processing

Moving from Farm Sector to Non-Farm Sector
- Boost to manufacturing Sector
- Labour Intensive Industries Promoted

Farmer's Income

Promotion of Food Processing industries
- Reduced Post Harvest losses
- Contract Farming
- Employment Generation.

Encouraging Allied Sectors
- Supplement Farm's Income
- More resistant to Climate change and other calamities.

Remunerative Prices against their produce
- Improved Storage Infrastructure
- Reduced Post Harvest losses
- MSP Reforms
- APMC Reforms (Alternative market channels need to be improved)
- Boosting Agri-Exports.

Increase Productivity
- Timely & Adequate Credit
- Increased Insurance Coverage
- Increased Irrigation Cover. (+ Micro-Irrigation)
- Technological Factors
- Land Reforms (Digitisation, land lease)

# FOOD PROCESSING SECTOR

Food processing refers to a process which transforms the raw product of agriculture and Allied activities, where it involves a value addition in such a way that the original physical properties undergo a change and the final product has a commercial value and suitable for human and animal consumption.

Raw Material (Agriculture/Allied Activities)

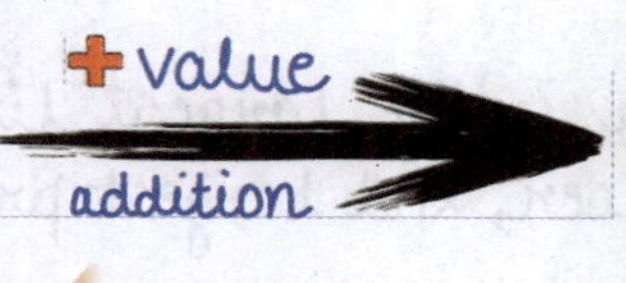


Finished Products (undergoes change in physical properties + (Commercial product)

## Why value addition?

- Boost shelf life of Food. (present food contamination)
- Safety of food (chemically, microbiologically
- Product which are attractive and market-oriented. (meeting the consumer demand)

## What type of Value Addition?

- Primary Processing (Low-value addition)
- Secondary Processing (High-value addition)

## Significance of Food Processing Industry

### Economic

- Contribution to GDP (~8%)
- Boosting Farm Income
    - Higher value addition
    - Decrease post harvest losses
- Employment Generation (As per ASI- Annual Survey of Industries Report, 12% of the work force in registered manufacturing is employed in food processing sector).
- Facilitating the transition from farm jobs to non-farm jobs
- Boosting Agri Exports (~ 11% of total export in 2021-22.
- Agricultural Diversification (Environmental Consequence decrease)

### Social

- Helps in controlling Inflation decrease.
- Nutritional Security (Hidden hunger)
- Decrease Distress migration
- Increase Women's livelihood
- Decrease Farmer's suicide.

# Growth Drivers of Food Processing Industry

01 Huge Market: The market size of the industry is projected to reach 482 billion $ by 2025 from 258 billion $ in 2020.

02 Increased demand of Processed Foods: (Rise in per Capita Income + increased urbanisation + Changing lifestyle)

03 Increased health awareness

04 Abundance of raw material: India is the largest livestock owner, largest milk producer, largest cereal producer, 2nd largest producer of spices.

05 Increase E-Commerce Start-ups.

06 High potential of agri-exports.

07 Pro-active Government support to give a boost to food processing.
- → PLI Scheme (Production Linked Incentive)
- → PM Kisan SAMPADA Yojana.
- → PM formalisation of Micro processing enterprises.

08 Increasing penetration of organised retail stores providing consumers with access to diverse product.

09 High level of agricultural production - large livestock base, wide variety of crops and a long coastline that help in increasing marine production.

10 MSME playing a vital role in India's food processing chain through various advancements in skill technology.

11 Online food ordering business is witnessing an exponential growth.

12 India is processing less than 10% of its agricultural output and therefore presenting immense opportunities for increasing these progressive levels and leading to investments in this sector.

## Status of Food Processing Industry

- Inspite of large production base, the level of processing is low (<10%).
- Approximately 2% of the fruits and vegetables, 8% marine, 35% milk and 2% of poultry is processed.
- This indicate a huge untapped economic potential.
- India has the highest livestock population but only about 1% of the total meat production is converted to value added products.
- 775% of FPI is in unorganised sectors.
- At present, India's agricultural exports predominantly consist of raw materials which are then processed in other countries.

# SUPPLY CHAIN MANAGEMENT

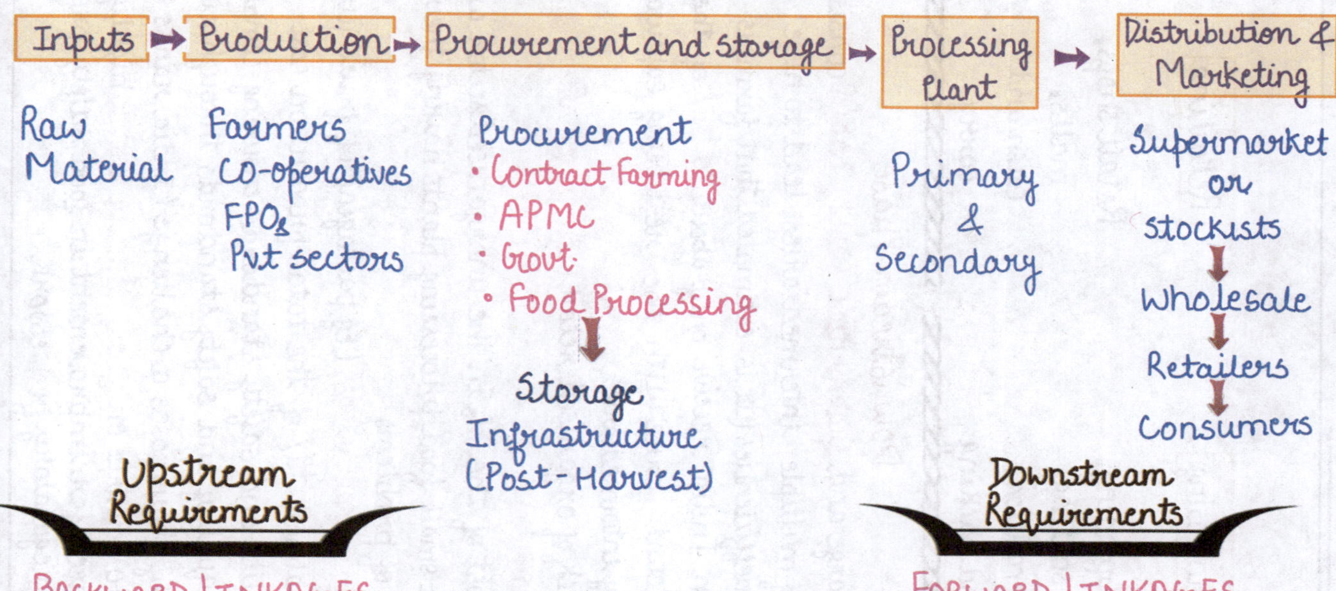


BACKWARD LINKAGES

FORWARD LINKAGES

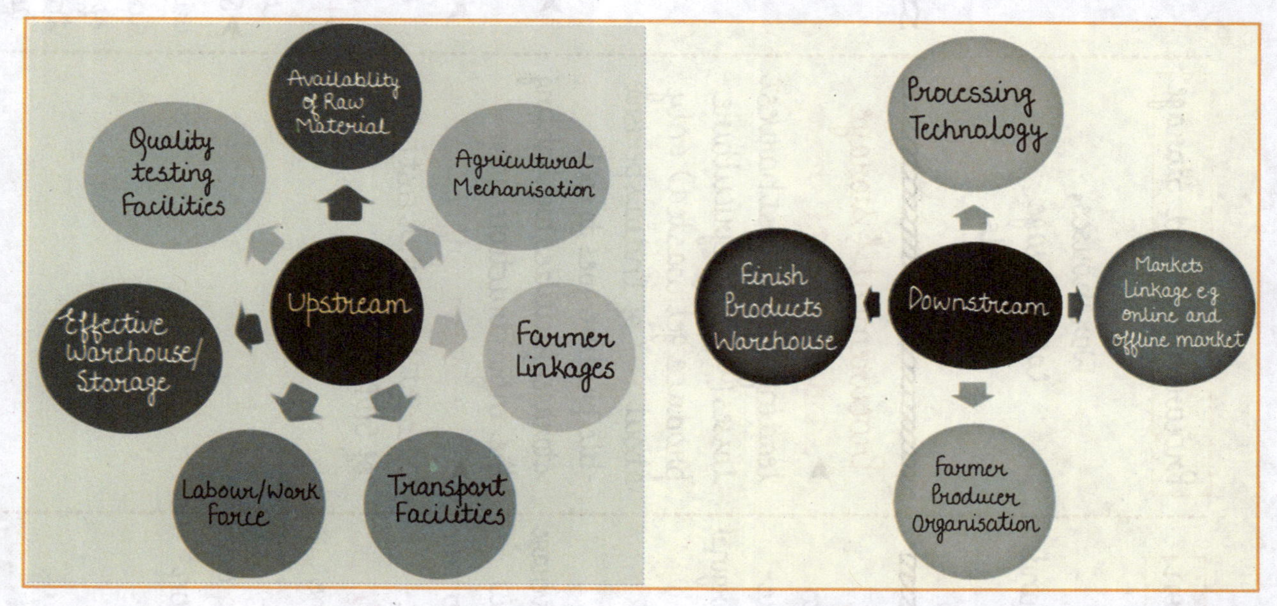


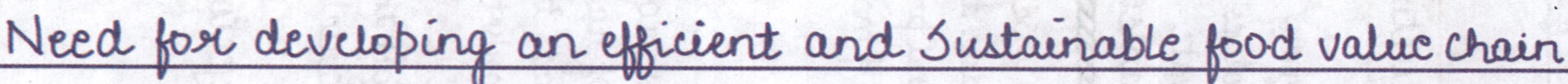


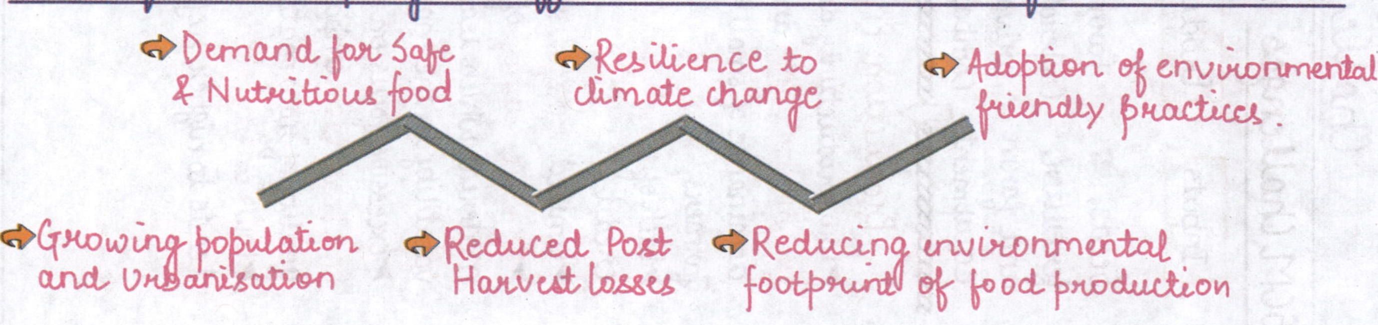

# Challenges in Supply Chain Management (SCM)

## SCM Challenges

| Inputs | Production | Procurement and storage | Processing | Retailing |
|---|---|---|---|---|
| Seeds, fertilizer and farm equipment | Farmer, Cooperatives and private Companies | Warehouses, Cold storage and soils | Grading, sorting, million and packing | Retail shops, malls, Cash and Carry. |

### Production Phase

- Low productivity due to fragmented land and pre-dominance of small & marginal farmers.
- Lack of timely & adequate credit.
- Limited irrigation coverage
- Erratic supply of raw material which leads to price volatility in the market.
- Excessive focus on fertilizers and pesticides impact the quality of raw material.
- Low quality standards also leads to higher rejection.

### Procurement & storage

- Inadequate cold storage leading to high post harvest losses (~30% of agriculture produce get wasted) only about 10% of India's perishable produce goes to cold storage facilities highlighting the infrastructure gap.
- Poor logistic infrastructure account for higher cost (~14% of GDP).

### Downstream Phase

- Large and fragmented supply chain consisting of multiple intermediaries lead to huge inefficiencies (It is estimated that farmers in India receive only about 30-35% of the retail price with the rest being captured by intermediaries.
- Lack of organised retail (low penetration of super markets)
- Most of the FPs in the unorganised sector which are small food processing plants having their own set of problems
- High packaging cost (Eg packaging of fruit juice cost almost 19% of the total production cost.
- Quality and safety standards- ensuring compliance with quality and safety standards throughout the supply chain poses a challenge (India ranks 77 out of 140 countries on food security index highlighting the need for improvement in food safety practices and regulatory fr ework.

## Challenges with the small Food Processing Units

01 Small processing units are generally debarred from the facilities of packaging, cold storage and logistics.

02 Use of harmful fertilizers impact the quality of food which make these units unable to pass through quality checks.

03 Small units do not follow the internationally recommended standards of packaging and labelling.

04 Poor skill levels and lack of manpower hamper the competitiveness of small processing units.

05 The small processing unit lack basic technalgies for food Processing and most of the processing is manual.

06 The small processing unit do nat go for certification of food products by bodies like FSSAI which leads to poor acceptance of their product and make them uncompe-titive in national and international markets.

07 The individual small units are unable to invest in marketing and branding impacting the performance of the sector.

08 These small units are unable to compete with the large processing unit that make them economically unviable.

## Futuristic Reform Measures

**Agriculture Reforms**

- Increasing Productivity
- Crop Diversification
- Sustainable Agriculture Practices

↓ PM PRANAM

**Post-Harvest Infrastructure**

- Logistic cost reduced
- Infrastructure creation reduced

↓ PMKSY (Mega Food Parks)

**Increased Competitiveness/ Formulisation of Small FP Plants**

- PMFME
- One District-One Product Scheme

## Government Initiatives

- **Mega Food Parks Scheme:** It is a government initiative aimed at developing large-scale food processing hubs across the country.
  - It was launched in 2008-09 to give a major boost to the food processing sector by adding value and reducing food wastage at each stage of the supply chain with a particular focus on perishables.
  - Under the scheme, the **Centre provides 50 per cent of the project cost, up to Rs 50 crore.**
  - The Scheme is based on the "Cluster" approach and envisages creation of state of art support infrastructure in a well-defined agri/horticultural zone for setting up of modern food processing units in the industrial plots provided in the park with a well-established supply chain.
  - A Mega food Park typically consists of supply chain infrastructure including collection centers (cc), primary processing centers (ppc) central processing centers (cpc), cold chain and around 25-30 fully developed plots for entrepreneurs to set up food processing units.

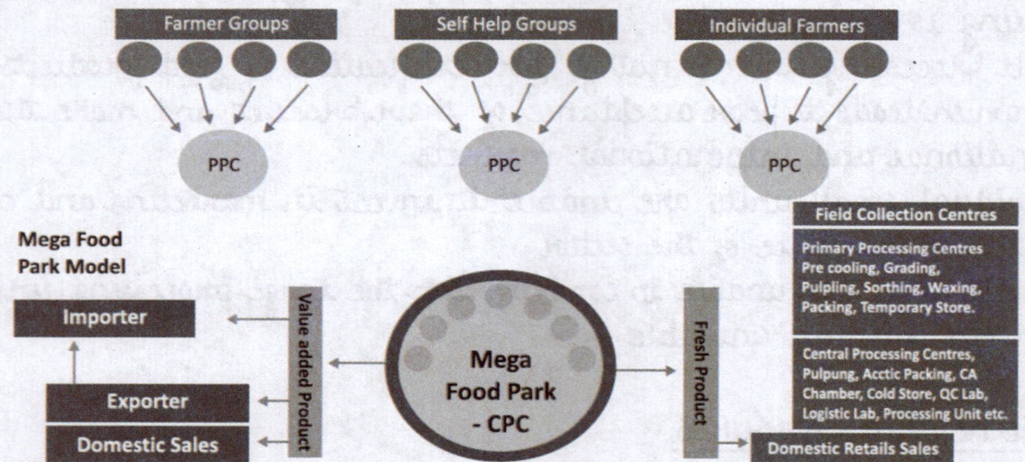


- **PM Formalisation of Micro Food Processing Enterprises Scheme (PM-FME Scheme):** Ministry of Food Processing Industries (MoFPI), in partnership with the State/ UT Governments, has launched an all India centrally sponsored scheme for providing financial, technical and business support for upgradation of existing micro food processing enterprises.
  - **About:** The scheme aims to enhance the competitiveness of new and existing individual micro-enterprises in the unorganized segment of the food processing industry and promote formalization of the sector.
- **One District, One Product (ODOP):** It is initiated as a transformational step towards **realizing the true potential of a district, fueling economic growth, generating employment and rural entrepreneurship,** taking to the goal of **Atmanirbhar Bharat**.
  - It is aimed at **fostering balanced regional development** across the country, enabling **holistic socio-economic growth** across all regions.
  - **Objective:** To focus on District of the country as unit for converting into a **manufacturing and export hub** by identifying products with **export potential** in the district.
- **Pradhan Mantri Kisan SAMPADA Yojana:** It is a comprehensive package which will result in creation of modern infrastructure with efficient supply chain management from farm gate to retail outlet.

## PYQs Corner

*(Write the Answer and Get Free Evaluation)*

1. Elaborate the scope and significance of the food processing industry in India.[150 Words] [10 Marks] [2022]

2. What are the main bottlenecks in upstream and downstream process of marketing of agricultural products in India?[ 250 Words] [15 Marks] [2022]

3. Elaborate the policy taken by the Government of India to meet the challenges of the food processing sector? [250 Words] [15 marks] [2019]

4. What are the reasons for poor acceptance of cost-effective small processing unit? How the food processing unit will be helpful to uplift the socio-economic status of poor farmers? [150 Words][10 Marks] [2017]

5. What are the impediments in marketing and supply chain management in developing the food processing industry in India? Can e-commerce help in overcoming this bottleneck? [200 Words][12.5 Marks] [2015]

Edict-2: Industrial Sector

CHAPTER 10

# INDUSTRIAL POLICIES

**Moving from Farm Sector to Non-Farm Sector**
- Boost to manufacturing Sector
- Labour Intensive Industries Promoted

Farmer's Income

**Promotion of Food Processing industries**
- Reduced Post Harvest losses
- Contract Farming
- Employment Generation.

**Encouraging Allied Sectors**
- Supplement Farm's Income
- More resistant to Climate change and other calamities.

**Remunerative Prices against their produce**
- Improved Storage Infrastructure
- Reduced Post Harvest losses
- MSP Reforms
- APMC Reforms (Alternative market channels need to be improved)
- Boosting Agri-Exports.

**Increase Productivity**
- Timely & Adequate Credit
- Increased Insurance Coverage
- Increased Irrigation Cover. (+ Micro-Irrigation)
- Technological Factors
- Land Reforms (Digitisation, land lease)

# INDIA'S STRUCTURAL TRANSFORMATION

## Structural Transformation

- As a country develops, it undergoes 'structural change'. Usually with development, the share of agriculture declines and the share of industry become dominant.
- At higher levels of development, the service sector contributes more to the GDP than the other two sectors.
- In general, it follows the below trend as experienced by many developed countries such as US, UK etc. or by developing countries like China etc

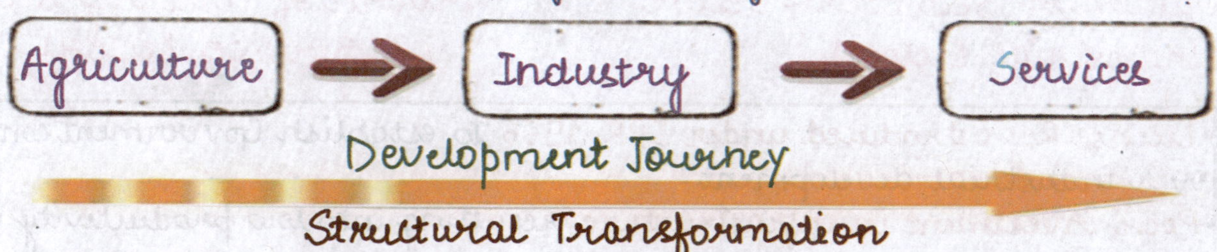


| | | |
|---|---|---|
| • Low productive | Semi-productive | Highly productive |
| • Unskilled labour | Semi-skilled labour | Skilled labour |
| (Underdeveloped Countries) | (Developing countries) | (Developed Countries) |

- Occupational Transformation: Such transformation also involve the transfer of labour from farming to sectors- particularly manufacturing and modern services - where productivity, value addition and average incomes are higher.

## India's unique Structural Transformation

- India shifted directly from Agriculture to Services bypassing the industrial sector.
- The difference is while most developed countries entered the phase of pre-dominance of services in their economies after going through a phase of industrialization and growth of manufacturing sector, India's industry failed to show similar growth and it arrived into service sector dominance straight away.
- As per PLFS 2021-22, agriculture still employ around 46% of the working force inspite of its contribution to only 16% of the GVA. Thus, India witnessed a slow change in occupational structure from agriculture to service sector.

| Sector | Contribution in GDP | | Contribution in Employment | |
|---|---|---|---|---|
| | 1950-51 | 2021-22(GVA) | 1951 | 2019 |
| Agriculture | ~52% | 18.8% | ~72% | ~43% |
| Industry | ~14% | 28.2% | ~11% | ~25% |
| Services | ~34% | 53% | ~17% | ~32% |

## Reasons for India's Unique Structural Transformation

There are various factors that led to India's unique structural transformation and it can be broadly divided into 2 categories.

- Slowdown of Secondary Sector (Industrial Sector)
- Growth of Tertiary Sector (Service Sector)

### Slowdown of Secondary Sector (Industrial Sector)

- License Raj introduced under IPR, 1956 to establish Government control over industrial development.
- Poor investment in infrastructure resulting into low productivity of industries.
- High cost of doing business which include high taxes, bureaucratic red tape and high energy costs.
- High logistics cost amounting to 14% of GDP while it is 8.14% of GDP in USA (Economic Survey 2022-23)
- Poor access to credit and thus finding it difficult to invest in new technologies and expand their operations.
- Low adoption of technology prevented the industries to reduce its cost of production and thus could not compete with big MNCs.
- Protectionist policies has discouraged the companies to adopt technologies resulting in lack of innovation and productivity & high production cost.
  - This prevented the domestic companies to compete with big MNCs.
- Low labour productivity as compared to other developing countries due to prevalence of rigid labour laws.

| Commanding role of public sector | No Economies of Scale | Inward looking strategy |
|---|---|---|
| • IPR 1956 | • Industrial Licenses | • Closed economy |
| • Nationalisation | • MRTP Act 1969 | • FERA 1973 |
| • Socialism | • Reservation of Sector for SSI | • Import Substitution (High import Tariffs) |

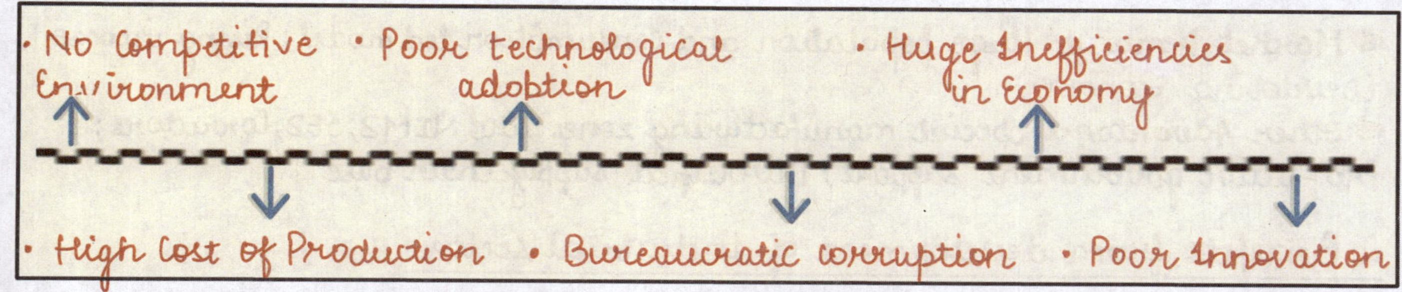


**Growth of Tertiary Sector (Service Sector)**

- **Impact of Globalisation**: Resulted in the demand of many services such as banking, telecommunication, tourism, financial service and thus Service Sector in India showed the rapid growth.
- **Large and well educated labor force**, which was well-suited for the Service sector particularly the IT and BPO sectors.
- **Low capital requirement** as compared to the industry sector. This has made it easier for entrepreneurs to set up service-based businesses, leading to a growth in service sector.
- **Government policies** including tax breaks, subsidies and investment in infrastructure to support the growth of service sector.

## Implications of Structural Transformation

Stagnant manufacturing Sector (Around 16% of the GDP)

Net importing (Widening of CAD)

Low agricultural productivity

Increased informalisation of Labour

Jobless Growth (Low employment elasticity)

Rising income inequalities

**Need to give greater Push to the industrial Sector**

- Tapping the potential of Industrial Development
- Benefits from the development of Industrial sector.

### 1. Tapping the potential of Industrial Development

- **Natural Resources**: Vast Mineral Reserves, Rapid growth of renewable energy.
- **Human Resources**: Demographic Dividend and large labour force; cheap labour as compared to other countries.

- **Market Demand**: Huge population and consumption led model; Rising income (Developing Economy)
- **Other Advantages**: Special manufacturing zones like NIMZ, SEZ, Corridors; Pro-active government support; Diversified supply chain base.

## 2. Benefits from development of Industrial Sector

- **Economic Benefits**: Boost to Economic Growth; Boost to other Sectors; Employment Generation (Reaping Demographic Dividend); Positive Trade Balance; Attract Investment - FDI Inflow; Higher Tax Revenue; Higher Exports = Brings Foreign Exchange.
- **Social benefits**: Balanced Regional Development; Poverty Alleviation; Reduction of Income Inequality; Boost to handicraft and ethnic textiles.

# TIMELINE FOR INDUSTRIAL POLICIES

## 1. On the Eve of Independence

Britain's colonial policies (One Way Free trade + Britain as importer of raw materials and exporter of manufactured goods to feed Britain's Industrial Revolution. + Lack of government Intervention + Limited supply of technical and managerial skills.

- Deindustrialisation (Destruction of Indian handicraft & artisanal industry).
- Underdeveloped industrial sector with a very weak infrastructure.
- Preponderance of consumer goods industries vis-a-vis producer goods industries resulting in lopsided industrial development.
  - In 1953, the ratio of consumer goods to producer goods worked out to be 62:38.
- Lopsided Industrial Development - Industries were concentrated only in a few regions and cities of the country resulting in wide regional disparities in income.

When India achieved independence in 1947, the national consensus was in favour of rapid industrialisation of the economy which was seen not only as the key to economic development but also to economic sovereignty.

### Objectives of Industrial Policy

The main objective of industrial policy of the government are.

- To maintain a sustained growth in productivity.
- To enhance gainful employment.
- To achieve optimal utilisation of human resources.
- To attain international competitiveness.
- To transfer India into a major partner & player in the global arena.

## 2. 1st Industrial Policy (IP) – Industrial Policy Resolution, 1948

- ✓ It was the first IP adopted by independent Indian government. It defined the broad contours of the policy delineating the role of state in industrial development both as an entrepreneur & as an authority.
- ✓ The Industrial (Development & regulation) Act, 1951 was passed to implement the IPR, 1948.

## 3. 2nd IPR, IPR 1956

- Emphasized on heavy goods (Capital Goods) based industrialization strategy.
- Nehru-Mahalanobis Strategy.
- State led Industrialisation
  - Reservation of sectors for public sector.
  - System of industrial licenses (License Raj)
- Import Substitution Strategy.
  - High tariffs and putting quotas on imports.
- Balanced regional development.
- IPR 1956 classified industry into 3 Categories.

  a) Schedule A consisting of 17 industries was the exclusive responsibility of state (This is known as reservation of industries for public sector). At present only 2 industries are reserved for public sector – Atomic energy + railway operations.

  b) Schedule B consisting of 12 industries was open to both public and private sector. However such industries were progressively state owned.

  c) Schedule C All other industries not included in these 2 schedules constituted the 3rd category which were left open to private sector. However the state reserve the right to undertake any type of industrial production. The private sector was kept under state control through the system of licences.

## 4. Industrial Policies during 1970s/1980s

- MRTP Act, 1969 (Monopoly Restricted Trade Practices)
  - To curb the formation of large monopolies
  - Reservation for small scale industry.

- FERA Act, 1973 (Foreign Exchange Regulation Act)
  - To regulate the foreign investment in our country.
- Nationalisation – Banking/ Aviation/ Insurance
  - Public Sector taking control of private sector industries.

**Consequences of various Industrial Policies = Structural Problem within Sector**

Commanding role of public sector
- IPR, 1956
- Nationalisation
- Socialism

+

No Economies of Scale
- Industrial licences
- MRTP Act, 1969.
- Reservation of sector for SSI

+

Inward looking Strategy
- Closed Economy
- FERA, 1973
- Import substitution (High Import Tariffs)

- No Competitive Environment
- Poor Technological Adoption
- Huge Inefficiencies in Economy
- High cost of Production
- Corruption (Nexus)
- Poor Innovation.

## 5. Industrial Policy, 1991

1. Dereservation of Public Sectors: Sectors that were exclusively reserved for public sector were reduced. Presently only 2 sectors – Atomic energy & Railway operations are reserved exclusively for public sector.
2. De-licensing: Abolition of industrial licensing for all projects except for the following industries where an industrial licence is currently required:
   i. Electronic airspace and defense equipments.
   ii. Specified hazardous chemicals
   iii. Industrial Explosives
   iv. Cigar, Cigarattes of tobacco and manufactured tobacco substitutes.
3. Disinvestment: Reducing government stake in public sector enterprises (Covered Extensively in Fiscal Policy)
4. Liberalisation of Foreign Investment: 1st industrial policy in which foreign companies were allowed to have majority stake in India (FDI and FPI are covered extensively in External Sector)
5. Foreign Technology Agreement: Automatic Approvals for technology related agreements.
6. MRTP Act was replaced by the Competition Act, 2002 and a new statutory body 'Competition Commission of India (CCI) was constituted

## Impact of IPR, 1991

- **Slow Industrial Growth** - Despite the liberalisation efforts. The industrial growth rate in India remained sluggish. According to Annual Survey of Industries (ASI), the average growth rate of industrial production between 1991-2000 was around 6.7% which was lower than the average annual growth rate of 8.6% between 1981-1990.
- **Unequal Distribution of Benefits** - The benefits of the industrial policy were concentrated in certain sectors and regions leading to an unequal distribution of growth. CII - Confederation of Indian Industry highlighted that sectors such as software services and telecommunications witnessed significant growth while traditional industries like textile and small scale manufacturing faced challenges and job losses.
- **Jobless Growth** - Despite the policy aim of creating employment opportunities, the actual impact on job creation was limited.
- **Persistent Informal Sector** - The industrial policy didnot adequately address the issue of informal sector which continues to dominate Indian economy. According to National Commission for enterprises in unorganised sector, informal sector accounted for about 92% of total employment in 2010 indicating that the policy did not effectively promote formalisation.
- **Regional Disparities** - The industrial policy failed to address regional disparities & promote balanced industrial development across the country.
- **Inadequate Infrastructure** - The existing infrastructure remains deficient & is utilised sub-optimally resulting in high logistics cost, adversely impacting competitiveness of India's Industrial exports. According to World Bank's logistic performance Index, India is ranked 38th out of 139 countries in 2023
- **Outdated Technology** - Insufficient public investment in research and development sector continue to pose a serious challenge in acquisition of advanced technology for production.

# MANUFACTURING SECTOR

## National Manufacturing Policy (NMP), 2011

- Aims to increase the share of manufacturing to 25% of the country's GDP and generate additional 100 million job by 2022 (Present share is around 17%)
- Envisages the creation of National Investment and Manufacturing Zones (NIMZs)

### About NIMZ:

- **Objectives**: Developed as integrated industries township with state of the art infrastructure and land-use on the basis of zoning; clean and energy efficient technology; necessary social infrastructure; like development facilities etc to provide a productive environment to person transitioning from the primary sectors to the secondary and tertiary sectors.

## Make in India, 2014

- Aims to transform the country into a leading global manufacturing and investment destination.
- Implemented by the Department for Promotion of Industry and Internal Trade.
- Some objectives as of National Manufacturing Policy 2011- increase the share of manufacturing sector in the country's GDP from 16% to 25% and create 100 million additional jobs by 2022.
- Consists of four pillars:

| 01 New Processes | 02 New Infrastructure |
|---|---|
| → Ease of Doing Business<br>→ Delicenceing and deregulation of the industry. | → Intends to develop industrial corridors, strengthen existing infrastructure, etc |
| **03 New Sectors** | **04 New Mindset** |
| → Identified 27 sectors in manufac-turing, infrastructure and service activities | → Partner industry in the country's economic development and approach will be of a facilitator & not regulator. |

## Production Linked Incentive (PLI) Scheme

- It is a financial initiative launched by the Indian government to boost domestic manufacturing and make it globally competitive.
- It began in March 2020, covering mobile manufacturing and IT hardware initially and IT hardware initially, and has since expanded to include 14 sectors such as pharmaceuticals, telecom, food products, automobiles, textiles, and drones.
- Under the PLI scheme, eligible companies receive financial incentives or subsidise based on their incremental production or sales.
- **Objective:** To boost the competitiveness of Indian manufactures, attract investment, create employment opportunities, and enhance exports in targeted sectors.

## Reasons for the subpar performance of the Manufacturing Sector

Over last 30 years the share of manufacturing sector in the GDP remained stagnant at around 16-17% due to the various problems in the sector:

- **High compliance cost leading to "Dwarfism":** Economic Survey in the past talked about the "regulatory cholesterol" in the country. It breeds informal, sub-scale and uncompetitive enterprises.

- **Inverted Duty Structure:** It leads to the situation, where it is better to import finished goods rather than immediate goods are raw materials for manufacturing the goods.
- **Free Trade Agreements (FTAs):** Though, FTAs tend to increase trade, but many of India's recent FTAs have benefited the other partner more.
  - >>> Ex: India-ASEAN trade agreement led to the increase in India's trade deficit with ASEAN.
- **Global Competition:** India's manufacturing sector faced a stiff competition from other developing countries like Bangladesh, Pakistan and Sri Lanka in case of textile.
- **Infrastructural Bottlenecks:** The current logistic cost of India is around 14% of GDP, which is very high in comparison to U.S and Europe, where it ranges between 8-10%.
- **Human resource with poor skill set:** It is estimated that only 5% of India's workforce is formally skilled (South Korea 96%). It affects the quality of workers.
- **Land acquisition and environmental clearance:** Land acquisition act, made acquiring of land very difficult. Repeated PILs and court's interventions also affect the growth of setting up of manufacturing facilities.
- **Poor expenditure on Research & Development:** India's expenditure on R&D has remained stagnant at around 0.6-0.7% of GDP (Economic Survey), Israel & China spends 4.3% & 2.1% respectively.
- **Intellectual Property Protection and enforcement:** Poor patent protection and enforcement affect investment and innovation climate in the country.
- **Growing Protectionism:** There is a rise of protectionist tendencies in western economies. The export market which helped in the growth of Asian tigers, is no more supportive.
- **Restrictive labor law:** It discourages employers from hiring workers on a regular basis. It has probably also led to entrepreneurs choosing to stay away from labor intensive sectors.
- **Absence of Incentives for raising efficiency:** Focusing attention or internal liberalization without adequate emphasis on trade policy reforms resulted in 'Consumption-led growth' rather than 'investment' or 'export-led growth'.
- **Slow technology adoption** has led to low productivity and higher costs adding to the disadvantage of Indian products in international markets.
  - >>> Productivity as measured by value added per worker and average wages in manufacturing in India are only one-third of that in China.

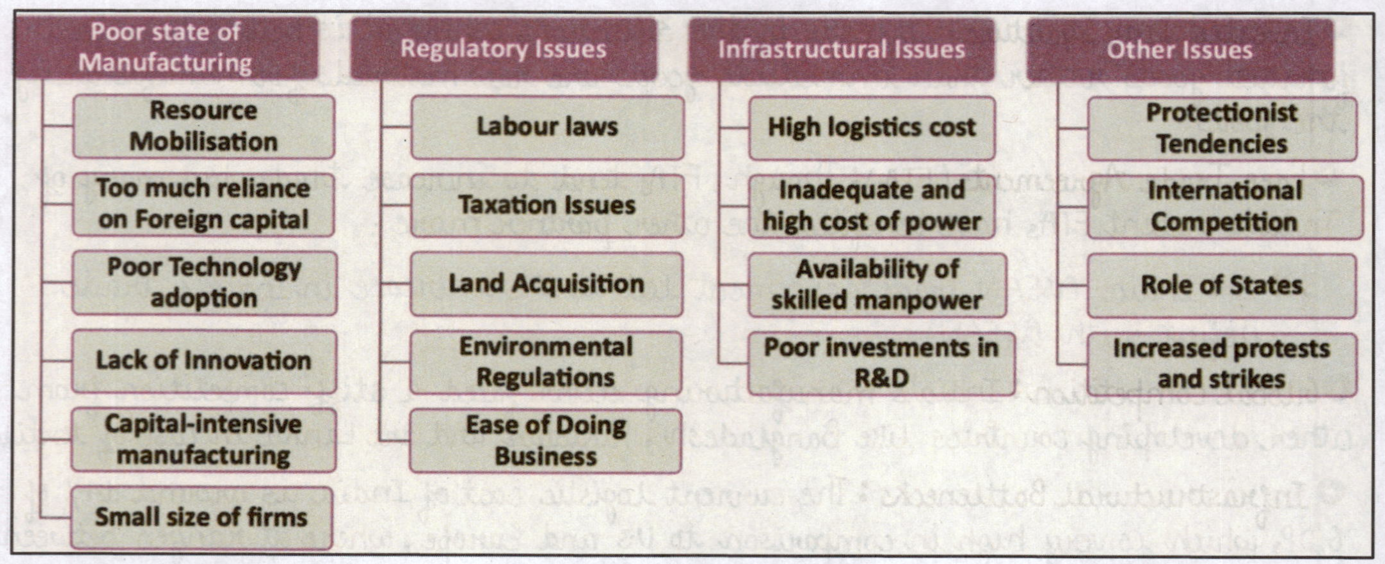


## Reform Measures

- Rationalization of policies related to labor laws, land acquisition, insolvency and exit law and contract enforcement.
- Increasing investment on R&D: It will help in the development of cutting-edges technologies and increasing competitiveness.
- Improving the infrastruture implementation of National Infrastructure pipeline can help speed up infrastructure delivery.
- Promote the growth of labor-intensive industries: Economic Survey also supported the idea of supporting textile (especially technical textiles), leather industries etc. due to India's competitive advantage and their labor-intensive nature.
- Promote MSMEs: MSMEs account for 8% of GDP, 45% of manufacturing output and 40% of exports. There is need to increase the credit accessibility, and large support for their growth and expansion.
- Filling the skill gap among the demography dividend.
- Bank recapitalization: Rising numbers of non-performing assets hamper bank's leading ability, which turn affect the growth of Indian industries.
- Improving the availability of power to the sectors which is the 2nd most important obstacle for manufacturing firms as per World Bank.

### Sectors for Labour-intensive Manufacturing

There are two groups of industries that hold the greatest potential for job creation and export growth.

01 Traditional unskilled labour-intensive industries such as textile, clothing, footwear and toys.

→ Economic Survey 2016-17 show that apparel sector is the most labor-intensive, followed by footwear.

» Apparels are 80-fold more labor-intensive than autos and 240-fold more jobs than steel. Leather goods are 33-fold more labor-intensive than autos and 100-fold more jobs than steel.

→ Women-centric sector: Apparels and leather sector offer tremendous opportunities for creation of jobs, especially for women. The opportunity created for women implies that these sectors could be vechiles for social transformation.

02 Huge potential to emerge as a major hub for final assembly in a range of products, referred to as "network products".

→ The Economic Survey 2019-20 advised that by integrating "Assemble in India for the world" into Make in India, India can raise its export market share to about 3.5 per cent by 2025 and 6 per cent by 2030, which is highly feasible.

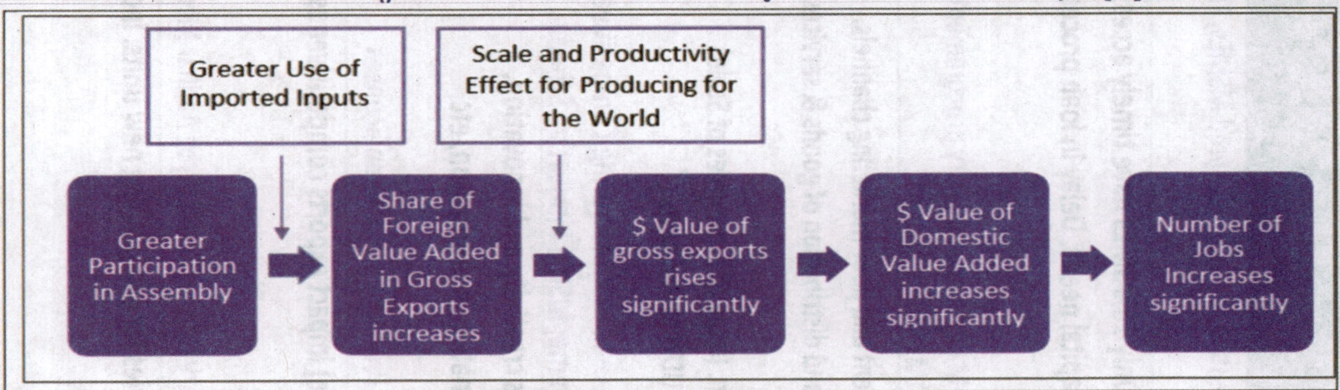


# MSME SECTOR

MSME definition get revised in 2020 which resulted in large number of medium enterprises:

| Composite Criteria: Investment and Annual Turnover | | | |
|---|---|---|---|
| Classification | Micro | Small | Medium |
| Manufacturing & Service | Investment < 1cr & Turnover < 5cr | Investment = 1-10cr & Turnover = 5-50cr | Investment = 10-50cr & Turnover = 50-250 cr |

## MSME → Growth Engine

01 Contribution to GDP (30%)

02 Contribution to manufacturing GVA (35-38%)

03 Employment Generation (11.1cr workers) [2nd largest employer after agriculture]

04 Contribution to Exports (45%)

05 Emphasis on Inclusive Growth

→ Rural dominated MSMEs (>50%) - promote rural industrialisation.

→ Around 20% of MSMEs are owned by the women

→ Social Inclusion (around 66% of MSMEs are around by socially backward sections)

| Problem Areas | Government Initiatives |
|---|---|
| **Access of Credit** | 59 minute portal, 2% interest subvention for GST registered MSMEs, TReDS, Udyami Mitra Portal , MSME Samadhaan, MUDRA Scheme |

- **Informal Loans: 90% of MSMEs are dependent on informal sources. Only 16% SMEs have timely access of finance.**
- **Procedural Challenge: Lack of sufficient collateral and high working capital needs. Delay in loan processing**
- **Delayed payments from ancillary clients and large buyers.**

| Problem Areas | Government Initiatives |
|---|---|
| **Access of Market** | E-Commerce companies, ONDC, GeM portal, compulsory procurement from MSMEs by PSUs, MSME Sambandh, SFURTI; RAMP; Digitalisation (UDYAM Platform); ONDC |

- **Low outreach and non-availability of new markets. Ineffective advertisement and poor marketing channels.**
- **Lack of skilled manpower and therefore, no innovation in the production and distribution of goods & services.**
- **Difficult for MSMEs to sell products to government agencies**
- **Competition from MNCs and other big industries in the era of globalisation. (Issue of Economies of Scale)**
- **Lack of formalisation. Barely 15% of MSME units have registered with the UDYAM Platform.**

| Problem Areas | Government Initiatives |
|---|---|
| **Technology Access** | CGTMSE; Financial assistance for Lean Manufacturing Competitive Scheme (LMCS); Digital MSME Scheme; Credit Linked Capital Subsidy Scheme; MSME Innovative Scheme |

- **Limited human resources and weak financial standing which impedes creativity and innovation.**
- **Lower adaptability of new technology such as digital presence, automation in production, etc.**

| Problem Areas | Government Initiatives |
|---|---|
| **Quality and Export Issues** | Zero Defect, Zero Effect Scheme; Product certification licenses |

- **Low quality products and low productivity (due to poor infrastructure) impact exports competitiveness**
- **Inadequate access of raw materials.**

| Problem Areas | Government Initiatives |
|---|---|
| **Ease of Doing Business** | Labour Reforms, improved regulatory compliances, Udyog Aadhar Memorandum (UAM), CHAMPIONS Portal |

- **Regulatory Cholesterol: Cumbersome government procedures and rules for establishing new units. Increasing the compliance cost.**
- **Red-Tapism: Bureaucratic delays in getting clearances.**
- **Poor insolvency and poor litigation system in the country**

## Futuristic Measures

- Incentivizing 'infant' firms rather than 'small' firm: With the appropriate grandfathering of existing incentives, they need to be shifted away from dwarfs to infants based on the age criterion.
- Sunset clause for incentives of five to seven years after which the firm should be able to sustain itself.
- Focus on High Employment Elastic sectors such as manufacture of rubber and plastic products, electronic and optical products, transport equipment, machinery, basic metals and fabricated metal products, chemicals and chemical products, textile and leather & leather products.
- Easy access to Finance and Credit: Institutional finance/credit from banks & other financing institutions should be promptly available without long and cumbersome procedures.
- Stepping up Infrastructural and Support Facilities: Deficiencies in basic infrastructural facilities like water, power supply, road/rail and telephone connectivity etc. should be addressed on priority basis.
  - Use of solar or renewable energy as an alternative source should be encouraged in rural areas on subsidized basis.
- Access to Modern Tools and Technology for increased productivity and quality product for competitive advantage.

**PYQs Corner**
*(Write the Answer and Get Free Evaluation)*

1. Faster economic growth requires increased share of the manufacturing sector in GDP, particularly of MSMEs. Comment on the present policies of the Government in this regard. [150 Words] [10 Marks] [2023]
2. Account for the failure of manufacturing sector in achieving the goal of labour-intensive exports rather than capital-intensive exports. Suggest measures for more labour-intensive rather than capital-intensive exports. [150 Words] [10 Marks] [2017]
3. "Industrial growth rate has lagged behind in the overall growth of Gross-Domestic-Product (GDP)in the post-reform period" Give reasons. How far the recent changes is Industrial Policy are capable of increasing the industrial growth rate? [250 Words] [15 marks] [2017]
4. Normally countries shift from agriculture to industry and then later to services, but India shifted directly from agriculture to services. What are the reasons for the huge growth-services vis-à-vis industry in the country? Can India become a developed country without a strong industrial base?[200 Words] [12.5 Marks] [2014]

Edict-3: Infrastructure

# CHAPTER 11

# INFRASTRUCTURE AND INVESTMENT MODELS

## INFRASTRUCTURE

- Infrastructure Sector refer to basic Services/Systems which are critical for an economy and have multiplier impact on the economic growth
- The National Statistical Commission headed by Dr. C. Rangarajan attempted to identify infrastructure based on some characteristics. The Rangarajan Commission indicated six characteristics of infrastructure Sector. These characteristics are:

a. Natural Monopoly

b. High Sunk Cost: A cost that had already been incurred and thus cannot be recovered.

c. Non-tradability of Output: Non tradable good or Service is one which is produced and sold at the same location.

d. Non-rivalness (up to congestion limits) in consumption: Non-rivalness implies that the cost of providing a good or Service to an additional individual is zero.

e. Possibility of Price exclusion: Price Exclusion means that the enjoyment of benefits is contingent on payment of user charges.

f. Bestowing externalities on Society.

# Categorization of Infrastructure

**Physical Infra**
- Logistic sector
- Transportation
  - → Roads
  - → Railways
  - → Airports
  - → Ports

**Energy Infra**
- Coal
- Natural Gas
- Renewable Energy
- Biofuels

**Digital Infra**
- Digital Payments
- Indiastack

**Social Infra**
- Health
- Education
- Skill Development

**Urban Infra**
- Sanitation
- Drainage system
- Solid waste disposal

## Infrastructure and Economic Growth

Investment in infrastructure is essential for more rapid and inclusive growth:

- **Multiplier Impact:** Investment in infrastructure leads to industrial development, thereby stimulating the growth in the economy. Eg: PM Gati Shakti Scheme
  - World Bank study: 1% increase in stock of infrastructure leads to corresponding 1% increase in GDP of a nation.
- Reduction in logistics cost by lowering production and transportation costs. This improves the competitiveness of Indian goods in the International markets. Eg - Bharatmala scheme
  - NITI Aayog: 4 10% decrease in indirect logistic cost has the potential to increase the exports by 5-8%
- Rippling effect on various sectors of the economy. Reliable power supply attracts foreign investment in sectors like manufacturing and IT. Eg: UDAY Scheme
  - UDAY Scheme aimed for financial turnaround for Discoms
- Boost to FDI inflows as the investment in infrastructure leads to improved ease of doing business
  - According to the World Investment Report 2022, India has ranked 7th among the top 20 host countries
- Growth in digital infrastructure will give a strong push to the economic growth. Eg - Digital India Initiative
  - Digital economy is expected to be $1 trillion economy by 2025-26.

## Promotion of Inclusive Growth

- Employment Generation: Eg - Deen Dayal Upadhyay Grameen Kaushalya Yojana (DDU-GKY)
- Addressing regional imbalances Eg - Krishi UDAN Scheme.
- Rural Development: Eg Pradhan Mantri Gram Sadak Yojana.
- Reduction of poverty and Income inequality: Eg - Pradhan Mantri Jan Aarogya Yojana
- Promotion of MSME: Eg - Startup India, Standup India.
- Gender Equality: Eg - Beti Bachao, Beti Padhao.
- Agriculture development: Eg - Pradhan Mantri Krishi Sinchayee Yojana (PMKSY)
- Improvement in Social indicators Eg: Poshan Abhiyan 2.0

## Concerns in the Infrastructure

1. **Infrastructure Deficit:** India has the second largest infrastructure deficit in the world
2. **Inequality in the access of infrastructure**
   - Inter-regional
   - Rural-Urban
   - Gender based
   - Digital divide
3. **Huge infrastructure financing gap (>5% of the GDP)**
4. **Sector specific challenges**
5. **Delay in timely completion of projects due to various reasons:**
   - Lack of coordination among multiple departments
   - Issue of land acquisition and environmental challenges
   - Lack of expertise and technology etc.
6. **Huge number of stalled projects (high sunk cost)**
7. **Poor quality of infrastructure** (Unreliable power supply, Poor drainage system causing urban floods)

# Roadblocks in key sectors

## HIGHWAYS

- Delays in land acquisition; lenders stop lending midway
- Tendering of projects to low-traffic entity
- Unclear exit policy for road developer; NHAI is a developer as well as the regulator which causes a conflict of interest in case of arbitration so there is a need for a clear distinction of roles for NHAI

## PORTS

- Multiple changes in tariffs setup by the Tariff Authority for Major Ports make it difficult to evaluate the cost of projects
- Delays in tariff fixation

## AIRPORTS

- Lack of consistency in tariff methodology and concession tariff framework
- Switching from single till tariff method to hybrid till creates difficulty in assessing the cost of projects
- Delays in the passage of tariff orders cause problems in the timely execution of projects

## WIND

- Inconsistent policy at Central and State govt level
- Accelerated depreciation leads to non-viability
- State regulators do not honour renewable purchase obligation

## TELECOM

- Lack of predictability
- Inconsistent policy and regulatory framework; govt refuses to honour PPAs signed earlier
- Aggressive bidding to some extent

## POWER

- Coal block deallocation causing execution delays and losses to project developers
- New auction-based coal linkage approved by government in 2017, uncertainty remains regarding the validity of old contracts
- Inconsistency in the interpretation of PPA
- Inconsistency in Central & State regulation, for instance, the Central electricity Act allows open access, but State governments do not adhere to it causing the problem in execution
- Unstable financial health of State utility causes a delay in the payment cycle

## GREENFIELD PROJECTS

- Land acquisition delay
- Nature of developers have been contractors which leads to low-cost bidding making the project unviable
- Bank loans are given out for **10/15/18 years** but the interest reset clause poses a high risk on overall investment return evaluation, sometimes **8%** interest rates are increased up to **14-15%** rendering the project unviable

## BROWNFIELD PROJECTS

- Government questions the validity of existing projects (eg, with rates of solar energy slashing, will the contracts entered on higher tariffs remain valid or not?)
- There is a strong need for the ability to have more credible infrastructure developers and partners

**UNIFIED LOGISTICS INTERFACE PLATFORM (ULIP) IS DESIGNED TO ENHANCE EFFICIENCY AND REDUCE THE COST OF LOGISTICS BY CREATING A TRANSPARENT, ONE-WINDOW PLATFORM**

# PM GATI SHAKTI YOJANA

- Government of India has launched the ambitious Gati Shakti Yojana or National Master Plan for Multi-Modal Connectivity Plan with an aim of coordinated planning & execution of infrastructure projects to bring down logistics costs.
- It is a digital platform that connects 16 ministries - including Roads and Highways, Railways, Shipping, Power, Petroleum & Gas, Telecom, etc - to institutionalize holistic planning for major infrastructure projects.

**National Infrastructure Pipeline (NIP)**

Consists of project and programme with an allocation of INR 111 lakh Crore for infrastructure development

- Launched in 2019 that includes economic and social infrastructure projects.
- Includes both greenfield and brownfield projects.
- Top 3 Sectors: Energy (24%) > Roads (19%) > Urban infrastructure (16%)
- Funding breakup: Centre (39%) : States (40%) ; Private Sector (21%)

- Subsumes the NIP that was launched in 2019.
- It incorporate the infrastructure schemes of various ministries and state governments such as Bharatmala road projects, Sagarmala waterways plan, ports and the UDAN scheme
- PM Gati Shakti Yojana intends to remove long standing issues such as disjointed planning, lack of standardisation, problems with clearances & timely creation and utilisation of infrastructure capacities.

## Envisaged Benefits

- Increased pace of infrastructure ▶▶ Bridging the infrastructure deficit.
- Improved connectivity ▶▶ Seamless and efficient network of transportation infrastructure across various modes.
- Focus on last mile connectivity ▶▶ Balanced regional development
- Reduced logistics cost ▶▶ Increased exports and boost economic growth.
- Integrated Planning (Digital Platform) ▶▶ Faster project completion
- Eliminate silo-based working ▶▶ Improving the quality and reducing the cost of infrastructure
- Higher investment ▶▶ Enhanced job creation.
- Building next generation infrastructure ▶▶ Improves Ease of Living as well as Ease of Doing Business
- Optimum utilisation of country's resources
- Increase cargo handling capacity ▶▶ Reduce the turnaround time at ports to boost trade

PM Gati Shakti envisages integrating existing and proposed infrastructure development initiative through following six pillars

- Comprehensiveness: Include all the existing and planned initiatives of various ministries with one centralised portal
    - Each and every department will now have visibility of each other's activities providing critical data while planning & execution of projects in a comprehensive manner
- Prioritization: Through this, different departments will be able to prioritize their projects through cross-sectoral interactions.
- Optimization: National Master Plan (NMP) will assist different ministries in planning for projects after identification of critical gaps.
- Synchronisation: Individual ministries and department often work in silos which often resulted into project delays.
    - Gati Shakti will help in synchronizing the activities of each departments, as well as of different layers of governance, in a holistic manner by ensuring coordination of work between them.
- Analytical: The plan will provide the entire data at one place with GIS based spatial planning and analytical tools having 200+ layers, enabling better visibility to the executing agency.
- Dynamic: All ministries and Departments will now be able to visualize, review and monitor the progress of cross-sectoral projects, through the GIS system, which will be updated on a regular basis on the portal.

## The master plan

The PM Gati Shakti aims to break inter-ministerial silos in infrastructure development. It will be achieved through integrated planning and coordinated implementation between different government departments.

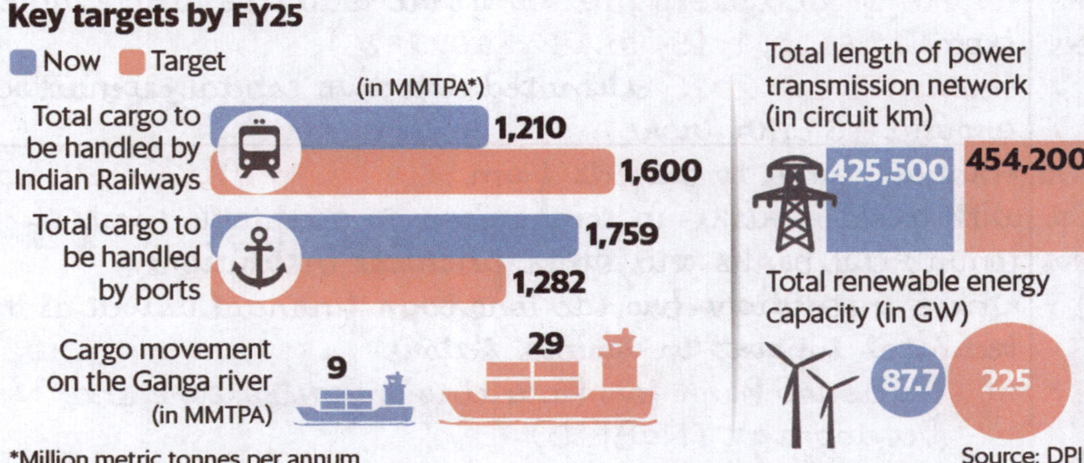

# INFRASTRUCTURE FINANCING

- Infrastructure development is a prerequisite for economic growth, productive investment, job creation and poverty reduction.
  - Poor infrastructure remains the biggest hurdle to sustaining a fast pace of economic growth and job creation in the future.
- India's biggest challenge is the huge infrastructure financing gap, which is estimated to be more than 5% of GDP.
  - Infrastructure projects involves huge investments, long gestation periods, procedural delays and delayed returns. This makes infrastructure financing complex.

## Sources of Infrastructure Financing

- Budgetary Resources
- Development Finance Institutions
- Banks led Debt based funding
- Public Private Partnerships (PPP)
- Asset Monetisation
- InvITs and REITs
- Equity & IPO
- External Sources
- Bond Market
- External Sources such as FDI, ECBs

| | |
|---|---|
| Budgetary Resources | • Share of capital expenditure in the total expenditure increased from 11% (2014-15) to 19% (2022-23)<br>• Budget 2024-2025 estimated Effective capital Expenditure of around 15 Lakh crore. |
| Development Financial Institutions (DFIs) | • Provide funds to projects from medium to long gestation periods with greater risks - in comparison to acceptable limits of commercial banks and other financial institutions<br>• These institutions provide long term financial as well as the technical support to various sectors.<br>Eg - National Bank for Financing Infrastructure and Development (NaBFID). |

| | |
|---|---|
| Banks-led debt-based funding. | • Dominant source of debt finance for infrastructure projects but banks typically offer short term to medium-term loans while infrastructure projects need long term funds. |
| Public Private Partnership (PPP) | • Agreement between government and private sector for the provision of public assets and public services.<br>• It allows large scale government projects, such as roads, bridges, or hospitals, to be completed with mix of public and private funding. Eg - HAM, BOT, EPC etc. |
| Viability Gap Funding (VGF) Scheme | • Viability Gap Finance means a grant to support projects that are economically justified but are not financially viable<br>• A grant under VGF is provided as a capital subsidy in order to attract the private sector players to participate in PPP projects that are otherwise financially unviable. |
| Asset Monetization | • Objective is to unlock the value of investments in public sector assets by tapping private sector capital and efficiencies which can thereafter be leveraged for augmentation/greenfield infrastructure creation.<br>• National Monetisation Pipeline was launched in 2021-22 for resource mobilisation through monetisation of brownfield, but underutilised infrastructure assets. |
| Infrastructure Investment Trusts (InvITs) | • These trusts pool small sums of money from a number of investors to invest in infrastructure assets that give cash flow over a period of time. Part of this cash flow is distributed as a dividend back to investors. Eg - National Highways Infra Trust, Power Grid Infrastructure Investment Trust, etc. |
| Capital Market | • Equity and IPO: Funds can be raised via the dilution of equity or raising directly from the public through IPO.<br>• Bond Market: Eg - Corporate bonds, infrastructure bonds, green bonds, municipal bonds. |
| External Sources | • FDI: FDI upto 100% under automatic route is permitted in projects for construction and maintenance of roads, highways, vehicular bridges, toll roads, vehicular tunnels, ports and harbors.<br>• External Commercial Borrowings (ECBs): Corporates can borrow from outside upto $750 million under automatic route.<br>• Issuance of Masala bonds or rupee denominated bonds to eliminate foreign exchange risk. |
| Other Sources | Such as Infrastructure Debt funds (IDFs), National Infrastructure Fund (NIIF), India Infrastructure Finance Company Ltd (IIFCL) etc. |

# Challenges in infrastructure Financing

**Approach 1: Budgetary Resources**
1. Limited Fiscal space. (BE 2024-25 estimates FD = 5.1% GDP)
2. Higher expenditure tilted towards Revenue Expenditure. (>80% of Expenditure is Revenue Exp)

**Approach 2: Banks led Debt based funding**
1. Asset liability mismatch
2. Higher NPAs (Fourbalance sheet problem)

**Approach 3: Development Finance Institutions (DFIs)**
1. Funding constraints
2. Failed DFIs in past such as IFCI.

**Approach 4: Public Private Partnerships (PPP)**
1. Subdued Investment in
2. PPP projects, due to various challenges - Financing, Procedural, Policy

**Approach 5: Asset Monetisation**
1. Asset specific challenges such as Regulated tariffs in power sector assets; Higher valuation of most assets.

**Approach 6: InvITs & REITs**
1. Nascent stage and low awareness.

**Approach 7: Funds such as NIIF, IDFs.**
1. Nascent stage
2. lower penetration of insurance and pension funds due to their obligation to invest a substantial portion of their funds in government securities.

**Approach 8: External Sources**
1. Global economic slow down making it difficult to access external resources
2. FDI concerns such as Ease of doing business, Regulatory uncertanity etc.

**Approach 9: Equity Market**

**Approach-10: Bond Market**
Poor corporate Bond Market

# Reforms needed in Infrastructure Financing

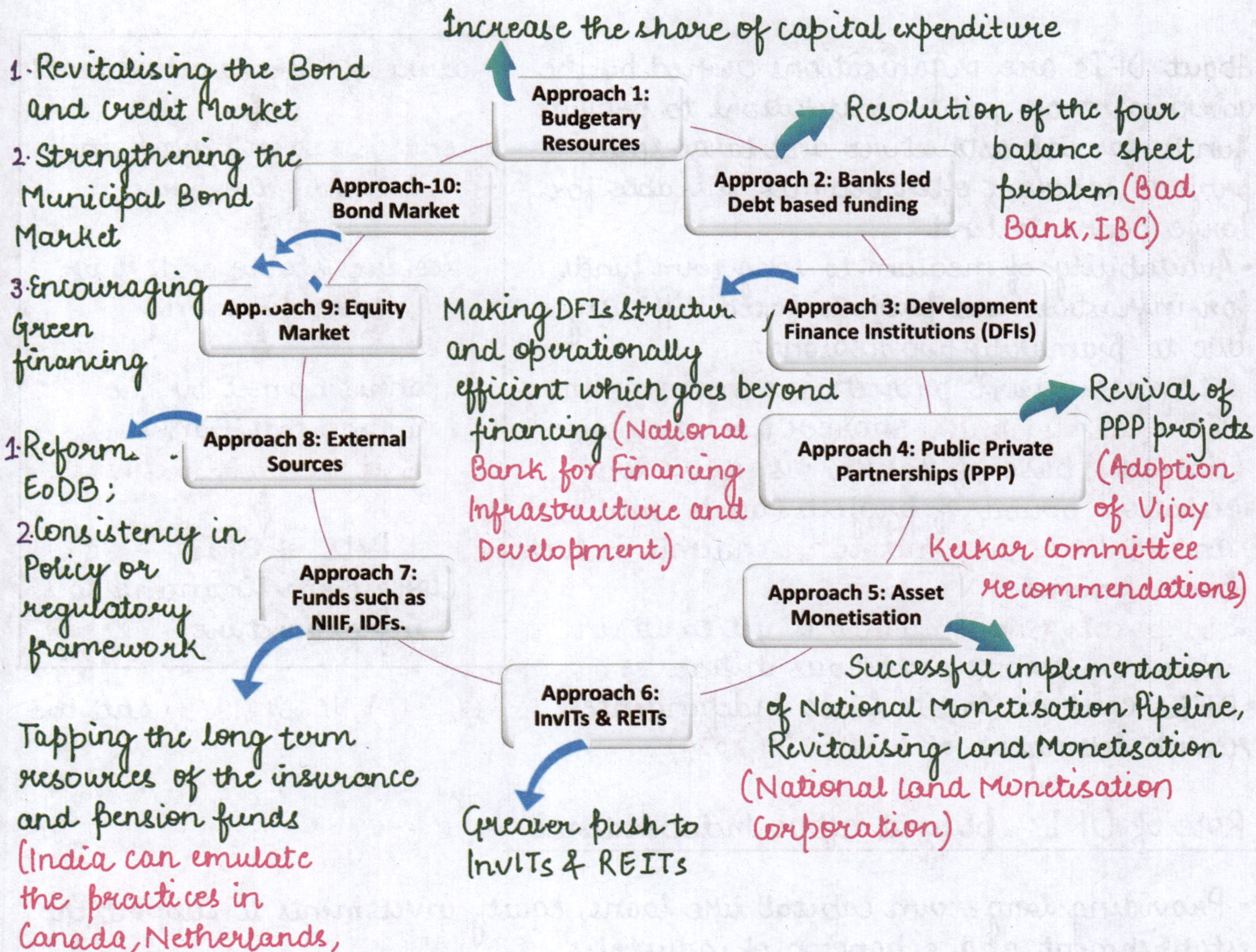


## Other reforms required

- Reasonable user charges: It is necessary for augmenting infrastructure financing, financial viability of infrastructure service providers, and for environmental and resource use sustainability.
- Developing Risk Mitigation instruments: Exploring credit guarantees, viability gap funding, and partial risk guarantees to mitigate risks for private players in infrastructure projects.

# Development Finance Institutions

**About:** DFIs are organisations owned by the government or public institutions to provide funds for infrastructure and large scale projects, where it often becomes unviable for large banks to lend.

- Availability of medium to long term funds for infrastructure projects faced difficulty due to primarily two reasons:
  1. Infrastructure projects are predominantly financed by banks. Shorter term resource (liability) base of Banks, vis-a-vis long gestation period of projects (assets) makes an asset liability mismatch endemic in such bank finance.
  2. Corporate bond market is yet to attain vibrancy despite numerous initiatives.

Nature of Infrastructure Assets
↓
Long gestation period and delayed returns
↓
Requires stable and long term financing
↓
Cannot be met by the Commercial Banks (Asset liability mismatch)
↓
Role of DFIs (long term financing to infrastructure)

- DFIs exist in India since independence: IFCI (1948), ICICI (1955) and the recent setting up of NaBFID (2021)

## Role of DFIs played after Independence

- Providing long-term capital like loans, equity investments to support the establishment and expansion of industries.
  Eg- Infrastructure Development Finance Company Ltd (IIFCL)
- Risk Assessment and Management to evaluate the feasibility and profitability of industrial ventures, thereby promoting responsible lending practices.
- Sector Specific focus enabled targeted financial support to industries that were considered critical for India's economic growth and social development.
- Technical and managerial assistance going beyond the financial support.
  Eg- NABARD.
- Catalyzing private investment by participating as equity partners, offering guarantees and extending credit enhancements particularly in sectors with high capital requirements and longer gestation periods.
  Eg- SIDBI offers partial risk guarantees for infrastructure projects.
- Development of Capital Markets through the mobilization of funds from

individual and institutional investors and channeled them into industrial projects, facilitating the growth of financial sector and fostering investment opportunities.

## Challenges faced by DFIs (leading to their failure)

- Funding Constraints: DFIs have faced difficulties in raising long term funds from the market, particularly during periods of economic uncertainity or when interest rates are high.
- Asset Quality and Non-Performing Assets (NPA) eroded the profitability and financial stability of DFIs, limiting their ability to lend and support new projects.
- Systemic issues: During the 1970-80s, DFI got discredited for mounting NPAs, allegedly caused by politically motivated lending and inadequate professionalism in assessing investment projects for economic, technical and financial viability.
- Financial Sector reforms (Post-LPG): The role of DFIs diminished as commercial banks started offering long term financing as DFIs lacked the operational efficiency and wider reach of commercial banks.
- Narasimhan Committee (1991) recommended disbanding of the DFI, and the existing DFI were converted into commercial banks. Eg- IDBI converted into commercial bank.
- Governance and Efficiency: Some DFIs have faced governance challenges, including issues related to transparency, accountability and effective management practices.

**Case study**

- IFCI in India and KFW in Germany were both created in 1948. Unfortunately, the irony is that KFW is currently running with an asset portfolio of something like US$ 26 billion whereas IFCI is reporting losses accumulated over time.

## NATIONAL BANK FOR FINANCING INFRASTRUCTURE AND DEVELOPMENT (NaBFID)

- Established in India in 2021 to address specific shortcomings in the infrastructure financing landscape.
- About: Set up as a corporate body with authorised share capital of 1 lakh crore rupees.

- Ownership: Shares of NaBFID may be held by central government; multilateral institutions; sovereign wealth funds; pension funds; insurance, banks, & financial institutions and any other institution prescribed by central government.
    - Initially the central government will own 100% shares of the institution, which may be subsequently reduced to 26%.
- Role: NaBFID will have both financial and development objectives
    - Financial objectives will be to directly or indirectly lend, invest or attract investment for infrastructure projects located entirely or partly in India.
    - Development objective include facilitating the development of market for bonds, loans and derivatives for infrastructure financing.

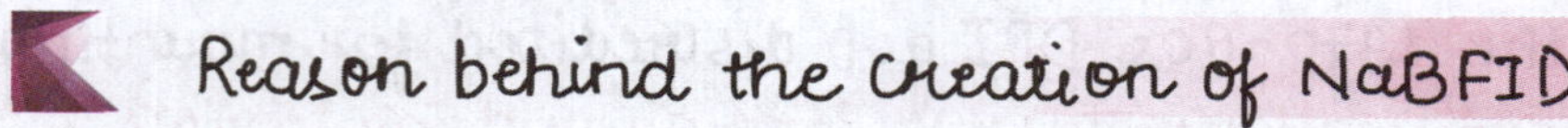

## Reason behind the creation of NaBFID

- High NPAs in banking sector led to renewed policy attention on setting up DFIs
- Bridging the gap in infrastructure financing needs especially after the NIP which envisages more than Rs. 100 lakh crore investment on infrastructure projects.
- Need for specialised DFIs to handle the unique challenges of infrastructure project as compared to earlier DFIs which may have broader mandates or cater to specific sectors.
- Development of bond market by issuing infrastructure bonds and promoting participation from institutional investors like pension funds & insurance companies.
- Promoting innovation in infrastructure financing by exploring new financing instruments, credit enhancement mechanisms, etc. to attract private capital and make infrastructure projects more attractive to investors.
- Reduction in stalled infrastructure projects which have high sunk cost to the economy.
    - Out of 6835 projects identified in December 2019 under NIP, only about 225 have been completed and the remaining face, among other things, funding issues.
- Achieving the target of $5 trillion economy by providing the much-needed finance on infrastructure projects.

## NaBFID is different from the earlier DFIs in the following manner

- Mandate and focus: NaBFID has a specific mandate for infrastructure financing.

- Earlier DFIs like IDBI or IFCI had broader mandates encompassing various Sectors such as agriculture, housing etc potentially leading to a Scattered focus

- Financial Resources: wider range of funding sources beyond government support by raising additional funds from the market both internationally and domestically.
  - Earlier DFIs heavily relied on budgetary allocations from the government, making them vulnerable to changes in government priorities and limited resources.
- Beyond financing by playing a developmental role that includes facilitating the development of bond market and develop innovative financing instruments such as InvITs or IDFs.
  - The focus on innovation was largely missing with the earlier DFIs.
- Ownership and Governance: NaBFID is expected to have a professional & autonomous governance structure which is governed by a board of directors comprising professionals from the finance and infrasfrasture Sectors (Government stake to be reduced by 26%)
  - Earlier DFIs in India were either wholly owned by the government or had a Significant government stake have been Subject to more bureaucratic processes or political interference.
  - NaBFID's governance structure is designed to ensure independence in decision-making to facilitate faster project approvals and implementation.
- Risk management techniques and tools to assess and mitigate risk associated with infrastructure projects.
  - Earlier DFIs often grappled with non-Performing assets (NPAs) due to inadequate risk management practices.
- Outside the purview of investigative agencies: NaBFID, as per the Act, will remain outside the purview of the 3Cs namely- CAG, CVC, CBI, enabling faster decision-making and bringing professionalism in functioning of NaBFID.
- leveraging Technology and digital platforms for project appraisal, monitoring and evaluation, making its operations more efficient and transparent compared to earlier DFIs.

Conclusion: Establishment of NaBFID reflects a focussed approach to infrastructure financing and development, with an emphasis on professional governance, financial sustainability and technology integration.
These aspects distinguish it from earlier DFIs in India and highlight intention to address the evolving needs and challenges of infrastructure Sector in the country.

# Asset Monetisation

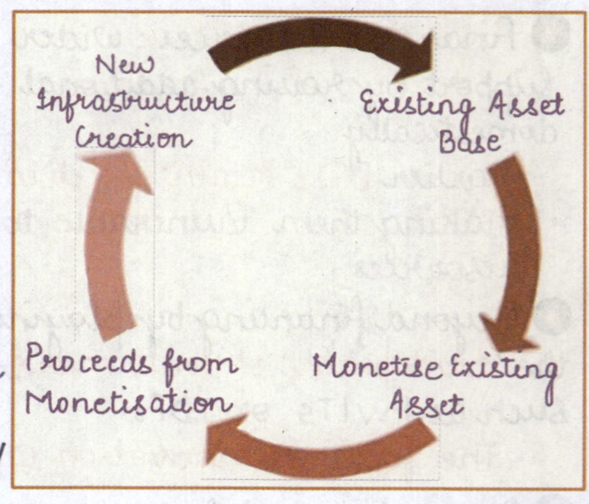


- It is a process of creating new sources of revenue for the government by unlocking the economic value of unutilised or underutilised public assets.
- Strategic objective is to unlock the value of investments in public sector assets by tapping private sector capital and efficiencies which can be leveraged for greenfield infrastructure creation.
- In the process, it helps public sector authorities/ entities in easing fiscal constraints and freeing up the balance sheets for taking up more greenfield infrastructure creation.

## National Monetisation Pipeline

- National Monetisation Pipeline (NMP) is an initiative by the Government of India for resource mobilisation through monetisation of brownfield but underutilised infrastructure creation.
  - Rs 6 lakh crore of assets will be monetised over 4-year period (2022-25)
  - Top 5 sectors = Roads (27%) > Railways (25%) > Power (15%) > Oil & Gas companies (8%) > Telecom (6%)

## Benefits of Asset Monetisation

- Resource mobilisation to bridge the infrastructure financing gap and NIP funding requirements.
- Fiscal Consolidation: Revenue generation for the government, reduced public sector burden and freeing up balance sheets for more greenfield creation.
- Social infrastructure: The freed resources can then be directed towards other priority areas like healthcare or education.
- Unlocking the economic potential of underutilised public assets.
- Economic Growth: Boosting new infrastructure development can stimulate economic activity, creation of jobs and improving overall productivity.
- Attracting private sector due to the leasing of brownfield assets (minimal risk)
  - This can bring in fresh investments, new technologies and improved management practices, leading to a more efficient infrastructure network.

- Generating Investment Avenues: Creates an enabling environment for participation of long term institutional investors in infrastructure asset management.
- Improved efficiency in the operation and maintenance of assets resulted into effective and efficient public service delivery.

### Achievements under NMP

Mining Sector: The monetisation of assets in 2023-24 has been led by the mining sector, particularly coal blocks and other mines.
NHAI as the second biggest contributor to brownfield asset recycling, is likely to achieve around Rs 45000 crore in the fiscal year 2024-25.

## Challenges in the Successful implementation of NMP

- Issue of Taxpayer's money: Concerns about potential double charges on public assets at the time of creation of public assets and utilisation of assets.
- Monopolisation: A significant criticism of the NMP is that the transfer would end up creating monopolies, leading to a rise in prices.
- Social impact: Increased user fees or reduced access for low income communities can impact the service delivery to the poor and marginalised section of the society.
- Labour issues: Transfer of public assets to private hands can raise concerns about job security for existing government employees.
- Asset-specific challenges: Issues such as low level of capacity utilization in gas and petroleum pipeline networks, regulated tariffs in power sector assets, low interest among investors in national highways below four lanes etc. will create specific challenges.
- lack of identifiable revenues streams in less-profitable sectors can impact the monetisation in those sectors.
- Data security and privacy: Some public assets may hold sensitive data and therefore, monetisation agreements include robust data security and privacy protections.
- Valuation and transparency: Concerns exist about fair pricing and potential undervaluation, leading to questions about transparency and potential for corruption.
- Regulatory uncertainity can deter potential investors as the legal and regulatary framework for asset monetization is still evolving in India.
- High valuation of most assets is likely to limit the number of potential bidders to few industrial or sectoral conglomerates.

- This can create issues of coordinated bidding, raise concerns of crony-capitalism and undermine the real value of assets.

Financing issues: Success of NMP depends upon structured financing models such as REITs and InvITs. Poor awareness among the investors may make it difficult for REITs/InvITs to raise money.

The above challenges might undermine resource mobilisation possible under NMP. Following measures can help in optimum resource mobilisation:

- Efficient and effective dispute resolution will help improve the attractiveness of projects and assets.
- Transparent Bidding is crucial to bringing in competitive and competent bidders, efficient price discovery and best management practices.
- Investor friendly Taxation and unpredictable policies such as retrospective taxation should be avoided.
- Establish a robust monitoring and evaluation system to track the performance of asset monetization projects.
- Dealing with cronyism by making the bidding conditions such that, people eligible to bid are not a small, predetermined set.
  - The high capital intensity of the project itself makes it difficult to everyone to bid but ensuring sufficient participation on the government's part is important.

NITI Aayog Recommendations

- Recommended bringing in policy and regulatory changes to scale up monetisation instruments like Infrastructure Investment Trusts (InvITs) and Real Estate Investment Trusts (REITs) as a critical element for success of the National Monetisation Pipeline (NMP)
- Bringing InvITs under Insolvency and Bankruptcy Code (IBC)
- Tax efficient and user friendly mechanisms are needed.

## Conclusion

Asset monetisation needs to be viewed not just as a funding mechanism, but as an overall paradigm shift in infrastructure operations, augmentation and maintenance considering the private sector's resource efficiencies and its ability to dynamically adapt to the evolving global and economic reality

# PUBLIC PRIVATE PARTNERSHIP

## Public Private Partnership

- Public Private Partnerships (PPPs) in infrastructure refer to the provision of a public asset and service by a private partner who has been conceded the right (the "Concession") for the purpose, for a specified period of time, on the basis of market determined revenue streams, that allow for commercial return on investment.

- According to World Bank, PPP is a long-term contract between a private party and a government entity, for providing a public asset or service, in which the private party bears significant risk and management responsibility, and remuneration is linked to performance.
- This collaboration or partnership is built on the expertise of each partner that meets clearly defined public needs through the appropriate allocation of 4R's.

  - Resources
  - Risks
  - Responsibilities
  - Rewards.

### Need for PPP in infrastructural projects

- Bridging gaps in infrastructure financing: PPPs attract private sector investments, supplementing limited government funds and reduces the burden on public finances (Decline in fiscal deficit)
  - World Bank estimates that India needs to invest $1.5 trillion annually in infrastructure by 2030 to meet its development goals.
  - Eg- the Hyderabad Metro Rail Ltd (HMRL), the largest metro project in the world to be implemented in the Public Private Partnership (PPP).
- Improved efficiency: Private companies often bring in better project management practices, technological advancements and operational efficiency, leading to faster project completion and improved service delivery.
  - Eg- PPP has helped NHAI clock 29.81 km/day (in 2014-15, the rate was 16.61 km/day)
  - Better quality of infrastructure by mechanism of accountability and responsibility owing to presence of private players. Eg- Kamlapati Railway station.
- Extracting long term value for money through appropriate risk transfer to the private sector over the life of the project - from design/construction to operation/maintenance.

- Capacity building: PPPs enable governments to tap into the private sector's expertise and resources, filling capacity gaps and accelerating project delivery.
  - Bangalore International Airport, developed through a PPP arrangement, benefitted from private sector expertise in airport design, construction and operations.
- Reduced corruption and wastage in government projects.
- Innovation in the infrastructure sector leading to a more sustainable and resilient infrastructure network.
- Other benefits: Cost-effectiveness through competitive selection, higher productivity by linking payments to performance and demand-centric delivery of projects.

### Successful PPP Examples

- Delhi and Mumbai International Airports: The privatisation of these major airports in the early 2000s is a prime example of successful PPPs.
- Golden Quadrilateral Highway Project: This massive highway project connecting major Indian cities was developed using a PPP model, leading to a more efficient national transportation network.
- Adani Mundra Solar Power Plant: This large scale solar power plant in Gujarat is a testament to the potential of PPPs in promoting renewable energy development.

### Failures of PPP

- Delhi Airport Metro Express project faced operational and financial problems, leading to the termination of PPP agreement with Reliance Infrastructure and subsequent government takeover of the metroline.
- Gurgaon Expressway: This highway project faced issues due to unrealistic traffic projections and delays in acquiring land. The Concessionaire, GMR infrastructure, eventually exited the project in 2015.

## Types of PPP Models

1. Build, Operate and Transfer (BOT-Toll): Conventional model in which private partner is responsible to design, build, operate (during the contracted period) and transfer back the facility to the private sector.
   - Private sector bring the finance for the project and allowed to collect revenue from the users.

2. Build, operate and Transfer (BOT-Annuity): Similar to the BOT (Toll) Model with only difference that private Sector will get fixed annual payments from the government unlike the BOT (Toll) under which private sector was collecting revenue from the users.

3. Engineering, Procurement and construction (EPC). Kind of PPP model in which the project cost is fully covered by the government and the private developers were supposed to design, construct and hand over the project to the government.

4. Hybrid Annuity Model (HAM): Type of PPP based on risk sharing where Government contributes 40% of the project cost and 60% of the cost is borne by the developer.

- Government agency collects the revenue from the project and pay annuity to the developer of the project
- Mix of both EPC and BOT model

| Models | Asset Ownership | Concession Period | Capital Risk | Revenue/ Commercial Risk | Responsibility of Private Player |
|---|---|---|---|---|---|
| BOT (Toll) | **Operationally private** | **Typically 15-30 years** | **Private – High** | **Private – High** | **Financing, Construction, Toll Collection, Operation and Maintenance** |
| BOT (Annuity) | **Operationally private** | **Typically 15-30 years** | **Private – High** | **Private - None** | **Financing, Construction, Operation and Maintenance** |
| EPC | **Public** | **Not Applicable** | **Private – High** | **Private – None** | **Engineering, Procurement & Construction** |
| HAM | **Operationally private** | **Typically 15-30 years** | **Private – Medium** | **Private - None** | **Less Financing, Construction, Operation and Maintenance** |

## Challenges faced in the Successful implementation of PPP projects.

**FINANCING ISSUES**

- Issues including aggressive bidding, under pricing of projects, huge dependency on commercial banks for financing leads to the delay of cancellation of PPP projects.
- Delay in Infrastructure have resulted in poor recovery from projects, thereby making these companies overleveraged and NPA increase in banking Sector.
  - This leads to vicious cycle of lower credit to PPP projects.
- Bureaucratic red tapism, economic slowdown & frequent renegotiations increase the project cost.
- Poorly developed corporate bond market

## CAPACITY AND PROCEDURAL CHALLENGES

- Lack of capacities at various levels of government to properly plan and prepare PPP projects resulting into poorly drafted contracts.
- Requirement of multiple clearances at the Centre, State and local levels resulting in serious delays. Land acquisition and environment clearance are the major contributing factors.
- Inadequate Regulatory framework and inefficiencies in the approval process have been considered as serious disincentives for developers and contractors.
- Weak institutional framework: Lack of clear guidelines, bureaucratic delays and complex approval processes can stall projects and discourage private participation.
  Eg- The Mumbai Trans-Harbour link project faced delays due to environmental clearances and land acquisition issues, leading to cost escalation and investor uncertainty.
- Lack of transparency in bidding processes and unclear project monitoring mechanisms can raise concern about corruption and inefficiency.
  Eg- There have been allegations of favouritism and unfair competition in awarding contracts in the past.

## POLICY, REGULATORY AND INSTITUTIONAL GAPS

- Absence of a dedicated PPP policy guiding all stakeholders of PPP project.
- Misaligned Goals and expectations: Government's priority of social welfare vs private partner's focus on profit can lead to disagreements on project scope, quality and user charges.
  Eg- Delhi Metro Airport Express line.
- Risk allocation issues: Unclear risk allocation or too much risk transferred to the private sector is a major cause of increasing project cost and project delays.
- Dispute Redressal: Absence of regulator or multiple regulators leads to slow or ineffective dispute redressal mechanism.
  - Disputes are bound to rise in PPP projects due to the long term nature of PPP contracts, uncertain market conditions, lack of capacity at both government and private player level etc.
- Institutional issues: India sometimes lacks the strong institutions needed for effective PPPs. Weak regulatory frameworks and a lack of skilled manpower can hinder project execution.

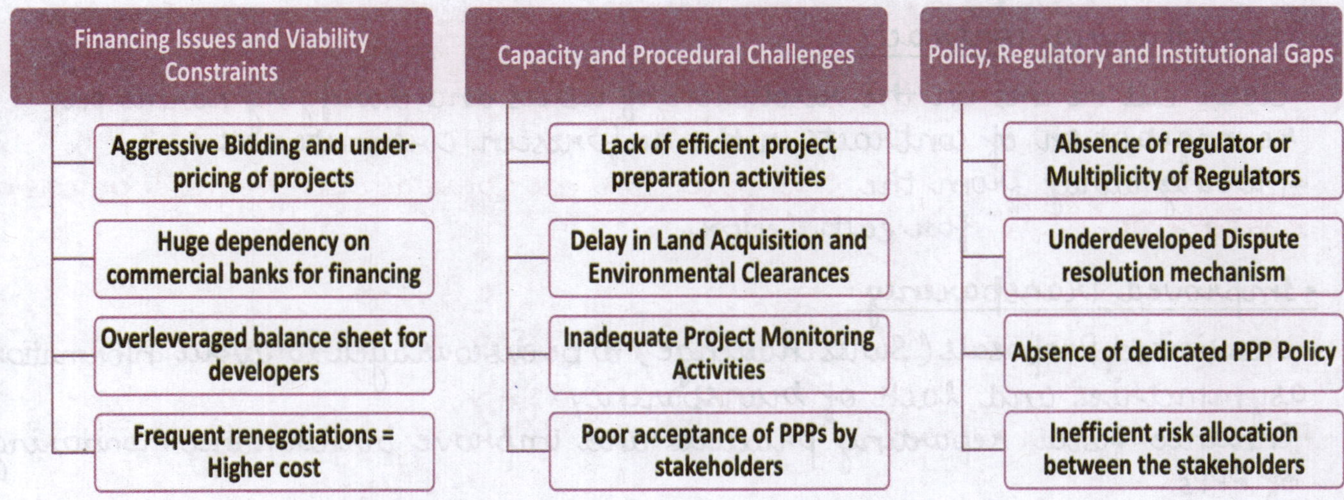


## Reform Measures (Vijay Kelkar Committee Recommendations)

- **Focus on Service delivery:** PPP Contracts should shift their focus from fiscal benefits to Service delivery for citizens by setting clear performance benchmarks and ensuring user satisfaction.
- **Improved risk allocation** by adopting a balanced approach to risk sharing between public and private partners.
  - This involves a thorough assessment of potential risks and assigning them to the party best equipped to manage them.
  - PPPs should not be used by the government as a means to evade its responsibility for Service delivery to citizens.
- **Policy and legal recommendations**
  - Some countries have a legal framework for PPPs in the form of PPP Act/ law/Policy. MoF may develop and publish a national PPP policy document or formulate a PPP law if feasible.
  - Amend Prevention of corruption Act, 1988 to distinguish genuine errors from acts of corruption.
- **Institutional Capacity building:**
  - Build the capacity of all stakeholders involved in PPPs, including regulators, authorities, consultants and financing agencies.
  - Set up an institution for invigorating private investments in infrastructure, providing guidance for a national PPP policy and developments in PPP.
  - Strongly endorses the 3P India (3PI), which can function as a centre of excellence, enable research and review and roll out activities to build capacity.
  - Infrastructure PPP Project Review Committee (IPRC) to evaluate PPP projects.
  - Infrastructure PPP Adjudication Tribunal (IPAT) for dispute resolution.
  - Set up independent regulators in Sectors engaging in PPPs.

- **Strengthening contracts:**
  - Clear cut norms on the resolution of issues and clarifying norms on re-negotiation of contracts in the unforeseen circumstances.
  - Moving away from the One-size-fits-all approach to PPP model concession agreements (MCAs) for each sector.
- **Improved Transparency:**
  - Unsolicited Proposals ("Swiss challenge") to be discouraged to avoid information asymmetries and lack of transparency.
  - Enhance fiscal reporting practices and improve performance monitoring of PPPs.
- **Funding:**
  - Explore innovative financing mechanisms to attract private investment in PPP projects like zero-coupon bonds or allowing for greater participation from institutional investors.
  - There is an urgent need in India to tap pension and insurance markets to fund its infrastructure requirements.
  - Prudent utilization of viability gap funds where user charges cannot guarantee a robust revenue system.

### Factors to be considered for designing a concession agreement

A concession agreement, which channelizes investment, is a contract that gives a company the right to use resources for a specified purpose and operate a particular business granted by a government with specified terms.

- Scope of the project including the nature of the infrastructure or service to be provided, the duration of the concession period and performance targets to be achieved.
- Investment requirements including the amount of capital to be invested, the source of funding and the return on investments.
- Clear delineation of responsibilities among the public and private sectors.
- Fair allocation of risks and rewards between the public and private parties this includes defining the mechanisms for sharing revenues, cost overruns and other contingencies.
- Transparency and competitive bidding (having enough players) in the award of concessions, thus preventing crony capitalism.
- Consistent with the regulatory and legal framework of host country, including laws related to taxation, labour, and the environment.

- Ownership and management of assets: The final ownership should lie with the government whereas management can be devolved to private sector.
- Fair valuation of the asset to prevent the underpricing of public assets.
- Monitoring mechanism through which the enforcement of the terms and conditions of the contract is ensured, and the market standard is followed.
- Time period of the partnership after which the partnership is allowed to be reassessed both from the perspective of government and private player.
- Clear norms and guidelines for the renegotiation of contracts in the unforeseen circumstances.
- Dispute redressal mechanism in the case of disputes between the public and private parties.
- Consultation with stakeholders such as local communities, civil society organisations, and other relevant parties to ensure that the project is socially and environmentally sustainable.
- Service delivery on time and targeted delivery system is another factor to be considered.

## PYQs Corner

*(Write the Answer and Get Free Evaluation)*

1. The Gati-Shakti Yojana needs meticulous coordination between the government and the private sector to achieve the goal of connectivity. Discuss. [150 Words] [10 Marks] **[2022]**
2. Why is Public Private Partnership (PPP) required in infrastructural projects? Examine the role of PPP model in the redevelopment of Railway Stations in India. [150 Words] [10 Marks] **[2022]**
3. "Investment in infrastructure is essential for more rapid and inclusive economic growth." Discuss in the light of India's experience. [250 Words] [15 Marks] **[2021]**
4. Explain how Private Public Partnership arrangements, in long gestation infrastructure projects, can transfer unsustainable liabilities to the future. What arrangements need to be put in place to ensure that successive generations' capacities are not compromised? [200 Words] [12.5 Marks]**[2014]**
5. Adoption of PPP model for infrastructure development of the country has not been free of criticism. Critically discuss the pros and cons of the model. [200 Words] [10 Marks] **[2013]**

Edict-4: Growth and Development

CHAPTER 12

# ISSUES RELATED TO GROWTH AND DEVELOPMENT

## GDP AND ITS LIMITATIONS

- Gross Domestic Production (GDP) is the final value of goods and Services which is produced within the geographical boundaries of a country during a specified period of time.
- Higher GDP growth rates are generally associated with increased employment opportunities, improving living standards and higher per capita income, thus it is synonymous with enhanced quality of life.

### Importance of GDP

- Per Capita Income is used by economists to gauge quality of life in a country.
- Indicator of the health of an economy.
- Linked with employment generation.
- Comparison of economic performance of various countries across the world.

### Limitations of GDP as a measure of Welfare

Welfare refers to the sense of well-being which is influenced by economic and Non-economic factors. It is assumed to treat the higher value of GDP of a country as as index of greater well-being of the people of the country but GDP has limitations in measuring well-being:

- Does not capture any type of inequalities in society: Income inequality, Gender inequality or Caste inequality as GDP only focuses on the per capita income.
  Alternate Approach: Gender Inequality Index, Inclusive Development Index etc.
- Environmental costs such as pollution or climate change are not included in GDP.
  Alternate Approach: Green GDP.

- **Leisure time:** People value leisure time but is not included in GDP.
  Alternate Approach: 'Net Economic Welfare (NEW)' popularised by Paul Samuelson
- **Does not capture non-monetary transactions** such as raising children, volunteering or caring for the elderly.
- **Ignores Informal Economy** which can be significant in many developing Countries.
  - This exclusion may lead to an underestimation of the true economic output and employment generated by these informal activities.
- **Human Development:** GDP doesnot measure the factors which leads to human development like education, health etc which severely impacts quality of life being lived by the people.
  Alternate Approach: Human Development Index (HDI)
- **It counts every expenditure as positive and does not discriminate welfare enhancing activity** from welfare-reducing activity.

## Determinants of Economic Growth

| Economic Factors | Non-Economic Factors |
|---|---|
| → Availability of Natural resources such as land, water Minerals etc.<br>→ Human Resources: India has 62.5% of its population in the age group of 15-59 years and will be at peak around 2036 when it will reach approximately 65%<br>→ Skilled labour forces as per Industry 4.0 requirements<br>→ Investment - GDP Ratio of around 29%<br>• Higher Capital Formation which has a multiplier impact in Growth<br>→ High domestic savings rate providing the resources for higher private investment (More than 30% in Indian economy)<br>→ Foreign Direct Investment (FDI) can help in improving the capital formation.<br>→ Efficient utilisation of resources (Incremental Capital Output Ratio (ICOR) should be low)<br>→ Technological adoption can reduce the production cost.<br>→ Government Policies: Tax and regulatory policies, FDI liberalisation policies such as PLI schemes, Atmanirbhar Bharat etc.<br>→ Ecosystem of Entrepreneurship & Innovation. | → Political Stability: Unstable political environment may reduce investment & the pace of economic development.<br>Eg: Pakistan, Sri Lanka in recent times.<br>→ Addressing governance issues such as Regulatory cholesterol, red tapism, corruption etc.<br>→ Social Institutions such as caste system can burden the economy with inefficiencies in the allocation of labour and other critical minerals. |

# APPROACHES TO DEVELOPMENT

| Growth | Development |
|---|---|
| • Uni-Dimensional i.e. Focus only on monetary aspects such as Per Capita Income or ↑se in GDP. | • Multi-dimensional i.e. focus on improving standard of living such as removal of poverty, improved health & education facilities, etc |
| • Measures only quantitative change. | • Measures qualitative change. |
| • Focus on Economy | • Focus on peo . |
| • Does not capture externalities such as gender inequalities, environmental implications, etc. | • Growth is a pre-requisite for development but it goes beyond just measuring growth. |

## 1. World Development Report (WDR, 1991)

• Economic Development is defined as a sustainable increase in living standards that encompasses material consumption, education, health and environmental protection

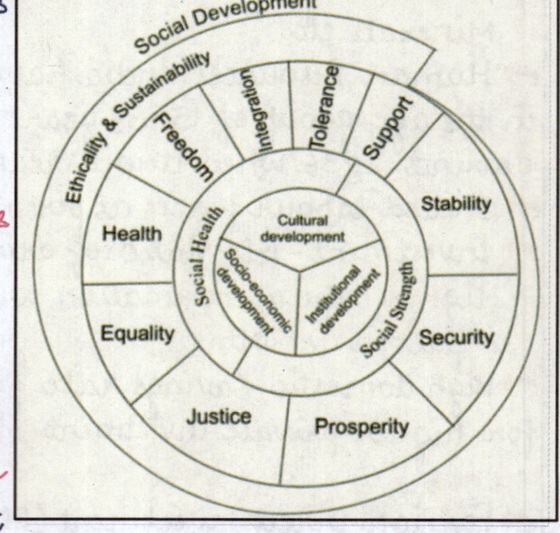


• The overall goal of development is therefore to increase the economic, political and civil rights of all people across gender, ethnic groups, races, religions and countries.

## 2. Amartya Sen's Conception of Development

• Development is the process of expanding human freedom. It is " the enhancement of freedom that allow people to lead lives that they have reason to live.

• Hence, development requires the removal of major sources of unfreedom: Poverty, tyranny, poor economic opportunities, systematic social deprivation, neglect of public facilities, intolerance and overactivity of repressive states.

• Freedom are not only the primary ends of development but among its principle means.

Political freedom, in the form of free speech and elections, help to promote economic security.

Social opportunities, in the form of education and health facilities, facilitate economic participation

Freedom

Economic facilities in the form of opportunities for participation in trade & production, can help to generate personal abundance as well as public resources for social facilities.

With adequate social opportunities, individuals can effectively shape their own destiny and help each other.

## 3. Human Development Approach

- This approach gives a central role to the ability of people to be agents of their own lives. People are not passive objects of generous social welfare provisions but are active agents.
- Concerned both with building up human capabilities (through investment in people) and using these human capabilities fully through an enabling framework for growth and development.

4 Pillar Approach of Human Development

**Sustainability**
Refers to sustainability in all spheres- social, Political and financial

**Productivity** Least cost method of achieving goals through interventions that maximise opportunities for individuals & communities through optimal use of human & institutional resources.

**Equity**
Refers to the concept of justice, impartiality and fairness; and incorporates the idea of distributive justice, particularly in terms of access to opportunities and outcomes to all human beings.

**Participation & Empowerment**
People are both the ends as well as the means to development. Empowerment is about processes that lead people to perceive themselves an entitled to make life decisions.

## Economic Growth vs Human Development

- India is the world's 5th largest economy in nominal GDP but is the 3rd largest in GDP on PPP basis. It has grown rapidly since 1991 with an average economic growth of 7% in last 30 years & currently India's economy is more than $3.7 trillion economy.

But this growth has not resulted into a corresponding increase in its Human Development Index (HDI)

- India ranks 134 out of 193 countries on the global HDI (Human Development Report 2023-24). India is ranked worst among the BRICS economies and below than most of its neighbours such as Srilanka (78), Bangladesh (129), Bhutan (125) etc
- High Inequalities: Oxfam Report
  - Top 1% has greater than 40% of nation's wealth.
  - Bottom 50% have 3% of nation's wealth.
  - Increase in number of Billionaires (102 in 2020; 166 in 2022)
- High Poverty: Global MPI = 16%
  Niti Aayog MPI = 15%
- India's poor rank in Global Hunger Index, 2023 (111 out of 125 countries) and is home to over 190 million hungry people.

## Reasons

1. Jobless growth as India's growth is led by Service Sector
   a. Employment elasticity has fallen from close to unity in the 70s to 0.4 in the 90s to less than 0.1 in the present times.
2. Less Employment Opportunities + Increasing India's Youth population
3. Unique structural transformation bypassing growth of industrial sector.
   (Stagnant manufacturing sector of 16%) ➡ leads to less Employment.
4. Capital intensive manufacturing rather than labour intensive.
5. Low public investment on social infrastructure (India spends 3% of GDP on education and 2% of GDP on health).
   ⇩
   - Poor learning outcomes, low employability of graduates, low productivity & consequent low wages. Economic survey highlighted this via 'Learning Poverty'.
   - Numerous health issues such as malnutrition, poor hygiene, & inadequate healthcare infrastructure.
6. Systematic social discrimination against certain groups such as SCs & STs.
7. Widespread corruption affecting the distribution of resources and opportunities leading to lack of trust in government and Institutions.
8. Mismatch in availability of skills: low availability of skills as required by fourth Industrial Revolution.
9. Slow growth in Productivity (low Productivity): Hampers income of 45% of the population.

## 4. Sustainable Development Approach

- Described as development which "meet the needs of the present without compromising the ability of future generations to meet their own needs" (Our Common Future 1907)
- UN adopted 17 SDGs and 169 targets which aim at eradicating poverty in all forms and seek to realise the human rights of all and achieve gender equality.

**Three core elements of Sustainable Development**

| Economic Sustainability | Social Sustainability | Environmental Sustainability |
|---|---|---|
| • Focus on equal economic growth that generates wealth for all without harming the environment<br>• Eradicating poverty in all its forms and dimensions. | • Foster gender equality, development of people, culture & communities to help achieve a reasonable and fairly distributed quality of life, healthcare & education across the globe. | • Prevents nature from being used as an inexhaustible source of resources and ensures its protection and rational use. |

## Need for Sustainable Development

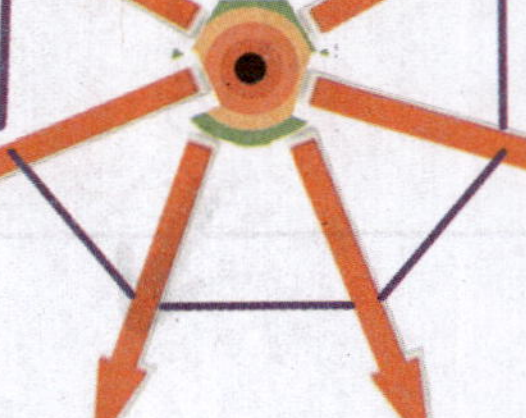

1. Fight against climate change and protecting biodiversity.
2. Contributing to wellbeing of our communities
3. Sustainable economic growth.
4. Innovation, digitalization and quality for our customers
5. Good governance, transparency and stakeholders engagement.
6. Promoting in the supply chain
7. Workplace health and safety & personal development

# INDIA's PROGRESS TOWARDS SDGs

## India's Initiatives

### NITI Aayog's SDG India Index

- Monitoring of States Progress

### Sampanna Bharat, Samriddha Bharat (Prosperous and Vibrant India)

- Faster Economic Growth (Target of $5 Trillion by 2025)
- World's 5th largest economy

### Sashakt Bharat, Sabal Bharat (Empowered and Resilient India)

(lifted more than 415 million people out multidimensional poverty between 2005-06 to 2019-21)

- Poverty Eradication Programs
- Education Programmes (NEP)

### Satat Bharat, Sanatan Bharat (Sustainable India)

- Renewable Energy (Panchamrit - COP 26)
- Compressed Biogas Plants
- Ethanol-blending programme (Target 20% by 2025)
- International Solar Alliance

### Swachh Bharat, Swasth Bharat (Clean and Healthy India)

- Sanitation (SBA) (Sanitation coverage in India improved from 39% in 2014 to 100% in 2019).
- Nutrition (POSHAN Abhiyan 2.0)
- Universal Health Coverage (Ayushman Bharat providing Rs 5 Lakh per family to approximately 55 Crore beneficiaries).

### Samagra Bharat, Saksham Bharat (Inclusive and Entrepreneurial India)

- Social inclusion through universalising access to nutrition, health, education and social protection
- Financial Inclusion (PM Jan Dhan Yojana)
- Aadhar Coverage (More than 92% of population)
- Developing Capabilities & fostering innovations (Skill Development programs, Start Up India, Stand Up India)

# CHALLENGES IN ACHIEVEMENT OF SDGs

## Structural

- Slow Economic Growth
- Not adhering to Sustainable Development (Over Exploitation of natural resources)
- Rapid Urbanisation. (Demand-Supply Gap in Infrastructure, housing & other Services)
- Regional Variance in Development between states and between rural and Urban areas

## Implementation

- Financing SDGs require significant investment.
- Governance Issues
  - One-Size-Fits-All approach
  - Lack of Co-ordination
  - Slow release of Funds
  - Inadequately trained Human resources.
- Technological Backwardness.
- Lack of Awareness and poor participation by marginalised communities.

## Monitoring

- Unquantifiable Targets
- Poor Grievance Redressal Mechanism
- Irregular Data reporting on outcomes and lack of Capacity of Data preparation at state levels.

## Solutions

### Structural

- Faster Economic Growth
- Environment Impact Assessment
- Urban Infrastructure
  - Smart Cities
  - AMRUT.
- Targeted Programs
  - Localising SDGs
  - Aspirational Districts

### Implementation

- Raising Funds
  - Issuing Municipal Bonds
  - Multilateral Institutions' Funds
- ICE Activities
  - Information
  - Communication
  - Education.
- Focus on 3As (Awareness, Actions, Accountability)

### Monitoring

- Quantifiable Targets
- Robust Grievance Redressal mechanism
- Involvement of Civil Society

## 5. Rights-Based Approach to Development

➡ 'Basic Needs' approach: It was pursued till 1990s under which basic requirements of beneficiaries were identified and either supported initiatives to improve service delivery or advocated for their fulfilment.

➡ 'Rights-Based approach: Emphasis upon fulfilment of the rights of the people rather than needs of beneficiaries.

- An unfulfilled need leads to dissatisfaction, while a right that is not respected leads to violation.
- A Right-based approach develops the capacity of duty bearers (government) to meet their obligations and encourage right holders to claim their rights.

➡ People's participation: It recognizes that people are actors in their own development, rather than passive recipient of services.

➡ Two-way relationship

- Individuals & communities informed about the rights and participate in the decisions that affect them.
- Government to develop the capacity and the political will to fulfill their commitment to human rights.

➡ Implementation in India: India has followed the path of rights based social welfare policies to guarantee the social rights of the people – Right to Information Act (2005); Right to Education (2002); Right to work (MGNREGA Act, 2005) and Right to Food (NFSA 2013).

## 6. Women-led development

- Meaning: Refers to development approach where women take on leading roles and actively participate in shaping and driving the economic, social and political progress of a society or community.
  - Under this development model, women are not just beneficiaries of development, instead they set the agenda for development and are key participants in development planning & decision making as leaders and equal participants.
- Government Initiatives: 106th CAA (Women Reservation Act); Stand Up India Scheme; PM Mudra Yojana; Beti Bachao Beti Padhao; Paid Maternity leave to 26 weeks; PM Ujjwala Yojana; Swachh Bharat Mission (SBM); Mission Shakti; Abolition of Triple Talaq, etc.
  - India has signed several UN conventions, including the convention on Elimination of all Forms of Discrimination against Women (CEDAW), Beijing Platform for Action and the Convention on Rights of the child, among others.

Important Facts

- The presence of girls/women in Science, Technology, Engineering and Mathematics (STEM) is 43%, which is one of the highest in the world.
- 46% of elected representatives in rural local bodies in India are women.
- More than 80% of nurses and midwives in India are women.
- More than 70% of the loans under PM Mudra Yojana have been sanctioned to women.
- Similarly 80% of beneficiaries under Stand-up India are women, availing bank loans for green field projects.
- About one-fourth of space scientists in India are women.
- In India, about 15% of unicorn start-ups have atleast one women founder. The combined value of these women led unicorns is over 40 billion dollars.

# INDIA'S DEVELOPMENT CHALLENGES

## GOVERNANCE DIMENSIONS

- Issue of Corruption: Transparency International's 2023 Corruption Perception Index ranked India at 93rd out of 180 countries.
- Ineffective implementation of rural programmes due to bureaucratic inefficiencies, red tapism, procedural delays, corruption etc.
- Weak Coordination among the government departments and between centre and state governments
- Policy paralysis creating uncertainities and discouraging private sector investment.
- Other governance issues: Poor capacity building, ineffective accountability mechanisms, weak grievance redressal mechanism, one size fits all policy formulation etc.

## ECONOMIC DIMENSIONS

- Poverty: As per MPI 2023, 14.96% of the population are multidimensionally poor between 2015-16 and 2019-21.
- Economic Inequality: Just 5% of Indians own more than 60% of country's wealth, while the bottom 50% of the population posses only 3% of the wealth. (Oxfam Inequality Report, 2023)
- Unemployment and Underemployment: While India's unemployment rate stood at 6.4% (April-June 2023) [CMIE], a significant portion of the workforce is underemployed, lacking opportunities for full time work or jobs that utilize their skills.
- Industrial Development: India's manufacturing sector contributes around 17% to the GDP (as of 2022), compared to China's 27%.
- High logistics costs: India's logistics cost is around 14% of the world which is one of the highest in the world, reducing the export competitiveness

| SOCIAL DIMENSIONS | ↱ Education and Skill Development. India has 4.7% of its workforce trained in formal skills, compared to 52% in the US, 80% in Japan, 96% in South Korea, according to the 2015 National Policy on Skill Development and Entrepreneurship.<br>↱ Healthcare: India's Infant Mortality Rate (IMR) has declined to 30 per 1000 live births (National Health Profile 2023) but lacks behind the global average of 23.<br>↱ Social Issues: NCRB reported over 3 lakh cases of crimes against women in 2021, highlighting the prevalence of gender based violence.<br>↱ Nutrition Indicators based on NFHS-5<br>• Stunting: High among children in rural areas (37%) than urban areas (30%) in 2019-21.<br>• Obesity: Increased from 21% (NFHS-4) to 24% among women and 19% (NFHS-4) to 23% among men.<br>↱ Drinking water: less than half of the total households in rural areas have exclusive access to the principle source of drinking water (2018 NSSO Survey).<br>↱ Sanitation:<br>• Drainage: 31.7% of rural households and 82.5% of urban households had 'improved drainage facility (NSSO 69th round Survey)<br>• Garbage disposal: 32% in rural households and 75.8% in the urban households had some garbage disposal arrangements. |
|---|---|

Other Dimensions

➡ Imbalanced regional development: Urban-Rural Divide, unplanned urbanisation, inter-state disparity in the development process.

➡ Climate change: India is one of the most vulnerable countries to climate change, with extreme weather events like heatwaves and floods causing economic losses and displacing population.

➡ Emerging Technologies: Automation and Artificial Intelligence pose challenges for the Indian workforce, requiring investment in skill development and digital literacy programs to bridge the skill gap.

➡ Internet penetration: According to ICRIER's State of India Digital Economy 2024 report, while 'India as a nation is highly digitalised the average indian is not'.

• India's gender gap in internet connectivity is at 10%, higher than world's average of 9% and the rural-urban divide is at 58%, higher than world's average of 49%.

• According to IAMAI's Internet in India Report, 2023, at 759 million, 52% Indians have access to internet.

➡ Protectional trade policies and trade barriers imposed by developed economies can limit India's export opportunities and hinder its economic integration with global markets.

# INDIA'S DEVELOPMENT POLICIES

| Colonial Regime | Nehruvian Legacy (1947-65) | 1965-1991 | Post 1991 |
|---|---|---|---|
| **Agriculture**<br>• Land Revenue System<br>• Commercialisation<br>• Low State Investment<br>**Industrial Development**<br>• Britain's Industrial Revolution<br>• India = Raw material based Industries.<br>**Foreign trade**<br>• One way free trade<br>• British Monopoly over trade<br>• Export of Raw material like Cotton, Jute, Indigo etc.<br>**Infrastructure Development**<br>• Railways<br>• Roads<br>• Telegraph | **State of Indian Economy on the Eve of Independence**<br>• Vicious Cycle of Poverty.<br>• Low levels of Saving & Capital Formation.<br>• Mainly Rural & Agrarian Economy<br>• Unbalanced Occupational Structure<br>• Illiteracy very High<br>• Widespread Communicable Disease; No Self-Reliance.<br>↓<br>Models of Economic Development<br>↙ Capitalist Model — Democracy (Liberalism)<br>↘ Socialist Model — Erstwhile USSR<br>↓<br>India's Economic Development Model<br>↓<br>**Strong Public Sector** (Supported/Complemented by Private Sector)<br>↙ Domestic Factors ↘ International Factors | **1960s: Era of Dangerous Decade**<br>1. 2 wars with Neighbours<br>2. Drought & Famine Conditions (Food Insecurity)<br>3. Balance of Payment Crisis<br>4. Emergence of Naxalism<br>**Policies Adopted**<br>1. New Agriculture Strategy (Led to Green Revolution)<br>2. Directly-targeted Poverty Alleviation Program launched (Removal of Trickle-down)<br>3. Indira's Socialism (Stricter version of Nehru's Socialism)<br>• Role of public sector increased<br>• MRTP Act / FERA Act<br>• Bank / Insurance company's Nationalisation<br>↓<br>(3 Annual Plan + 4 FYPs later) (7 FYPs)<br>↓ | 1. Structural Problems<br>2. Immediate BoP Crisis, 1991<br>↓<br>LPG Reforms<br>↙ Partly due to Reforms needed ↘ Partly due to IMF Condition<br>↓<br>Liberalisation<br>(Removal of barriers/Constraints)<br>↙ Internal level — Privatisation (Increase in role of Pvt. Sector in Economy)<br>↘ External level — Globalisation (People, goods, Service & Capital movement across nations)<br>**1. Industrial Sector Reforms**<br>• MRTP removal; Public Sector De-reservation; PSUs' Dis-investment, Industrial Licensing Abolition; FDI liberalisation (FERA → FEMA)<br>**2. Financial Sector Reforms**<br>• De-regulation of Interest Rates; New Institutions created (SEBI, PFRDA, TRDA) |

↓

Impact on Economy

1. Stagnating Agriculture
2. Commercialisation
3. Deindustrialisation (Raw material based Industries feeding Britain's Industrial Development)
4. Exporter of Raw Materials
5. Drain of Wealth resulting into reduced investments in Indian industries

↓

**Indian Economy = Complementary Economy to Britain.**

- Independence movement (left ideology in 1920s)
- Karachi session, 1931
- Bombay Plan 1944

- Great Depression (New Deal Program)
- Emergence of Keynesian Economics
- Erstwhile USSR became an economic superpower

↓

Planned Model

- High Planned Expenditure (Priorities) + Resource Mobilisation (Optimal Allocation)

↓

FYPs (Growth; Modernisation; Equity; Self-Reliance)

↓

1. Agriculture vs Industry debate (Heavy industrialisation)
2. Public vs Private Sector (Public-Major role)
3. Import Substitution Industrialisation Strategy (Mahalanobis Model)

↓

Industrial Policy Resolution, 1956 + Promotion of Labour Intensive & cottage Industries + Land Reforms in Agriculture.

↓

**Trickle Down Growth Model**

1. Structural Problems
- Agriculture ↓
  - Land Fragmentation; low Productivity; Input-Intensive (Green Revolution)
- Industrial Sector ↓
  - Low Productivity
  - → Import Substitution; MRTP; FERA; SSI Reservations; License Raj.
- Continuation of inward developmental path - FERA
- Gradual Erosion of fiscal prudence → Increasing fiscal Deficit.

+

2. Immediate crisis, 1991.
- Twin Deficit Issue → FD and CAD increasing
- Gulf crisis (High Oil prices)
- Loan shortage + NRI withdrawals

↓

BOP Crisis (Import cover of just 2-3 weeks was left)

↓

**LPG Reforms**

3. Trade Reforms
- Reduction in Import tariffs; WTO membership (MFN status Extension)

4. Public Sector Management
- Decrease in Fiscal Deficit;
- PSU Autonomy (Navratna, Miniratna, Maharatna)

↓

Critical Analysis of LPG Reforms given in the next page.

# Critical Analysis of LPG

**Background**

- In return for the $7 billion loan to manage the 1991 Balance of Payment (BoP) crisis, IMF expected India to liberalise and open up the economy by removing restrictions on the private sector, reducing the role of the government in many areas and removing trade restrictions between India and other countries.
- Thereafter, India announced the New Economic Policy (NEP), 1991 with wide ranging structural reforms introducing liberalisation, privatisation and globalisation.
- It was aimed to liberalize the economy, promote growth, attract foreign investment and improve the overall business environment which have catapulted Indian economy to become 5$^{th}$ largest economy in the world.

**Impact of Economic Reforms**

- **Increased Economic Growth:** LPG reforms helped in increasing the rate of economic growth in India. From 1991 to 2020, India's GDP grew at an average rate of 6.7% compared to an average rate of 3.5% in the previous three decades.
- **Higher Foreign Investment:** LPG reforms opened up several sectors of the Indian economy to foreign investment leading to an increase in foreign direct investment. According to Ministry of Commerce & Industry, FDI inflows into India increased from $98 million in 1990-91 to $84 billion in 2021-22.
- **Improvement in Industrial Productivity:** According to a study by the Reserve Bank of India, the productivity of the Indian manufacturing sector increased by 6.8% annually between 1991 and 2006.
- **Expansion of the Service Sector:** LPG Reforms led to the growth of the services sector in India, which became a major contributor to the country's GDP. Its contribution to India's GDP increased from 37.2% in 1990-91 to 54.3% in 2020-21.
- **Increase in Consumerism:** LPG Reforms led to an increase in consumerism in India as people had access to a wider range of goods and services. According to NSSO, the average monthly per capita expenditure of Indian households increased from Rs. 206 in 1987-88 to Rs. 2,446 in 2017-18.
- **Trade Liberalisation:** India's trade openness increased from a meagre 13 per cent in 1990-91 to 42 per cent in 2020. The exports, driven by the devaluation of the rupee in 1991 and further depreciation in later years, have increased from $17.96 billion in 1990 to $324.43 billion in 2019.
- **Impact on Forex Reserves:** There has been a significant improvement in forex reserves, which are now sufficient to cover more than 12 months of imports as per the Economic Survey 2022-23.
- **Impact on Social Indicators:** There have also been improvements in literacy rates, gross enrolments ratio and life expectancy, among others. Overall, human development has improved in India.
- **Faster rate of poverty eradication:** In the post-reform period, poverty declined faster in the 2000s than in the 1990s Poverty declined by 1.36 percentage points per annum after 1991, compared to that of 0.44 percentage points per annum prior to 1991.
    - Around 415 million people in India climbed out of poverty between 2005-06 and 2019-21, with the incidence of poverty falling from 55 per cent to just over 16 per cent over this period, according to the Global Multi-dimensional Poverty Index 2022.

**Economic Reforms resulting in sectoral imbalances and inequalities**

Sectoral imbalances are in the form of growth inequities in various sectors. The growth has been concentrated only in some areas in the services sector such as telecommunication, IT, finance, entertainment, travel and hospitality, trade etc., whereas vital sectors such as agriculture and manufacturing industry continue to struggle.

- Post-reforms, **economic growth was disproportionately led by service sector.** The share of services in GDP has risen from 28% in 1950s, 44% in 1990s to 54% in 2000s.
- Reforms **did not lead to sustained growth of the manufacturing sector**. After an acceleration in the mid- 1990s, growth slowed in the decade's second half. Contribution of manufacturing sector in GDP has remained almost stagnant.
- **The share of agriculture in GDP declined** after economic reforms. Data shows that agricultural share in GDP have declined by 7.3% since 1991 reforms.

**Evidence shows that inequalities have increased post-economic period as discussed below:**

- According to World Inequality Database, the top 1% of India's population held 22% of the country's wealth in 1991 which increased to 42.5% in 2018 while the wealth of bottom 50% of the population decreased from 14% in 1991 to only 3% in 2022.
- Another report, by Council of Social Development, reported six-fold increase in India's wealth inequality between 2000 and 2017.

- **The Gini coefficient** measured in terms of consumption for rural areas increased from 0.29 in 1993-94 to 0.31 in 2011-12 and from 0.34 to 0.39 in urban areas. The India Human Development survey revealed that the Gini coefficient in income (rural + urban) was 0.52 in 2004-05 and increased to 0.55 in 2011-12.
- **Economy witnessed a period of jobless growth:** India experienced job growth of 3% per annum in the 70s at a time when India's economy grew at 3-3.5% per annum but over the last 3 decades India's economy grew at over 5-8% per annum but job growth has been close to 1% p.a.

**Key areas of Reform 2.0**

- **Macro-Economic Reforms:** It should include controlling current account deficit, balancing growth and inflation, increasing tax revenues by broadening the tax base, and managing debt by setting up a separate Debt Management Office.
- **Social Sector Reforms:** Should focus on reducing wealth and income inequality by raising the minimum wage, reducing gender pay gap, raise female labor force participation rate (FLFPR) and focus on health, education and skilling.
- **Market Reforms:** Should include - infrastructure development, factor markets reforms including land, labor and energy reforms, industrial and bureaucratic reforms (PSUs, PSBs), easing regulations toward ease of doing business and encouraging new-generation entrepreneurs and start-ups by creating opportunities.
- **Financial Sector Reforms:** Strengthening the financial sector is crucial for sustained economic growth. Credit to Gap ratio need to be improved to fuel a rapid economic growth.
- **Strong push to manufacturing:** India's manufacturing sector has not kept pace with other major economies and is stagnant at around 16% of the GDP. Reforms should focus on improving the competitiveness of domestic manufacturing and promote labor-intensive manufacturing.
- **Agricultural Reforms:** Should focus on integration of the agricultural market, rationalization of supply chain, encouraging the formation of cooperatives and boosting agricultural exports.
- **Environment and climate change:** Should focus on pursuing mitigation priorities in environment targets (NDCs), designing better disaster management systems, improving legal framework for environment regulation and forest management.
- **Improvement of Infrastructure especially physical and logistics infrastructure** which reduces the cost of production and thus, making Indian goods competitive in the international market. **Digital transformation is also required** as it can drive innovation, increase efficiency and create new business opportunities.
- **Skill development of youth population** focusing on new emerging technologies such as AI, Machine Learning, etc. in the background of Fourth Industrial Revolution.
- **Ease of Doing Business** aimed to attract foreign investment and boosting the overall productivity of an economy.
- **Governance and Anti-Corruption Measures:** Strengthening governance, promoting transparency, and implementing effective anti-corruption measures are essential for fostering investor confidence and ensuring a level playing field for businesses.

## Critical Appraisal of NITI Aayog

- The setting up of NITI Aayog in 2015 replaced the Planning Commission, which was established in 1950. NITI Aayog is a think tank that provides strategic and technical advice to the government on policy matters.
- It is different from its predecessor in many perspectives from a centralized top-down approach to decentralized bottom-up approach with an aim to realize the idea of Minimum government and maximum governance.

**NITI Aayog has shifted planning perspective in many ways:**

- **Shift from centralized planning:** NITI Aayog has shifted the focus from centralized planning to decentralized planning. The institution promotes co-operative federalism and encourages states to take ownership of their development. **Example: Aspirational Districts Programme** which aims to improve the quality of life in 115 districts.
- **More involvement of states:** NITI Aayog involves state governments in the planning process by creating a platform for dialogue between the Centre and the states. This has led to a more collaborative and cooperative approach to development planning. **Example: School Education Quality Index, State Health Index, Composite Water Management Index.**
- **Emphasis on evidence-based policy:** NITI Aayog has a data-driven approach to policy making, which involves the use of evidence-based research and analysis. This helps to ensure that policy decisions are based on accurate information. **Example: Digital India initiative.**

- **No 'One-size Fits All' approach:** India is a diversified country and its states are in various phases of economic development along with their own strengths and weaknesses and in this context, a 'one size fits all' approach to economic planning is obsolete.
- **Focus on innovation and entrepreneurship:** NITI Aayog promotes innovation and entrepreneurship as a means to achieve economic growth and development. It has launched several initiatives, such as the Atal Innovation Mission, to support startups and entrepreneurs.
- **Convergence than Silos:** The work of NITI Aayog also includes cutting across the silos within the government, for example, still, the maximum number of malnourished children in the world are in India. **POSHAAN ABHIYAAN by NITI** Aayog is best placed to achieve this convergence and push the agenda forward.
- **Promoting Economic Reforms:** NITI Aayog has been actively involved in the reforms in economy like agricultural sector in India. It has advocated for the implementation of various reforms, such as the model Agricultural Land Leasing Act and the Pradhan Mantri Fasal Bima Yojana, to improve the productivity and income of farmers.
- **Greater emphasis on social sectors:** NITI Aayog has placed a greater emphasis on social sectors such as health, education, and social security. **Example:** SDG index
- **Shift towards outcome-based monitoring:** NITI Aayog has shifted the focus of monitoring and evaluation from inputs and outputs to outcomes. This helps to ensure that policies and programmes are achieving their intended objectives. **Example: Output-outcome monitoring framework**
- **Emphasis on sustainable development:** NITI Aayog has placed a greater emphasis on sustainable development and environmental conservation. **Example: E-Mobility, Atal Bhujal Yojana**
- **Encouraging private sector and civil society participation:** NITI Aayog has encouraged greater private sector participation in development planning through initiatives such as the Public-Private Partnership (PPP) model. This helps to leverage private sector resources and expertise for public good. **Example: NGO DARPAN**

### Achievements of NITI Aayog

- **Co-operative and Competitive Federalism:** Number of steps have been taken by NITI Aayog to **foster cooperative federalism through structured support initiatives** and engagement with the States/UTs on a continuous basis. These include meetings between the Prime Minister/Cabinet Ministers and all Chief Ministers; subgroups of Chief Ministers on subjects of national importance; sharing of best practices; policy support and capacity development of State/UT functionaries; launching of the Aspirational Districts Programme for development of backward districts
  - It **encourages healthy competition among states** through transparent rankings, in various sectors, along with a hand-holding approach. Some of the indices launched by NITI Aayog are School Education Quality Index, State Health Index, Composite Water Management Index, Sustainable Development Goals Index, India Innovation Index and Export Competitiveness Index.
- **Adoption of holistic and long-term planning:** NITI Aayog has developed a comprehensive Vision Document, Strategy, and Action Agenda for India's development. The documents provide a roadmap for achieving the long-term vision and goals of the country and involve the identification of key challenges, opportunities, and specific policy interventions to address them.
- **Policy formulation:** NITI Aayog has played a crucial role in the formulation of various policies and initiatives in India. It has been instrumental in the formulation of the National Health Policy, the National Nutrition Mission, and the Atal Innovation Mission, among others.
- **Digital Transformation :** NITI Aayog has been at the forefront of India's digital transformation, spearheading initiatives such as the National Health Stack, National Strategy for Artificial Intelligence, and Digital India. These initiatives are aimed at leveraging technology to improve service delivery, enhance transparency, and promote innovation.
- **Balanced Regional development:** The programme has achieved significant success in improving development outcomes in these districts, with several districts recording improvements in areas such as health, education, and agriculture. For instance, in 10 indicators of health, 73 Aspirational Districts have surpassed the state averages.
- **Ease of Doing Business:** NITI Aayog has been instrumental in improving India's ranking on the Ease of Doing Business index. Through its close collaboration with state governments, NITI Aayog has implemented several reforms aimed at simplifying regulatory processes and improving the ease of doing business in India.
- **Sustainable Development Goals:** NITI Aayog has been actively involved in implementing the United Nations' Sustainable Development Goals (SDGs) in India. It has developed a comprehensive SDG Index for India, which tracks progress across 16 SDGs. NITI Aayog has also launched several initiatives for example: E-Amrit for e-vehicle
- **Agricultural Reforms:** NITI through its Model land leasing law, Agricultural Marketing and Farmer Friendly Reforms Index is working to transform agriculture in India.

### Challenges before NITI Aayog

- **Coordination with States:** One of the biggest challenges faced by NITI Aayog is ensuring effective coordination with state governments. While the think tank has made significant progress in promoting cooperative federalism, there is still a need to improve the level of engagement with state governments to ensure that policies are implemented effectively.

- **Limited financial resources:** NITI Aayog has limited financial resources at its disposal, which can limit its ability to implement its plans and initiatives. This is especially challenging in a country like India, where there are several competing demands for resources.
- **Data Availability:** NITI Aayog's policy recommendations are heavily reliant on data, and there have been challenges in accessing timely and reliable data. This has impacted the think tank's ability to make evidence-based policy recommendations in certain areas.
- **Implementation of Policies:** Another challenge faced by NITI Aayog is the effective implementation of policies. While the think tank has played a key role in formulating policies, the implementation of these policies often falls under the purview of other government departments, which can result in delays and suboptimal outcomes.
- **Balancing Interests:** NITI Aayog often needs to balance the interests of various stakeholders, such as state governments, industry bodies, and civil society organizations. This can result in competing priorities and trade-offs, which can be difficult to manage.
- **Capacity Building:** NITI Aayog needs to build capacity within its own organization as well as in other government departments to effectively implement policies.
- **Lack of monitoring power:** NITI Aayog does not have any monitoring power over ministries and thus, effective implementation of policies and programmes becomes difficult.

## PYQs Corner

*(Write the Answer and Get Free Evaluation)*

1. Why did human development fail to keep pace with economic development in India? [150 Words] [10 Marks] [2023]
2. Define potential GDP and explain its determinants. What are the factors that have been inhibiting India from realizing its potential GDP? [150 Words] [10 Marks] [2020]
3. Despite consistent experience of High growth, India still goes with the lowest indicators of human development. Examine the issues that make balanced and inclusive development elusive. [150 Words] [10 Marks] [2019]
4. "Access to affordable, reliable, sustainable and modern energy is the sine qua non to achieve Sustainable Development Goals (SDGs)". Comment on the progress made in India in this regard. [150 Words] [10 Marks] [2018]
5. How are the principles followed by the NITI Aayog different from those followed by the erstwhile Planning Commission in India? [250 Words] [15 Marks] [2018]
6. Among several factors for India's potential growth, savings rate is the most effective one. Do you agree? What are the other factors available for growth potential? [150 Words] [10 Marks] [2017]

Edict-4: Growth and Development

CHAPTER 13

# INCLUSIVE GROWTH AND FINANCIAL INCLUSION

## INCLUSIVE GROWTH

- "Inclusive Growth refers both to the pace and pattern of growth, which are inter-linked and must be addressed together" - World Bank.
  - Pace: Faster Economic Growth
  - Pattern: Broad based (Benefit to all Sections of the society.

Inclusive Growth refers to the economic growth that is distributed fairly across Society and creates opportunities for all. It refers to 'Broad-based', 'Shared', 'pro-poor growth'.

### Dimensions of Economic Growth

**INCLUSIVE GROWTH**

- High, efficient and Sustained growth to create productive jobs and economic opportunity.
- Social Inclusion to ensure equal access to economic opportunity
  - Investing in education, health & other Social Services to expand human Capacity
  - Eliminating market and institutional failures and Social exclusion to level the playing field.
- Social Safety nets to protect the chronically poor and to mitigate the risk of transitory livelihood shocks.

**GOVERNANCE AND INSTITUTIONS**

## Core Components of Inclusive Growth

- Inclusive Growth is a multi-dimensional concept which includes several interrelated elements:

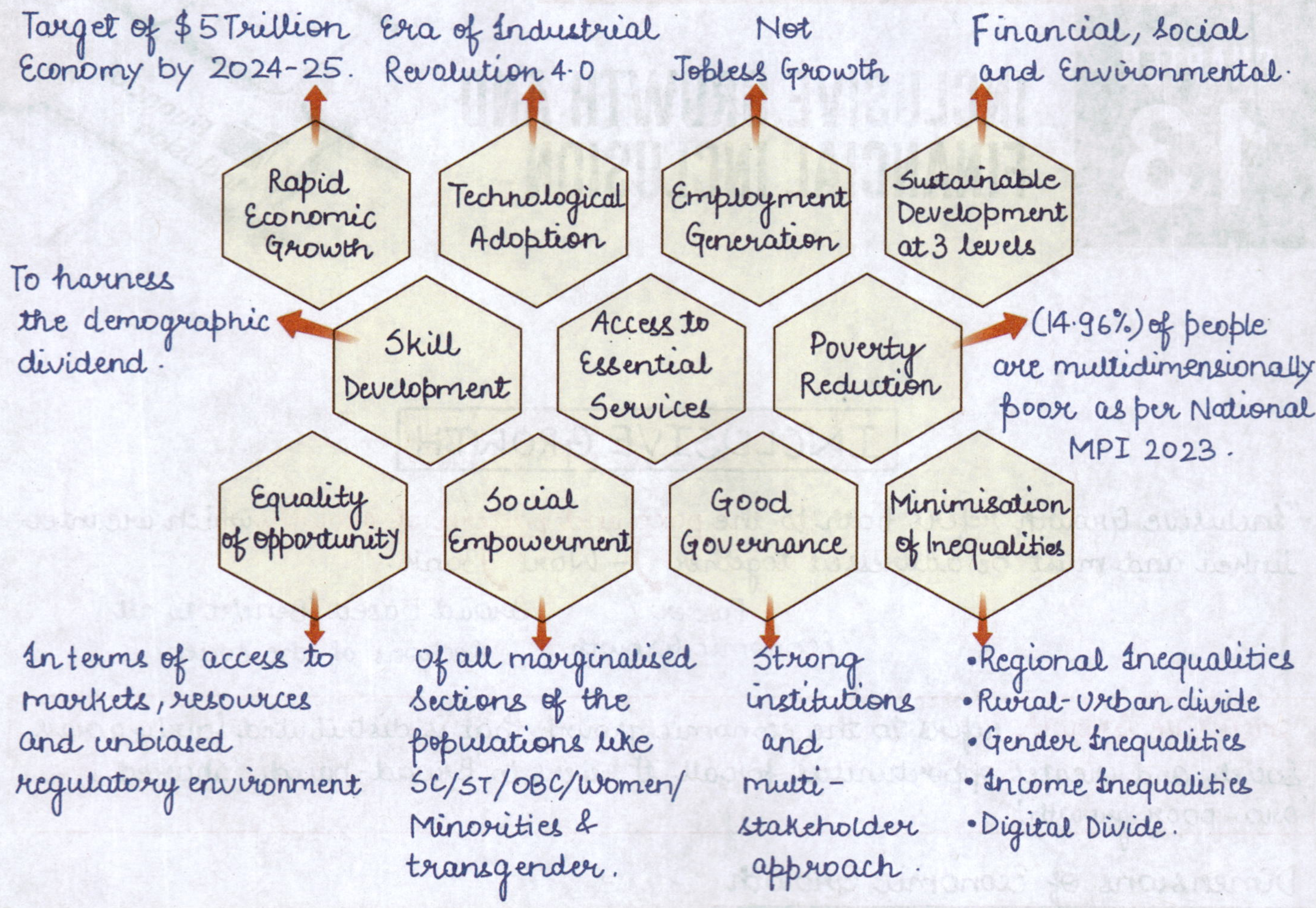


## SOCIAL INFRASTRUCTURE AND INCLUSIVE GROWTH

- Social Infrastructure covers a range of foundational services and facilities that meet the social needs by building strong communities, and contributes towards a good quality of life in areas such as health, education, recreation, skill development etc.
- As per a World Bank report, countries that sustained high growth for long periods put substantial effort into educating its citizens and deepening its human capital.
- Investment in human capital through education, training, health and medical facilities yields additional output and economic returns.
- Economic growth theory also sees human capital as an important source of economic growth.
- Achievement of UN SDGs: 17 SDGs and 169 targets envisaged in the Agenda 2030, are closely interrelated with social infrastructure as observed by Economic Survey.

Investment in Various components of Social Infrastructure lead to inclusive and Sustainable growth in India in the following ways:

| Aspects | Government Initiatives |
|---|---|
| • Education: Changes in knowledge, skills, values & attitudes to enable a more sustainable and just Society for all. | • RTE Act, 2009; National Education Policy 2020 |
| • Health: Higher longevity and more productivity resulting into faster economic growth. | • Ayushman Bharat - PM Jan Aarogya Yojana, National Health Mission etc. |
| • Skill Development: Harnessing the Demographic Dividend through upskilling and re-skilling. (India has 62.5% of its population in the age group of 15-59 years which is ever increasing and will be at the peak around 2036 when it will reach approximately 65%) | • National Skill Development Mission, Deen Dayal Upadhyaya Grameen Kaushalya Yojana. |
| • Women Empowerment: IMF estimates that equal participation of women in workforce will increase India's GDP by 27%. | • Mahila Shakti Kendra, Nai Roshni, Stand up India. |
| • Environmental Conservation: Ensuring clean air & water and efficiency in resource use are central to equitable growth. | • Net zero emissions by 2070, 50% energy from renewable Sector |
| • Justice: Efficient and credible criminal justice System. | • E-courts, Alternative Dispute Resolution Mechanism. |
| • Social Security cover especially to the unorganised Sector | • Unorganised workers Social Security Act, 2008; Atal Pension Yojana, Janani Suraksha Yojana. |

## INTER-GENERATIONAL AND INTRA-GENERATIONAL EQUITY

| Inter-Generational Equity | Intra-Generational Equity |
|---|---|
| • Development of resources by one generation to enhance economic sustainability for the future generation. It signifies the rights and interests of the present and future generations regarding the resources of the Earth. | • Deals with the equity among the same generations. It includes fair utilization of global resources among the human beings of the present generations. |

| Issues of Inter-generational Equity | Issues of Intra-generational Equity |
|---|---|
| • Global warming and Climate Change resulting into higher frequency and intensity of extreme weather events like heatwaves, floods and droughts.<br>• Mindless Deforestation to fulfill the needs of rapid industrialisation resulting into destruction of loss of habitat, biodiversity loss and deprivation of traditional rights.<br>• High debt of the countries translates to higher tax burden on the future generations.<br>• Over-exploitation of resources - land, water, Minerals, Energy etc has led to resource depletion. | • Income Inequality: Richest 1% in India now own more than 40% of Country's total wealth, while the bottom half of the population together share just 3% of wealth between 2012 and 2021 (Oxfam Report 2023)<br>• Rural-Urban Inequality: In 75% rural household, the monthly income of the highest earning member is less than Rs 5000 (SECC 2011)<br>• Gender Inequality: Male literacy rate is about 82% and female literacy rate is 65.5% according to Census 2011.<br>• Oxfam report highlighted that female workers earn only 63 paise for every 1 rupee earned via male workers.<br>• Digital Divide: Only 15% rural households had an internet connection (Oxfam Inequality Report, 2021)<br>• Developed vs Developing countries: Eg - Inequitable access of COVID-19 Vaccine; Transfer of burden of climate change to developing countries.<br>• Resource Exploitation: Imbalance in the resource distribution, ongoing environmental degradation and depletion of resources. Eg - Global North and Global South. |

## Constitutional Provisions

**Preamble**
- Justice - Social, Economic, Political
- Equality - of status & opportunity

**DPSPs**
- Socialist Principles - Article 38, 39, 39A, 41, 42, 43, 43A, 47 1st part.
- Gandhian Principles - 40, 43, 43B, 46, 47, 48.
- Liberal-Intellectual Principles - 44, 45, 48, 48A, 49, 50, 51.

- 4 goals of Planning - Growth with Equity / Modernisation / Self reliance.
- XI FYP explicitly mentioned Inclusive growth for the 1st time.
- XII FYP - faster, Sustainable and more inclusive growth.

# INCLUSIVE GROWTH : STRATEGY, GOVERNMENT INITIATIVES & CHALLENGES

| Strategy | Components | Government Initiatives | Challenges |
|---|---|---|---|
| High Efficient & Sustained economic growth | • Faster Economic growth<br>• Infrastructure Creation<br>• Tech advances<br>• Employment Generation<br>• Poverty Reduction<br>• Financial Inclusion<br>• Sustainable Development. | • Agriculture Reforms<br>→ PM Krishi Sinchai Yojana<br>→ E-NAM<br>→ Soil Health Card (SHC)<br>• Industrial Sector<br>→ Make In India (MII)<br>→ Production Linked Incentive (PLI) scheme<br>→ MSME Sector<br>• Service Sector<br>→ Digital India Mission<br>• Infrastructure<br>→ Roads (Bharat Mala)<br>→ Ports (Sagar Mala)<br>→ Railways<br>→ Digital (5G Auction)<br>• Labour Intensive<br>→ Apparel, Leather, Textile<br>• Financial<br>→ PM Jan Dhan Yojana<br>→ PM Mudra Yojana<br>• Sustainable<br>→ Renewable energy generation (Alternative energy) | • Low agricultural productivity + Rainfed agriculture<br>• Weak Global economic outlook (Decreased Exports)<br>• Infrastructure financing → Stagnant Private Investment + Constraints on public Investment.<br>i) Increased Fiscal deficit<br>ii) Increased Debt<br>• Financial Inclusion<br>• Jobless growth → Informalisation of Labour (>90%)<br>• High Poverty - India is having the largest number of multi dimensionally poor world-wide (22.8 Cr)<br>According to Global MPI 2022, India is having 16.4% of population multidimensionally poor in 2019-20.<br>• Greater than 50% energy coming from fossil fuels. |

| Strategy | Components | Government Initiatives | Challenges |
| --- | --- | --- | --- |
| Equality of opportunity for social inclusion | • Social Infra.<br>• Access to essential services<br>• Women Empowerment<br>• Balanced Regional Development. | • Education<br>→ NEP 2020 (Early childhood Care & Education) + RTE 2009<br>• Healthcare<br>→ Ayushman Bharat Mission<br>→ Mohalla Clinics<br>• Women Empowerment<br>→ Gender Budgeting.<br>• Balanced regional development<br>→ Tax Concessions, Tax Holidays etc<br>• Skill Development<br>→ PM Kaushal Vikas Yojana | • India's dismal ranking in various social indicators.<br>- HDI:<br>i. A decent standard of living (GNI per Capita)<br>ii. Long and health life (life expectancy at Birth)<br>iii. Knowledge → a) Mean Years of Schooling<br>b) Expected Years of Schooling.<br>HDI rank declined to 132 out of 196 countries<br>- MPI: Largest number of poor people.<br>- GII. 122.<br>- Poor ranking in GHI indicates food security concerns. |
| Social Safety Net | • Social Security<br>• Redistribution of resources | → Atal Pension Yojana<br>• Insurance Schemes<br>→ PM Jeevan Jyoti Bima Yojana<br>→ PM Suraksha Bima Yojana<br>• Redistribution of resources<br>→ MGNREGA.<br>• Subsidies | • Schemes are mainly for organised/formal sector. |
| Governance and Institutions | • Good Governance → Multi-Stakeholder Approach | → RTI Act<br>→ 73rd and 74th CAA. | • Issue of transparency and accountability.<br>• Bureaucratic apathy & Corruption<br>• Poor capacity building. |

# India's Progress towards Inclusive Growth

1. Moved beyond 'Hindu Rate of Growth' – From an annual average growth rate of 3.5% during 1950-80, the growth rate of Indian economy accelerated to around 6% in 1980s - 1990s. Era of 2000 saw an impressive growth of 8%.
2. Poverty Reduction – Overall Poverty ratio of Indian economy declined from 45% in 1993-94 to 22% in 2011-12, as per the Tendulkar Committee.
3. Expansion in per Capita Income – Since 1947, India has achieved tremendous progress in raising the income level of an average Indian citizen from ₹7,513 to ₹92,565 (2018-19).
4. Rapid Development of Infrastructure – Government undertook various measures across different modes of transport which resulted in significant infrastructure creation in economy. Eg-Golden Quadrilateral Project in roads sector.
5. Social Development Indicators – Literacy rates have increased significantly from 18% during 1950s to 73% during 2011.
6. Improvement in Alternate Energy Sources – Renewables & hydropower contributes >40% of power generation.
7. Vast Improvement witnessed in Financial Inclusion – Under PM Jan Dhan Yojana.

**TOWARDS AN INCLUSIVE GROWTH**

| | |
|---|---|
| Economic Growth | 1. Improving India's Tax-GDP Ratio (From around 11% to at least 22% of the GDP)<br>2. Structural reforms to increase private investment – Ease of Doing Business reforms, FDI reforms, financial sector reforms etc. |
| Employment Generation | 1. Promotion of labour intensive industries such as apparel & textile, leather and footwear, network products etc.<br>2. Formalisation of workforce |
| Resource Allocation | 1. Increased allocation on various welfare schemes<br>2. Special attention to backward states by creating a favourable investment climate through improved rural connectivity, establishment of law and order, etc |
| Sustainable Agriculture | • Raising agricultural productivity through the adoption of agricultural technology and infrastructure |
| Skill Development | • Upgradation of skills in accordance with the requirements under Industrial Revolution 4.0 |
| Socio-Economic Infrastructure | • Ensure 3As (Available, Accessible, Affordable) in delivery of essential services such as health, Education, drinking water.<br>• Comprehensive social safety net especially for unorganised sector |

# FINANCIAL INCLUSION

• Financial inclusion has been defined as "The process of ensuring access to financial services, timely and adequate credit for vulnerable groups such as weaker sections and low income groups at an affordable cost.

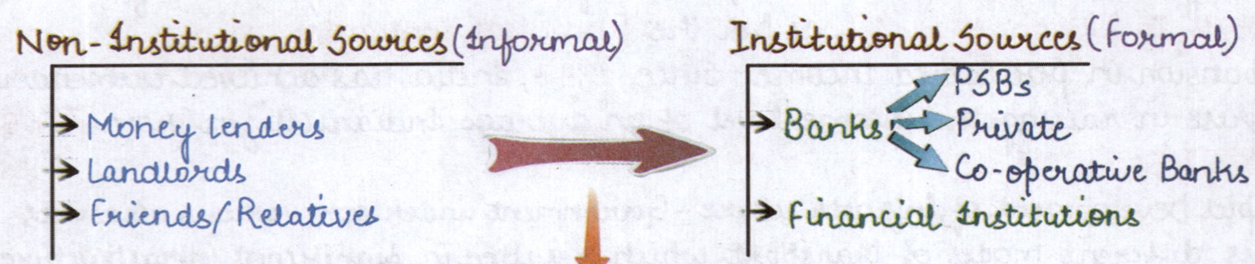


(Financial Inclusion) FI → Measures taken to shift the people from non-formal sources to formal sources

• The main concept of Financial inclusion is to ensure availability of financial services in the most accessible and affordable manner.

• It is more than just opening of bank accounts and comprises of the following financial services:

- Bank accounts for savings and transactional purposes.
- Investment option for wealth creation.
- Insurance facilities (life and non-life) etc
- Low cost credit for productive, personal and other purposes.

ACCESS
- Contingency Planning
  - Retirement Savings
  - Buffer Savings
  - Insurable
- Credit
  - Business Livelihood
  - Emergency Loans
  - Housing Loans
  - Consumption Loans
- Wealth Creation
  - Savings & Investments based on household's level of financial literacy and risk

## Need of Financial Inclusion

Non-Institutional Sources (Informal) ⟹ Issues in taking loan from these sources

1. High Interest Rate (IR) which is outside the regulation of government.
2. High IR combined with low literacy levels result into taking another loan to repay the previous loan. This result in Debt Trap like situations.
3. Moneylender forces the farmers:
   a. To sell their produce at very low prices
   b. Work on their land as forced labour and at very low wages.

   This results into a very high effective real interest rate charged upon the farmers which ultimately leads to the confiscation of farmer's land.
4. Stagnation of agriculture resulting into high poverty (Inter-generational cycle of Poverty)

Institutional Sources (Formal) ⟹ Benefits to various stakeholders.

- Benefits to Individual

1. Savings account → Culture of Savings account created ↴
Results in Economic Growth

2. Access to Credit
➠ Innovation / Technological
➠ Entrepreneurship
➠ Higher Employment Generation
➠ Poverty reduction

3. Access to Insurance
➠ Protects / Cushion them at the time of crisis.

4. Gender Equality
➠ Financial empowerment of women - Economic Empowerment
➠ Decreased Gender Inequality

5. Access to Investment options
➠ Wealth generation ↴
Beating the Inflation

6. Investment in Social Infrastructure → Health, Education, Skill development, and various Social Services like Sanitation, Drinking Water. ⇒ Breaking the Cycle of Inter-generational Poverty

- Benefits to Economy

7. Formalisation of Economy (People coming under Government regulation)
↳ Increased Tax Net ⇒ Increased Tax Revenue
i) Government Spending Increased → Increase in Demand → Leading to increase in GDP
ii) Welfare Schemes or Subsidies → Poverty reduction.

8. Savings → Financial Services ↴
Mobilised in Various productive activities → Increase in GDP

9. Enabler of achieving IG
➠ Poverty reduction; Increase in Employment; Gender Inequality decrease; Social Services; Faster Economic Growth.

- Benefits to Government

• Reduction in Subsidies cost (Reduced Leakage); Raising resources to finance fiscal deficit;
• Boost tax revenue → More Expenditure for welfare program (Minimising Inequalities)

- Benefits to Bank

• Attracting low cost deposits to reduce dependence on bulk deposits from Corporates.
• Opportunity for the banks to cross-sell various products → New business avenues.

## Achievement of SDGs

☛ Financial Inclusion is increasingly considered as a key driver of economic growth and poverty alleviation.

☛ Accessibility to formal finance like banking can promote job creation, reduce vulnerability to economic shocks & increase investments in human capital.

☛ Importance of FI is visible from the fact that seven of the 17 UN SDG considers financial inclusion as a key enabler for achieving sustainable development.

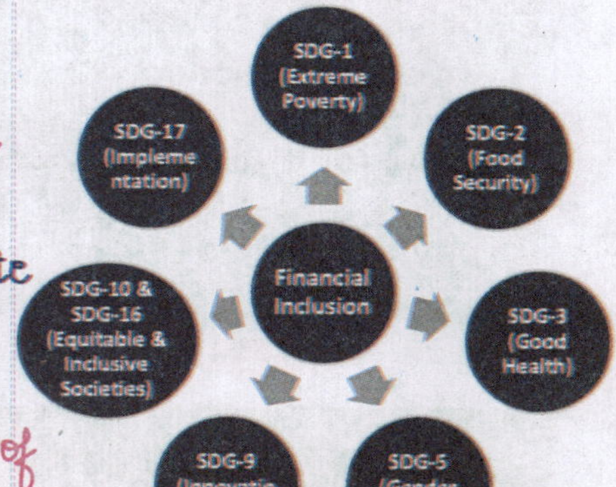

# Gateway to Financial Inclusion

## How to get there?

**UNSERVED**

- Have no basic bank account
- Have no (or restricted) access to financial services
- Rely on a cash economy

**Banks**
**Microfinance Institutions**
**Mobile Network Operators**
**Card Companies**
**Postal Networks**
**Financial Cooperatives**

**SERVED**

- Have a transaction account
- Use broad range of financial services

### What's needed to get there?

- Broader inclusion
- Customer-centered product innovation
- Financial capability
- Strong consumer protection
- Better financial infrastructure
- More & interoperable access points
- Enabling legal & regulatory frameworks
- Public & private sector commitment
- Open & balanced playing field

## How Financial Inclusion Creates Opportunities

### Individuals

**Can more easily:**

Manage expenses
Smooth consumption
Mitigate shocks & risks
Invest in education & health
Save for the future
Make safe & secure payments

Greater social & economic well-being

### Businesses

**Can more easily:**

Thrive & grow
Mitigate shocks & risks
Invest in people & assets
Reduce transaction costs
Make safe & secure payments

Higher profits, competitiveness & growth

### Economies

**Can more easily:**

Allocate resources
Diversify economic participation
Create jobs & innovate
Increase national savings
Gain efficiencies
Raise competitiveness

Higher economic growth, decreased inequality (income, gender)

## Approaches of Financial Inclusion

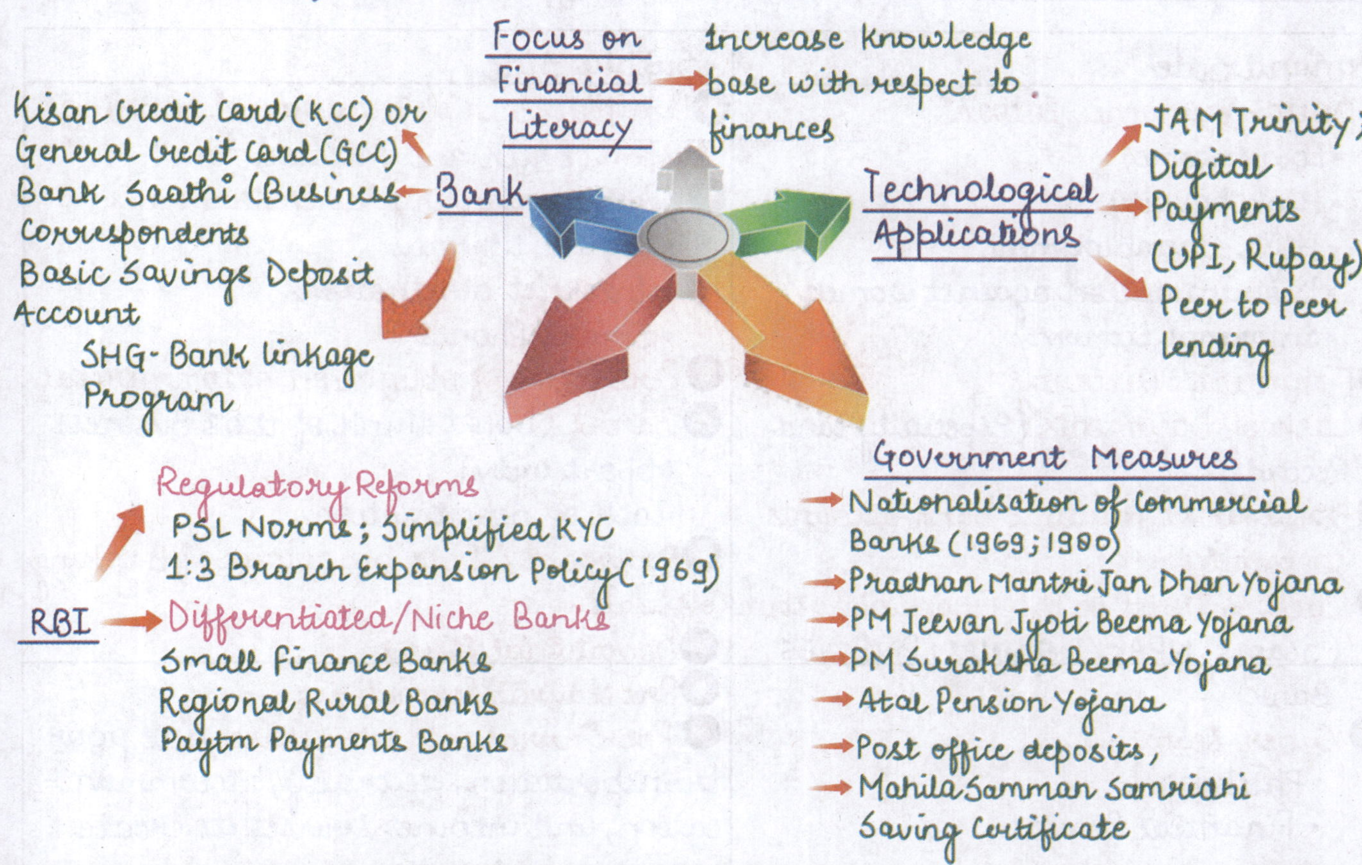


## Extent of Financial Inclusion

- India still has the second largest unbanked population in the world & as per Global Findex Report, 2017, over 190 million Indian adults still do not have a bank account.
- Around 20% of the bank accounts are inoperative and 8.2% of PM-JDY are zero balance accounts.
- 31% of Jan Dhan Accounts are duplicate accounts.
- Today Indian women stand at the forefront as the country witnessed a sharp fall in gender gap in terms of bank accounts. This gender gap was 6% in 2017, a decline from 20% in 2014.
- According to the Global Findex Survey 2021, of the women owned accounts in India, 32% are inactive.
- As per NFHS-5, women's access to credit remains low and only 11% ever taken a micro-credit loan.
- India's score in the annual financial index, which is published by RBI is 56.4 out of 100.

## Reason for Financial Exclusion

| Demand Side | Supply Side |
|---|---|
| **Socio-Economic Factors**<br>• Low Income<br>• High poverty<br>• High Unemployment<br>• Discrimination against women<br>• Informal Economy<br>**Financial Illiteracy.**<br>**Lack of Documents** (Especially land Records)<br>**Don't want multiple bank accounts in family.**<br>**Lack of Trust in the Financial System** (Scams, NPAs/Defaults; PNB, YES Bank)<br>**Cyber Scams**<br>• Phishing<br>• Financial frauds | **Limited reach of Traditional Banking System** (Brick and Mortar)<br>**Limitations in Digital Instruments**<br>• Digital literacy<br>• Internet penetration<br>• Smart Phones.<br>**Perception of obligation of commercial Banks** (Don't think of it as Business opportunity)<br>• Lack of Sensitization<br>**Arrogant/Rude behaviour of Banking officials.**<br>**Operational Issues**<br>**Procedural Formalities.**<br>**Poor rural infrastructure** like poor transportation, electricity, telecommunication, and internet services etc create operational hurdles. |

**Self - reported barriers to use of formal accounts**

Non- account holder reporting barrier as a reason for not having an account (%)

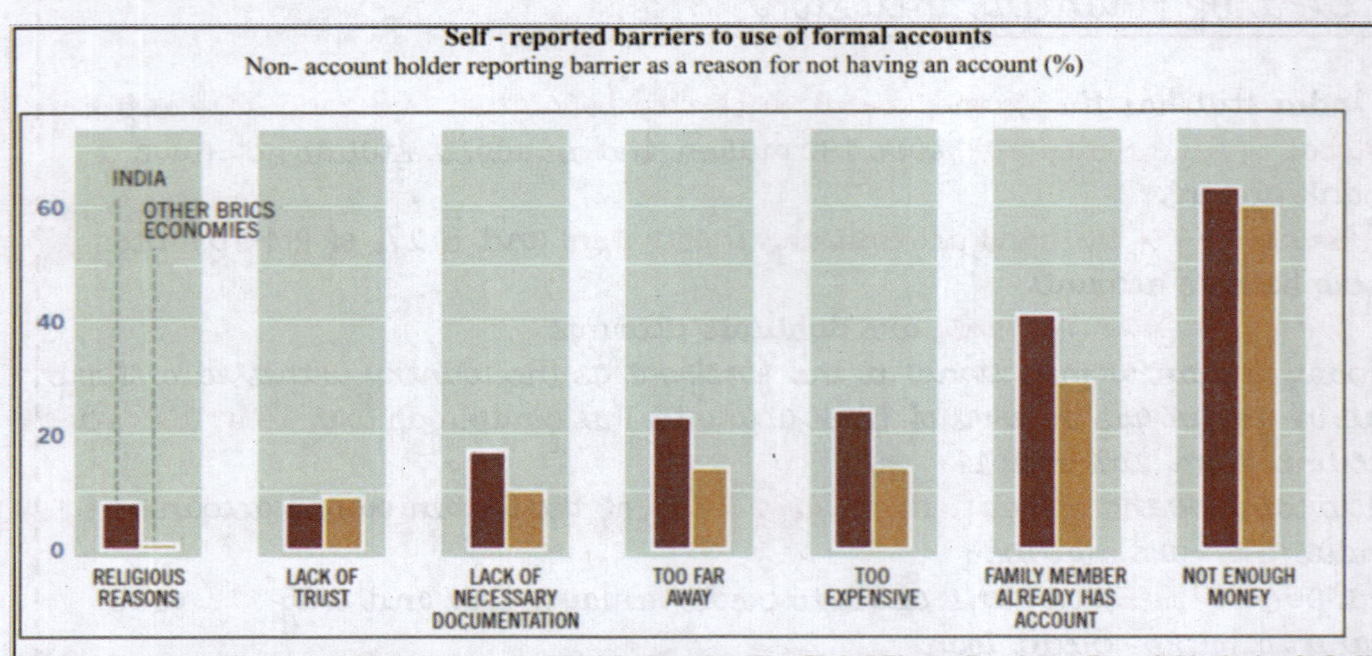


**Source: Demirguc-Kunt, Asli; Klapper, Leora; Randall, Douglas, The Global Findex Database: financial inclusion in India**

***Note: Respondents could choose more than one reason. Other BRICS economies comprises Brazil, Russia, China, South Africa.***

# MICROFINANCE

- Microfinance is defined as financial services such as savings account, insurance funds and credit provided to poor and low income clients so as to help them increase their income, thereby improving their standard of living.
- Basic feature: No collateral is required for Microfinance loans. This helps persons with little or no assets to access credit.
- Core Idea: A small loan will provide access to the larger economy to people who typically live outside the scope of institutions on which the mainstream economy rests.
- Evolution: The concept of microfinance has been highlighted since 1970s with an aim to uplift the poor section of the society and to enhance economic growth.
- Institutional Support: It is being promoted in India by agencies like NABARDs via microfinance institutions (MFIs), formation of Self Help Groups (SHGs) among others.
- Channels of Microfinance: There are two channels through which microfinance is being operated in India: SHG-Bank Linkage Programme (SBLP) and Micro Finance Institutions (MFIs)

**Products and Services of Micro finance**

| | | |
|---|---|---|
| Savings | Mortgage loans | Livestock loans |
| Insurance | Business loans | Emergency loan |
| Leasing | Consumer loans | General loans |

**Mushrooming Market of Microfinance**

Credit to marginal and sub marginal farmers as well as other small borrowers

Going beyond credit and providing a helping hand to the rural areas

Commercial Banks to open branches in rural areas

Simplification of procedure for granting loans to small borrowers

Strengthening the SHG-Bank Linkage program

Effective implementation of business facilitator and correspondent models

- Evolution of Microfinance in India:

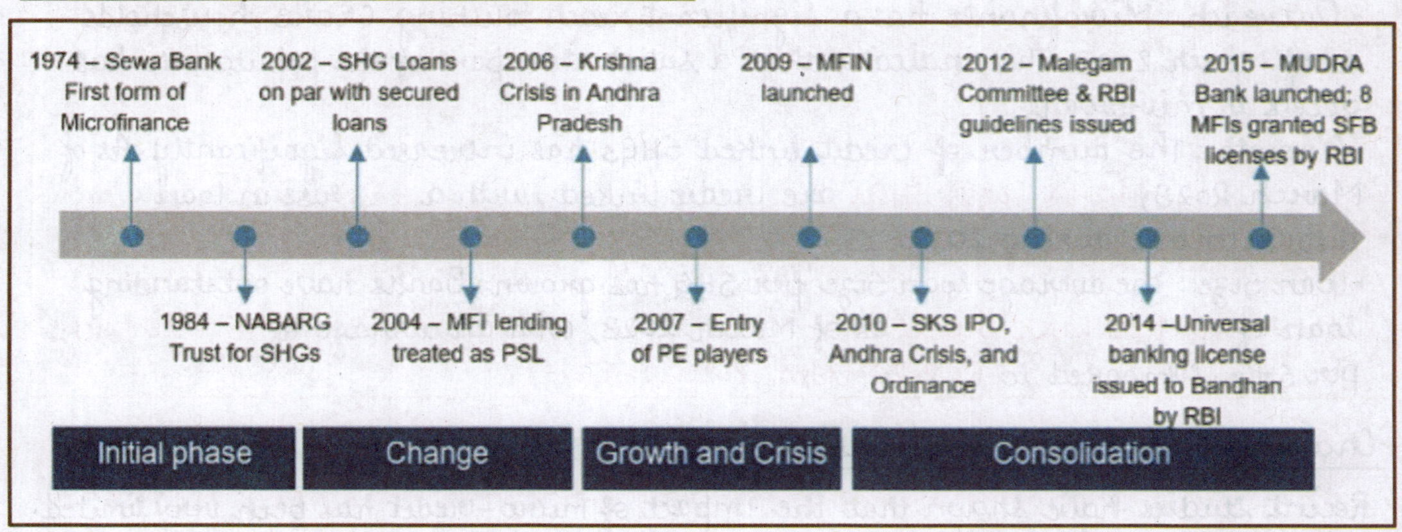

## Importance of Microfinance for Indian Economy

- Improved Financial Inclusion by providing access to credit and other financial Services to those who have been excluded from the traditional banking System.
- Cheaper Interest rate than informal loans coupled with reduction in economic vulnerability + SHG-linked programme have been Successful in mobilising voluntary Savings from poor households.
- Boosting Entrepreneurship → Higher economic growth and employment generation (including Self employment)
- Higher level of asset creation and income Security → Poverty Alleviation (Bringing people out of poverty trap.
- Anti-poverty Vaccine for the people living in rural areas.
- Women Empowerment as microfinance can help women become more economically independent and improve their social standing.
  - According to NABARD, the SHG-Bank linkage programme covers 14.2 crore of families through 119 Lakh SHGs (87% of which are women) as of March 31, 2022.

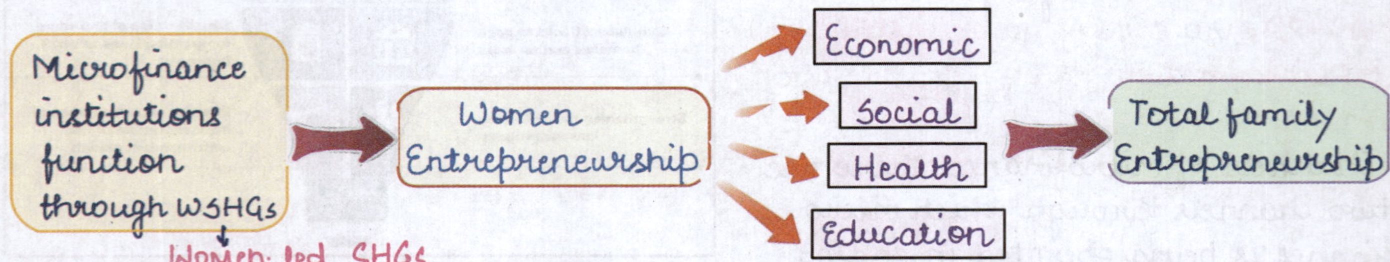


- Improving agricuture productivity and Support rural development

Achievement of Microfinance (Based on NABARD

- Outreach: Microfinance has a significant reach touching crore households as of March 2023. This indicates that a substantial part of the population has access to microloans
- Growth: The number of credit linked SHGs has increased significantly. As of March 2023, 42.96 Lakh SHGs are credit linked, with a 46% rise in loan disbursements during 2022-23.
- loan Size: The average loan Size per SHG has grown. Banks have outstanding loan of Rs 1.88 lakh crore as of March 2023, with an average of Rs 7.20 Lakh per SHG, compared to Rs 2.24 lakh in 2022-23

## Challenges of Micro-Credit Institutions

Recent studies have shown that the impact of micro-credit has been very limited. Various reasons can be attributed to this Such as:

☛ **Overindebtedness:** Borrowers may take loans from multiple MFIs to repay existing ones leading to a debt trap. This can be caused by factors like aggressive lending practices, limited financial literacy and unforeseen circumstances. Eg: 2010 microfinance crisis in Andhra Pradesh.

Solution: Financial literacy Programs – Partner with NGO or government agencies to educate borrowers on loan terms & responsible borrowing practices.

☛ **High NPAs in Post-pandemic Period:** The overall NPA of sector shot up from 4.5% as at end-March 2020 to 14% in September 2022 (RBI's Financial Stability Report 2022)

Solution: Integrate MFIs with credit bureaus to track a borrower's total debt across institutions, preventing over-borrowing.

☛ **High Interest Rates** charged by MFIs due to the high cost of servicing small loans. This can create a debt trap for the borrowers making it difficult for them to repay loan.

Solution: MFIs should transparently inform borrowers regarding the interest rate charged on the loan.

☛ **Regional Imbalances:** About 60% of total SHG credit linkages in the country are concentrated in Southern states compared to poorer states like Jharkhand, Bihar.

Solution:
- Utilize mobile technology and digital platforms to reach geographically remote borrowers.
- Encouraging MFIs in areas of low microfinance penetration by providing financial assistance.

☛ **Credit Linkage Gap:** Despite a rise in loan disbursements, a significant number of SHGs are not linked to formal credit institutions.

Solution: Streamline the loan application process and capacity building for SHGs to make it easier for them to access formal credit

☛ **Heavy dependence on banks for borrowing:** Funds available from these banks are typically for short-term, generally 2 years. Moreover, banks tend to disburse loans at the end of financial year to meet the targets. This can create issues for MFIs if there is delay in repayment of loans by borrowers.

☛ **Weak Governance:** Many MFIs are not willing to convert to a corporate structure; hence there is lack of transparency. This also limits their ability to attract capital.

Solution: MFIs should look for other sources for funding their loan portfolio e.g., by converting to for-profit company (NBFC).

☛ **Poor Regulation:** Andhra Pradesh crisis (2010) exposed the need for stricter regulations to prevent malpractices.

Solution: Strengthening the regulatory framework – RBI should continue to monitor and regulate the micro-finance sector to ensure that it operates in a fair and transparent manner.

Limited Impact of MFIs on poverty alleviation

Solution: MFIs should provide complete range of products including credit, savings, remittances, financial advice and non-financial services like training & support. It will enable underserved people with access to all financial services.

## SELF-HELP GROUPS

- SHGs are registered/unregistered entities which usually have a membership of 15 to 20 members from very low income families, usually women.
- It can be defined as informed, self-governed, peer-controlled information group of people with similar socio-economic background and having a desire to collectively perform common purpose (improving their living condition)
- They mobilise savings from members and uses the pooled funds to give loans to the needy members.
- SHGs rely on the notion of "Self-Help" to encourage self employment and poverty alleviation.

- SHGs follow Panchsutras

Conduct of regular meetings

Timely repayment of loans

Regular savings within the group.

Maintenance of proper book of accounts

Internal lendings based on demand of members.

- Dr. C. Rangarajan Committee in its report on 'Financial Inclusion in the country' identified 4 major reasons for lack of financial inclusion: Inability to provide collateral security, Poor credit absorption capacity, inadequate reach of the institutions and weak community network.

Strong Community Network (Through SHGs)

- Accessing credit to the poor and critical role in poverty alleviation
- Build Social Capital among the poor especially women resulting into women empowerment.
- Improved standard of life such as higher literacy levels, better healthcare & better family Planning

## SHG-Bank Linkage Programme



- Under this programme, banks were allowed to open saving accounts for SHGs.
- Banks also provide loans to the SHGs against group guarantee and the quantum of loan could be several times the deposits placed by such SHGs with the banks.
- Banks should consider entire credit requirements of SHG members, namely.
  a) Income generating activities
  b) Social needs like housing, education, marriage etc.
- The recovery rates of loans are good and banks have found that the transaction cost of reaching the poor through SHGs is considerably lower than direct lending by the bank.
- Based on NABARD report on 'Status of Microfinance in India 2021-22', SBLP touches 14.2 crore households through 119 lakh SHGs.

### SHGs as a tool of poverty alleviation and women empowerment

| | |
|---|---|
| 1. Improved Financial Inclusion | • Creating a pool of savings. |
| 2. Asset creation | • Maximising income. |
| 3. Change in the use of loan from personal consumption to income generating income. | • Employment opportunities (Breaking the vicious cycle of inter-generational poverty transfer. |
| 4. Training and Capacity building of SHGs | • Higher skills and employability. |
| 5. Alternate source of employment | • Reduced dependency on Agriculture (increased agricultural productivity) |
| 6. Higher expenditure on Education, Health etc | • Improved Social Infrastructure. |
| 7. Voice of the Marginalised sector | • Ensure social justice. |
| 8. Critical role in social audit. | • Reduced corruption and effective implementation of government schemes |
| 9. Social Integrity. | • Encourage collective efforts for combating practices like dowry, alcoholism. |

10. Gender Equality and Women Empowerment.
   a) Political Empowerment by increasing women participation in election.
   b) Economic Empowerment: Addressing the issue of Feminisation of Poverty' and making financially independent.

c) Social Empowerment: Reduced child mortality, improved maternal health, better nutrition etc → Enhances the self esteem

## Issues of SHGs

SHGs are important tools of microfinancing. Over the years SHGs have achieved tremendous progress in bringing about social and economic upliftment in the life of its members. Only a minority of the SHGs are able to raise themselves from a level of micro-finance to that of micro entrepreneurship.

- Poor Market linkages and forward integration hamper the growth of SHGs.
- Limited training, capacity building and skill upgradation: There is a lack of appropriate training plans, quality training and expert training institutions.
- Regional Disparities. The Southern region registered the highest share at 36% followed by Eastern region (27.4%) and western region (11.4%) in the percentage share of SHGs savings linked during 2021-22.
- Lack of Rural Banking facilities: There are about 1.2 lakh bank branches & over 6 lakh villages. Moreover, many public sector banks and microfinance institutions are unwilling to provide financial services to the poor as the cost of servicing remains high.
- Internal conflicts with SHGs and lack of strong group dynamics can hamper decision making and hinder overall group functioning.
- Inadequate financial assistance to meet their actual requirements as found in most of the SHGs.
- Sustainability concerns after the withdrawal of initial support from NGOs or government agencies. The withdrawal of support often leads to their collapse indicating lack of strategies for long-term financial independence.
- Membership bias: SHGs might not always include the poorest families, potentially leaving them without access to financial and social benefits.
- Patriarchal Attitudes: Traditional social norms may discourage women from participating in SHGs limiting their economic opportunities.
- Poor progress in improvements in income. Though there has been social empowerment of the poor, the economic gain to bring about a qualitative change in their life has not been satisfactory.
- Recognition of beneficiaries: Identifying and including the poorest remains a challenge.
- Lack of Market Linkages. Poor market linkages and forward integration hamper the growth of SHGs.

Government recognition and mainstreaming of the initiative has often been perceived as an indicator of Success but Such recognition has been a double edged Sword.

1. It provided the thrust required to expand quickly.
2. Becomes vulnerable to government management practices
   a. Target-Oriented quick group formation
   b. Pre-determined criteria for identifying beneficiaries.
   c. Forming groups without assessing affinity among members.
   d. Tendency to further Separate each caste or community for group formation, especially for subsidy distribution.

## 2nd ARC Recommendations for Strengthening SHGs

- Government as a facilitator and promoter by creating a Supportive environment for the growth and development of the SHG movement.
- Expanding SHG movement of credit deficient areas of the country Such as Madhya Pradesh, Rajasthan, North Eastern states.
- Rapidly expanding financial Infrastructure including strengthening NABARD's presence, will improve the access to credit in these regions.
- Extension of SHGs to Urban/Peri-Urban areas: Efforts should be made to increase income generation abilities of Urban poor as there has been a rapid rise in Urbanisation & many people remain financially excluded.
- SHG-Bank linkage model with a mentor SHPI deserves to be encouraged as the preferred mode for financial intermediation throughout the country.
- Need-Based Financial Products: Commercial Banks and NABARD in collaboration with state government need to innovate & design new financial products for these groups
- Training/Capacity building of government functionaries so that they develop a positive attitude & treat the poor and marginalised as viable and responsible customers and as possible entrepreneurs.
- Leveraging Technology to reduce cost of reaching out to poorest of the poor.

## Other Measures to be Taken

01 Strengthening market linkages and forward integration is essential for Sustainable livelihoods.

02 Efforts should be made to enhance the skills and Capacities of SHG members.

03 Ensuring uniform financial management systems at all levels of SHGs is crucial for growth in bank accounts, financial literacy and the absorption capacity of Community members.

## PYQs Corner

*(Write the Answer and Get Free Evaluation)*

1. Is inclusive growth possible under market economy? State the significance of financial inclusion in achieving economic growth in India. [150 Words] [10 Marks] **[2022]**

2. Explain intra-generational and inter-generational issues of equity from the perspective of inclusive growth and sustainable development. [150 Words] [10 Marks] **[2020]**

3. "Micro-Finance as an anti-poverty vaccine, is aimed at asset creation and income security of the rural poor in India". Evaluate the role of Self Help Groups in achieving the twin objectives along with empowering women in rural India. [250 Words] [15 Marks] **[2020]**

4. It is argued that the strategy of inclusive growth is intended to meet the objectives of inclusiveness and sustainability together. Comment on this statement. [250 Words] [15 Marks] **[2019]**

5. What are the salient features of 'inclusive growth'? Has India been experiencing such a growth process? Analyze and suggest measures for inclusive growth. [250 Words] [15 marks] [2017]

6. Comment on the challenges for inclusive growth which include careless and useless manpower in the Indian context. Suggest measures to be taken for facing these challenges. [150 Words] [10 Marks] **[2016]**

7. Pradhan Mantri Jan-Dhan Yojana (PMJDY) is necessary for bringing unbanked to the institutional fiancé fold. Do you agree with this for financial inclusion of the poorer section of the Indian society? Give arguments to justify your opinion. [200 Words] [12.5 Marks] **[2016]**

9. Comment on the challenges for inclusive growth which include careless and useless manpower in the Indian context. Suggest measures to be taken for facing these challenges.[200 Words] [12.5Marks] **[2016]**

Edict-4: Growth and Development

# CHAPTER 14

# POVERTY, INEQUALITY AND UNEMPLOYMENT

## CONCEPT OF POVERTY

- UN Human Rights Council defines poverty as "a human condition characteristics by the sustained or chronic deprivation of the resources, capabilities, choices, security and power necessary for the enjoyment of an adequate standard of living and other civil, cultural, economic, political and social rights.

| Traditional View (Uni-Dimensional) | Present View (Multi-dimensional |
|---|---|
| • Lack of financial resources and unable to fulfill even its basic necessities of life.<br>• Emphasis on minimum standard of living rather than reasonable level of living. | • Poverty goes beyond monetary deprivations by including access to social infrastructure - Health, education etc and basic essential services such as sanitation, drinking water etc. |

## Multi-dimensional Poverty Index

- Global MPI is a poverty measure that reflects the multiple deprivations poor people face in the areas of education, health and living standards

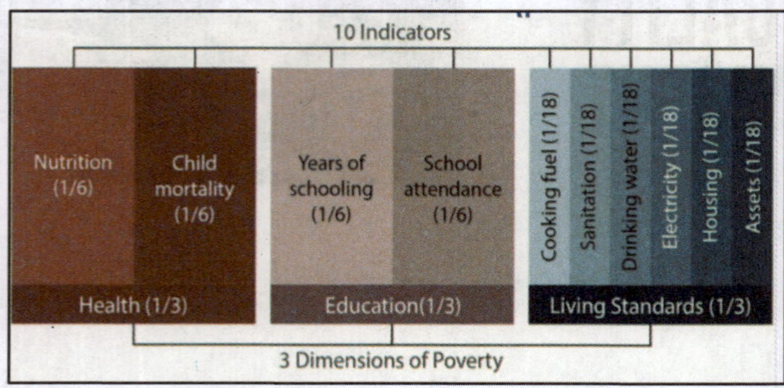


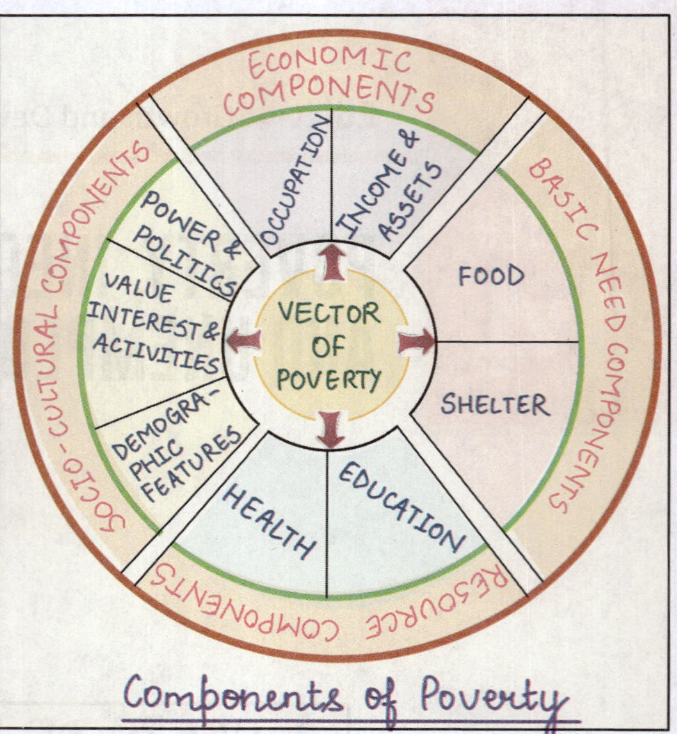


Components of Poverty

- First launched in 2010 by UNDP and Oxford Poverty Human Development Initiative.

- A person is multidimensionally poor if he/she is deprived in one third or more of the weighted indicators.
- Reflects both the incidence of multi-dimensional poverty and its intensity

## National MPI, 2023

- It is an important Public Policy tool which monitors multi-dimensional poverty & leads to evidence based policy making.
- It captures multiple deprivations & thus its broader in nature
- 2nd edition of MPI is published by NITI Aayog based on National Family Health Survey - NFHS 5 (2019-21)
- 3 Equally weighted dimensions and 12 indicators (2 more than Global MPI.
- India's population in multi-dimensional poverty decreased to 14.96% in 2019-21
- Rural Poverty > Urban Poverty
  (19.20%) (5.27%)
- Uttar Pradesh saw the largest decline in the number of poor individuals.

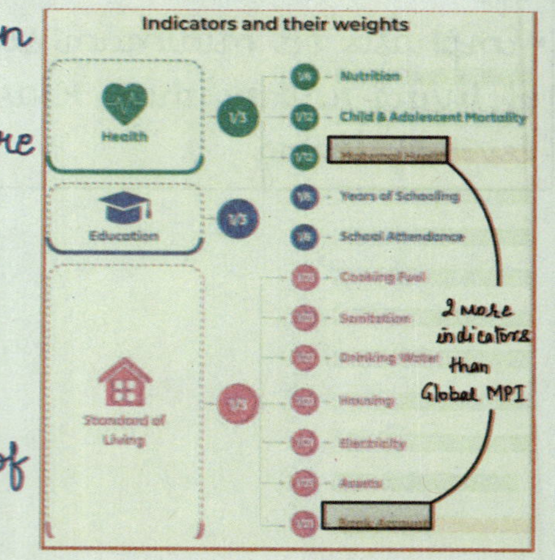

# Causes of Poverty

| Historical | Economic | Socio-cultural | Politico-Administrative |
|---|---|---|---|
| • Exploitative land Revenue Policies<br>• One way Free trade<br>• Drain of wealth<br>↓<br>Deindustrialisation<br>↓<br>Increased Unemployment<br>↓<br>Overburdened Agriculture Sector<br>↓<br>• low productivity<br>• Disguised Unemployment<br>↓<br>High Poverty | • Failure of Trickle-Down Growth Model<br>• Slow Growth rate during 1960s-1980s (Hindu Rate of Growth ≈ 3.5%)<br>• Tertiarisation of Economy + Stagnant manufacturing sector.<br>↓<br>Jobless Growth (Reduced Employment Elasticity)<br>• Slow Pace of Inclusive Growth<br>• low productivity in Agriculture<br>• Informalisation of Labour<br>• Inadequate and ineffective social security schemes | • Population increase (World's largest)<br>• low investment in Social infrastructure<br>Health = 2%<br>Education = 3%<br>• Social Deprivation<br>→ Feminisation of Poverty<br>→ Ruralisation of Poverty<br>→ Castetisation of Poverty<br>• Systemic Deprivation of certain sections<br>• More Pressure on resources<br>• Persistent regional disparities<br>• Digital Divide | • Lack of Political will.<br>• Bureaucratic Apathy<br>• Corruption<br>• Governance Issues<br>→ One-Size-fits-All approach<br>→ Centralised planning<br>→ Lack of Sensitisation<br>→ Capacity Building.<br>• Lack of Coordination (working in Silos)<br>• Mistargeting of Beneficiaries (Inclusion & Exclusion error<br>↓<br>Leakages and Misutilisation of public funds |

## Types of Poverty

| Parameters | Absolute measure of Poverty | Relative Measure of Poverty |
|---|---|---|
| Definition | • Refers to a condition when household income is below a necessary level to maintain basic living standard such as food, clothing or shelter | • Defined from social perspective i.e. living standards compared to economic standard of population living in sorroundings |
| Purpose | • Assessing the number of people living below the poverty line and monitoring changes over time. | • Analyzing income inequality trend, comparing poverty levels across region/countries & evaluating the impact of economic growth and policies on income distribution. |
| Measurement | • Fixed Poverty line is calculated based on the cost of a basket of essential goods and services. | • Measured using Gini coefficient calculated through Lorenz curve. |
| Income Inequality | • Doesnot consider income inequality within the society. | • Consider income inequality & the distribution of resources within society |
| Policy Implication | • Helps in targeting resources and interventions to alleviate absolute poverty. | • Highlight disparities & the need of redistributive policies to address relative poverty. |

## Poverty Line Estimation (PLE)

- Poverty estimation in India is carried out by NITI Aayog's Task Force through the calculation of poverty line based on the data captured by National Statistics office under the Ministry of Statistics and Programme Implementation (MoSPI).
- Poverty line estimation in India is based on consumption expenditure and not on the income levels.
- Consumption Expenditure is required on the basket of goods and services necessary to satisfy basic human needs known as 'Poverty Line Basket (PLB)'
- Price levels for consumption of goods & services in PLB varies from state to state and therefore, official poverty lines are higher in some states than in others.

## Various Committees

- Dadabhai Naoroji (Poverty and Un-British Rule in India) made the earliest estimation of poverty line. The poverty line proposed by him was based on the cost of a subsistence or minimum basic diet.

National Planning Committee, 1938: It was based on a minimum standard of living perspective in which nutritional requirements were implicit.

Planning Commission Working Group (1962): Poverty line in India was quantified for the 1st time in terms of minimum requirement of individuals but excluded the expenditure on health and education. (It was assumed that it will be provided by the state)

Dandekar and Rath (1971) It made the 1st Systematic assessment of poverty in India based on National Sample Survey data.

- It was the first to establish the consumption levels required to meet a minimum calorie requirement, normally of an average of 2250 Calories per capita per day.

Alagh Committee (1979): Official poverty counts began for the 1st time in India based on the approach of this task force.

- This Committee constructed a separate poverty line for rural and urban areas on the basis of nutritional requirement and related consumption expenditure.
- Caloric Requirement: Rural (2400 calories per day) and Urban (2100 calories per day)

Higher calorie requirement because rural people do more physical work.

| Criteria | Lakdawala Committee | Tendulkar Committee | Rangarajan Committee |
|---|---|---|---|
| Constituted | 1993 | 2004-05 | 2012 |
| Criteria | • Caloric intake based on consumption expenditure<br>• Presumption of provision of health & education by the state only | • Shift from calorie consumption to nutritional outcomes<br>• Incorporation of private expenditure on health and education. | • Consumption basket that includes food components such as calorie, protein & fat intake & essential non-food item groups (Education, Clothing, Health, Housing & Transport. |
| Poverty Line | • Separate Poverty line Basket for rural and Urban India | • Uniform all India Poverty Line Basket across rural and Urban India | • Separate Consumption Basket for rural and Urban India |
| Data Collection Poverty | • Uniform Reference Period<br>• State-specific Poverty lines using CPI-IW in urban areas and CPI-AL in rural areas. | • Mixed Reference Period<br>• Daily per-capita expenditure of Rs 27 and Rs 33 in rural & urban areas | • Modified mixed reference period.<br>• Daily per capita expenditure of Rs 32 and Rs 47 in rural and urban areas. |

## Reason for Estimation of Poverty Line

1. Identification of poor population. This helps in better targeting of resources.
2. Allocation of expenditure on various poverty alleviation measures taken by the government.
3. Tracking the performance of welfare schemes.
4. Helps in fulfilling SDG-1.
5. Fulfilling the constitutional goal of Justice-Economic.

## Parameters in the Poverty Line Estimation

- Poverty line Basket (PLB) → It consists of Goods and Services which needs to be consumed, based on that whatever expenditure has been incurred, that is known as consumption Expenditure.
  - Earlier consists of minimum subsistence level of diet
    - Now → Multi-dimensional poverty

**Food Components**

1. Calorie requirement
2. Nutrition requirement

**Non-Food components**

Health, Education, Conveyance, Rent, Transport, Clothing.

## Reduction in Poverty levels over time with respect to Rural and Urban Poverty

- Based on the estimation of Tendulkar committee, there has been a decline in poverty level from 45.3% in 1993-94 to 21.9% in 2011-12.
- Rural poverty witnessed a significant decline in poverty from 50.1% in 1993-94 to 25.7% in 2011-12 while urban poverty declined from 31.8% to 13.7% in the same period.

| Year | Lakdawala | | | Tendulkar | | | Rangarajan | | |
|---|---|---|---|---|---|---|---|---|---|
| | R | U | T | R | U | T | R | U | T |
| 1993-94 | 37.3 | 32.4 | 36.0 | 50.1 | 31.8 | 45.3 | – | – | – |
| 2004-05 | 28.3 | 25.7 | 27.5 | 41.8 | 25.7 | 37.2 | – | – | – |
| 2009-10 | – | – | – | 33.8 | 20.9 | 29.8 | 39.6 | 35.1 | 38.2 |
| 2011-12 | – | – | – | 25.7 | 13.7 | 21.9 | 30.9 | 26.4 | 29.5 |

- As per Global MPI Report 2022, the incidence of poverty fell from 36.6% in 2015-16 to 21.2% in 2019-21 in rural areas and from 9.0% to 5.5% in urban areas.
- According to the update by World Bank of Indian poverty using the new poverty line of $2.15 per day, 10% of Indians were poor in 2019, down from 22.5% in 2011. Rural India had more poor than the urban: 11.9% in rural areas and 6.4% in urban areas.
  - Extreme poverty is 12.3% points lower in 2019 than in 2011, with greater poverty reductions in rural areas.

# POVERTY ALLEVIATION MEASURES

| Trickle down Growth Model | Directly Targeted Poverty Alleviation | Basic-Needs Approach | Rights-Based Approach |
|---|---|---|---|
| Big Farmers / (Green Revolution)<br>Big Industries (Nehru-Mahalanobis Strategy)<br>↓<br>Increased GDP → Increased Economic Growth<br>↓<br>Employment Generation<br>↓<br>Benefits trickle down to lowest strata<br>↓<br>Unsuccessful<br>(Benefits did not adequately Trickle Down) | "Garibi Hatao" Slogan<br>Employment Generation programmes<br>↓<br>Emphasis upon<br>Self Employment / Wage Employment<br>↓<br>Employment Generation<br>↓<br>Increased Income<br>↓<br>Poverty Reduction<br><br>Eg: • Swarn Jayanti Shehri Rojgar Yojana<br>• Integrated Rural Development Program | Focus on providing basic needs to the people.<br>Eg: Integrated Child Development Scheme<br>• Mid-Day Meal<br>• PDS<br>• Sarva Shiksha Abhiyan<br>• 'Food For Work' program<br><br>People = Passive Beneficiaries<br><br>Government's policies to lift people out of poverty | Similar to Amartya Sen's Capability Approach<br>Change towards People's Rights.<br>People = Active Participants (Rights / Entitlements of people)<br><br>Government has a natural obligation of Poverty Alleviation<br>Eg - National Food Security Act.<br>• Right to Education<br>• MGNREGA<br>• PM Jan Dhan Yojana<br><br>Empowering people so that they themselves lift out of poverty |

## Change in Poverty Alleviation Measures in the Post-LPG Era

While earlier poverty alleviation measures have resulted in the reduction of poverty levels, there has been faster reduction in poverty in post-LPG era

In the post reform period, poverty declined faster in 2000s than in 1990s.

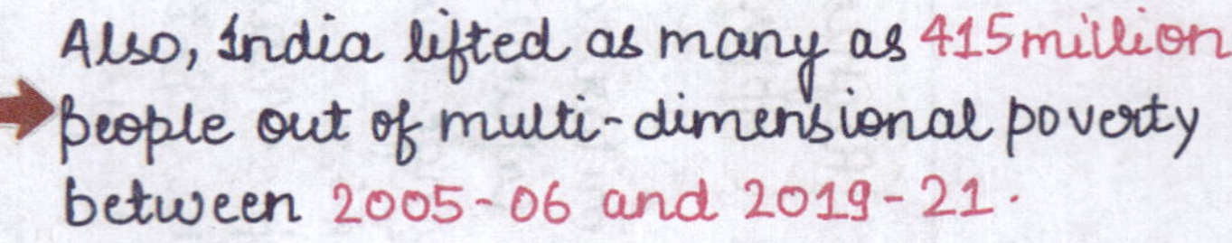

Also, India lifted as many as 415 million people out of multi-dimensional poverty between 2005-06 and 2019-21.

Poverty declined by 1.36% points per annum after 1991, compared to that of 0.44% points per annum prior to 1991.

- This has been due to various changes in policies adopted in post-LPG Era

**Shift from Welfare to Rights-Based Approach:**

- MGNREGA generated over 279-crore person-days of employment, benefitting more than 12 crore households since its inception (Ministry of Rural Development)
- The Right to Education (RTE) ensured free and compulsory education for children aged 6-14 years, benefitting over 22 crore children (Ministry of Education)

**Emphasis on Skill Development and Entrepreneurship:** Government initiated several programs to enhance vocational training and promote self-employment. Eg: Skill India Mission, Start up India, Stand Up India.

**Shift towards Inclusive Growth** in the post-LPG era as a means to alleviate poverty. Eg: XI and XII FYPs explicitly mentioned about achieving Inclusive Growth

**Targeted Programs and Identification of Beneficiaries:** Eg: Antyodaya Anna Yojana (AAY) identified the poorest households and provided them with heavily subsidized food grains, benefitting over 2.5 crore families (Ministry of Consumer Affairs)

**Focus on Human Development and not just Growth:**

- National Health Mission (NHM) improved access to healthcare services, resulting in the decline of Maternal Mortality Rate (MMR) from 301 in 2001-03 to 97 in 2023 (Ministry of Health and Family Welfare)
- The Sarva Shiksha Abhiyan (SSA) achieved significant progress in achieving universal elementary education, with the Gross Enrolment ratio in primary Education reaching 97.4% in 2022 (Ministry of Education)

**Financial Inclusion and Social Security:** Pradhan Mantri Jan Dhan Yojana (PMJDY) facilitated financial inclusion, with over 43.04 crore bank accounts opened and deposits worth more than ₹1.46 lakh Crore (Ministry of Finance)

**Asset Creation and Employment Generation:** PM Awas Yojana aimed to provide affordable housing to all by 2022, with over 1.12 crore houses sanctioned and

77 lakh houses completed (Ministry of Housing and Urban Affairs)

- **Use of Technology**: Eg: Direct Benefit Transfer (DBT) resulted in transfer of ₹17.02 lakh crore across various schemes, benefitting over 64 crore beneficiaries, efficiency and transparency of welfare programs (Ministry of Finance)
- **Public Private Partnerships (PPPs)** were encouraged in sectors like healthcare, education and skill development to enhance service delivery and leverage private sector expertise.
- **Decentralization of community participation**: Gram Sabha and Village Development Committees were involved in planning and implementation of programs like PMGSY and MGNREGA.
- **Monitoring and Evaluation**: Regular evaluations, such as Social Audit under MGNREGA, helped in identifying gaps and improving implementation.

## Issues and Challenges in Poverty Alleviation Programmes

- Multi-dimensional Poverty: It is a multi-dimensional menace which needs convergence and synergy from all level of institutions which is generally lacking.
- Targeting and Identification: Many poverty alleviation programs rely on income thresholds or socio-economic indicators to identify beneficiaries. However these criteria can be subjective & prone to errors, leading to inclusion and exclusion errors
- Governance Challenges such as corruption, bureaucratic inefficiencies, lack of capacity and accountability and inadequate infrastructure can hamper the smooth delivery of benefits & services to intended beneficiaries.
- Leakage at different levels had led to diversion of resources meant for deprived ones
- Focus on immediate relief: Poverty alleviation programs often focus on providing immediate relief or income support. However sustainable poverty reduction requires a focus on building livelihoods and empowering individuals to become self-reliant.
  Eg: Providing access to education, skill training, healthcare and productive assets, as well as facilitating market linkages & entrepreneurship opportunities.
- Social and Cultural Factors: Deep rooted social inequalities, gender discrimination, caste based hierarchies and cultural barriers can impede poverty reduction efforts
- Persistent Regional Disparities continue to pose a challenge in poverty reduction, with certain states and regions experiencing higher poverty rates compared to others
  Eg: States like Bihar, Uttar Pradesh, and Jharkhand still face significant challenges in reducing poverty rates (Official Poverty Estimates)
- Marginalised Communities often face social exclusion, discrimination and limited access to resources and opportunities.
- Informal Sector Employment: The informal sector, which employs a significant portion of the population, often lacks Job Security, social protection and adequate wages.

- **Climate Change and Vulnerability:** Climate Change impacts, such as extreme weather events, natural disasters, & agricultural challenges, disproportionately affect the poor and vulnerable communities.
- **Digital Divide:** Poor are not able to reap the benefits of digital technologies.
- **Other factors** like Jobless growth, high inflation etc.

### NITI Aayog Strategy to Combat Poverty

Sustained rapid growth that is also employment intensive | Making anti-poverty programs effective

1. Employment - Intensive Sustained Rapid Growth: First, by creating jobs that pay steadily rising real wages which directly dents poverty and secondly, it leads to growth in government revenues which in turn allow the expansion of Social expenditures at faster pace.
   Eg: Emphasis on labour intensive Sectors such as Apparel, footwear, food processing, electronic and electrical appliances, other light manufactures, construction and retail trade.
2. Making Anti-poverty Programs more effective such as Public Distribution System (PDS), Midday Meal Scheme, MGNREGA and Housing for All.
   Eg: MGNREGA can be made more effective by allowing it to impart skills.

## FEMINISATION OF POVERTY

About: 'Feminisation of Poverty' term coined by Diana Pearce in 1976 → refers to a phenomenon in which women are disproportionately represented among the world's poor and highlights the trend that women are more likely to experience poverty as compared to men.

- About 19.7% of people living in female-headed households live in poverty compared with 15.9% in male-headed households.
- World Economic Forum's Global Gender Gap Report 2021 India's gender pay gap is around 20-30% as per wage index.
- Agricultural Census 2015-16 → In India women own only about 12.7% of agricultural land.

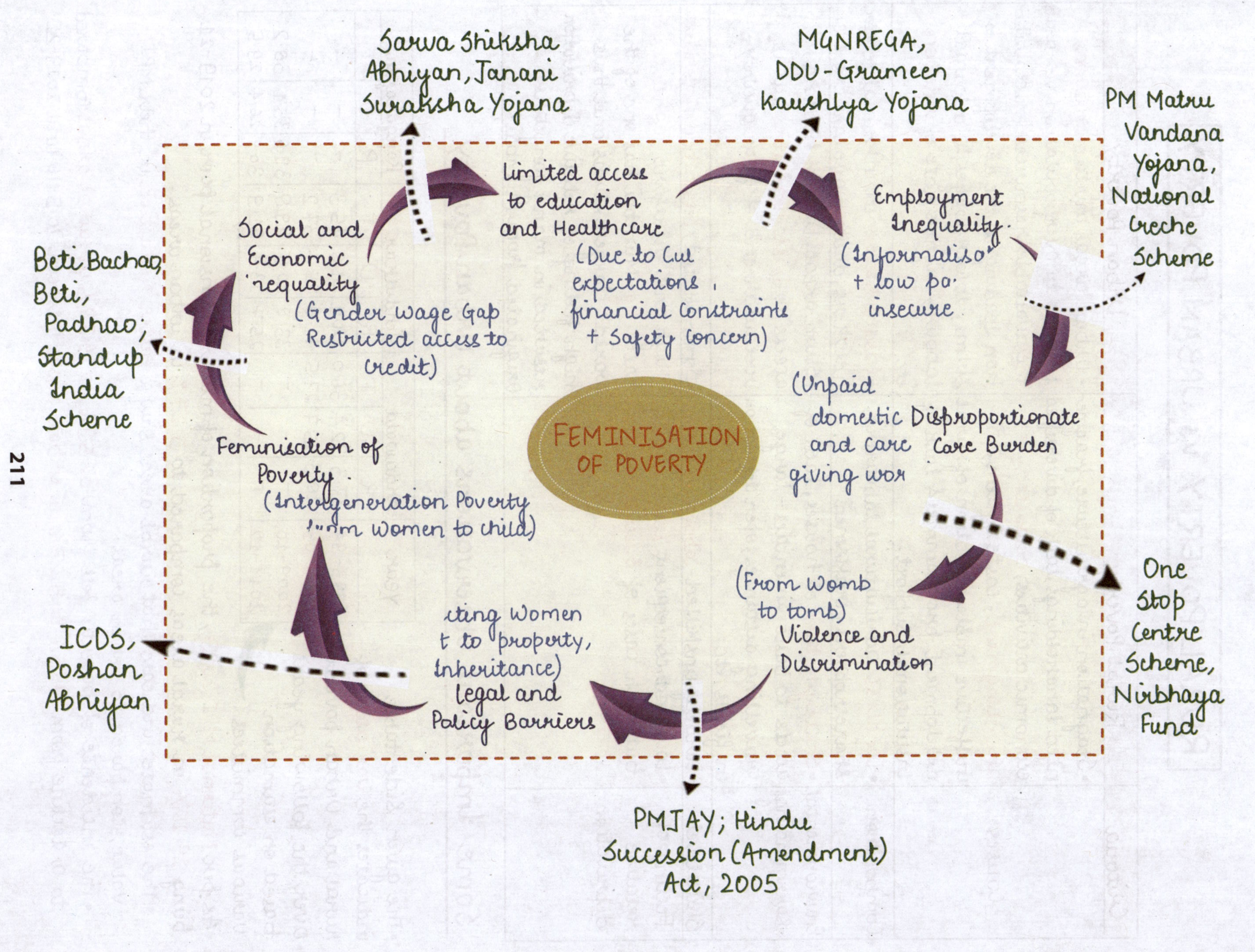
FEMINISATION OF POVERTY
Social and Economic 'nequality
(Gender wage Gap Restricted access to credit)
Limited access to education and Healthcare
(Due to Cul expectations, financial constraints + Safety concern)
Employment Inequality
(Informaliso + low pa insecure
Disproportionate Care Burden
(Unpaid domestic and care giving wor
Violence and Discrimination
(From Womb to tomb)
legal and Policy Barriers
ting women t to property, inheritance)
Feminisation of Poverty
(Intergeneration Poverty from women to child)
Sarwa Shiksha Abhiyan, Janani Suraksha Yojana
MGNREGA, DDU-Grameen Kaushlya Yojana
PM Matru Vandana Yojana, National Creche Scheme
One Stop Centre Scheme, Nirbhaya Fund
PMJAY; Hindu Succession (Amendment) Act, 2005
ICDS, Poshan Abhiyan
Beti Bachao, Beti, Padhao; Standup India Scheme

# RURAL POVERTY vs URBAN POVERTY

| Criteria | Rural Poverty | Urban Poverty |
|---|---|---|
| Causes | • Stagnation in agriculture, fragmented landholdings, lack of diversified economic activities, disguised unemployment, caste system, ineffective implementation of rural development programmes & lack of institutional support. | • Urban areas invite migration leading to overpopulation vis-a-vis the available resources for exploitation leading to the development of slums, lower wages to informal labour, higher rate of inflation etc. |
| Composition | • Landless agricultural labourers, sharecroppers, craftsmen | • Casual labour in informal sector, hawkers, daily wage earners, etc. |
| Environmental Sorroundings | • Shabby nature of houses, lack of access to basic amenities - large travelling distances, open defecation in fields, etc. | • Slum areas, lack of housing; access to basic amenities but is irregular and of poor quality. |
| Skill level | • Largely unskilled - labour intensive | • Semi-skilled; less labour intensive. |
| Feeling of relative deprivation | • Low and consequent lesser crime but high cases of suicides. | • High and therefore higher crime rates. Eg: Mumbai has one of the world's largest slums and thus high feeling of relative deprivation resulted in many gangsters originated from Mumbai. |

## Some Important Observations about Urban Poverty

• The given side table indicates the variation of rural and urban poverty over the following years based on estimation various committees:

| Year | Lakdawala | | | Tendulkar | | | Rangarajan | | |
|---|---|---|---|---|---|---|---|---|---|
| | R | U | T | R | U | T | R | U | T |
| 1993-94 | 37.3 | 32.4 | 36.0 | 50.1 | 31.8 | 45.3 | – | – | – |
| 2004-05 | 28.3 | 25.7 | 27.5 | 41.8 | 25.7 | 37.2 | – | – | – |
| 2009-10 | – | – | – | 33.8 | 20.9 | 29.8 | 39.6 | 35.1 | 38.2 |
| 2011-12 | – | – | – | 25.7 | 13.7 | 21.9 | 30.9 | 26.4 | 29.5 |

• As per National MPI 2023, the proportion of multi-dimensional poor in 2019-21 being 19.28% in rural areas compared to 5.27% in urban areas.

- The estimates indicate that rural areas saw a faster reduction in their MPI value, compared to urban areas.
- The incidence of poverty fell from 32.59% to 19.28% in rural areas compared to a decline from 8.65% to 5.27% in urban areas between 2015-16 and 2019-21.

- Today one in every six of India's urban households live in slums, a number forecast to rise exponentially over the coming years.
  - Most slum dwellers do not have access to clean water, sanitation and healthcare facilities. They face a constant threat of eviction, removal, confiscation of goods and have virtually no social security cover.
  - Some 54% of urban slums do not have toilets; public facilities are unusable due to lack of maintenance.
- Migration towards urban centres has increased, indicating that economic reforms have not been effective in creating jobs in small and medium towns as well as rural areas.

## Reasons behind the increasing Urbanisation of Poverty

01 **Push-Pull Factors**: The causes of urban poverty can be linked to the lack of infrastructure in rural areas (push factor), forcing inhabitants of these regions to seek out work in India's mega-cities (pull factor).
- The urban poor is largely the overflow of rural poor who migrate to urban areas in search of alternative employment and livelihood.

02 **Lack of Skills** to participate in the emerging employment opportunities in different sectors of urban economy.

03 **Indebtness**: Unemployment or underemployment and the casual nature of work in urban areas lead to indebtedness, that in turn, reinforces poverty.

04 **Informalisation of Labour**: Jobless growth witnessed after LPG Reforms led to increased informalisation of labour which created irregular income among the urban workers.

05 **Increasing Gig Economy**: Recent boost to gig economy while generated employment opportunities have also posed challenges for gig workers such as no fixed employment terms, uncertain income according to the whims & fancies of employer and many more. Eg: Blinkit Gig worker protest in 2023 against the reduction in fee per delivery

06 **Inflation** intensifies the hardship and deprivation of lower-income groups.

07 **Unequal distribution** of income and assets has also led to persistence of poverty in urban India.

# FORMS OF INEQUALITIES IN INDIA

- **Income Inequalities**: Oxfam India's report, "Survival of the Richest: the India Story," Says that between 2012 and 2021, 40% of the wealth created in India has gone to just 1% of the population and only a mere 3% of the wealth has gone to the bottom 50% (Total number of billionairs in India increased from 102 in 2020 to 166 in 2022)
- **Extreme hunger**: India's ranking in Global Hunger Index 2023 declined to 111 out of 123 countries.
- **Financial Exclusion**: Bank Savings are there for 62% upper caste households whereas this is 49% for SC households. Hence, ability to invest in technology is lower for SC households.
- **Educational Inequalities**: The rapid shift to e-learning prompted by the pandemic has resurfaced long standing issues of inequality and digital divide in India that must be addressed by future economic, education and digitalization policies.
- **Gender Inequalities**: India stood at rank 122 out of 191 countries with a score of of 0.490 in the Gender Inequality Index 2021.
  - Female LFPR in India (Based on PLFS 2022-23) stands around 37% also there is a considerable gender wage gap which contribute to gender inequality in country.
- **Caste Inequalities**: Higher poverty levels among SC (42.93%) & ST (42.7%) compared to other groups.
  - There is a Significant disparity in graduate percentages among different caste groups, with the general category having the highest (14.54%)
- **Urban poor**: There are large Swathes within the informal workforce who would be facing inequalities in health, income and employment.
  - Health-Income-Employment triple insecurity faced by the urban poor has grown exponentially as they live in densely populated urban neighbourhood where diseases spread much faster, generating further income losses & job uncertainities.

## Reasons for increasing Inequality in India

→ **Agricultural wages**: Stagnation in agricultural wages owing to stagnation yields, crop failures, post harvest damages and climate risks have impacted income level of nearly 50% of the population that draws Sustenance from agriculture.

→ **Skewed growth**: A considerable share of economic growth was cornered by the Service Sector that employed nearly a third of the population. On the contrary, agriculture grew at less than 3% in the last few decades.

→ **Regional disparity**: Incomes remain Subdued in the relatively backward states of Rajasthan, Bihar, Chhattisgarh etc. which have lagged behind in GSDP growth owing to Infrastructure deficit and governance deficit.

→ Failure of Trickle down Effect: Employment grew merely by 0.5% per annum from 2004-05 to 2011-12 → the period that saw the highest growth of GDP by 8.5% per annum.

→ Informalisation of Economy: As per ILO data, 81% of total employment is informal in nature. The contractual labourers remain outside of the ambit of labour laws and are bereft of social security and fair wages.

→ Capital-led growth: Growing economic inequalities due to over-reliance on capital and finance as the drivers of growth and neglect of labour.

→ Inefficient Re-distribution: With only 6 out of 100 individuals paying taxes (only 5% Indians pay taxes) and tax to GDP ratio being 11% (Economic Survey), India is not efficient at redistribution of wealth. The income gap between rich and poor also worsens due to prevalent tax evasion, black money.

- Heavy reliance on consumption taxes like GST increases inequality and is regressive in nature because poor people pay a larger share of their incomes.

→ Low investment in Public Health: India's investment in public health are among the lowest in the world and most cities lack any kind of public primary health services

→ State's withdrawal from the welfare expenditure leaving the domain open to private sector which further exacerbated inequality.

## Measures needed to Contain Inequality

☛ Improving the state of Agriculture by investing in irrigation technologies, preventing fertiliser overuse etc., to ensure remunerative prices for farmers - through MSP reforms, eliminating middle men by promoting platforms like e-Rashtriya Kisan Agri Mandi etc and to promote research to improve farm productivity.

☛ Employment Oriented growth: Promoting labour intensive industries such as leather, & apparel as suggested by NITI Aayog, can be instrumental in raising incomes of bottom 50%

☛ Tax Efficiency: India needs to improve tax to GDP ratio and bring it on par with emerging economies (23%). This can be done by lowering income tax evasion and generation of black money, simplifying tax procedures to improve compliance etc.

☛ State to be dominant provider of merit goods such as health, nutrition, Education.

- Public sector spending in these sectors need to increase to around 6% of GDP which currently stands at around 2%.
- Increased social spending has been shown to reduce inequality by 20% across OECD countries.

☛ Preventing deprivation: Enforcing laws against eviction & exploitation such as LARR, Forest Rights Act can also avoid impoverishment of people while also ensuring income security through land and forest resources

☛ Women Empowerment: Higher wages and stronger labour rights - especially for women workers who tend to work in the lowest paid and most insecure jobs - are key to reducing inequality.

# FORMAL vs INFORMAL EMPLOYMENT

## Categorization of the Workforce

**Based on Employment Status**

- NSO classified the worker on the basis of Employment status into 3 categories:

i. Self Employed Workers → Informal
ii. Casual / Contract labour → Workforce
iii. Regular / Salaried labour → Formal Workforce

**Based on Sector in which they are employed**

→ Informal / Unorganised
→ Formal / Organised.

### Based on Employment Status

- **Self Employed Workers**: People who operate their own farm or non-farm enterprises with an essential feature of autonomy (in deciding how, where & when to produce) and economic independence (in respect of choice of market, scale of operation and finance) for carrying out operation.
- **Casual Labour**: A person who was casually engaged in other's farm or non-farm enterprises & in return received wages according to the terms of daily or periodic work contract.
- **Regular Wage/Salaried Employee**: Person who worked in other's farm or non-farm enterprises and in return received salary or wages on a regular basis. This category included not only persons getting time wage but also persons receiving piecewage or salary and paid apprentices (Full time and part time)

### Organised or Unorganised Sector

| Organised Sector | Unorganised Sector |
|---|---|
| It is a sector where the employment terms are fixed & regular and the employees get assured work. | The sector is characterised by small and scattered units, which are largely outside the control of the government. |
| The Job is regular and has fixed working hours. | Jobs are low paid and often not regular. |
| Workers enjoy the security of employment. | Employment is not secure |
| Employees are entitled to various medical and other social benefits. | No benefits are available for the workers. |
| Eg: Government employees, Registered industrial workers etc. | Eg: Shopkeeping, Farming, Domestic works, etc. |

# Need for generating Employment in the Formal Sector

- **Implementation of the labour laws** which envisages protection of labour rights in the formal Sector. There is greater exploitation of workers who are outside the reach of the labour legislation.
  Eg: No fixed working hours or workers are dismissed without any compensation in the unorganised Sector.

- **Better Wages and Social Security Protection**: The workers in the formal Sector form trade unions and bargain with employers for better wages and other Social Security measures.
  - Workers and enterprises in the informal Sector do not get regular income; they do not have any protection or regulation from the government.

- **Skill Development of Employees**: The Employers in the formal Sector are motivated to invest in the upgradation of Skills of employees while the informal employment does not result into any upgradation of Skills.

- **Improved production of Goods/Services**: Contract workers do not feel as much loyalty to the company as regular workers would, reducing employers' incentive to invest in their training
  - There is evidence that hiring Contract workers today hurts a firm's productivity tomorrow as Contract workers do not accumulate "firm specific human capital".

- **Reduced Gender Disparity**: Women constitute the majority of informal participants characterized by lower paying, income volatility and the lack of a robust Social Safety net.

- **Increased tax returns**: Formalisation leads to more tax revenues with an increase in tax to GDP ratio. There will be reduction in generation of black Money
  - With increased tax revenue, government can invest in Social infrastructure like education, health, Skill development etc.

- **Reduction of Poverty**: Unorganised Sector workers had a much greater rate of poverty in the organised Sector than their counterparts.

- **Prevention from the impact of Disaster/External Crisis**: Many Natural Disasters such as floods, drought, famine, earthquakes and so on have devastating effects on informal Sectors. This problem is exacerbated by lack of Social Security.
  Eg: Unequal impact of COVID-19 on Migrant workers and formal IT Professionals.

# ESTIMATES OF UNEMPLOYMENT

- The following are the agencies involved in the collection of employment data and their sources for the data. These sources may be classified into three broad categories: Household Surveys, Enterprise and Industry Surveys & data from government schemes.

1. Household Surveys: These are the primary method of generating employment and and Unemployment data. There are 3 types of Surveys:
   a. Employment - Unemployment Surveys (EUS) by NSSO. Replaced with Periodic Labour Force Surveys.
   b. Annual Labour Force Survey by Labour Bureau.
   c. Decennial Population Census by Office of Registrar General of India and Census Commissioner.
2. Enterprise Surveys:
   a. Economic Census: This census cover the entire universe of non-agricultural established regardless of size or sector. It extends to both industrial and service establishments.
   - 7th economic census was launched in 2019 and was conducted by the Ministry of Statistics and Programme Implementation (MoSPI).

   b. Annual Survey of Industries (ASI): Conducted by NSO. It uses the enterprises registered under the Factories Act, 1948 and takes into account only organised sector establishment (≥ 10 workers)

   c. Quaterly Employment Survey (QES): Conducted by the Labour Bureau that would provide the employment estimates employing 10 or more worker in the organised segment of 9 sectors.
   - Manufacturing, Construction, trade, transport, Education, health, IT/BPO, Accomodation and Restaurant and Financial Services.

   d. MSME Census to capture the employment in all MSMEs.
3. Government Schemes: Administrative data and government schemes are also potential source for gathering data on job creation.
   - The former includes data from EPFO, ESIC, NPS and other similar sources relating to large private organisations.

## Deficiencies in the existing Surveys

- Low frequency and time lag between data collection and availability of results: Typically data collection takes place once every five years & the results usually become available with a lag of more than a year. This delay makes the data less relevant as policy inputs.

- Census data is collected only once in ten years, the estimates are available after much time lag. So, these estimates rarely form the basis of formulation of employment policies.
- Enterprise Surveys do not adequately cover the Self-employed & farm workers
- Economic Census fails to capture the entire non-agricultural workforce as it covers only those with 10 or more workers and thus, its coverage is very limited.
- Annual Survey of industries has several gaps such as outdated sample frame, limited coverage and time lag in collecting data.
  - Further available fields for drawing samples for such surveys often do not cover small, unorganised enterprises & therefore leave out worker employed by them
- Sources in administrative datasets are even more partial in coverage than enterprise surveys.
- Jobs generated in education and health sectors are particularly important from the viewpoint of job creation and they can provide valuable data. But this source is limited by its highly partial coverage

## Periodic Labour Force Survey (PLFS)

- India's first computer-based survey launched by NSO in 2017.
- Constituted based on the recommendations of a committee headed by Amitabh Pundu.
- Estimate key employment & unemployment indicators (WPR, LFPR, UR)
  - → Quarterly release → Urban Areas → (Based on 'Current Weekly status')
  - → Annual release → Rural and Urban Areas → Based on both 'Usual Status' and 'Current Weekly status'

| Indicator | 2017-18 | 2022-23 | Trend |
|---|---|---|---|
| **Labour Force Participation Rate (LFPR)** | | | |
| - Total LFPR | 49.8% | 57.9% | Increased |
| - LFPR in Rural Areas | 50.7% | 60.8% | Increased |
| - LFPR in Urban Areas | 47.6% | 50.4% | Increased |
| - Male LFPR | 75.8% | 78.5% | Increased |
| - Female LFPR | 23.3% | 37.0% | Increased |
| **Worker Population Ratio (WPR)** | | | |
| - Total WPR | 46.8% | 56.0% | Increased |
| - WPR in Rural Areas | 48.1% | 59.4% | Increased |
| - WPR in Urban Areas | 43.9% | 47.7% | Increased |
| - Male WPR | 71.2% | 76.0% | Increased |
| - Female WPR | 22.0% | 35.9% | Increased |
| **Unemployment Rate (UR)** | | | |
| - Total UR | 6.0% | 3.2% | Decreased |
| - UR in Rural Areas | 5.3% | 2.4% | Decreased |
| - UR in Urban Areas | 7.7% | 5.4% | Decreased |
| - Male UR | 6.1% | 3.3% | Decreased |
| - Female UR | 5.6% | 2.9% | Decreased |

## Status of Employment Trends

01. Latest annual findings of PLFS (2022-23) observed the following employment trends.

LFPR

Urban Areas: Increased from 47.6% in 2017-18 to 50.4% in 2022-23.

Rural Areas: Increased from 50.7% in 2017-18 to 60.8% in 2022-23.

Male: Increased from 75.8% in 2017-18 to 78.5% in 2022-23.

Female: Increased from 23.3% in 2017-18 to 37% in 2022-23.

- **Unemployment Rate**: It shows that the Unemployment rate at 3.2% in 2022-23, compared with 4.1% in 2021-22. In Rural Areas, UR decreased from 5.3% in 2017-18 to 2.4% in 2022-23, while for Urban areas it decreased from 7.7% to 5.4%.
- **Dominant Share of Employment in Agriculture**: The Sectoral Composition of the workforce shows that 45.6% of the workers in India are engaged in agriculture & allied activities, 30.0% in Services and 23.7% in industry.

## 02 India Employment Report (Institute for Human Development and International Labour Organisation)

- **The report has flagged concerns about poor employment conditions** - The slow transition to non-farm employment has reversed; Women largely account for the increase in self-employment and unpaid family work; youth employment is of poorer quality than employment for adults, wages and earnings are stagnant or declining.
- Informal employment has risen. Nearly 90% of the workforce is informally employed.
- Self-Employment remains the primary source of employment - 55.8% in 2022. Casual and regular employment has accounted for 22.7% & 21.5% respectively.
- Female Labour Force Participation rate (LFPR) in India remains among the World's lowest. There is a considerable gender gap - Women's LFPR (32.8%) in 2022 was 2.3 times lower than men's (77.2%).
  - India's low LFPR is largely attributed to low female LFPR, which was much lower than the world average of 47.3% in 2022, but higher than South Asian average of 24.8% as per ILO Data.
- Structural Transformation: There has been a reversal of the slow transition towards non-farm employment after 2018-19.
  - The share of agriculture in total employment fell to around 42% in 2019 from 60% in 2000 and this shift was largely absorbed by construction and services.
  - The share of manufacturing in employment has remained almost stagnant at 12-14%
  - Since 2018-19, this slow transition has stagnated or reversed with the rise in the share of agricultural employment.
- Youth Employment: There has been a rise in youth employment, but the quality of work remains a concern, especially for qualified young workers.
  - Youth Employment and underemployment increased between 2000 and 2019.

# JOBLESS GROWTH

### Less Number of Jobs

- India experienced job growth of 3% per annum in 70s, when India's economy grew at 3-3.5% per annum but over last 3 decades India's economy grew at over 5-0% per annum but job growth has been close to 1% per annum.
- Employment Elasticity has fallen from unity in 70s to 0.4 in 90s to less than 0.1 today.

### Informal Jobs

- Nearly 90% of the workforce is informally employed

### Low Female Labour Force Participation Rate

- There is a considerable gap - Women's LFPR (32.8%) in 2022 was 2.3 times lower than men's (77.2%) (Based on India Employment Report, 2014)

## Reason for the Jobless Growth

- Tertiarization of Indian Economy (Service Sector constitutes more than 50% in the GDP).
- Stagnant manufacturing sector (contributing only 14-16% of the GDP).
- Less focus on labour-intensive industries such as textiles & apparel, leather & footwear, network products etc.
- Slow occupation transformation (Nearly 45% the workforce is employed in Agriculture
- Impact of Globalisation: Decline in formal public sector employment; market competition encourages contractual labour; etc.
- Government Policies that promote dwarfism (Eg: Small scale industries reservation) held back job creation and productivity.
- Fourth Industrial revolution and automation poses dangers to present formal sector jobs.
- Lack of Skill Development of Employees hindering the participation in formal sector (Eg: 2015 Report on National Policy on Skill Development and Entrepreneurship estimated that only 4.7% of total workforce in India had undergone formal skill training compared with 52% in US, 80% in Japan, & 96% in South Korea.)
- Low Human Development Parameters which negatively affected the efficiency of the workforce and its potential to engage in high productivity employment opportunities (India ranked 134 in HDI 2024).

## Reason for Low Female LFPR.

➔ Lack of Suitable Job opportunities especially for women in rural areas after the fall of farm Jobs & lack of economic opportunities in non- farm employment.

➔ Increased Mechanization: Nearly 12 million Indian women could lose their Jobs by 2030 owing to automation (McKinsey Global Institute Report)

➔ Increased women literacy by getting enrolled for higher studies in colleges reduced the workforce participation.

➔ Effect of household income: With increasing household incomes, especially over the last 3 decades, the need of a "Second income" reduced.

- This reduced women's participation especially in Subsidiary activities (Secondary income') due to change in preferences. This effect is especially seen in urban women workforce.

➔ Gender Discrimination: For every woman, 90% of the inequality she faces would be caused by discrimination because of gender.

- Higher Education: As of 2010-19, only 2% of working age women received formal vocational training, of which 47% did not join labour force (NSSO, 2018-19)
- Skill training: Women form only 17% of cloud computing, 20% of engineering and 24% of data/artificial intelligence Jobs. (WEF 2020)
- Wages: WEF's gender gap report 2022, where India was ranked at 135th position out of 146 countries.

➔ Familial Responsibilities. Unpaid care work continues to be a women's responsibility, with women spending on average five hours per day on domestic work.

- women regularly sacrifice wages, career progression and education opportunities to meet family responsibilities, Safety Considerations etc.

➔ COVID-Effect: Massive Job losses for women, especially informal workers, and slower recovery of women-led micro businesses.

- Deepened gender digital divides, disrupted girls' schooling and placed millions of female health workers at risk.

➔ Under-reporting of women's work (Economic Survey 2022-23)

➔ Other factors: lack of Sanitation, Sexual harassment at workplace, unsafe travelling, poor child care facilities and care homes for elderly etc has prevented women from working in industries.

## Measures to be taken to address Jobless Growth

- Government has undertaken various measures in the past such as implementation of Goods and Services tax, digitalisation of economy, launch of E-Shram portal, Codification of labour codes, Gender Budgeting (2005-06) & many other Schemes Such as PM SVANidhi - Micro Credit Scheme for street Vendors.
- National Education Policy (NEP), 2020 has set the goal to achieve 100% enrolment

of girls in schools by 2035 and 50% in higher education institutes.
Other measures which can also be taken to tackle jobless growth.

➡ Rapid and Inclusive growth with high employment elasticity has to be central to any employment strategy → will generate more jobs.

➡ Strengthening of MSMEs which employ 40% of informal workforce will contribute to economic recovery, job creation, & economic formalisation.
Eg: Growth of Stronger industrial clusters and MSMEs will create more employment per unit of capital, and support inclusive growth.

➡ Decentralisation of Industrial Activities is necessary for balanced regional development.

➡ Development of rural areas puts a check on the migration towards cities.
Eg: Implementing more schemes like Providing urban amenities to Rural Areas, Shyama Prasad Mukherjee Rurban Mission.

➡ Investment in Human Capital: There is an urgent need to increase investment in Sector such as education, health and education
Eg: Interim Union Budget 2024-25 emphasised the need for 6% of GDP in Indian Education Sector.

➡ Development of Skills through a combination of apprenticeships and training institutes run by private sector → essential to address academic-industry mismatch.

➡ Technological Interventions can enhance productivity, through increased market access, real time information, quick dispute resolution, & development of transparent mechanisms.
Eg: India's Edtech Sector is beneficiary of the same

➡ Comprehensive Data of Informal Sector: It is necessary to build a comprehensive statistical base on various dimensions of the informal economy as an integral part of National Statistical System, enabling policy makers to make informed decisions.

➡ Promoting labour Intensive Industries such as food processing, leather & footwear, wood manufacturers & furnitures, textiles & apparel & garments. Eg: Economic Survey 2019-20 Suggests integrating "Assemble in India" under "Make in India" particularly in network products → Boost to India's Export.

## GIG ECONOMY

- A Gig Economy is a free market system in which temporary positions are common and organisations contract with independent workers for short term engagements.
- Gig workers have a non standard work arrangements with their employers and share a non traditional employer-employee relationship.
- Newly passed labour codes for the first time in India have defined Gig and

platform workers.

- Code on Social Security, 2020 [Section 2 (35)] defines a gig worker as 'a person who performs work or participates in a work arrangement and earn from such activities outside of traditional employer-employee relationships'.
- Gig workers can be broadly classified into two categories: Platform and non-platform based workers.
  - The Social Security Code defines a platform worker as "a person engaged in or undertaking platform work". A Platform worker implies a worker working for an organisation that provides specific services using an online platform directly to individuals or organisations. Eg: Ola or Uber drivers, Swiggy or Zomato delivery agents etc.
  - Non-Platform gig workers are generally casual wage workers and own-account workers in the conventional sectors, working part time or full time.
- Gig workers can also be classified on the basis of skills - High skilled, medium skilled and low skilled workers.
  - According to the NITI Aayog Report, at present, about 47% of gig work is in medium-skilled jobs, about 22% in high skilled jobs, and about 31% in low-skilled jobs.
  - Trends show that concentration of workers in medium skills is gradually declining and that in low skills and high skills is increasing.

**NITI Aayog Report on Gig Economy**

- India's Gig workforce expected to expand to 2.35 crore by 2029-30 (2021-22 = 77 lakhs)
- An estimated 56% of New Employment in India is being generated by Gig Economy companies.

## Drivers for growth of Gig Economy

Demographic factors - Large and growing number of young, educated & ambitious Indians who are seeking to improve their livelihood & side income generation.

Growth of E-commerce → Increased demand for delivery & logistic services

Emergence of Startup culture → Hiring of contractual labour → Reduce cost

Higher demand for flexible work to balance personal & professional lives.

COVID-19 Pandemic also gave a boost to the gig economy.

Penetration of Smartphones & affordability of high-speed internet → Growth of online platform & thus, platform workers.

Economic liberalisation → Increased competition & open markets which encouraged growth of gig economy.

## Challenges faced by the Gig workers.

➔ Largely an Urban phenomenon (Access to internet services and digital technology can be a restrictive factor) → Exacerbating income inequality.

➔ Job and Income Insecurity: Gig workers do not get benefit from labour regulations pertaining to wages, hours, working conditions & right to collective bargaining.

Eg: Protest by Blinkit workers in 2023. There are regular protests by Ola and Uber workers.

➔ Lack of access to many workplace entitlements.

➔ Occupational Health and Safety Risks which have been aggravated in the background of quick commerce culture (10 min delivery)

➔ Skills mismatch: According to ILO surveys, workers with higher educational achievements are not necessarily finding work commensurate with their skills.

➔ Increased Stress among the gig workers due to pressure from algorithmic management practices and performance evaluation on basis of ratings.

➔ Social Isolation: Gig workers may not have the same social connections and support systems as traditional employees, as they often work independently and may not have a physical workplace.

➔ Lack of Data makes it difficult for policy makers to understand its size, scope and impact on economy and workforce.

## NITI Aayog Recommendations to address the challenges

➔ Platform India Initiative: Establish a program similar to Startup India, specifically focused on supporting platform businesses. This includes simplifying regulations, provide guidance and offering financial incentives.

➔ Financial Inclusion: Improve access to credit for Platform workers & aspiring platform owners through specially designed financial products. Facilitate access to venture capital and loans for platform businesses at various stages

➔ Skill Development: Partner with relevant authorities to create platform-specific skilling programs to train gig workers & foster micro-entrepreneurship within the platform ecosystem.

➔ Social Inclusion in the new-age digital economy: Promote participation in the platform economy for underprivileged groups like women and people with disabilities. Partnering with Civil Society Organisations (CSOs) can facilitate skill development, access to resources & financial inclusion for these groups.

➔ Social Security: Explore options for providing social security benefits to gig workers. This might include paid leaves, insurance schemes, pension plans and income support programs to address work irregularity & ensure minimum earnings

- Data Collection: Conduct Separate Surveys to accurately estimate the size and characteristics of the gig workforce. Collect data on contract types, technology usage, and other relevant factors to create better policies for this growing sector.
- RAISE framework for Operationalising the Code on Social Security (CoSS), 2020: As central and State governments draw up rules and regulations under CoSS 2020, they could adopt the five pronged RAISE approach to ensure realisation of full access to Social Security for all gig and platform workers.

Recognise the varied nature of platform work to design equitable schemes

Ensure benefits are readily accessible to workers.

Allow augmentation of Social Security through innovative financing mechanisms.

Support workers to subscribe to government schemes and welfare programmes through widespread awareness campaigns.

Incorporate, while designing schemes, specific interest of platforms, factoring the impact on job creation, platform businesses and workers.

- Linking Women Empowerment with Gig Economy: There is a need to build right physical and social infrastructure that supports the engagement of women in the gig workforce.

## Social Security Code, 2020 provisions for workers

- The Code on Social Security, 2020 gives a legal identity to term "gig worker". The Code defines gig workers as a person who performs work or participates in a work arrangement and earns from such activities outside of traditional employer-employee relationship.
- Section 114 of Code mentions that Central Government may frame & notify suitable Security schemes for gig & platform workers. Matters covered in Section 114 of Code are; a. life and Disability cover; b. Accident Insurance; C. Health and maternity benefits; d. Old age protection; e. Creche; f. Any other benefits by the government.
- The Code recommends that schemes may be funded through a combination of contributions from Union and State governments, as well as gig platform aggregators.
- The National Social Security Board will have oversight of welfare of gig economy workers, & will include representatives of both aggregator companies and gig workers.

The Code also mandates that the Union government establish a Social Security Fund for gig economy workers.

# AUTOMATION AND EMPLOYMENT

| Positives | Negatives |
|---|---|
| Newer Job opportunities in emerging fields. Eg: Big Data Analytics, Cloud and Cyber Security Services, internet of things. | Widespread Job losses → Especially in repetitive & mundane tasks (Eg: Entry level jobs in IT Sector). • Automation threatens 69% of Jobs in India (World Bank 2016) |
| Enhancing the productivity of employees by automating repetitive task and enhancing focus on tasks that require creativity & problem solving skills. | Impact on specific Sectors such as Customer Services, IT/ITES etc. |
| Promoting entrepreneurship and innovation. | Higher impact on female workforce. Skill mismatch due to changing job requirements. |
| Improving the Safety of workers engaged in hazardous industrial operations | Widening of income inequality between the high skilled & low-skilled workers. |
| Increased demand for training programs, certifications, & educational initiatives that focus on AI-Related Skills. (Learn, Unlearn and Re-learn) | Dislocation of labour from their home places in search for alternative livelihood opportunity. |

## Steps to prevent the adverse impacts of Automation

- Comprehensive adoption of AI to reap its benefits and challenges. Eg: National strategy for Artificial Intelligence (AI) developed by NITI Aayog.
- Reskilling & Upskilling Programs: Implementation of comprehensive training program which includes promoting digital literacy, data analytics, & other AI related skills.
  - Budget 2023-24 launched PM Kaushal Vikas Yojana 4.0 to impart skill training to the youth according to the needs of Fourth Industrial Revolution.
- Realigning Education System: Expose students to cutting edge technologies like robotics, AI, machine learning, Nano technology, etc. Eg: National Education Policy, 2020 is a step in this direction.
- Social Security Measures for workers affected by AI-driven job displacement which can include unemployment benefits, income support, & healthcare provisions to ensure smooth transitions for affected individuals. Eg: Robot Tax proposed by Bill Gates.
- Encourage entrepreneurship and innovation by providing resources, funding and mentorship to individuals and startups working on AI-related solutions

- Foster collaboration between the government, private sector and civil society organisations to develop AI strategies and policies that prioritize job creation, worker protection and social impact.
- Investment in AI Research and development to advance state of art technologies, encourage innovation and support the growth of AI startups & entrepreneurship. Eg: AIRAWAT (AI Research, Analytics and Knowledge Assimilation Program).

## PYQs Corner

*(Write the Answer and Get Free Evaluation)*

1. Most of the unemployment in India is structural in nature. Examine the methodology adopted to compute unemployment in the country and suggest improvements. [150 Words] [10 Marks] **[2023]**

2. Economic growth in the recent past has been led by increase in labour productivity. Explain this statement. Suggest the growth pattern that will lead to creation of more jobs without compromising labour productivity. [250 Words] [15 Marks] **[2022]**

3. "The incidence and intensity of poverty are more important in determining poverty based on income alone". In this context analyse the latest United Nations Multidimensional Poverty Index Report. [250 Words] [15 Marks] **[2020]**

4. 'Despite implementation of various programmes for eradication of poverty by the government in India, poverty is still existing.' Explain by giving reasons. [150 Words] [10 Marks] **[2018]**

5. 'Poverty Alleviation Programmes in India remain mere show pieces until and unless they are backed by political will'. Discuss with reference to the performance of the major poverty alleviation programmes in India. [250 Words] [15 Marks] **[2017]**

6. "An essential condition to eradicate poverty is to liberate the poor from deprivation." Substantiate this statement with suitable examples. [250 Words] [15 Marks] **[2016]**

7. How globalization has led to the reduction of employment in the formal sector of the Indian economy? Is increased in formalization detrimental to the development of the country? [200 Words] [12.5 Marks] **[2016]**

9. The nature of economic growth in India in recent times is often described as a jobless growth. Do you agree with this view? Give arguments in favour of your answer. [200 Words][12.5 Marks]**[2015]**

10. Though there have been several different estimates of poverty in India, all indicate reduction in poverty levels over time. Do you agree? Critically examine with reference to urban and rural poverty indicators. [200 Words][12.5 Marks]**[2015]**

Edict-5: Mobilisation of Resources

CHAPTER 15

# GOVERNMENT BUDGETING

## FISCAL POLICY

- Fiscal Policy refers to the use of government spending, taxation & borrowing to influence the overall state of the economy.
- It is one of the key tools available to the government to manage economic activity, stabilize the economy and achieve certain macroeconomic objectives.
- Also known as Keynesian economics, this theory basically states that governments can influence macroeconomic productivity levels by increasing or decreasing tax levels and public spending/expenditure.

### Importance of Fiscal Policy

| Promotion of Economic Growth | Ensure Social Justice |
|---|---|
| 1. Infrastructure development which boosts investment enhances productivity & facilitates economic growth.<br>Eg: Capital Expenditure during Interim Budget 2024-25 is 11.11 Lakh crore<br>2. Stimulate private investment through tax incentives, Subsidies and other measures that reduce the cost of investment and promote business expansion.<br>Eg: Launch of PLI Schemes. | 1. Progressive taxation policies which helps in the redistribution of wealth & minimizing income inequality. Eg: Multiple slabs in income tax regime (2023-24)<br>2. Investment in education & healthcare to enhance human capital, improve Social well-being and promote equal opportunities. |

| | |
|---|---|
| 3. Promoting Consumption by individuals. Eg: Increase in tax exemption limit from Rs 2.5 lakh to 3 lakh<br>4. Allocation of resources for research and development activities to foster innovation, technological advancement, and productivity growth.<br>5. Promotion of MSMEs that play a crucial role in job creation, fostering entrepreneurship & driving economic growth.<br>6. Boost Exports. Eg: Foreign Trade Policy, 2023. | 3. Subsidies and Welfare Programs which aims to alleviate poverty, improve access to basic amenities and ensure social inclusion.<br>Eg: The government has pegged total subsidies on food, fertilisers and fuel at ₹5.22 lakh crore in its revised estimate (RE) for FY23.<br>4. Directed towards rural development, agricultural support and employment generation in rural areas.<br>5. Promote financial inclusion by expanding access to banking services, microfinance and affordable credit for marginalised sections of society. |

Is improving the growth performance of the economy and ensuring social justice contradictory?

While the objectives of improving growth and ensuring social justice may have different focus areas, they are not as such contradictory.

- Inclusive growth and equitable distribution of resources can foster sustainable economic development.
- A thriving economy with reduced inequalities can generate more opportunities for all segments of society, leading to social progress and stability.
- Economic Growth can have positive spill over effects on social welfare.
  - It generates tax revenues that can be used to fund social programs, infrastructure development and public services
  - It also provides opportunities for skill development, education & entrepreneurship, contributing to social mobility and improved quality of life.
  - Sustained economic growth can lay the foundation for social welfare
- However, it is important to note that challenges may arise in balancing these objectives:
  - Rapid Economic Growth without adequate attention to social welfare can lead to unequal distribution of wealth, exclusion and social unrest.
  - On other hand, excessive focus on social welfare without supporting economic growth can strain public finances, impact fiscal stability, hinder investment & entrepreneurship and limit resources available for long term sustainable development.

# BUDGETING

- Budget or the annual financial statement is a statement of estimated receipts and expenditures of the government in respect of every financial year
- Budgeting refers to the process of planning, allocating & controlling financial resources by the government for a specific period.
- It is a manifutation of the government's fiscal policy and represents choices, policies and philosophies of the government.
- It enables effective resource utilisation, supports economic growth, and ensures accountability in the allocation and management of public funds.

## Functions of Budget

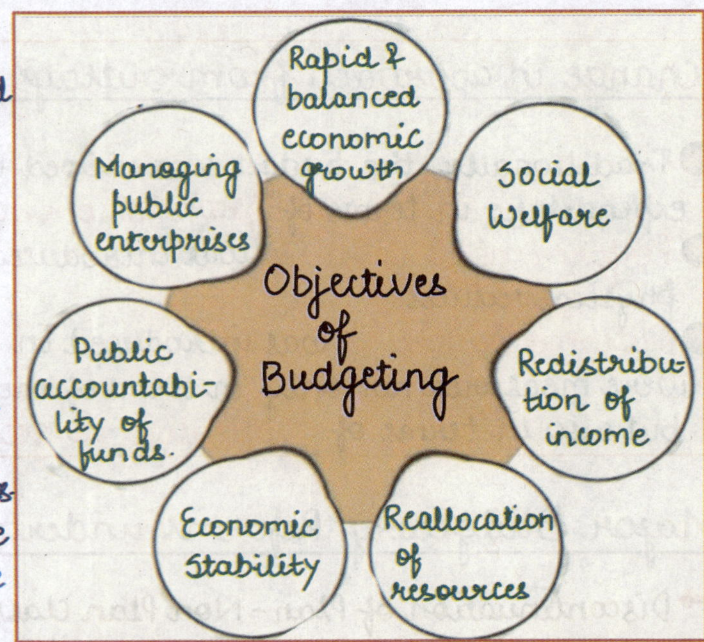


- Instrument of control: Budgets are used to evaluate the progress of various departments. If a department is not on targets, corrective action can be taken.
- Coordination: The budgetary process involves all departments of government and achieve coordination among them.
- Punitive action. Budgets can be used as tools of punitive action by reducing the allocation of under-performing departments
- Change: Budgets can be used to institute change. Eg: A government can introduce incentives like performance-related bonuses to improve employee productivity.
- Redistribution of resources: Budgets can be used to redistribute resources from rich to poor, between regions, between generations, or between workers & non-workers. Eg: Welfare Schemes or Subsidies.
- Public accountability: Budgets serve as a platform for public accountability of funds.

## Evolution of the Budgetary Process in India

- 1968: Ministries started bringing out a Performance Budget.
- 1983: Zero-based budgeting was adopted by the DoST, later made compulsory for all ministries
- 1996: Introduction of Participatory budgeting, first by Kerala Government

- Participatory budgeting allows people to deliberate and negotiate over the distribution of public resources and empowers them to better understand their rights and duties as citizens as well as the responsibilities of government

- 2003: Adoption of FRBM Act.
- 2005: Outcome Budgeting was introduced
- 2007: Inclusion of Gender Based Budgeting.
- 2014: Abolition of Planning Commission was removal of distinction between Plan and Non-Plan expenditure.
- 2016: Merger of Railway and General Budget and advancement of Budget by 1 month.
- 2017: Rationalisation of CSS and their expenditure.

## Change in approach from outlays to output to Outcome budget

- Traditionally, the budget was viewed merely as statement of receipt and expenditure in terms of financial outlays.
- Performance Budgeting was introduced in 1968 that link financial aspect to physical results.
- Outcome Budgeting was introduced in 2005-06 under which expected results were measured not only in terms of monetary units or physical infrastructure but also in terms of qualitative targets and achievements.

## Major Budgetary Reforms undertaken by the Government

- Discontinuation of Plan-Non Plan Classification in Budget 2017-18. Reform put greater emphasis on revenue and capital classification of government expenditure.
  - Economic Survey noted that there was a conception built over the years that plan expenditures were good while non-plans were not, which resulted in skewed budget allocations.
- Merger of Railway Budget with the main Budget in FY18 (Based on recommendations of Bibek Debroy Committee): The initiative looked to facilitate multi-modal transport between railways, highways and inland waterways.
  - The merger exempted Railways from paying dividends to the government Revenues.
  - It allowed the Ministry of Finance to ensure there is a coherent emphasis on capex across sectors in recent times.
- Shifting the date of Budget to February 1 from FY18: Advancing it by a

month paved the way to complete the Budget cycle before the start of next financial year and thus no need for the passage of vote on accounts.

- Ministries can also now plan better and execute schemes from the start of the financial year.

➡ Use of Technology to enhance the efficiency and transparency of budgetary processes. This includes the implementation of online platforms for budget preparation, execution and monitoring.

- The Public Financial Management System (PFMS) facilitates the direct transfer of funds from the central government to various implementing agencies, promoting transparency and reducing delays

➡ Emphasis on Outcome-oriented spending focusing on achieving measurable outcomes and impacts rather than just allocating funds. this encourages accountability and ensures that public resources are utilized effectively.

Eg: Atal Mission for Rejuvenation and Urban Transformation (AMRUT) is an example of outcome-oriented spending.

➡ Rationalization of Subsidies through JAM trinity and DBT transfer. This helps in better targeting of resources and avoiding wastage.

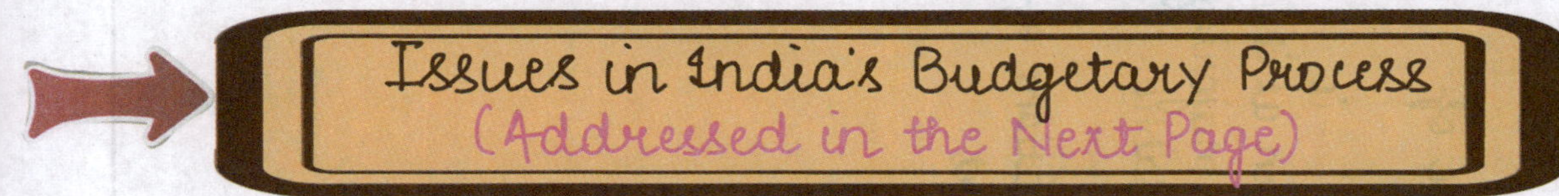


## Reforms Needed to Address Above Weaknesses

- Dealing with issue of Budget credibility through medium term Expenditure Framework facilitating sound macroeconomic forecasts and establishing a Fiscal Council to provide independent assessments of budget proposals.
- Enhancing budget transparency and accountability through steps like publishing a Pre-budgetary statement.
- Rectifying flaws in Gender Budget Statement.
- Establishing an independent Parliamentary Budget Research Office to bridge gap between the policies of the government and aspirations of general public.
- Inclusion of climate-responsive budgeting.

## Issues in India's Budgetary Process

| Budget Formulation | Budget Enactment | Budget Execution | Legislative Review. |
|---|---|---|---|
| Outcome budgeting is yet to emerge as a robust fiscal instrument.<br>Unrealistic budget estimates raises concern of budget credibility.<br>Mainly short-term approach.<br>Issues over credibility of Data.<br>Skewed focus towards revenue expenditure than Capital expenditure.<br>Low share of allocation under Gender Budgeting & other implementation issues.<br>Issues in mainstreaming participatory budgeting such as lack of public awareness, digital divide, lack of Capacity etc<br>Inadequate allocation in critical sectors like health, education etc | Limited discussion and practice of Guillotine.<br>Accountability is number driven as it requires the majority of only Lok Sabha.<br>Non-binding recommendations of DRSCs report. | Ad-hoc projects announcements.<br>Delay in implementation of projects.<br>March rush - skewed expenditure pattern.<br>Compliance with procedures rather than outcomes.<br>Lack of Coordination among multiple departments resulting into increased project cost.<br>Changing course of deficit management due to various FRBM amendments. | Limitations of CAG Audits: Post-Facto Analysis.<br>Limitations of Parliamentary Committees in ensuring accountability such as non-binding reports, lack of expertise etc.<br>Increased passage of Supplementary grants which passes without Scrutiny.<br>Off-Budget borrowings are outside the Scrutiny of the Parliament. |

# ZERO BASED BUDGETING

- **About**: Zero-Based Budgeting (ZBB) departs from the traditional budgeting by requiring each program/scheme to be justified from scratch, regardless of past budgets.
    - It involves a thorough analysis of costs and benefits, prioritizing programs based on their effectiveness and aligning resources accordingly.
- **Focus on efficiency and Necessity**: ZBB enables a disciplined and strategic allocation of resources, eliminating inefficiencies & ensuring funding is prioritized for high-value programs.

## Difference between ZBB and Traditional Budgeting

| Criteria | Traditional Budgeting | Zero-Based Budgeting (ZBB) |
|---|---|---|
| Budgeting Approach | • Uses previous year's budget as base | • Starts from a 'Zero-base' |
| Funding Allocation | • Based on historical budget figure | • Based on programme efficiency and necessity. |
| Budget Justification | • Often relies on incremental change | • Require Justification for all expenses. |
| Resource allocation | • May not align with current priorities | • Prioritizes resources based on Value and goals. |
| Decision-making process | • Often relies on the historical data. | • Involves a thorough analysis of costs and benefits. |
| Accountability | • May lack transparency in the spending | • Promotes fiscal responsibility and accountability |

## Benefits of ZBB

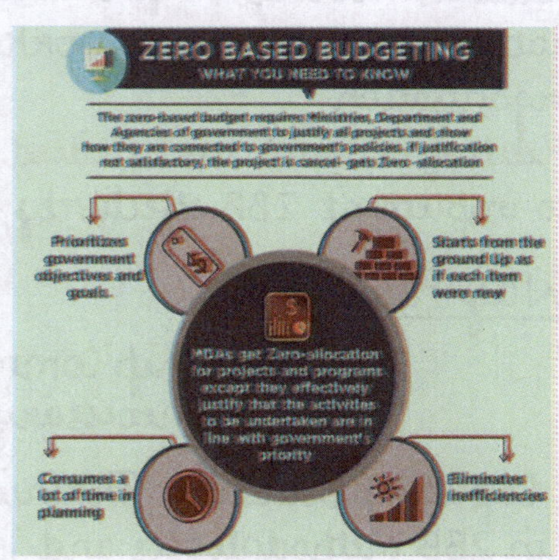


- **Efficiency**: ZBB helps in identifying inefficient or obsolete functions within the area of responsibility and may result in more efficient mechanisms.
- Reallocation of resources from low priority programmes to high priority programmes.
- Facilitate the identification of duplication of efforts among organisational units which result into the elimination of inefficient activities.
- Cost effectiveness as all expenditures, under this System are critically reviewed and Justified.
- Greater participation of personnel in formulation and ranking processes. This helps in promoting the level of Job satisfaction and thus, resulting in better control and operational efficiency in the organisation.

## Implementation of ZBB in India

- While not extensively adopted across all Sectors, there have been instances of ZBB being implemented at various levels of government & in specific organisations
- In India, zero-based budgeting was adopted by Department of Science and Technology in 1983
- In 1986, Indian government implemented zero-based budgeting as a system for determining expenditure budget.
  - The government made it mandatory for all ministries to review their programmes and activities and prepare their expenditure estimations based on zero-based budgeting concept.
- Additionally, some state governments in India have experimented with ZBB to enhance budgeting practices. Eg: Maharashtra, Karnataka etc.
- While the implementation of ZBB in India has not been widespread, these example demonstrate that there have been efforts to introduce this budgeting practice to improve resource allocation, enhance efficiency and prioritize program effectiveness

## Challenges associated in the Implementation of ZBB

- Time consuming and more complicated process as ZBB requires a thorough examination of every single expense.
- Organisational resistance as the adoption of ZBB challenges the past practices, methods, performances, attitudes, habits, etc. of the people working in the organisation
- Lack of Expertise and skilled managers to implement ZBB effectively.

- Data Availability and Accuracy as ZBB relies on accurate and comprehensive data on past expenditures and program effectiveness
- Neglecting long Term investments: The emphasis on justifying every expense can lead to prioritizing short-term cost savings over long term investments.
- Resource Intensive as implementation of ZBB often necessitates additional staff and skilled personnel.

## Way Forward

Leadership Commitment: Strong top-level support to drive necessary changes and overcome resistance

Capacity Building: Training officials in ZBB methodologies and Techniques

Gradual Implementation: Phased approach for learning, refining & modifying processes.

Stakeholder engagement: Encouraging dialogue, solicit feedback, & fostering collaboration.

Monitoring & Evaluation: Robust mechanisms to access impact and identify areas for improvement

# OUTCOME BUDGETING

- **About:** It is an approach to public finance management that focuses on measuring and evaluating the outcomes and impacts of government programs and policies, rather than just tracking inputs and outputs.
  Eg: Instead of measuring number of schools built (an input), Outcome Budgeting would assess the improvement in literacy rates or student performance
- **Purpose:** It ensures that public funds are allocated and utilized efficiently & effectively, leading to better service delivery, informed decision-making, resource optimisation, and enhanced accountability in public finance management.
- Introduced in India in 2005-06 as a revised version of the Performance budget, wherein certain ministries of the government were required to produce Outcome Budget

## Benefits of Outcome Budgeting

- Result Oriented Approach: It shift the focus from expenditure to results i.e specific outcomes and measuring performance against pre-defined goals.
- Improved Transparency and Accountability: By linking spending to desired outcome (Setting of clear targets), outcome budgeting makes it easier to track how effectively resources are used.
- Enables better resource allocation to those programs that have a higher likelihood of achieving desired outcomes.
- Evidence based policy making through continuous monitoring and evaluation of programs.
- Informed decision making and prioritisation of government spending.
- Citizen Centric Approach: Aligns government programs with citizen's needs and aspirations by ensuring that public funds are utilized for programs that address their priorities.

## Challenges for Policymakers

- Outcome Measurement
  - Defining and measuring outcomes can be complex, particularly in a country as diverse as India.
  - Linking specific outcomes to government interventions and policies requires rigorous data collection, monitoring and evaluation mechanisms.
  - Difficult to accurately attribute outcomes to specific government initiatives due to the presence of various contributing factors.
    → Scrutiny of the Outcome Budget for year 2013-14 to 2016-17 by the CAG revealed inconsistency in depicting scheme wise achievements (outcomes) against targets already set in previous year.

→ Audit noted that the Outcome Budget 2013-14 indicated unquantifiable targets like improvement of roads, bridges, drains, construction of market complexes, flyovers etc. but achievements or outcomes were not included in Outcome Budget of the following year i.e. 2014-15.

→ Many Outcome Budgets produced by ministries are in effect are 'Outlay Budgets'.

- Issue of data availability, quality & accuracy particularly at grassroot level.
- Political Pressures to focus on short term results while outcome budgeting requires a long term perspective.
- Behavioural and Cultural Shift: Implementing outcome budgeting requires a significant shift in the mindset and culture of bureaucracy
- Higher resource requirement for data collection, evaluation and monitoring Systems.
- The internal audit System in the ministries is weak in terms of professional expertise and inadequate manpower.
  - Thus, there is lack of independent, objective opinion to add value and improve the operation of Schemes

## Futuristic Measures

- Careful allocation of adequate resources to build the necessary infrastructure and capacity for effective outcome budgeting.
- Citizen engagement and Transparency: Policymakers need to engage citizens, Civil Society organisation and other stakeholders in budgeting process and make outcome data accessible to the public.
- Outcome Budgeting requires a robust institutional framework and coordination among various government department and agencies.
- Strengthening the capacity of government officials involved in outcome budgeting is vital for its successful implementation.
- Development of a robust framework that includes defining clear outcome indicators, setting realistic targets, establishing monitoring and evaluation mechanisms, enhancing data collection and analysis capacities and promoting a culture of evidence-based decision-making.

### Best Practice

- The Delhi government's Outcome Budget for 2017-18 shifts the bar for transparency and accountability in public spending to a new level.

# GENDER BUDGETING

## Need of Gender Budgeting

- Budget 2005-06 was very significant for women in the country, as for the first time the 'Gender Responsive Budgeting' was adopted.
- GRB is a method of planning, programming and budgeting that helps advance gender equality and women's rights.
- It is not an accounting exercise but an ongoing process of keeping a gender perspective in policy/programme formulation, its implementation and review.
- GB entails dissection of the Government budgets to establish its gender differential impacts and to ensure that gender commitments are translated in budgetary commitments.
- Rationale for Gender Budgeting: Recognition of the fact that national budgets impact men and women differently through pattern of resource allocation.
  - Women, constitute 48% of India's population, but they lag behind men on many social indicators like health, education, economic opportunities etc & therefore, warrant special attention due to their vulnerability & lack of access to resources.
- It allows gender specific grant allocations in various schemes. Eg: Schemes like Start-up India and Stand-Up India.
- Gender Sensitive plans: Gender responsive budget policies can contribute to achieve the objectives of gender equality, human development and economic efficiency.
- It is a powerful tool for achieving gender mainstreaming so as to ensure that benefits of development reach women as much as men.

## Evolution of Gender Budgeting in India

| 2001 - 2004 | 2005 - 2007 | 2007-2010 | 2010 - 2012 | 2012-2013 |
|---|---|---|---|---|
| Gender based analysis of Union and selected state budgets | Gender budget statement part of Exependiture budget | Charter on Gender budget cells issued | Integration of gender and outcome budget | Guidelines for State level gender budgeting issued |
| Note on gender budgeting issued as part of budget cicular from 2005-06 onwards | (i) women specific schemes (ii) pro-women schemes | Build capacity for gender budgeting at Central and State level line ministries | Targets / sub-targets for women to be included in outcome budgets | State level gender budget cells should also be set up |

• Since 2005-06, the Expenditure Division of the Ministry of Finance has been issuing a note on Gender Budgeting as a part of Budget Circular every year.

• This GB statement comprises two parts – Part A and Part B.

  • Part A reflects women specific schemes, i.e. those which have 100% allocation for women.

  • Part B reflects Pro Women Schemes, i.e. those where at least 30% of the allocation is for women.

• According to an IMF study, there are over 16 Indian states that have adopted gender-based budgeting, which is a good achievement.

• There are gender budgeting cells formed under 56 government departments/ministries to identify gender related goals & the approach to achieve them

• Ministry of Women and Child Development has also come up with guidelines for integrating gender budgeting into beneficiary-oriented schemes.

## Challenges

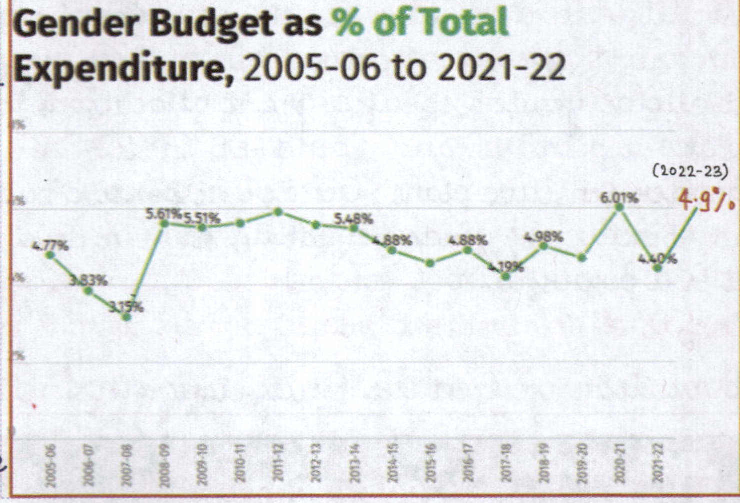


➔ Insufficient allocation on gender budget as a proportion of total expenditure of the Union Budget.

➔ Un-utilisation of Gender Budget: There are only a few "big budget" women exclusive schemes of Ministry of Women and Child Development (MWCD) like the Nirbhaya Fund & Beti Bachao Beti Padhao campaign.

➔ Concentrated in few sectors: Over the last decade, four ministries – Rural Development, Education, Health and Women & Child Development have received between 85-90% of Gender Budget expenditure this limits adoption of more holistic approach.

➔ Lack of Political Will and Resources for implementing gender budgeting effectively.

➔ Lack of Impact Assessment: Though it is mandatory to release the Gender Budget Statement (GBS), there are no accountability mechanisms mandating impact assessment of allocation for women beneficiaries.

  • Inadequate data hampers policy making as well as impedes impact study for analysis of outcomes.

➔ Inconsistent state-Specific approach: About 16 states in India currently undertake gender budgeting; however the quality of statements produced and allocation undertaken vary significantly among states, due to inadequate training of government officials.

→ Lack of dedicated human resources to implement interventions identified by Gender Budgeting Cells (GBCs)

→ Very little information is available in the public domain.

## Futuristic Measures

- Increase allocation for women focused Programmes: Despite an ambitious roadmap and MWCD's commitment to GRB at national level, the central government's gender budget has never been more than 1% of India's GDP.
- Improve targeting towards priority sectors which suffers from deepest gender inequalities.
- Ranking of States on the quality of gender budgets, impact analysis, & gender audits of these allocations akin to the ease of doing business.
- An Authority should be created for gender auditing, to conduct an annual impact impact assessment of budgetary allocations for all schemes, thus bringing accountability to the process.
- Capacity building across governments, corporates, public sector undertakings, NGOs and all involved agencies.
- National-Level Reporting Platform should be created under Ministry of Statistics and Programme Implementation, which will collect the disaggregated data by sex for understanding the impact and outcome of the gender budgeting initiative.

# EFFECTIVENESS OF FRBM ACT

- Fiscal Responsibility and Budget Management (FRBM) Act, 2003 was enacted to bring financial discipline in government spending.
- Key objectives of the Act:
  - Reduce Fiscal Deficit: It prescribes limit on fiscal deficit of 3% of GDP for central governments.
  - Enhance Transparency: Mandating the presentation of various fiscal documents alongside the Union Budget: Medium-Term Fiscal Policy Statement, Macro-economic Framework Statement, Fiscal Policy Strategy Statement.
  - Ensure long term macro-economic stability.
  - Intergenerational equity in fiscal management by preventing excessive debt burdens from being passed on to future generations.

## Reason for the introduction of FRBM Act

It was enacted in 2003 as rising government borrowing & the resultant government debt have seriously eroded the financial health of government.

- High revenue deficit due to higher expenditure on subsidies, salaries, defence etc. compelled the government to make big borrowing from early 1990s onwards.
- With inadequate revenues, government resorted to high level of borrowing. The borrowing again produced high interest payments. In this way, interest payments became the largest expenditure item of the governments.
- To arrest this financial weakness in its budget, the government has taken some serious deficit cut targets by introducing a law in form of the FRBM.

## Assessment of FRBM

- There was an improvement in the fiscal performance of both Center and States because of the implementation of the FRBM Act.
- States achieved the targets much ahead of the prescribed timeline. The Central Government was also on the right path of achieving this objective in the right time.
- However due to global financial crisis, this was suspended and consequently, the fiscal consolidation as mandated in the FRBM Act was put on hold in 2007-08.
  - This crisis period called for increased level of expenditure by government to boost demand in the economy. As a result of fiscal stimulus, the government has moved away from the path of fiscal consolidation.
- FRBM Act got amended in 2012 titled as FRBM 2.0 which brought new targets of fiscal deficit and aimed for elimination of effective revenue deficit. Post this government moved to the path of fiscal consolidation till 2018-19.
- With the COVID-19 pandemic impact on the economy and to undertake higher expenditure to give a boost to the economy, government announced 20 lakh crore stimulus package which led to a higher fiscal deficit much above than the targets.
- While FRBM Act has maintained some kind of financial discipline, there were two major instances → 2008-09 & 2020-21 where governments moved away from the path of fiscal consolidation because of boosting higher economic growth.

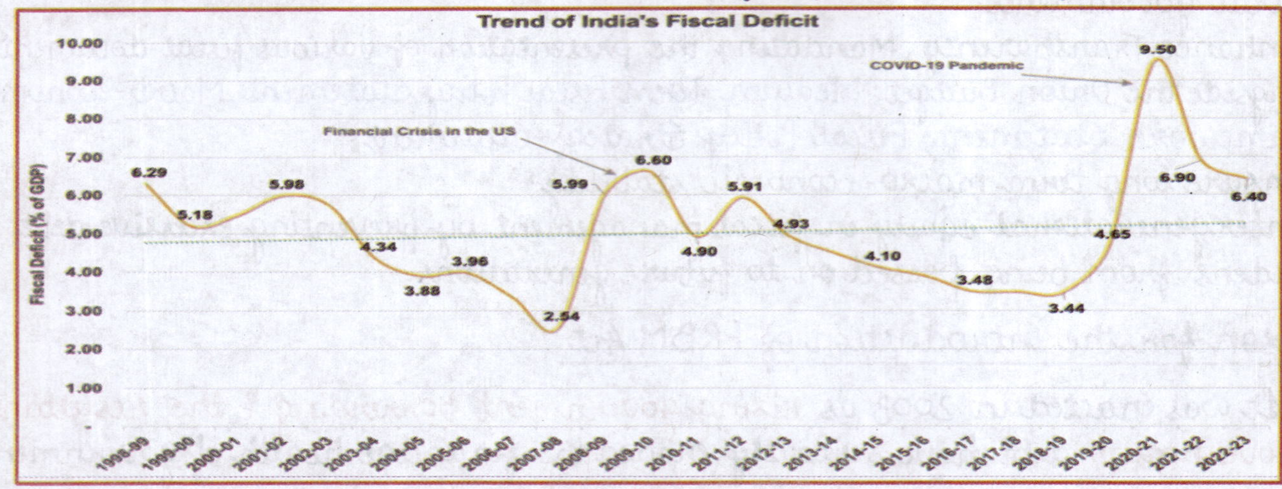

## Following are the possible implications of high Fiscal Deficit

1. High FD Could lead to higher inflation because of Increased government expenditure
2. High FD requires higher borrowings which could lead to higher interest cost and thus creating a vicious cycle leading to debt trap.
3. This involves the payment of principal and interest by the future generations thus transferring the burden on future generations.
4. High deficit can lead to crowding out of private investment.

## Issues in the FRBM Act

- **Undemocratic in its approach** as it denied freedom to future governments in respect of fiscal management.
  - Its aim was to bind future governments to a pre-specified fiscal policy framework which was in a way an anti-democratic measure.
- **Curb spending ability** especially on Social Sector expenditures on important segment like health and education. It also led to low levels of capital expenditure which can hamper economic growth and social progress.
- **Off-budget borrowings** are not accounted within the FD which disrupts entire purpose of the Act.
  - Solution: Optimize off-budget borrowings to a minimum, as these routes of funds are outside the Scrutiny of Parliament.
- **Escape Clause**: Frequent use can undermine the Act's effectiveness and make it difficult to achieve long term fiscal discipline.
- The Act might be **too rigid in its approach**, hindering the government's ability to respond to changing economic Situations.
  - Solution: More flexible framework is needed that allows for targeted spending during economic slowdowns (Cyclical nature of economy).
- The FRBM Act did not address the **problem of financing public expenditure** in a Serious manner.
  - Solution: FRBM Act could have provided for raising tax-GDP by making improvement in tax administration and collections & effective measures to rein in tax evasion.
- **No Independent agency** for giving fiscal forecasts & monitoring of fiscal targets.
  - Solution: Constitution of a fiscal council, as per the recommendations of N.K.Singh Committee and various finance commissions.
- **Focus on Deficit** but doesn't explicitly address the issue of overall government debt. High debt levels can still pose risks even with a lower deficit.
  - Solution: N.K.Singh Committee recommended Public debt to GDP ratio as the medium term anchor for fiscal policy in India.

- The Committee also recommended the enactment of a new 'Debt and Fiscal Responsibility Act' after repealing the existing Act.

➡ Lack of enforcement mechanism to penalize non-compliance. This can weaken its effectiveness if governments are not held accountable for exceeding deficit targets.

# FISCAL COUNCIL

- Fiscal councils are independent public institutions aimed at strengthening commitments to sustainable public finances through public assessment of fiscal plans and performance, evaluation and provision of macroeconomic & budgetary forecasts.
- The institution assist in caliberating sustainable fiscal policy by making an objective and scientific analysis.
- Fiscal councils can serve both ex-ante and ex-post functions such as:
  - Producing independent forecasts related to GDP growth, tax buoyancy, inflation rate.
  - Review the government's forecasts and assumptions related to tax collections, Fiscal Deficit, GDP growth etc (an ex-ante function)
  - Monitoring governments' fiscal performance including adherence

## Need Of Fiscal Council

➡ Mismanaged budgets: Historically budgets in India have consistently overestimated revenue growth and underestimated expenditure growth.
- Fiscal council will provide more accurate forecasts related to various parameters such as GDP, Tax Collection, Deficits etc.
- This is unlike the institutions like CAG which does post-facto analysis.

➡ Enhance the effectiveness of FRBM process & monitor adherence to fiscal rules.
- Case studies by IMF and OECD has confirmed that independent fiscal institutions effectively complement fiscal rules in monitoring their effective implementation and have contributed to improved fiscal performances.

➡ Provide a check on borrowing: Article 293(3) provides a constitutional check on borrowings of the state but there is no check on union govt. borrowings.
- Fiscal council will provide an annual assessment of overall public sector borrowing requirements & can also address the problem of off-budget borrowing.

➡ Independent and objective report can raise the level of debate and brings greater transparency and accountability of the government to the Parliament.

➡ Commission recommendations such as 15th Finance commission & N.K. Singh Committee.

• 15th FC stated that the absence of an Independent fiscal institution to assess and evaluate the fiscal plan as well as performance and forecasts published by governments has further diminished the capacity to monitor compliance.

➪ **International Experience:** 40+ developed and emerging market economies have found it necessary to have such an institution.

- Congressional Budget office in the US, office of Budget Responsibility in UK, Parliamentary Budget Office in Australia.

➪ **Discourage Populist Shift** of Government Expenditure and improve objectivity.

➪ **Promotes Co-ordination** among multiple agencies of government to provide harmonised fiscal statistics across government levels.

## Possible Functions of the Fiscal Council (Listed by 15th FC)

- Evaluating fiscal performances vis-a-vis targets across all levels of government
- Policy costing of new measures with significant fiscal implications.
- Providing multi year macro-economic & fiscal forecasts.
- Assessing appropriateness, consistency of fiscal targets in states
- Undertaking an independent assessment of long term fiscal sustainability.
- Assessing fiscal policy statements by government under fiscal responsibility legislations.
- Advising on the conditions for using escape clauses under fiscal responsibility legislations.

## Conclusion

- Fiscal Council bring an additional layer of legislative scrutiny, raise public awareness about their fiscal implications and makes the system more transparent and comprehensive

# TAX-GDP RATIO

- Tax-GDP ratio represents the size of the government's tax revenue expressed as a percentage of the GDP.
- While the ratio determines the extent to which the government is able to finance its expenditure from tax collections, it is also an indicator of tax compliance.
- Developed countries have a higher contribution of tax to their GDP.
- India's tax-GDP ratio has remained around 11% since many years which is lesser than the desirable target of 23% (this is the average of emerging economies) and much lower than OECD average of 34%.

## Reason for India's low Tax-to-GDP ratio

→ Low tax Base

- The exemption threshold of income tax has been consistently raised, much rapidly than underlying income growth. Eg: Budget 2023-24 raised the exemption limit of income tax from Rs 2.5 lakh to Rs 3 lakh.
- Various tax incentives such as tax exemption, tax cuts, preferential tax rates etc has led to large tax collection expenditure.

> - Ministry of Finance revealed that number of people who filed income tax returns stood at 6.0 crore in 2020-21. This means that only 4.8% of total population filed IT returns in 2021.
> - Of these, only 1.69 crore paid tax since 65% of the taxpayers earned less than Rs 5 lakh. So effectively, only 1.2% of population pays income tax as of now.

→ Structural Issues

- High cash, informal Economy: India is an informal economy (50% of GDP) with high cash in circulation (14.6% of GDP), which is difficult to track
  - Untraced transactions through illegal channels such as Hawala, lead to generation of black money and tax evasion
- Agriculture income is not taxed which employs maximum workforce. This results in a narrow tax base which is heavily reliant on other sectors of economy.
- Low participation of women in the workforce. (Around 37% as per PLFS 2022-23)

→ Tax Evasion

- Public distrust due to poor public service delivery, ineffective governance, corruption, etc. have created distrust on government resulting into the low willingness to pay taxes in India
- Corruption: lack of accountability, procedural loopholes and mild punishment can be cited as reasons for such corruption.

• Black Money which is generated from illegitimate sources is completely out of the tax system.

→ Weak Tax Administration is considered a key barrier to effective and fair tax collection in the country.

• Lack of technical expertise and lack of resources has reduced administrative capacity especially at state and local levels (Economic Survey, 2020 has highlighted that local bodies are not collecting property taxes adequately)

→ Lingering of contentious, adversarial tax issues: India has one of the highest number of disputes between tax administration and taxpayers, with lowest proportion of recovery of tax arrears.

Eg: Vodafone tax disputes involving Rs 20K crore lingered for more than 10 years

→ Loopholes in Double Tax Avoidance Agreements (DTAA) are often misused by the companies to re-route their investments (Called round tripping of funds)

Eg: Provisions for tax exemption from short term capital gains.

## Advantages of the Direct Tax Reforms

- Provide level playing field between large businesses and start-ups and young companies
- Widening of Tax Base → Increases the government revenue
- Attracts Foreign Investment
- Reduction of direct tax litigation → Reduced burden on judiciary and the government
- Reduced Base erosion and Profit shifting → Higher government revenue & reduced international arbitration
- Catalyst to Inclusive Growth
- Increases Ease of Doing Business (EoDB)

## Steps taken by the Government to boost Tax-GDP Ratio

1. Formalisation of the Economy. Eg- GST, Demonetisation & Increased Digitalisation.
2. Push to Digital Payments. Eg - UPI, Digital Rupee.
3. Increased Financial Inclusion. Eg - PMJDY, National Financial Inclusion Strategy
4. Measures taken to tackle Black Money. Eg - Voluntary Disclosure Scheme, Black Money (Undisclosed Foreign Income and Assets) Act (2015).
5. India agreed to a Global Minimum Corporate Tax.
6. Faceless Assessment Scheme ensures transparency, efficiency & accountability in income tax assessments by eliminating the human interface between the taxpayer and the income tax department.
7. Scrapping of Restrospective Taxation.

## Measures to Improve Tax-GDP ratio

- Simplified tax structure with optimum number of taxes, optimum tax rates, low concessions etc
  - Implementation of Direct Tax Code that will replace the income the Income Tax Act, 1961 (Akhilesh Ranjan Committee)
- Reduced tax litigation by reducing the discretionary power of tax department.
- Higher formalisation and digitalisation of the economy can increase tax base. Simplification of tax laws to make compliance easier.
- Bringing agricultural income into the tax net by setting a minimum threshold and by incentivising farmers to report their income.
- Fast Tracking of Disputes: Fast tracking of tax disputes, reducing discretion of taxman & creating a predictable dispute resolution mechanisms.
- Simplification of Direct Tax on cross border transactions to reduce base erosion and profit shifting & indirect transfers (Arbind Modi Panel on Income tax Returns).
- Need of Technology infusion in tax administration to improve efficiency of tax collection.

  Eg: Use of technologies like AI & Big Data analytics for analyzing databases

# BLACK MONEY

- Black Money refers to money that is not fully legitimate in the hands of the owner. It is mostly hidden from tax authorities. The source of black money can be legal or illegal
- Finance Ministry (2014): About 90% of unaccounted wealth, or black money, was lying within India and not outside
- Income Tax Department has detected total undisclosed credits worth Rs 20,353 Cr for 930 India-linked entities in the Panama and Paradise paper leak.

## Factors behind the generation of black money in India

- Tax Evasion (Significant Contributor to black money generation in India): Accounts for approximately 20-30% of India's GDP, resulting in substantial amount of unaccounted wealth (National Institute of Public Finance and Policy (NIPFP))
- Corruption: The corrupt practices, such as bribery and embezzlement, result in the accumulation of unaccounted wealth
- Parallel Economy where economic activities are conducted outside purview of legal regulations.

• According to a report by National Council of Applied Economic Research (NCAER), the size of parallel economy in India was estimated to be around 45% of GDP in 2017-18.

➜ Cash-Based Transactions: Cash-based transactions, particularly in sectors such as real estate and small businesses, facilitate the generation of black money

• Currently in circulation in India increased from around 8% of the GDP in 2000 to approximately 12% of GDP in 2020, indicating a significant reliance on cash transactions (RBI report).

➜ Illicit Activities such as smuggling, drug trafficking and illicit trade.

➜ Hawala Transactions, an informal and unregulated system of money transfer, also contribute to black money generation.

➜ Real Estate Sector: Around 30% of total value of real estate transactions in major Indian cities is conducted through unaccounted cash.

➜ Offshore Accounts and Tax Havens: Panama paper leak revealed the involvement of Indian individuals and entities in offshore tax evasion schemes.

## Efforts taken to curb Black Money

| POLICY & LEGISLATIVE MEASURES | ➜ Income declaration scheme and Pradhan Mantri Garib Kalyan Yojana: An amnesty scheme to encourage voluntary disclosure of black money and avoid prosecution after paying a fine of 50% on the undisclosed income.<br>➜ Prevention of Money Laundering Act (2002): Crack down on money laundering methods (hawala, shell companies)<br>➜ Benami Transaction Prohibition Act (1988): Ban anonymous property ownership<br>➜ Black Money (Undisclosed Foreign Income and Assets) Act (2015): Encourage disclosure of foreign black money.<br>➜ Demonetisation of Rs 500 and Rs 1000 was carried with the primary view of making black money useless. |
|---|---|

| INSTITUTIONAL MEASURES | ➜ Central Board of Direct Taxes (CBDT): Responsible for enforcing direct tax laws and tackling black money.<br>➜ Enforcement Directorate (ED): Investigates and prosecutes money laundering cases<br>➜ Financial Intelligence Unit (FIU): Coordinates efforts against terrorism financing, a major use of black money.<br>➜ Directorate of Revenue Intelligence (DRI): India's chief anti smuggling agency |
|---|---|

| INTERNATIONAL MEASURES | |
|---|---|
| | ➡ G20 Initiatives: Promotes automatic exchange of tax information & combat tax base erosion and profit shifting.<br>➡ Adoption of Global Minimum Corporate Tax Deal.<br>➡ DTAA Amendments: India-Mauritius and India-Singapore tax treaties amended to adopt source-based taxation of capital gains with a view to help curb tax evasion and tax avoidance. |

| Measures that can be taken to address the menace of black money in India | ➡ | Some Government Initiatives |
|---|---|---|
| • Strengthening of tax administration | ➡ | • Faceless E-Assessment Scheme, PAN-Aadhar interchangeability. |
| • Promotion of Digital Economy & reducing the dependence on cash transactions | ➡ | • Digital India, PMJDY, UPI, etc. |
| • Implementing Stricter Anti-corruption measures | ➡ | • Prevention of Corruption Act, CVC, CBI, etc |
| • Increased Transparency in Real Estate | ➡ | • Real Estate (Regulation and Development) Act (RERA). |
| • Strengthening Financial Intelligence units that can track and investigate suspicious financial transactions associated with black money | ➡ | • FIU-IND gather and analyse financial intelligence and share it with law enforcement agencies for further action |
| • International Cooperation to exchange tax info., track illicit financial flows and recover assets held abroad | ➡ | • Global Minimum Corporate Tax |
| • Strengthening of whistleblower protection by encouraging individuals to report cases of black money generation | ➡ | • Whistleblower Protection Act, 2014 |

# DISINVESTMENT

- Disinvestment is defined as the action of a government aimed at selling or liquidating its shareholding in a public sector enterprise in order to get the government out of the business of production and increase its presence and performance in the provision of public goods and basic public services such as infrastructure, health, education etc.
- There are mainly three types of Disinvestment:

Increased Privatisation →

| Criteria | Minority / Token Disinvestment | Majority / Strategic Disinvestment | Complete Privatisation |
|---|---|---|---|
| Ownership | Government > 51% | Government < 50% | Government = 0% |
| Government Voting Power | Majority of Voting power | Does not have majority voting power | None |
| Management Control | Government | Not to Government (Private Control) | Not to Government |
| Example | LIC 'IPO' | Hindustan Zinc limited | Air India |

- Strategic Disinvestment is defined as the sale of a substantial portion of the government's shareholding of a CPSE of upto 50% or higher along with the transfer of management control.

## Objective and Merits of Disinvestment

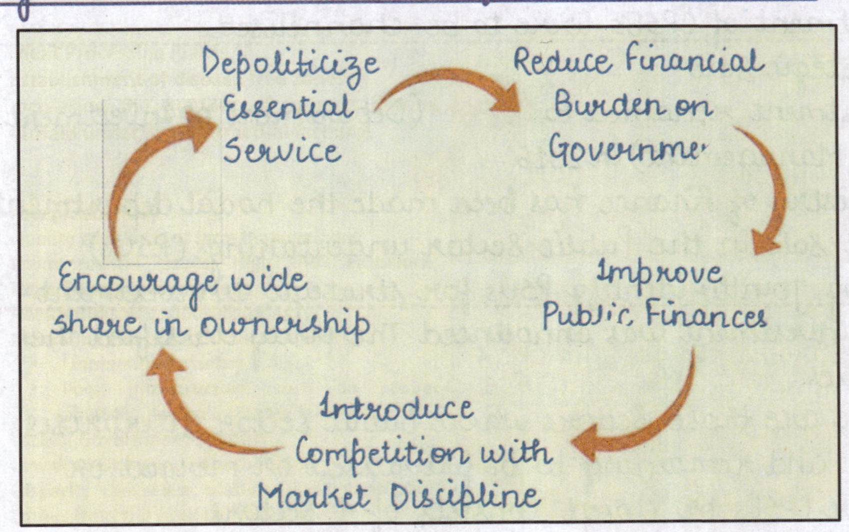


Reduce the Fiscal Deficit

Introduce New Management

Faster realization Value

Introduce Capital for the Company

- Reduce the burden on the government through the disinvestment of loss-making PSUs.
- Quick decision making linked with the competitive market changes

- Better Corporate Governance, exposure to competitive corporate responsibility, improvement in the work environment, etc.
- Market participation in the capital of PSUs through stock exchanges would enable the market to discover the latent worth of PSUs.
- Better Revival opportunities for loss making PSUs by asking the strategic partner to infuse fresh capital and exercising excellent management control over sick PSUs.

## Evolution of Disinvestment Policy

**1947**
- For the first four decades after Independence, India pursued a path of development in which public sector was expected to be engine of growth. (Reservation for public sector, compulsory licensing for private sector)

**1991**
- Liberalisation reforms undertaken in 1991 ushered in an increased demand for Privatisation/Disinvestment of PSUs.
- Focus on Minority/token disinvestment.

**1999-2000**
- Adoption of Strategic Sale.
- Department of Disinvestment was set up as a separate department in 1999 and was later named as Ministry of Disinvestment in 2001.

**2004-05**
- Radical departure from strategic sale
- It was decided that government may dilute its equity and raise resources to meet the social needs of the people.
- Department of Disinvestment was brought under Ministry of Finance.
- Government constituted 'National Investment Fund' in 2005, into which the proceeds from disinvestment of CPSEs were to be channelised.

**2014**
- Renewed push to strategic sale.
- Department of Disinvestment renamed to DIPAM (Department of Investment and Public Sector Asset Management) in 2016.
- DIPAM under the Ministry of Finance has been made the nodal department for the strategic stake sale in the Public sector undertakings (PSUs).
- DIPAM and NITI Aayog jointly identify PSUs for strategic disinvestment.

**2021-22**
- Policy on Strategic disinvestment was announced. The policy classified the sector into two categories:

1. Strategic Sectors: These are those sectors where public sector enterprises will be bare minimum and remaining to be privatised or merged or subsidiarised with other CPSEs or closed. Consists of 4 sectors.

i. Atomic Energy, Space and Defense ii. Transport and Telecommunications
ii. Power, Petroleum, Coal & other minerals iv. Banking, Insurance & Financial Services

2. Non-Strategic Sector: In this sector, CPSEs will be privatised, otherwise shall be closed.

## Rationale behind Strategic Sale in the recent past

- **Changing role of the Government (From Producer to Facilitator):** Strategic disinvestment is guided by the basic economic principle that Government should discontinue its engagement in manufacturing/ producing goods and services in sectors where competitive markets have come of age.
- Economic potential of PSUs may be better discovered in the hands of strategic investors due to various factors - infusion of capital, technology upgradation, better accountability and efficient management practices etc.
  - This would have a multiplier effect on other sectors of the economy.
- Additional source of income for the government which can bring down high fiscal deficit.
- **Impact of Privatisation:** Economic Survey 2019-20 based on comparative analysis of the before-after performance of 11 CPSEs that had undergone strategic disinvestment from 1999-2000 to 2003-04 observed that net worth, net profit, return on assets (ROA), Return on Equity (ROE), gross revenue, net profit margin, sales growth and gross profit per employee of the privatised CPSEs, on an average, have improved significantly in the past privatisation period compared to the peer firms.
  - The financial performance of many PSUs has improved drastically in many cases
    Eg: Hindustan Zinc saw its net profit shoot up from Rs 67 crore at the time of its sale in FY03 to Rs 9,698 Cr in FY19

## Missing Disinvestment Targets

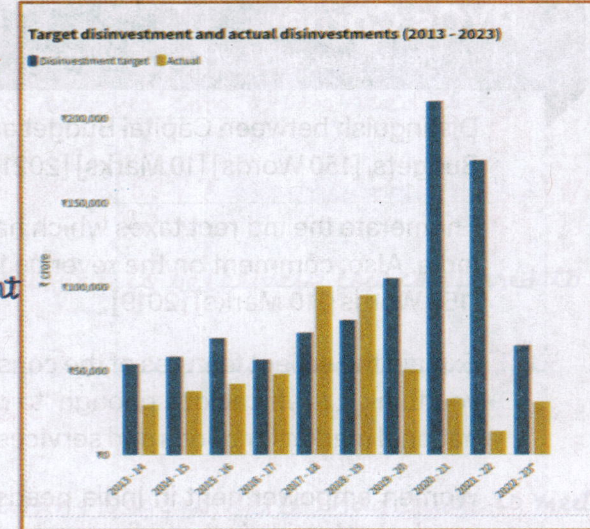


- While disinvestment targets have become aggressive, actual receipts have fallen short of the targets due to the following reasons:
- **Widening gap of estimates and revenue mobilization:** Since 2010, barring two years (2017-18 and 2018-19), the central government's actual receipts from disinvestment have consistently fallen short of the budget estimates.

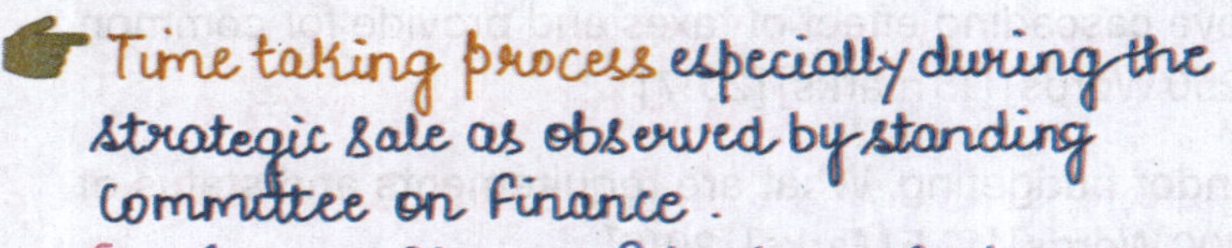

- **Time taking process** especially during the strategic sale as observed by standing Committee on Finance.
  Eg: Sale of Bharat Petroleum Corporation Limited (BPCL), approved in November 2019, is yet to be concluded.
- The strategic sale in many firms was called off due to a lack of bidders and lapses in the bidding processes.

- **Weak market Conditions** put the government on the backfoot for conducting share sale.
- **Poor participation** especially in the loss making units.
- Over the years, the policy of disinvestment has increasingly become a tool to raise resources in covering the fiscal deficit with little focus on market discipline or strategic objective.
- **labour Union protest** as disinvestment may lead to retrenchment of workers will be deprived of their livelihood.

### learning from the Privatisation Model of Singapore (Temasek Holdings Ltd.)

The government can transfer its stake in the listed CPSEs to a **separate corporate entity**.

- The entity would be managed by an **independent board** and would be mandated to divest the government stake in these CPSEs over a period of time.
- This will lend **professionalism and autonomy** to the disinvestment programme which, in turn, would improve the **economic performance** of the CPSEs

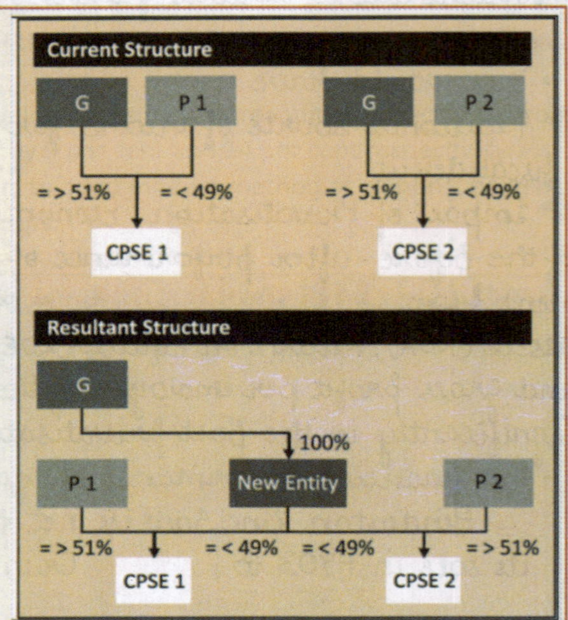


## PYQs Corner
*(Write the Answer and Get Free Evaluation)*

1. Distinguish between Capital Budget and Revenue Budget. Explain the components of both these Budgets. [150 Words] [10 Marks] [2021]
2. Enumerate the indirect taxes which have been subsumed in the goods and services tax (GST) in India. Also, comment on the revenue implications of the GST introduced in India since July 2017. [150 Words] [10 Marks] [2019]
3. Explain the salient features of the constitution(One Hundred and First Amendment) Act, 2016. Do you think it is efficacious enough 'to remove cascading effect of taxes and provide for common national market for goods and services'? [250 Words] [15 marks] [2017]
4. Women empowerment in India needs gender budgeting. What are requirements and status of gender budgeting in the Indian context? [200 Words] [12.5 Marks] [2016]
5. What were the reasons for the introduction of Fiscal Responsibility and Budget Management (FRBM) Act, 2003? Discuss critically its salient features and their effectiveness.[200 Words] [10 Marks][2013]

# CHAPTER 16 SPACE TECHNOLOGY

## SPACE TECHNOLOGY

- Space exploration is the discovery of celestial structures and phenomena in outer space by means of continuously evolving space technology and astronomical science.
- Early Era of Space Exploration was driven by a "Space War" between Soviet Union and United States.
- Space tech industry involves the development and application of technology for activities related to outer space, including satellite communication, exploration and space travel. It encompasses design, manufacturing and operation of spacecraft, satellites and other equipment used in space missions and applications.

| Snapshot of SpaceTech Industry | | | | |
|---|---|---|---|---|
| The global space industry was valued at USD 386 Bn in 2021 and is expected to grow to about USD 1 Trillion by 2040 | | | | |
| India occupies a meagre 2% of global market value. | India has potential to capture 9% of global market share by 2030 | India boasts world's 8th largest fleet of operational satellites. | From 1999 to 2022, 381 satellites from different countries have been launched from India. | **Application-wise Split of Indian Spacecrafts Launched by ISRO**<br>Earth Observation 40%<br>Communication 32%<br>Experiemental 12%<br>Navigation 11%<br>Planetary Observation and Space Science 5% |

## INDIAN SPACE RESEARCH PROGRAMME (ISRP)

- Driven by the vision of Dr. Vikram Sarabhai, ISRP aims to promote development and applications of space science and technology for National Development including socio-economic benefits with 2 important objectives :-
  1) Utilise outer space for peaceful purposes.
  2) Establish operational space services in a self reliant manner. E.g., Indigenous Space Launch Tech.

## Application of Space Technology

| End users | Application |
|---|---|
| Broadcasting | • Drivers: Today, there are 898 satellite TV channels, 7 DTH catering to ~101 Mn households.<br>• Increasing adaptation of entertainment services in rural areas.<br>• Extending satellite bandwidth to OTT players has the potential to increase the market size.<br>• Emerging Use-Cases: Ultra High Definition Broadcasting, Video on Demand Services, Integration with smart appliances, Personalized content streaming etc. |
| Disaster Management | • Disaster Response Management: In the event of floods, earthquakes, landslides, forest fires, droughts or cyclones and tsunamis, satellite imagery has been used to coordinate relief efforts and assess damages to property and lives.<br>• Emerging Use-Cases: Predicting forest fires, Snow cap/glaciers melting rate, Riverbank monitoring for flood prediction etc. |
| Infrastructure | • Terrain Mapping, Topographic Survey and Planning: driving initiatives such as Gati-Shakti can boost the effectiveness of the capital expenditure.<br>• This can aid in the better planning of roads, ports, industrial zones, power grids etc.<br>• Emerging Use Cases: Asset utilisation monitoring. Satellite image based Building Construction Information Model, etc. |
| Maritime | • Cargo: With ~95% of India's Merchandise trade being conducted through its ports; cargo emerges as an important and significant use case within maritime sector in India.<br>• Emerging Use Cases: Remote ship diagnostics, Integrated Fleet management, Autonomous Ship Navigation etc. |

| | |
|---|---|
| Agriculture | • Focus Area: Earth observation for crop insurance and monitoring for horticulture have a market potential of USD 1-35 billion over the next 5 years.<br>◦ With PM Fasal Bima Yojana. Government of India aims to increase the insurance penetration.<br>• Other areas: Integrated watershed management, Irrigation Management, Soil Mapping etc. |

## Space Technology as a Tool to Achieve Sustainable Development Goals (SDGs)

1) Earth Imaging Satellites:

- Goal 2: Ending Hunger: Satellite Imagery can estimate crop yield on a pixel-by-pixel basis - enabling farmers to better decide when to add water or fertiliser or when to harvest.
- Goal 6: Clean Water: Satellite images enable broad and efficient monitoring of reservoir water levels, providing early warnings of shortages that enables optimal usage.
- Goal 13: Climate Action: Often the earliest and clearest indications of climate change can be observed in very remote regions of the world.
- Goal 14: Life Below Water - Satellites can help track and stop illegal fishing by pairing vessel Automatic Identification System (AIS transponders)

2) Communication Satellites:

- Goal 3 and 4: Good Health and Well Being and Quality Education - Just 50% of Earth's 7.5 billion people have access to internet. A global network of communication satellites could enable internet connectivity to a clear majority of people.
  - With access to internet comes increased knowledge sharing, the benefits of best doctors & teachers via tele-medicine and digital and online education among others.

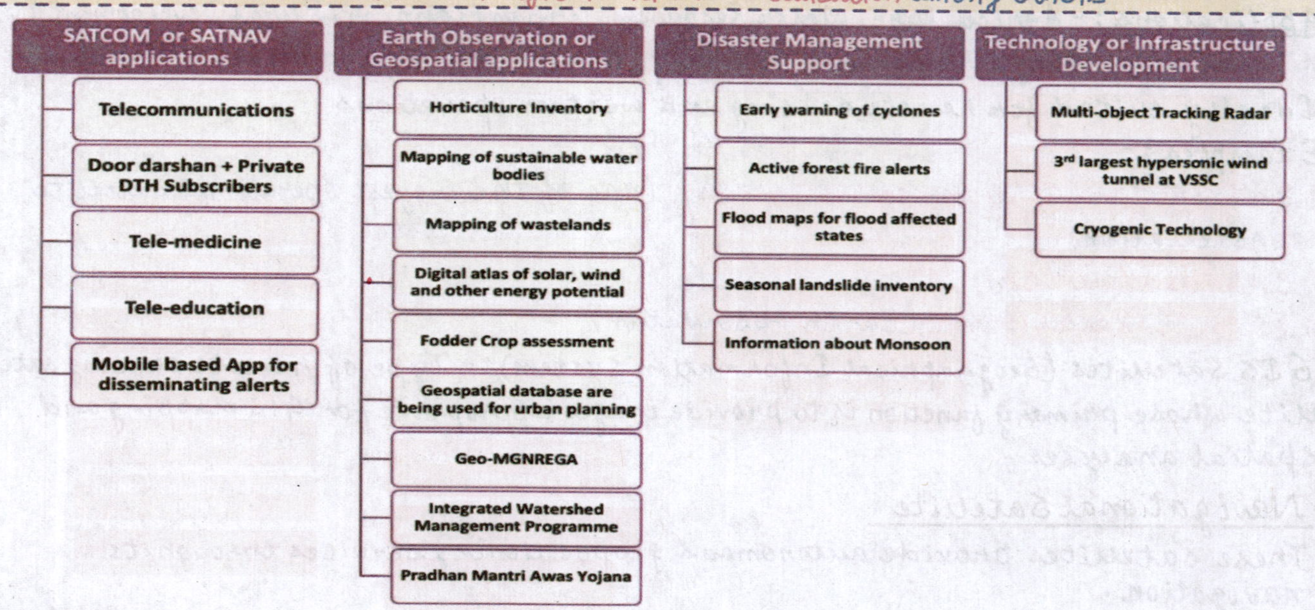

# TYPES OF SATELLITES

- Based on their application, satellite can be classified into 4 types:-
  1) Communication 2) Earth Observation 3) Navigational 4) Astronomical

## 1) Communication Satellites

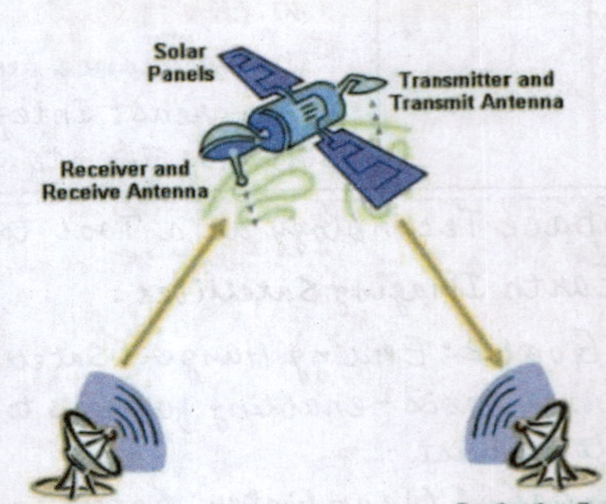


- Artificial Satellites that relays and amplifies radio telecommunication signals via a transponder, which creates a communication channel between a source transmitter and a receiver of different locations on earth.
- Uses :- Television Broadcasting, weather forecasting, disaster warning, societal application etc.
- Ideally suited for long distance communication.
- Examples - INSAT (Indian National Satellite System) series (Later GSAT) started in 1983 with insertion of INSAT-1B. GSAT-24, built by ISRO is the latest addition to INSAT/GSAT series launched in 2022.
- GSAT-9/ SAARC satellite - Launched under "Neighbourhood First Policy" in 2017 (cooperation in disaster management and telecommunication.
- GSAT-3/ EDUSAT - Launched in 2003 for promoting Tele-education.

## 2) Earth Observation Satellites

- The satellites monitor and supply necessary data in a spectral, spatial and temporal resolution for various issues and applications. Wide range of sensors are used in these satellites often referred to as Earth Remote Sensing Satellites.
- Applications :- Agriculture, Water Resources, Urban Planning, Rural Development, Mineral prospeiting, Environment, Forestry, Ocean resources and Disaster Management.
- Ideally suited for remote sensing and weather operations.
- Examples :-
  1) IRS System (Indian Remote Sensing) (one of the biggest operational satellite constellation).
  2) CARTOSAT, OCEANSAT
  3) RISAT, ResourceSat (Earth Observation)
- GIS Satellites (Geographical Information System) :- Type of remote sensing satellite whose primary function is to provide images appropriate for GIS mapping and spatial analyses.

## 3) Navigational Satellite

- These satellites provide autonomous geopositioning services through its navigation.

devices to determine their location (longitude, latitude and altitude/elevation) with precision.

- Two major types :-

(i) Global Navigation Satellite System (GNSS) – providing global coverage. E.g, Galileo (Europe); GLONASS (Russia); GPS (USA); BeiDou (China)

(ii) Regional Navigation Satellite System (RNSS) – autonomous coverage on a regional scale. E.g., India's IRNSS (aka NavIC), Japan's Quasi Zenith Sat.

### Navigation with Indian Constellation (NavIC)

- aka Indian Regional Navigation Satellite (IRNSS) – autonomous system that provides accurate real time positioning and time services.
- Operational in = 2018 (first launch = 2013)
- Developed by = ISRO (constellation of 7 satellite and a network of Ground stations 24x7).
- Orbits = GEO/ GSO (Orbital height = 35.786 Km)
- Coverage = India's landmass + upto 1500 Km (270 miles) from its boundaries.
- Services = (i) Standard Position Services (SPS) – civilian users
  (ii) Restricted Service (RS) – restricted users.

GAGAN (GPS Aided Geo Augumented Navigation) – satellite based augumentation system (SBAS) for Indian Airspace. ISRO + Airports Authority of India (AAI) implemented GAGAN. Interoperable with other international SBAS systems like USA's WAAS, European EGNOS, Japanese MSAS etc. It provides additional accuracy, availability and integrity and thus enhanced safety, necessary for various phases of flight.

## 4) Astronomical Satellites

- These are giant telescopes in orbit which are able to observe well without interference from the Earth's atmosphere and its infrared equipment is not confused by the heat of the Earth.
- These have upto 10 times better vision than the most powerful telescopes on Earth
- Applications : Used to make star maps, study mysterious phenomenon (like black holes, quasars), take pictures of far away celestial bodies, map different planetary surfaces.

### Astro Sat

- India's 1st dedicated multi-wavelength space observatory aimed at studying celestial sources in X ray, optical and UV spectral bands.
- Launched = 2015, Orbit = LEO (650 Km)
  Mission Duration = 5 years (minimum)
- Objectives :-

(i) Understand high energy processes in binary star systems – neutron stars, black holes

(ii) Estimate magnetic fields of neutron stars.

(iii) Detect X ray sources in the sky.

(iv) Deep field survey of universe in UV region.

- Different from Space Exploration probes because they collect their data from Earth's orbit. Probes are send out into deep space.
  - Astronomical satellites – Astrosat, Hubble, James Webb etc
  - Space Exploration Probes – Voyager 1, 2, New Horizons, Juno etc.

## Evolution of Space Technology

India's journey in space technology has been marked by significant progress and achievements evolving from humble beginnings to becoming a notable player in the global space community.

### Formative Phase (1960's to 1980's):

- 1962: Establishment of INCOSPAR to formulate and execute India's space program.
- 1972: ISRO was established superseding INCOSPAR to leverage space technology.
- 1975: India with the help of Soviet Union launched its 1st satellite Aryabhatta.
- 1980: ISRO developed its 1st Satellite Launch Vechile-3 (SLV-3), Placing Rohini satellite (RS-I) in orbit.
- 1988: ISRO started remote sensing programme with objective to apply space technology for socio-economic development.

### Conservative Phase (1990-2019):

- 1992: Anthrix Corporation established to explore commercial aspects of Satcom and launch services.
- 1994: India successfully launched its first PSLV. It enabled ISRO to launch LEO and GTO satellites plus facilitate the launch of foreign satellites.

Between 1990 to 2019, India experienced numerous advancements in space technologies and international partnerships. However, the space sector remained heavily protected and privatisation was discouraged due to national security concerns.

### Progressive Phase (2019 onwards)

- The New Space India Limited (NSIL), the commercial arm of ISRO was founded to enable Indian industries to take up high-technology space-related activities.
- Government announced the privatisation of the space sector and released the Spacecom 2020 Policy to facilitate public-private cooperation.
  - IN-SPACe (Indian National Space Promotion and Authorisation Centre) was also introduced to act as an interface between ISRO and private parties.
- Up to 100% FDI is allowed for satellite establishments and operations, subject to sectoral guidelines under the government route.
- ISRO will shift focus towards R&D, moving away from manufacturing of operational space system.

## Key challenges

- Bridging technology gaps and achieving self-sufficiency in critical areas remains a challenge.
- Infrastructure gaps that hinders quick prototyping and experimentation.
- A constant dearth of trained scientists, engineers and technicians to meet the demands of an expanding space program.
- Increasing Commercial Competition as the Global space industry is becoming increasingly commercialized.
- Hurdles for private sector participation like investor reluctance to back early-stage start ups, lack of awareness etc.

## Way Forward

- A single window approval process through a nodal body focused on the space economy would aid and ease the process that shall further help ease of doing business.
- Improve access to technology for the Industrial sector which will indirectly improve cost competitiveness and improve innovation potential.
- International Collaborations can provide access to new technologies, shared resources and diversified expertise
- Foster collaborations between government, space agencies and the private sector.
- Privatisation of manufacturing in the space sector will also help India capture a larger share of the global market.

# INDIAN SPACE POLICY, 2023

- Vision: " Augument space capabilities; Enable, encourage and develop a flourishing commercial presence in space" that suggests an acceptance that the private sector is a critical stakeholder in the entire value chain of the space economy.
- Key highlights of the Policy:

The policy creates four distinct, but related entities, that will facilitate greater private sector participation in activities that usually been the traditional domain of the ISRO.

1. InSPACE (Indian National Space Promotion and Authorisation Centre): Single window clearance and authorisation agency for space launches, establishing launching pads, buying and selling satellites and disseminating high resolution data among other things.
   - IN-SPACE will create a "stable and predictable regulatory framework" that will ensure a level playing field for the NGEs.

2. New Space India Limited (NSIL): Responsible for commercialising space technologies and platforms created through public expenditure as well as manufacturing, leasing or procuring space components, technologies, platforms and other assets from the private or public sector.

3. Department of Space: Nodal department for implementation of Indian Space Policy - 2023 and provides overall policy guidelines.

4. Rationalizing ISRO's role: As the National Space Agency, it will focus primarily on research and development of new space technologies and applications and for expanding the human understanding of the outer space.
   - ISRO will shift from manufacturing operational space systems to transferring mature systems to industries for commercial use.

## Role of the Private Sector:

- Non-Governmental Entities (NGEs) including the private sector can undertake end-to-end activities in the space sector, including the establishment and operation of space objects and ground based assets and related services, such as communication, remote sensing, navigation etc.
- NGEs can own, procure or lease satellites; provides communication service within and outside India; and disseminate remote sensing data domestically and internationally.
- They are allowed to design and operate launch vechiles and establish their infrastructure.
- NGEs can make filings with the International Telecommunication Union (ITU) and engage in commercial asteroid resource recovery.
- Security agencies can take NGEs to procure tailor-made solutions for specific requirements.

## Need of Introducing private players into the space sector:

1. India lags in the global space economy: The global space economy is valued at around USD 360 billion while India accounts for about only 2% of this economy.
2. Harnessing the full potential of India's space sector: Broadband, OTT and 5G promise significant growth in satellite based services.
   - With the right environment, India's space industry could grow to USD 60 billion by 2030, creating over 200,000 jobs.
3. Private sector revolution in Space Industry: Companies like Space X, Blue Origin and Virgin Galactic have transformed the space sector by reducing costs and turnaround times.
   - In India, private players have mostly been vendors or suppliers to the government's space program.

4. Enhancing security: Indian security and defence agencies procure earth observation data and imagery from foreign sources.
   - Dependence on foreign entities can compromise India's security.
5. Promoting self-reliance (Atma-nirbharta) in the space sector: More than half the transponders beaming TV signals into Indian homes are hosted on foreign satellites.
6. Promoting entrepreneurship in the space sector can unlock the potential of India's youth.
7. International Competitiveness: With the increasing global interest in space exploration, private companies can help countries remain competitive in the industry.
8. Flexibility: Private companies are often more agile and adaptable than government agencies, allowing them to respond more quickly to changing market demands and technological advancements.

## Advantages of the Indian Space Policy

- Provides clarity: Policy establishes a single regulatory body, IN-SPACe, to streamline the process and provide clarity to all involved parties.
- Fostering innovation: Encourages private sector participation, which brings new ideas, innovation and competition into the Indian space sector.
- Economic growth and job creation: As the private sector and startups gain more share in the space sector, it's expected to lead to economic growth and job creation.
- The policy could spur investments, create high tech jobs and contribute significantly to the Indian economy.
- Accessible and affordable space technology: With increased competition, space technology and services could become more accessible and affordable, benefiting various sectors like communication, navigation, earth observation and more.
- Encouraging environment for space startups, fostering entrepreneurship and innovation in the country.
- Streamlining regulations making it easier for businesses to navigate the regulatory landscape and encourages more entities to participate in space activities.

## Challenges in implementing Indian Space Policy

- Striking a balance between encouraging private sector investment and ensuring national security.
- Mobilisation of adequate funding and investment for private space ventures could be a challenge, particularly for capital intensive projects that may not have immediate revenue generation potential.

- Competition from global players: Indian space startups and private companies will face intense competition from established global players like Space X and Blue Origin.
- Developing a skilled workforce especially given the competition for talent from established global space companies.
- Streamlining regulations and ensuring a smooth clearance process could be challenging as the sector grows and diversifies.
- Infrastructure development for private companies to operate such as launch pads, ground stations and testing facilities require significant investment and planning.
- Establishing a smooth technology transfer process between ISRO and private entities could be challenging.
- International collaboration and compliance: Navigating International treaties, agreements and regulations in the space sector can be challenging for private companies.

## PYQs Corner

*(Write the Answer and Get Free Evaluation)*

1. What is India's plan to have its own space station and how will it benefit our space programme? [150 Words] [10 Marks] [2019]

2. Discuss India's achievements in the field of Space Science and Technology. How the application of this technology has helped India in its socio-economic development? [200 Words] [12.5 Marks][2016]

3. What do you understand by "Standard Positioning System" and "Precision positioning system" in the GPS era? Discuss the advantage India perceives from its ambitious IRNSS programme employing just seven satellites. [200 Words] [12.5 Marks] [2015]

CHAPTER 17

# DEFENCE INDIGENISATION

- Defence indigenisation refers to the strategic objective of a country to develop and enhance its own industrial and technological capabilities for producing essential defence equipments and equipments.
- It aims reduce dependency on foreign sources for military hardware and ensuring self-sufficiency in meeting the national security requirements.
- Defence Research Development Organisation (DRDO), Defence Public Sector Undertakings (DPSUs), Ordnance Factory Boards (OFB) and private organisation are playing a critical role in indegenisation of defence industries.

## India's Defence Indigenisation Journey: A Timeline

Overdependence on the Soviet Union, brought about a change in India's approach to defence industrialisation from license based production to production based on indigeneous design.

- Early Recognition (1950s-1960s): Wars of 1962, 1965 and 1971 highlighted the need to reduce dependence on foreign arms.
- Integrated Guided Missile Development Programme (1983): Launched under Dr. APJ Abdul Kalam to develop indigeneous strategic missile systems and concluded in 2008, significantly boosting India's missile capabilities.
  - Missile systems developed under this programme: Prithvi, Akash, Trishul, Nag and Agni (I, II, III).

- 1990s – Self Reliance Review Committee (SRRV) under A.P.J Abdul Kalam, had formulated a 10-year self-reliance plan under which, the self-reliance index (SRI), (defined as the percentage share of indigeneous content in total procurement expenditure), was to be increased from 30% in 1992-93 to 70% by 2005.
- Shift in Responsibility: The responsibility for indigenisation moved from the Department of Defence Production (DDP) and Directorate General of Quality Assurance (DGQA) to the Ordnance Factories Board (OFB) and the Armed Forces.
    - The Army and the Navy created 15-year Perspective Plans of Development
- Project 75 (1997): This project focused on developing submarines indigenously, emphasizing self-reliance in submarine construction and reducing dependence on foreign suppliers.
- Evolving DPP (2001 onwards): The Defence Procurement Procedure (DPP) has been continuously developed and refined since 2001.

## Need of Defence Indigenisation

- India's low share in the global market: Accounts for only 0.2 percent which goes against India's Balance of Payments.
    - Stockholm International Peace Research Institute (SIPRI) reports indicate that India ranked 23rd during the period 2017-21, with a marginal presence in the global arms market.
- Reduce India's imports and consequently, CAD will be reduced.
    - According to SIPRI, India is the world's largest importer of arms (more than the combined imports of both Pakistan and China) in the world from 2019 to 2023.
- Hostile Neighbours: India being surrounded by porous borders and hostile neighbours such as China, Pakistan etc., needs to be self-sufficient and self-reliant in defence production.
- Keeps intact the technological expertise and encourages spin-off technologies and innovation that stem from it.
- Development of military industrial complex: It is a network of individuals and institutions involved in the production of weapons and military technologies.
- Technology Transfer and Independence: It allows the nation to develop and maintain critical defence capabilities by facilitating technology transfer through foreign collaborations.

- Employment generation: As per government estimates, a reduction in 20-25% in defence related imports could directly create an additional 100,000 to 120,000 highly skilled jobs in India.
- Exports promotion: With the increasing defence indigenisation, India can widen its export base.
  - Ex- India is in the process of exporting Brahmos Cruise Missiles to the Philippines.
- Research and Development: Defence indigenisation promotes substantial investments in research and development (R&D) contributing to the growth of a defence industrial ecosystem in India and spin-off effects on other manufacturing sectors.

## Government Initiatives towards Defence Indigenisation

The Government has undertaken several initiatives and reforms to promote indigeneous design, development and manufacturing of defence equipment, aiming for self-reliance in defence manufacturing and technology.

1. Make in India: Launched in 2014, it aims to support domestic production, R&D and technological advancement in the realm of defence.
2. Defence Procurement Policy, 2018: Based on recommendations from the Dhirendra Singh committee, this policy introduced the "Buy (Indian-IDDM)"-Indigeneously Designed, Developed and Manufactured, as the most preferred way of defence goods acquistion.
   - Empowered the Defence Acquisition Council (DAC) with a "fast track" route for acquiring weapons
3. Innovations for Defence Excellence (IDEX), 2018 and IDEX Prime, 2022
   - Engages industries, particularly MSMEs, start-ups, individual innovators R&D institutes and academia.
   - Provides grants, funding and support for innovations and R&D.
4. Defence Industrial Corridors
   - Established two Defence Industrial Corridors in Uttar Pradesh and Tamil Nadu to create regional hubs for aerospace and defence.
5. Positive Indigenisation Lists
   - Prioritises procurement from domestic sources under the Buy Indian (IDDM) category with embargoes on imports
6. E-Biz Portal
   - Digitalized the application process for Industrial License (IL) and Industrial Entrepreneur Memorandum (IEM), enhancing efficiency.

7. Custom Duty and FDI policy
   - Imposed uniform custom duty on all Indian industries, public and private ensuring parity.
   - Allows composite foreign investment of upto 49% through the Government route (FIPB).
8. Vendor Development Guidelines
   - Introduced comprehensive guidelines for Outsourcing and Vendor Development to boost private sector, especially SME, participation in defence manufacturing for DPSUs and the Ordanance Factory Board (OFB).
9. Liberalisation of the sector: Simplification of the industrial licensing process, extended validity periods and liberalised FDI policy allowing up to 74% FDI under the automatic route.

**Impact of Government Initiatives:**

- Increased the share of domestic procurement: 54% in 2018-19, 59% in 2019-20, 64% in 2020-21 and 68% in the (2022-23) with 25% earmarked for private industry.
- Reduced defence procurement from foreign sources from 46% to 36% over four years (2018-19 to 2021-22)

**Indigenous Developments in Defence**

- INS Vikrant: First aircraft carrier to be built in India for Navy.
- Arihant: First indigeneous nuclear submarine was developed in association with BARC and DRDO.
- Tejas Aircraft: The lightest, smallest and tailless multi-role supersonic fighter aircraft in its class.
- Arjun Tank: A third-generation main battle tank developed by DRDO.
- Dhanush: First indigenous long-range artillery gun also known as the "desi Bofors."
- AGNI V: India's first intercontinental ballistic missile.
- Dhanush, Nirbhaya, Prithvi, Akash missiles have also been developed indigenously.
- Pinaka: Developed by armament Research Development Establishment (Pune).
- BRAHMOS: Joint Venture between India and the Russian Federation.

## Key Features of Defence Acquisition Procedure. 2020

1) Reservation for Indian Vendors
   - Allows up to 100% FDI in defence manufacturing (up to 74% through the Automatic route and beyond 74% through the Government route).
   - Encourages domestic industry participation, enhancing production capabilities.

2) Enhancement of indigenous Content:
- Emphasizes procuring indigenously manufactured products and technologies.
- Promotes self-reliance in defence production across various categories.

| Category | DPP 2016 | DAP 2020 |
|---|---|---|
| Buy (India-IIDM) | Min 40% | Min 50% |
| Buy (India) | Min 40% | Indigenous design-Min 50% Otherwise - Min 60% |
| Buy and Make (India | Min 50% of Make | Min 50% of Make |
| Buy (Global-Manufacturer in India | Category did not exist | Min 50% of Buy plus Make |
| Buy (Global) | Category didn't exist | Min 30% for Indian vendors. |

3) Make and innovation
- Supports indigenization efforts through initiatives like Make I/II/III, funded by both government and industry.
- iDEX facilitates the incubation of startups in the defence sector.

4) Buy (Global Manufacturing in India.
- Mandates that the entire or part of the manufacturing process for equipment, spare parts or Maintenance and Repair be conducted by the Indian subsidiary of foreign investors.

5) Ease of Doing Business
- Facilitates easier and faster operations and decision-making through the project Management Unit.
- Gives preference to manufacturers producing complete defence products rather than parts.

## Challenges Faced by Defence Indigenisation

1. Technological Gap: Critical components and subsystems often need to be imported, impacting the overall indigenisation effort.
   - Indigenous content of the LCA Tejas Aircraft is 59.7% by value and 75.5% by numbers.
2. R&D and Innovation: India's defence R&D budget is relatively low compared to global standards.
   - The spending on R&D as a percentage of the total defence expenditure has come down from 6.5% (2010-11) to the current 5.38% (2022-23) which hit a low of 4.62% (₹15,707 crore) in 2020-21.
3. Industrial Base: India's defence manufacturing base is still inadequate to meet the demands of a modern military.
4. Lack of Specialization: Many Indian defence companies lack the specialization required for high end defence products.

5. Limited Participation of Private Sector: Defence Public Sector Undertakings (DPSUs) still dominate a significant portion of defence production.
6. Procurement Process: India's defence procurement process is notoriously lengthy and bureaucratic, discouraging domestic industry.
7. Financial Constraints: Developing and producing defence equipment is capital-intensive, requiring significant investments.
8. Policy and Regulatory Environment: Frequent changes in defence policies can create uncertainities for the industry.

**Case Study: Tejas Light Combat Aircraft (LCA)**

- The development of the LCA, India's indigenous fighter jet, highlights many of these challenges. Despite being a significant achievement, the program faced delays, cost overruns and technological hurdles.
- While the LCA has entered service, it still relies on some imported components, underscoring the ongoing challenges in defence indigenisation.
    - Indigenous content of the LCA Tejas Aircraft is 59.7% by value and 75.5% by numbers. (Minister of State for Defence Subhash Bhamre in a written reply to Lok Sabha)

## Futuristic Measures

To achieve its goal of becoming a net defence exporter and reaching a target of US$ 5 billion in defence exports by 2025, India needs to implement several measures:

1. Strategic Planning: Create a detailed, long-term plan for defence indigenization that defines specific goals, deadlines and action steps.
2. Enhance Private Sector Contribution to atleast 50% of the total defence production.
    - Provides incentives and allocate large projects to private companies for the production of significant items, beyond just parts and components.
3. Technological Advancement: Chip industry should be developed and produced domestically using the software industry and technologies like artificial intelligence and cyber security.
4. Long-term Procurement Plans should be provided to industry for capacity building.
5. Strengthening Defence Public Sector Undertakings (DPSUs):
    - Grant greater autonomy to DPSUs while holding them accountable for performance.

- Professional Management: improve corporate governance and management practices in DPSUs.
- Strategic Partnerships: Encourage strategic partnerships between DPSUs and private industry.

6. Development of Defence Industrial Corridors with world class infrastructure.
7. Promotion of defense exports:
   - Focus on exporting high-value weapon systems like Aircraft carriers, Arjun Mark 2 tanks, LCA-Tejas and Light Combat Helicopters.
   - Comprehensive export deals that include weaponary, training and efficient maintainence services.
   - Leverage Defense Lines of Credit (LoC) to friendly foreign countries (FFCs) to facilitate defence exports.
   - Establish a dedicated Export Promotion Body to streamline and drive export related initiatives.
8. Defense Modernisation Fund: Establish a non-lapsable Defense Modernisation fund, as proposed in the budget 2023-24, to bridge the gap between projected requirements and budget allocations.

Cabinet Committee on Security (CCS) in March 2024 cleared a Rs 15000 crore project to design and develop the Advanced Medium Combat Aircraft (AMCA), India's fifth generation fighter multirole fighter jet. Only the US, China and Russia currently build fifth-generation fighters.

CHAPTER 18

# EMERGING TECHNOLOGIES

## The Fourth Industrial Revolution

- The Fourth Industrial Revolution (4IR) is a term coined in 2016 by Klaus Schwab, Founder and Executive Chairman of the World Economic Forum (WEF).
- It is characterized by the convergence and complementarity of emerging technology domains, including, nanotechnology, biotechnology, new material and advanced digital production (ADP) technologies.

### Different Types of Industrial Revolution (IRs)

→ 1st Industrial Revolution- Began in Britain in the last quarter of the 18th century with the mechanisation of the textile industry, harnessing of steam power and birth of the modern factory.

→ 2nd Industrial Revolution- Started from the last third of the nineteenth century to the outbreak of World War I and powered by developments in electricity transportation, chemicals, steel and mass production and consumption.

- Industrialization spread even further- to Japan after the Meiji Restoration and deep into Russia which was booming at the outset of World War I.
- During this era, factories could produce countless numbers of identical products quickly and cheaply.

→ 3rd Industrial Revolution- Began since 1970, it was digital and - applied electronics and information technology to processes of production.

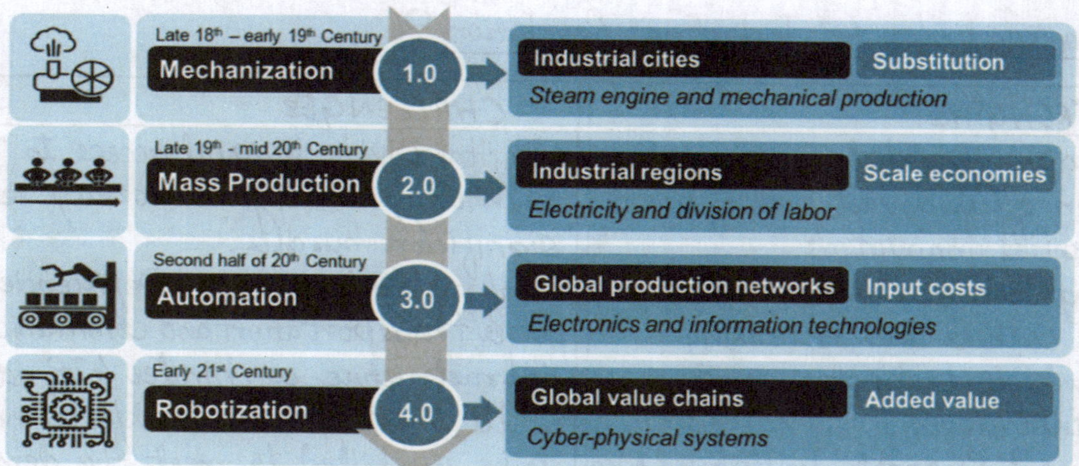


→ 4th Industrial Revolution- It is a way of describing the blurring of boundaries between the physical, digital and biological worlds. The four fundamental types of disruptive technologies (example below) that can be applied all along the value chain.

- Connectivity, Data and Computational power - cloud technology, the Internet, blockchain, sensors,
- Analytics and intelligence- advanced analytics, machine learning, Artificial Intelligence.
- Human-Machine Interaction- Virtual reality (VR) and augmented reality (AR), robotics and automation, autonomous guided vehicles.
- Advanced Engineering. Addictive manufacturing (such as 3-D printing), renewable energy, nanoparticles.

## Critical Analysis of 4th Industrial Revolution

(Green colour indicates positive impact and Red Colour indicates Negative impact)

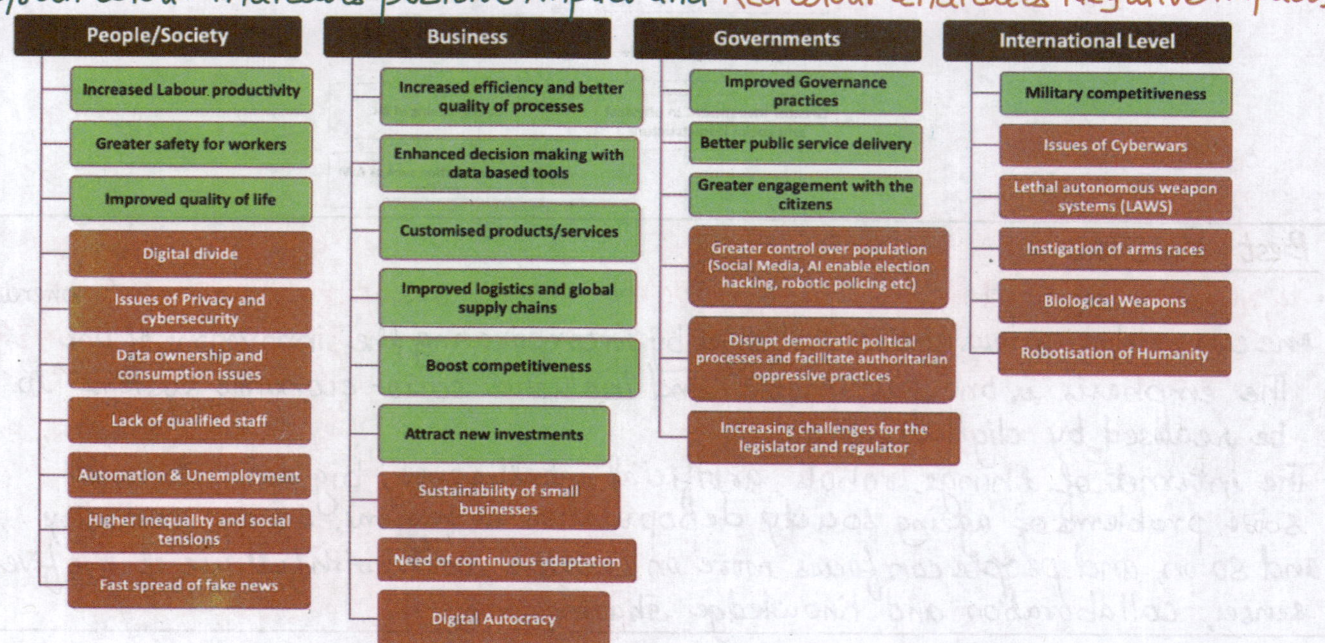

## Is India ready for 4th Industrial Revolution?

| STRENGTHS | CHALLENGES |
|---|---|
| • Demographic Divided- India's young population offers a vast pool of talent and potential innovators.<br>• Growing Tech Ecosystem - A thriving startup culture and increasing investments in technology and driving innovation.<br>• Government Support- Initiatives like Digital India, Make in India and Startup India are fostering a conductive environment.<br>• Global IT Services Industry- A strong foundation in IT services can be leveraged for 4IR technologies. | • Digital Divide- Unequal access to technology and digital literacy remain significant hurdles.<br>• Infrastructure Gaps- Deficiencies in power, transportation and communication infrastructure can hinder 4IR adoption.<br>• Skill Shortage- The workforce needs to be upskilled to meet the demands of emerging technologies.<br>• Data Privacy and Security Concerns:- Robust data protection frameworks are essential for trust and innovation. |

Reforms required for India to become a leader in 4.0

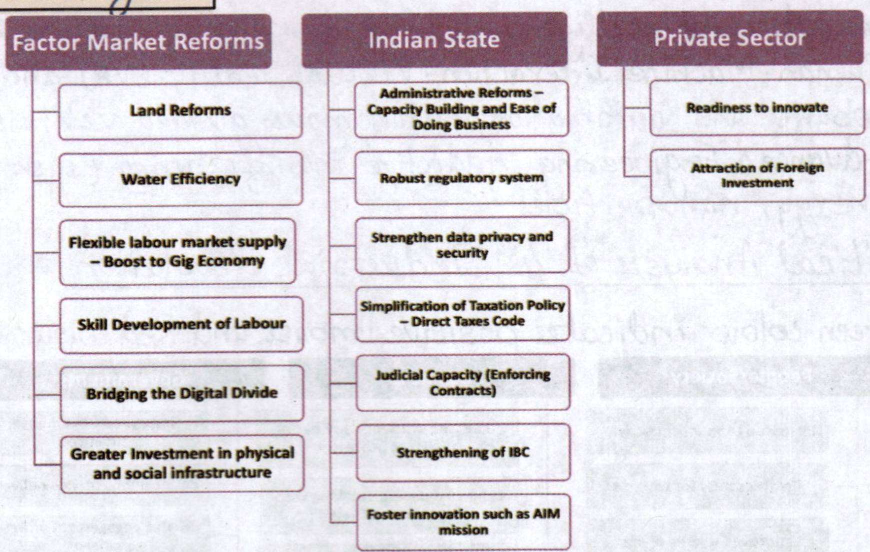


### Best Practices

- Japan has initiated the concept of "Society 5.0" or a super-smart society wherein one can resolve various social challenges by incorporating the innovations of the 4IR
- The emphasis is on "sustainable and inclusive socio-economic systems" to be realised by digitalisation.
- The internet of things, robots, artificial intelligence, big data, etc, will solve problems of ageing society depopulation in regions, income inequality and so on, and people can focus more on creative work with full use of the five senses, collaboration and knowledge sharing.

# ARTIFICIAL INTELLIGENCE

Artificial intelligence (AI) refers to the ability of machines to simulate human cognitive functions like thinking, perception, learning, problem-solving and decision-making.

- AI empowers computer systems to perform tasks independently that traditionally required human intelligence.
- AI Algorithms are trained on massive datasets, allowing them to identify patterns, make predictions and recommend actions. This functionality mirrors human capabilities but often with greater speed and accuracy.
- The term "Artificial Intelligence" was first coined in 1955 by Professor John McCarthy.

## Key Capabilities of AI:

- Learning- AI systems can learn from experience, constantly improving their performance over time.
- Reasoning- AI can used learned information to draw conclusions and solve complex problems.
- Image Recognition - AI systems can analyze and understand visual data, identifying objects and patterns within images.
- Language Processing- AI can understand and respond to human languages, enabling natural language interaction between humans and machines.
- Perspective Generation- AI can analyze data to create new insights and perspectives.

## Different Categories of AI

- Weak AI/ Narrow AI- It is a type of AI that is limited to a specific or narrow area. Weak AI simulates human cognition.
  - It has the potential to benefit society by automating time-consuming tasks and by analyzing data in a ways that humans sometimes can't.
  - For example, video games such as chess and personal

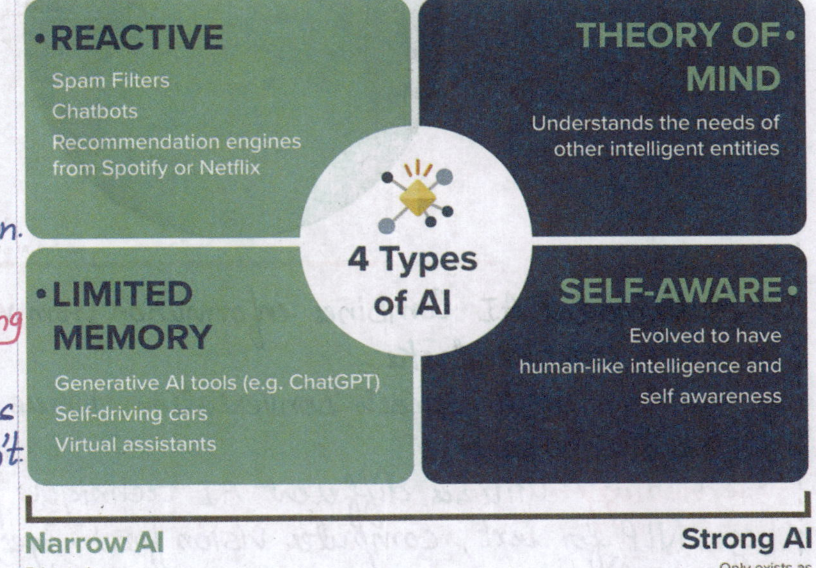

assistants such as Amazon's Alexa and Apple's Siri.

- Strong AI- These are systems that carry on tasks considered to be human-like. These tend to be more complex and complicated systems.
  - They are programmed to handle situations in which they may be required to problem-solving without having a person intervene.
  - These kinds of systems can be found in applications like self-driving cars.

## Dimensions of AI

01 Generative AI- Creates high-quality content like text, speech, and images using deep learning models.

Example- Open AI's Chat GPT, Google's Bard, DALL-E Krutrim (India)

Technology- leverages Natural Language Processing (NLP) for understanding and generating human language.

- GPT (Generative Pre-Trained Transformer): A Type of large Language Model (LLM)
  - LLMs are machine learning models trained on massive datasets for tasks like summarizing, translating and content creation.
  - Transformers: A specific neural network architecture with encoder and decoder components for processing information.
- Graphical Processing Units (GPUs) Provide the computational power for these Complex models.

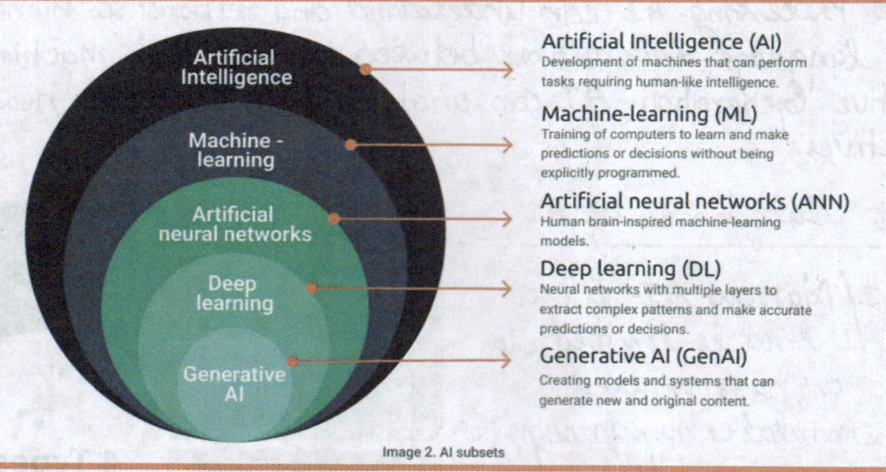

Image 2. AI subsets

02 Multimodal AI- Combines information from various sources (text, audio, video) to solve complex tasks.

- Example- Text-to-Speech conversation, where text is analyzed and converted into spoken language.
- Technology- Utilizes different AI techniques for handling different data types. (eg-, NLP for text, computer vision for images) and integrates them for a unified output).

**Frontier AI:-** Aims to create highly capable general-purpose AI models.
- Goals- To perform tasks beyond the capabilities of current specialized models.
- Technology- Still under development.

## Artificial Intelligence and its Application

1. **Supportive Mode:** AI as the assistant: AI acts as a supportive partner to human decision-making.
   - AI provides resources like predictive outputs, data analysis, and insights to augment human judgement.
   - This is ideal for tasks requiring human expertise and intuition, but where AI can streamline processes and reduce errors.
2. **Reimagining the Business-** AI Beyond Human limits: AI takes on tasks that surpass human cognitive abilities.
   - This frees up human specialists to focus on higher-level activities like interpreting results and developing strategies.
   - Ex: AI excels at analyzing massive datasets in fields like bioinformatics, enabling large-scale genome studies previously impossible.
3. **AI Takes the Wheel:** When Humans Should Step Back: AI can perform Tasks that pose a risk to human safety.

## Benefits and Application of AI

- **Economy-** AI is expected to add $967 billion to the Indian economy by 2035. It could create up to 8.2 million new jobs in India by 2025 (PWC study).
- **Healthcare-** AI driven diagnostics (For example IBM's Watson for Health, Google's Deep Mind Health), Early detection (Fitbit, iWatch etc), Treatment (AI driven robots) Drug research and discovery etc.
- **Education-** Automation of repetitive tasks (For ex IntelliMetric and Project Essay Grade tool), Practicals using AR and VR (Ex Practically by Hedrebad based firm), Counselling sessions (using chatbots), Evaluation (AI enabled digitized checking of handwritten answer sheets) etc.
- **Agriculture-** AI enabled Agricultural Robotics (to tackle labor challenges), Predictive Analytics (enables right decision making), AI for intelligent spraying of chemicals etc.
- **Energy-** AI managed smart grids, Anti-theft technology, Fault prediction, Maintenance facilitated by image processing, Energy efficiency (using Alexa, Google Nest) etc.
- **Financial services-** Personalised banking, fraud detection, Process automation, AI can be used to examine cash accounts, credit accounts and investment accounts etc.
- **Law Enforcement-** Facial recognition, Speech recognition, Predictive analytics etc.

## Concerns and Risk Associated with AI Development in India

| | |
| --- | --- |
| ECONOMIC DISRUPTION | • Job Displacement - artificial intelligence will replace some 85 million jobs by 2025 (WEF)<br>• Financial Market Volatility - AI-driven high-frequency trading in financial markets could exacerbate volatility and economic instability.<br>• Lack of trained professionals - According to NASSCOM, India houses a talent base of 416k AI professionals as opposed to the current demand of approximately 629K, a figure expected to surge to 1 million by 2026. |
| REGULATORY CHALLENGES | • Lack of universal definition - among regulators due to its global nature.<br>• Lack of transparency in AI systems can lead to users being unaware they are interacting with automated systems, impacting trust.<br>• Liability issues - Black box nature and self-learning ability of AI make it difficult to justify decisions and assign liability for errors.<br>  • The inability of seeing how deep learning systems make their decision is known as the black box problem. |
| SOCIAL BIAS | • AI Perpetuating Bias - Machine learning algorithms can inherit and amplify societal biases present in the data they are trained.<br>• Ex - Facial recognition algorithms have been shown to have higher error rates for women and people with darker skin tones. |
| Lack of Transparency | • Unforeseen Consequences: Opaque AI decision-making processes make it difficult to pinpoint who is accountable for negative outcomes generated by AI systems.<br>• Loss of Trust - A lack of transparency in AI-decision-making can erode trust in the technology, hindering its adoption. |
| IPR | • Copyright Infringement - AI-generated creative outputs like images or text could infringe upon existing copyrights, stifling artistic expression. |
| Data Privacy Concerns | • Data Collection and Misuse - The vast amount of personal data collection required for AI systems raises concerns about privacy violations and potential misuse of this information.<br>• Ex - Lawsuits against Silicon Valley giants for data and privacy breach in their AI systems |
| Regulation | • Dominance by Big Tech - The concentration of AI development power in the hands of a few big tech companies raises concerns about potential misuse and a lack of diversity in perspectives. |
| Security Risk. | • Misuse and Malicious Actors - AI systems could be intentionally misused for malicious purposes, such as spreading disinformation or cyberattacks. |

| | |
|---|---|
| | • Model Instability- AI models can deteriorate over time if the data they are trained on becomes corrupted or biased, leading to unintended consequences. |
| Ethical Concern | • Equality and Justice- The use of AI in areas like criminal justice raises concerns about fairness and potential discrimination against certain demographics.<br>• Human Dignity- AI development must consider the impact on human dignity and privacy, ensuring responsible creation and use of these technologies. |
| Challenges in AI in India. | • Lack of investment because of High implementation cost<br>• Super-intelligence- A sufficient intelligent AI system can redesign itself or can create a better successor system which creates fear.<br>• Data security and privacy issues.<br>• Limited AI expertise.<br>• Lack of AI and cloud computing infrastructure |

## Steps Taken to Regulate AI in India

1. India AI Mission- Aims to Establish an ecosystem for AI innovation through public-private partnerships.
   - Driving responsible, inclusive growth of India's AI ecosystem through democratization, data quality improvement, and indigenous AI capabilities development

### India AI Mission: Key Features

- India AI Compute Capacity- Build high-performance computing infrastructure for AI research startups.
- India AI Innovation Centre- Develop indigenous large language models and foundational models for critical sectors.
- India AI Database Platform- Provide easy access to quality, non-personal data for AI development.
- India AI Application Development Initiative- Promote real-world applications of AI in collaboration with government departments.
- India AI Future Skills: Expand AI education and training programs at all levels.
- India AI Startup Financing- Support and fund promising deep-tech AI startups.
- Safe & Trusted AI- Ensure responsible development and use of AI through ethical frameworks and tools.

- National AI programme- to promote the efficient and responsible use of AI.
- India AI portal- One-stop digital platform for AI-related developments in India.
- Global Partnership on Artificial Intelligence (GPAI)- It is a multi-stakeholder initiative which aims to bridge the gap between theory and practice on AI by supporting cutting-edge research and applied activities on AI-related priorities.
  - Secretariat- Hosted at the Organisation for Economic Cooperation and Development (OECD) in France.
  - Membership: 29 international partners, including India.
- National Strategy for Artificial Intelligence # AI For All strategy by NITI Aayog: It featured AI research and development guidlines focused on healthcare, agriculture, education, "smart" cities and infrastructure and smart mobility and transformation.

## Steps taken to Regulate AI Globally

- Bletchley Declaration- It aims to enhance global collaboration on artificial intelligence (AI) safety. It has a two-fold focus:
  - identifying shared AI-related risks and enhancing scientific understanding of these risks.
  - A collaborative approach to international research on frontier AI safety.
- European Union- It is working on draft Artificial Intelligence Art (AI act) to regulate AI from the top down.
- United States- White House office of Science and Technology Policy has published a non-binding Blueprint for the development, Use and Deployment of Automated Systems. (Blueprint for an AI Bill of Rights), listing principles to minimize potential harm from AI.
- Japan- Society 5.0 project, aiming to address social problems with innovation.
- China- China has established the "Next Generation Artificial Intelligence Development Plan" and published ethical guidlines for AI. It has also introduced specific laws related to AI applications, such as the management of algorithmic recommendations.

## Futuristic Reform Measures

**1. Ethical and Responsible AI:**

- **Prioritize Ethical Development:** Focus on fairness, transparency, accountability, and mitigating bias in AI systems → clear guidelines and regulations.
- **Data Governance:** Ensure data privacy and security through proper data collection, cleaning, labeling, and sharing practices.
- **De-biasing Training Data:** Ensure fairness by carefully curating training datasets with diverse representation and implementing feedback mechanisms to identify and address bias.

**2. Continued Innovation and Investment:**

- **Research and Development:** Invest in fundamental research on new algorithms and models to advance AI capabilities.
- **Data Quality and Accessibility:** Promote high-quality, diverse datasets for effective AI model training.

**3. Human-AI Collaboration:**

- **Focus on Collaboration:** Design AI to complement human capabilities, not replace them.

**Principles for responsible AI management**

1. Principle of Safety and Reliability
2. Principle of Equality
3. Principle of Inclusivity and Non-discrimination
4. Principle of Privacy and Security
5. Principle of Transparency
6. Principle of Accountability
7. Principle of Protection and Reinforcement of Positive Human Values

- **User-Centred Design:** Develop user interfaces that facilitate seamless interaction with AI systems.

**4. Domain-Specific Applications:**

- **Identify Impact Areas:** Prioritize specific domains where AI can have a significant positive impact (e.g., healthcare, education).
- **Tailored Solutions:** Develop AI solutions that address specific challenges in various industries.

**5. Workforce Development:**

- **Education and Upskilling:** Prepare the workforce for the AI-driven future through education and training programs.
- **Collaboration:** Encourage interdisciplinary collaboration between academia, industry, and government to support workforce development.

**6. International Cooperation:**

- **Global Standards:** Establish international standards for AI development and deployment to address global challenges.
- **Impact Assessment:** Collaborate internationally to assess the potential societal impact of AI systems.
- **Knowledge Sharing:** Promote knowledge sharing and best practices across countries and organizations.

**7. Regulation and Governance:**

- **Proportionate Governance:** Strike a balance between encouraging innovation and mitigating risks through appropriate regulations.
- **Risk-Based Approach:** Tailor regulations based on the potential risks posed by different AI systems.
- **Specific Use Cases:** Focus regulations on specific high-risk areas like autonomous vehicles or healthcare AI.
- **Human Oversight:** Maintain human oversight and control over AI systems.
- **Transparency and Explainability:** Develop transparent and explainable AI systems to understand their decision-making processes.
- **Multi-Stakeholder Approach:** Involve governments, industry, academia, and civil society in shaping effective AI regulations.

**8. Industry Self-Regulation:** Encourage companies developing AI to adopt ethical practices and self-regulate to ensure responsible use of their technologies.

# ROBOTICS

- Robotics is an inter-disciplinary branch of engineering that deals with design, development, operation and application of Robots as well as computer system for their control, sensory feedback and information processing. Robots are automated machines which can replace humans in dangerous environments or manufacturing processes, or resemble humans in appearance, behaviour and cognition.
- Word Robot comes from czech word "robota" which means 'forced labour' or 'work'
- Word Robotics was 1st used by Isaac Asimov in his science fiction story 'Liar' published in 1941. He only introduced the '3 laws of Robotics'.
- Law of Robotics are a set of laws, rules or principles, which are intended as a fundamental framework to underpin the behaviour of robots designed to have a degree of autonomy. The 3 laws are:

**What is a 'Bot'?**

An Internet bot (or web robot or bot) is a software application that runs automated tasks over the internet.

Most ubiquitous bots are the programs also called spiders or crawlers.

Chatter bot- simulate talk with a human

Shopbot- shops around the web on your behalf & locates best price.

Knowbot- program that automatically searches internet sites & gathers information from them.

1) A robot may not injury a human being, or through inaction, allow a human being to come to harm.
2) A robot must obey orders given by human beings except where such orders would conflict with the 1st Law.
3) A robot must protect its own existence as long as such protection does not conflict with 1st or 2nd laws.

- **Application of Robots**

Robots are being used across a range of sectors such as-

1) Warehouse Automation
2) Automotive Manufacturing

} Robots add precision, tirelessness & continuity in the manufacturing/management processes.

- Process Optimization - Helps to streamline workflows, reduce costs, ensure production, continuity, and improve operational efficiency.

3) Defence and National security.
   - for dangerous security tasks like Bomb Disposal, Reconnaissance etc. (eg- Daksha - India's current military robot.
   - DRDO looking to develop next generation Robotic soldiers.
   - Mine detection, deployment for surveillance activities on land, air, water surface and underwater environments or remotely operated vehicles.

4) Hazardous Industries

- BARC is using robots to clean radioactive water Tanks.

5) Mining & Mineral Exploration.

6) Marine Engineering (eg- Amogh an autonomous underwater vehicle. It is designated to inspect & repair bridges, pipelines & hulls of ships at the depth upto 15 meters. Endurance capacity = upto 3 hours.

7) Space Exploration (eg Vyommitra- humanoid robot on India's uncrewed test flight (Gaganyaan mission).

8) Health Sector. (eg- Robots being used in operation Theatres & rehabilitation centre. They assist various surgical procedures.

## Application in Agriculture

- Robots equipped with big data analytics and environmental sensors are transforming agriculture into a data-driven practice, enabling precision farming.
  - Application of the precise amounts of pesticides, herbicides or fertilizers to control weeds, pests and manage nutrients requirements.
  - Deployment for crop surveillance, weed control, monitoring soil health and detecting nutrient deficiencies.

## Challenges and Concerns in building Indian Robotics Ecosystem

- Skilled Human Resources: India lacks skilled engineers and technicians for robotics design, development and maintenance.
- Import Dependency- Heavy dependence on imported robotics components hinders domestic manufacturing and increases costs.
- High Costs- Customized solutions, import reliance and complex integration processes increase robotics costs, hindering adoption, especially among SMEs.
- Technological Immaturity- Insufficient foundational research and limited access to advanced manufacturing capabilities impede the development of sophisticated robotic systems.
- Collaboration Gaps- A lack of effective partnerships between government, industry, academia and startups hinders innovation and growth in the robotics ecosystem.
- Knowledge Gap- Limited understanding of robotics technology and its potential benefits hinders investment and adoption.
- Regulatory Hurdles- Absence of specific robotics regulations, coupled with high certification costs, creates a challenging environment for businesses, particularly startups and MSMEs.

- Infrastructure Constraints- Insufficient power supply and inadequate internet connectivity limit the effective deployment and operation of robots.
- Ethical Issues- Raise significant ethical questions, such as the use of autonomous weapons and algorithmic biases, especially in healthcare and law enforcement.
  - Issues include privacy infringements, biased decision making and intrusive surveillance.
  - Other issues like Robot suicide as happened in South Korea.
- Data and Algorithm Bias- Robots trained on large datasets may perpetuate societal biases.
  - Ex- Amazon's facial recognition software demonstrated gender identification bias in 2019.
- Capital Intensive Nature- limits the ability to scale up production, requiring significant investment in software, manufacturing processes, and production units.
- Job Displacement- Automation leads to job losses in industries like manufacturing creating socio economic challenges 300 million jobs could be lost or diminished due to this rapidly growing technology (Goldman Sachs)
- Cybersecurity Risks- Increased connectivity exposes robots to cyber-attacks.
  - In 2017, the "WannaCry" ransomware attack affected a US robot manufacturing facility.
- Safety Concerns: Industrial robot accidents can be fatal, necessitating better safety protocols and methods for human-robot collaboration.
  - In 2015, a worker at a Volkswagen factory in Germany was reportedly killed by a robot.

## Government Initiatives

| Steps undertaken | Description |
|---|---|
| **National Policy** | **Draft National Strategy for Robotics (NSR)** aims to position India as a global leader in robotics by 2030, recognizing its transformative potential.<br>Core Areas identified by NSR:<br>1. **Manufacturing** = Logistics & Warehousing automation, Process optimisation<br>2. **Healthcare** = Surgical robots, Telemedicine<br>3. **Agriculture** = Crop scouting, Spot spraying, etc.<br>4. **National Security** = Combat robots, Mine detection, etc. |
| **Research** | **Artificial Intelligence and Robotics Technology Park (ARTPARK):** Leverages AI and robotics for |

| | |
|---|---|
| **Centres** | innovation under the *National Mission on Interdisciplinary Cyber-Physical Systems* (NM-ICPS).<br>• **Centre for Advanced Manufacturing for Robotics and Autonomous Systems (CAMRAS):** Established to reduce reliance on imported robotics and autonomous systems, this centre focuses on domestic development.<br>• **I-HUB Foundation for Cobotics (IHFC), IIT Delhi:** Launched eight major projects in areas like medical simulators, healthcare robotics, rehabilitation robotics, and drone applications. |
| **Capacity Building** | • **FutureSkills Prime (MeitY):** Provides a robust online platform offering subsidized access to certified courses in AI, blockchain, robotics, cybersecurity, and more.<br>• **Atal Innovation Mission:** Atal Tinkering Labs (ATLs) provide dedicated innovation workspaces **with Do-It-Yourself (DIY) kits** on emerging technologies like robotics and IoT.<br>• **e-YANTRA:** Funded by the Ministry of Education, this robotics outreach program aims to harness young engineering talent to develop solutions in agriculture, manufacturing, defence, and other sectors. |
| **Made-in-India Robots** | • **DAKSHA:** An automated mobile platform with stair-climbing capabilities designed for handling Improvised Explosive Devices (IEDs).<br>• **Vyommitra:** The spacefaring humanoid robot being developed by ISRO for the Gaganyaan mission.<br>• **MANAV:** India's first 3D-printed humanoid robot with vision and sound processing capabilities, allowing it to walk, talk, and dance based on human commands. |

## Strategic Recommendations to create Robotics

| Recommendations | Description |
|---|---|
| **Enhancing Research and Development (R&D)** | • Increase funding availability for robotics research.<br>• Promote collaboration with **Centres of Excellence (CoEs)** for AI and Cyber-Physical Systems.<br>• Establish platforms for global research partnerships.<br>• Attract and retain skilled professionals in the robotics field.<br>• Fund **Moonshot Projects** to drive groundbreaking innovation in robotics. |
| **Demonstration and Testing** | • Develop infrastructure and facilities for robot testing, validation, and certification.<br>• Ensure responsible and safe adoption of robotics technology. |
| **Commercialization and Supply Chain Development** | • Implement fiscal and non-fiscal interventions to support robotics startups.<br>• Develop supporting infrastructure for the robotics industry.<br>• Enact policy measures to increase domestic value addition and promote exports. |
| **Adoption and Awareness** | • Promote the penetration and adoption of robots in India.<br>• Provide fiscal and non-fiscal support for market expansion.<br>• Create a regulatory framework for robotics.<br>• Conduct awareness campaigns to educate the public and industries about the benefits and responsible use of robotics.<br>• Improve access to network infrastructure to facilitate the deployment of robotic systems. |
| **Capacity Building** | • Focus on building capacities across the innovation lifecycle.<br>• Provide training and education in robotics and related fields to develop a skilled workforce.<br>• Ensure India has the talent and expertise needed to compete globally in the robotics market. |
| **Two-Tier Institutional Framework** | • Establish a two-tier institutional framework to facilitate the implementation of the National Strategy on Robotics, termed the '**National Robotics Mission.**' |
| **Alignment with India AI Vision** | • Ensure that the National Strategy on Robotics aligns with the broader **India AI vision** and supports the objectives of **Cyber-Physical Systems**. |

| Fostering Innovation | • **Robotic Innovation Unit (RIU):** Establish an RIU to create a dynamic robotics ecosystem in collaboration with industry players and startups.<br>• **R&D Centre of Excellence**: Create a dedicated R&D centre to lead cutting-edge discoveries and technological breakthroughs in robotics. |
|---|---|
| Enhancing Regulatory Landscape | • **Demonstration Centres**: Establish centres to showcase the latest robotics innovations and serve as platforms for testing and refining technologies before wider implementation.<br>• **Regulatory Sandboxes**: Implement sandboxes to encourage experimentation with novel robotics technologies in controlled environments.<br>• **Standardization and Safety**: Develop a standardized mechanism to ensure safety and quality in robotics development |
| Financial and Skill Development Support | • **Innovation Fund**: Create a dedicated fund to support innovation and accelerate technological progress in robotics.<br>• **Fiscal Incentives**: Implement incentives to attract investments and stimulate growth in the robotics sector.<br>• **Technical Training**: Develop comprehensive training modules to equip the workforce with the necessary skills for operating and maintaining robots. |

## PYQs Corner

*(Write the Answer and Get Free Evaluation)*

1. Introduce the concept of Artificial Intelligence (AI). How does AI help clinical diagnosis? Do you perceive any threat to privacy of the individual in the use of AI in healthcare? [150 Words] [10 Marks] [2023]

2. What are the areas of prohibitive labour that can be sustainably managed by robots? Discuss the initiatives that can propel the research in premier research institutes for substantive and gainful innovation. [200 Words] [12.5 Marks] [2015]

CHAPTER 19

# NANOTECHNOLOGY

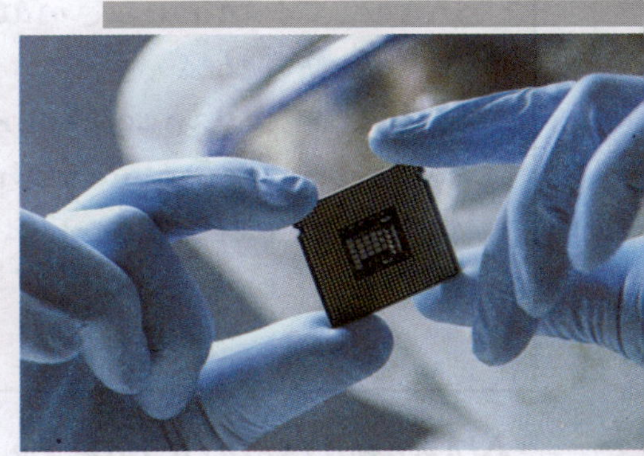

## NANOTECHNOLOGY

- Nano means 'Dwarf' [1 Nanometer = 10-9 Metre (one billionth of a metre)].
- Nanotechnology = Manipulation of matter within nano scale range from 1 to 100 nm and developing new materials with special properties.
- New material thus developed may be stronger, lighter, more precise. At nano size, these new materials may exhibit extraordinary properties that are different from its original properties.

  E.g., Aluminium, which is otherwise stable becomes combustible at nano sizes. Gold, which is otherwise golden yellow becomes reddish brown in colour and soluble in water at nano sizes.

Thus, Nanotechnology aims at utilising these unique properties of Nanoparticles to develop new applications of nano materials that were not possible originally.

| |
|---|
| 1 nm – 1 Glucose Molecule |
| 10nm – 1 DNA Strand |
| 100nm – Virus size |
| 1000nm – Bacteria size |
| 1 lac nm – 1 Hair Strand |
| 10 lac nm – 1 Ant |

- In 1959, Richard Feynman (Nobel Prize winning American physicist), presented a concept of nanotechnology at Caltech. His ideas have proven correct, making him "Father of Modern Nanotech."
- In 1974, Prof. Norio Taniguchi coined the term 'Nanotechnology.'
- In 1981, scanning tunneling microscope (STM) was invented which made it possible to "see" individual atoms. Later Atomic Force Microscope (AFM) made it possible for Nanotechnology to become reality

| Top Down Approach | Bottom-Up Approach |
|---|---|
| → Break down bulk materials to obtain nanoparticles.<br>→ Utilizes advance techniques such as precision engineering and lithography.<br>→ Material deposition is employed to achieve the desired structure. | → Build nanostructures from individual atom or molecules.<br>→ Relies on physical and chemical methods for synthesis of nanostructures.<br>→ Self-assembly driven by chemical-physical interactions organizes nanostructures precisely. |

- Nanomaterials can be available naturally and present in nature. Example-
  - → Nanosize scales in the wings of butterfly.
  - → Corals, spider silk, clay, opal, virus, biomolecules.
- Matter can be manipulated and therefore artificial nanoparticles can be developed and they can be both Organic and inorganic in nature.
  - Organic – Graphene, Fullerence, CNT, Inorganic – Gold-spherical, hollow-Nanocages, Silver, iron, copper, aluminium, tungsten, titanium etc

## *GRAPHENE

- Basic allotrope of carbon in which C-atoms are linked together in a hexagonal lattice arrangement.
- Properties of Graphene
  - → Exceptional Mechanical, Electrical and Thermal properties.
  - → Exceptionally strong yet light weight
  - → Near perfect conductor of electricity.
  - → Optically Transparent and Hydrophobic (water repelling)

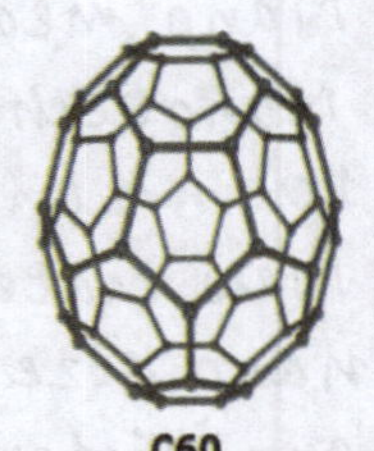


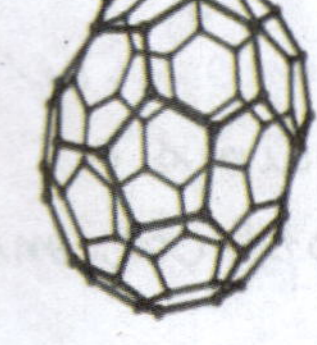


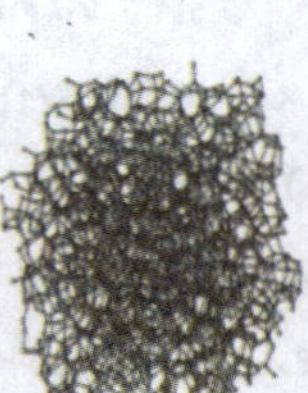


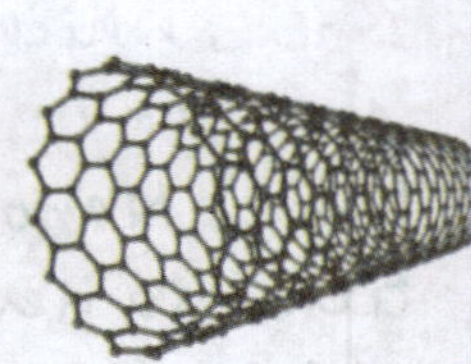


Fig: Carbon Allotropes

- Applications
  - → Utilised for making Electronic Skins used especially in Robotics.
  - → In Wearable Electronics in health care technology and improve the efficiency of energy harvesting devices.
  - → Desalinization of water as it may block salt molecules and let the water pass through the Graphene layer.
  - → Used to improve quality of Touchscreens in electronic devices. Ex: Smartphones.
  - → Being able to repel water, it can prevent and delay the oxidisation reaction that occurs in rusting. Thus, it can make Automobiles component rust free.

## * CARBON NANOTUBES (CNT)

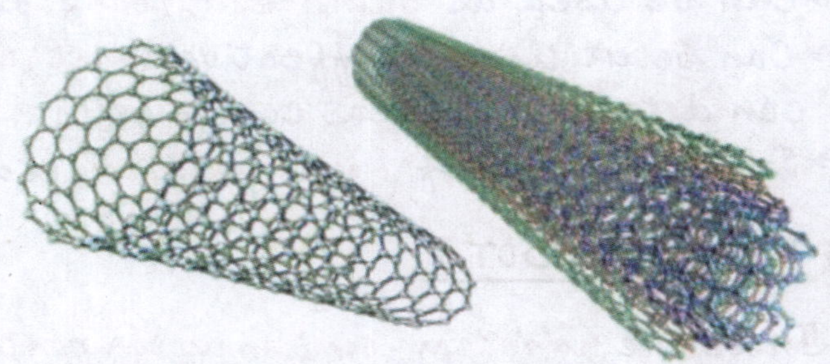

Single- and multi-walled carbon nanotubes.

- CNT is also a form of carbon allotrope in which Graphene sheets are rolled in cylindrical tube like structure. Developed by Sumio Lijima in 1991.
- CNT may be single-walled (SWCNT) or Multi-Walled (MWCNT) in which CNTs are arranged concentrically within each other. MWCNT can slide within each other without any friction making finest and smallest Rotational Motors.
- Properties :- → Ultimate high-strength nanomaterials.
  → May be the best heat conducting materials ever Known.
- Applications

→ Used in manufacturing of stabproof and bulletproof nanomaterials.

→ Used in Medical science as scaffhold to support and reinforce tissue repair, accelerating healing process.

→ CNT is replacing Silicon and Germanium based computer chips with Nanochips containing CNTs, developing Nano circuits with enhanced speeds and storage capacities.

→ CNTs intrinsically have an enormously high surface area and with the ability to attach essentially any chemical species to their sidewalls, can provide unique catalyst supports.

→ Can be used in effectively dispersing heat as they are extremely good conductors of heat and therefore can function as Heat Sinks.

→ Bucky paper (accumulation of CNTs in a flat sheet like structure) can be used as effective fireproof coating making valuables fireproof.

## * FULLERENCE

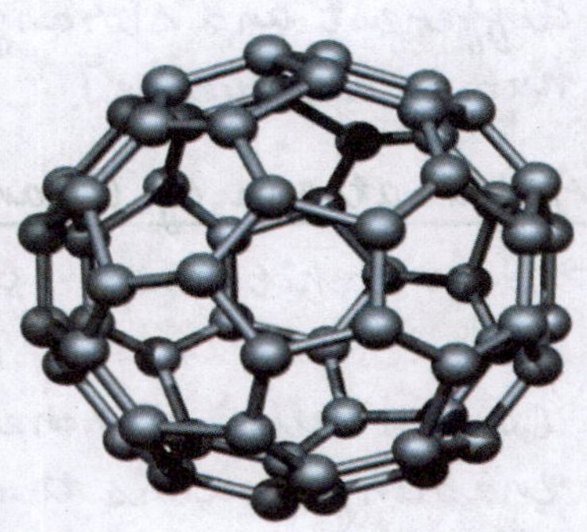

- An allotrope of carbon in which Graphene sheets are rolled into spherical ball like structure. Family of such closed mesh topology ($C_n$) is named after Buckministerfullerence ($C_{60}$) named after the American architect and inventor Buckminster Fuller.
- Properties :

→ Extraordinary mechanical strength and electrical conductivity.

→ Unique property to "absorb heat and light" and get activated.

- Types of Fullerences :- Buckyball clusters ($C_{20}$), $C_{60}$, $C_{70}$, CNT etc.

• **Applications:**

→ Can be used as superconductors and also absorbent for gases.

→ Can be utilised as effective constrast agents in biomedical applications that can detect and treat cancer cells.

→ In preparation of Ferromagnets, etc.

## * QUANTUM DOTS

• These are nanoscale semiconductor particles (1-100nm) with unique optical and electrical properties.

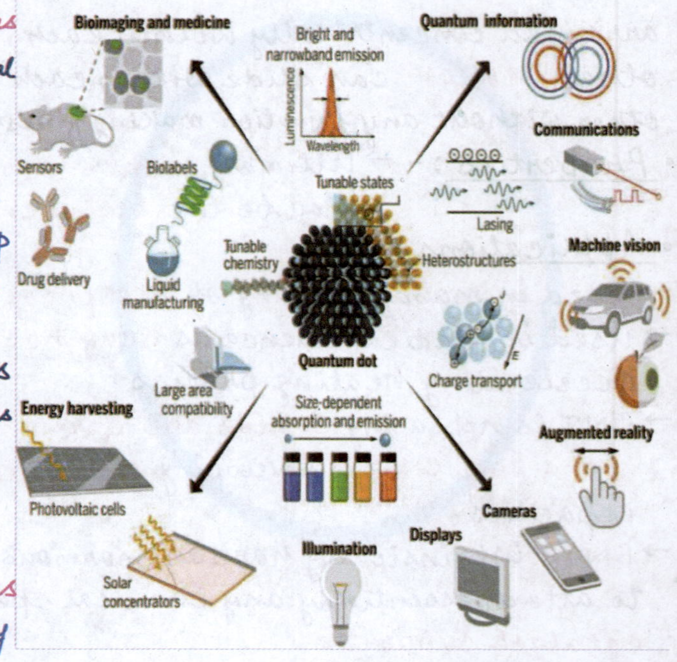


◦ Quantum dot is a crystal that often consists of just a few thousand atoms. In terms of size, it has a some relationship to a football as a football has to the size of Earth.

• Quantum Dots are like Jails for electrons where electrons are trapped which enables us to harness the quantum effects that electrons exhibit.

• Nobel Prize in Chemistry, 2023 was awarded to Moungi Bawendi, Louis Brus and Aleksey Yekimov – for the discovery and synthesis of Quantum Dots.

• In the Nanoworld, things really do behave differently. Once size of matter is reduced to nanoscales, a strange phenomena starts to occur – Quantum Effect (that determines its unique characteristics)
[Quantum Theory: The motion and behaviour of very small particles are radically different and strange, when compared with any familiar object in normal human experience].

• **Applications of Quantum Dots:-**

→ QDs exhibit specific opto-electronic properties and thus can be used for fluorescene imaging where QDs are injected in body which when encounters cancer cells, attaches to it and lights them up under light of certain frequency enabling doctors to accurately target these cells.

→ Can be designed to release drugs in response to a certain trigger like pH or temperature (Targeted Drug Delivery).

→ In Photonics and Solar cells etc.

## * NANOROBOTS

- Nanorobotics describes the technology of producing machines or robots at the nanoscales.
- Nanobots is an informal term to refer to Engineered Nano Machines.
- These carry out very specific function and are ~50-100nm wide.
- They can be used very effectively for Targeted Drug Delivery (reducing chances of possible side-effects).

## Major Applications of Nanotechnology

**ELECTRONICS**

→ Nano-RAM: Non-volatile RAM (Random Access Memory) based on CNT deposited on a chip-like substrate. Its small size permits very high density memories.
→ Nano Optomechanical SRAM (Static RAM): This shows faster read/write time as compared to a MEMS memory.
→ Chip fabrication can be done by Nanolithograpgy (this technology is fabricating nanometer-scale structure).
→ The transistors are made up of nanowires, which brought revolution in communication and information technology.
→ Nanorods for display technique are the future technology which consume less electricity and emit less heat.

**AGRICULTURE AND FOOD**

→ Nano-sensors can detect harmful bacteria or contaminants in food such as E. coli or Salmonella ensuring safer consumption and preventing foodborne illness.
→ Nanoencapsulation techniques and nanocarrier can protect and deliver essential nutrients such as vitamins or anti-oxidants, ensuring their stability and targeted delivery to improve the nutritional value of food products.
→ Can help in increasing agricultural productivity develop drought-resistant crops and enhance post harvest storage methods – contribute to food security.
→ Contribute to precision farming → monitor moisture levels, nutrient content and pest infestation allowing farmers to precisely manage irrigation, fertilizer and pest control for optimal crop growth.
→ Sensors for food-borne pathogens.

### Liquid Nano Urea

Recently, Indian Farmers Fertiliser Cooperative limited (IFFCO) introduced world's first liquid nano urea for farmers across the world. It is a potential chemical nitrogen fertilizer.

**Benefits :-**

1) Improved Agricultural Produce with reduced urea consumption as the efficiency of LNU is as high as 85-90% to deliver Nitrogen to plants in comparison to 25% of conventional use.
2) Higher shelf life as no issue of caking on coming in contact with moisture.
3) An average 8% increase in yield is witnessed
4) Significant reduction in urea imports
5) Reduce soil, water and air pollution from urea.

**SECURITY**

- → Nano-fertilisers can deliver nutrients directly to the plant roots, improving nutrient absorption and reducing fertiliser runoff, leading to increased crop yields and reduced environmental pollution.
- → Hybrid Polymers used in packaging and to reduce spoilage.
- → Nanoemulsions – reduce bacteria on produce.
- → Nanoparticles based on Titanium Dioxide – used as microbial agents.
- → Nano Fertilizers.

**ENERGY**

- → Solar Paints or Photovoltaic Paints can replace solar panels. Applying solar paints to any surface will enable it to capture energy from the sun and transform it into electricity. This can be used in houses and cars.
- → Nanogenerators (wind power generation) have thin flexible sheets which when bent can generate potential power.
- → Nanobatteries used to help rechargable lithium ion batteriers last longer.
- → Nanomaterials to optimize combustion and reduce friction.
- → Nano-catalysts for improved food efficiency.

**HEALTHCARE & MEDICINE**

- → Nanotech detectors for heart attack.
- → Nanocarriers for eye surgery, chemotherapy etc.
- → Diabetic Pads for regulating blood sugar levels
- → Nanoflares for detection of cancer cells.
- → Nanosponges absorbing toxins from blood
- → Nanopores to make DNA sequencing more efficient
- → Nanochips to check plaque in arteries
- → Synthetic bone has been developed by the molecular level manipulation of calcium and phosphate through nano-particulate
- → Silver nano-crystals material kill bacteria and prevent infection.
- → Targeted drug delivery using nano capsules.
- → Nanobots material can clear the blockage in arteries and solve heart attack risk in human body.

**OTHER**

- → Environment: Nanotechnology innovations address environmental pollution challenges by creating materials and technologies for water and soil remediation.
  - The nanotechnology can be used to remove industrial water pollutants in the groundwater through chemical reactions at a cheaper rate.
  - Nanotechnology sensors and solutions also have the potential to detect, identify, filter and neutralise harmful chemical or biological agents in the air and soil.

BENEFITS

→ Transport: Nanotechnology contributes to manufacturing lighter, smarter, efficient and greener automobiles, aircraft and ships.
- Materials made of carbon nanotubes can reduce the weight of the spaceships while retaining or increasing the structural strength.

## Application of Nanotechnology in Food Industry

### Food Processing

- **ATTACKING AGENT** — Improves consistency & prevent lump formation.
- **NANO ADDITIVES & NEUTRACEUTICALS** — Improve nutritional value of food.
- **GELATING AGENT** — To improve of food texture
- **NANO CAPSULATION & NANOCARRIERS** — To protect aroma, flavor and other ingredients in food

### Food Packaging

- **IMPROVED PACKAGING** — Use of Nanoparticles to improve physical performance of food
- **ACTIVE PACKAGING** — Nanoparticles as antimicrobial agent.
- **SMART PACKAGING** — Nano-biosensors for pathogen detection.

## Concerns of Nanotechnology

### Environmental Concerns:

- **Toxicity:** Nanoparticles due to their small sizes, can enter the environment and potentially harm ecosystems.
  - For instance, titanium dioxide nanoparticles, common in food and cosmetics have been found to accumulate in the livers and spleen of rodents.
- **Bioaccumulation and Biomagnification:** Nanoparticles can accumulate in living organisms and potentially magnify their concentration in the food chain, posing risks to higher-level predators, including humans.
- Some nanoparticles are highly persistent in the environment, making them difficult to degrade, leading to long-term environmental problems.

### Health Concerns:

- **Toxicity:** Nanoparticles can accumulate in various organs and induce toxicity leading to long-term safety concerns.
  - Some nanoparticles have been shown to cause lung damage.
- Certain nanoparticles can penetrate biological barriers, leading to cellular damage and adverse health effects.
- Ethical considerations arise regarding access to nanomaterial treatments, affordability and equitable distribution, especially in developing countries.

## ⊟ Ethical Concerns:

- **Dual-Use Technology:** Nanotechnology has the potential for both beneficial and harmful applications.
    - There are concerns about the misuse of nanotechnology for military or terrorist purposes
- **Economic Inequality:** The high cost of nanotechnology research and development could exacerbate economic inequality, as access to these technologies might be limited to wealthy nations or corporations.
- **Environmental Justice:** The potential environmental risks of nanotechnology could disproportionately affect marganalised communities.
- **Surveillance and security:** Nano enabled surveillance technologies raise concerns about government surveillance, erosion of civil liberties and the potential for misuse by authoritarian regimes.

## ⊟ Social Concerns:

- **Workforce Displacement** as automation and technological advancements replace traditional jobs.
    - This shift could exacerbate socio-economic inequalities and contribute to unemployment rates in certain sectors.
- **Social Justice and access:** Access to the benefits of nanotechnology may be unequal, exacerbating existing social disparities.
- **Regulatory challenges:** The rapid pace of technological innovation may outpace regulatory oversight, leading to gaps in accountability and enforcement.
- **Privacy Concerns:** Nanotechnology enables the development of advance surveillance devices, raising concerns about invasion of privacy and erosion of personal freedoms.
    - For instance, nano-sized sensors embedded in everyday objects could collect sensitive data without individual's Knowledge.
- **Public Discussion** for ensuring responsible development in nanotechnologies.
    - Addressing environmental, health, and safety concerns related to nanoparticles is crucial for their sustainable use.

# INDIA'S INITIATIVE

1) **9th Five Years Plan:** 1st time promoted research in nano materials.
2) **National Science and Technology Initiative (NSTI), 2001:** Set up by DST (Department of Science and Technology) to focus on issues related to infrastructure development, research and application programmes related to nano-materials including drug delivery, gene targeting and DNA chips.

3) Nano Mission

- Launched in 2007 under the Department of Science and Technology.
- Aimed to promote basic research, human resource development, infrastructure development and international collaborations in nanotechnology.
- Provided funding for various research projects, infrastructure development and human resource development programs.

4) Nanoelectronics Innovation Council set up by MeitY.

5) Indian Nanoelectronics Users Programme (INUP) by MeitY for understanding research and skill development.

6) Institute of NanoScience and Technology (INST) – Mohali – An autonomous institute supported by DST, Govt. of India.

7) National Centers for Nanofabrican and Nanoelectronics (NCNNs): Established at IISc Bangalore and IIT Bombay to provide state-of-the-art facilities for nanotechnology research and development.
   - These centres facilitate research and developmental activities for both academic and industry.

8) Thriving Innovation Ecosystem: Over 30 companies, including big names like TCS, Bharat Biotech, Sun Pharma and Tata Chemicals are actively involved in developing nanotechnology products and applications.
   - Startup Support: Nano-incubators are providing crucial resources and funding to tech startups and young researchers with promising ideas in nanotechnology.

9) Global Collaboration: Established collaborations with countries like the USA, Italy, Germany, Japan and Israel.
   - Multilateral Engagement: Participating in nanotechnology projects led by UN agencies.

**Achievements of India in the field of Nanotechnology**

- Energy Efficient Electronics: Researchers at IISc Bangalore fabricated nano-electronic transistors using carbon nanotubes, offering a more efficient alternative to silicon-based transistors.
- Quantum Computing Potential: IIT Bombay's development of logic gates using nano-scale components paves the way for future quantum computers.
- Targeted Drug Delivery: IIT Bombay scientists have created nanotechnology based drug delivery systems like nanoparticles and nano capsules for targeted drug delivery and controlled release.
- Vaccine Development: Bharat Biotech leveraged bioinformatics, molecular modelling, and nanotechnology to develop Covaxin, India's first indigenous COVID19 vaccine.
- Water Treatment: Tata Chemicals created Tata Swach, a low cost nanofiltration device that purifies water without electricity.

## PYQs Corner

*(Write the Answer and Get Free Evaluation)*

1. What do you understand by nanotechnology and how is it helping in health sector? [150 Words] [10 Marks] **[2020]**
2. Why is nanotechnology one of the key technologies of the 21st century? Describe the salient features of India Government's Mission on Nan science and Technology and the scope of its application in the development process of the country. [200 Words] [12.5 Marks] **[2016]**

# CHAPTER 20

# HEALTH AND BIOTECHNOLOGY

## ONE HEALTH APPROACH

- One Health approach is a collaborative effort that recognizes the interconnectedness between the health of humans, animals and environment.
- It derives its inspiration from One-Health Joint Plan of Action of Quadripartite- FAO, UNEP, WHO, and World Organisation for Animal Health (WOAH).

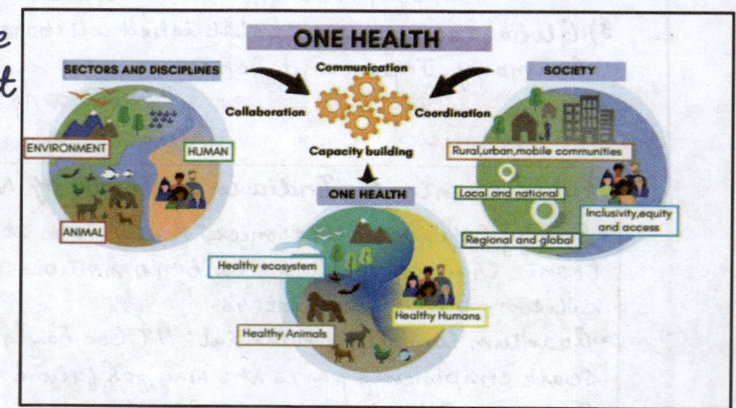


### Collaboration
It brings together experts from various disciplines, such as human health, animal health and environmental science.

### Disease Prevention
It aims to prevent diseases at source, considering their zoonotic nature and means of spread.

### Addressing Global Health Threats
One Health is particularly important for tackling zoonotic diseases like rabies, avian influenza and COVID-19.

### Promoting Sustainability
By addressing the health of ecosystems, One Health approach helps ensure a healthy environment for all living things.

## Need of One Health Concept

- **Emerging Infectious Zoonotic Diseases**- Over 60% of emerging infectious diseases are zoonotic, meaning they are transmitted from animals to humans.
  Ex- Ebola, SARS, and COVID-19.
- **Disease Surveillance**- Integrating human, animal and environmental health monitoring helps in early detection and control of outbreaks.
- **Antimicrobial Resistance (AMR)**- Coordinated efforts in all sectors are required to develop and implement effective AMR mitigation strategies.
- **Food Safety and Security**- Healthy livestock and poultry are essential for safe and sufficient food supplies.
  - Sustainable farming and responsible use of pesticides + fertilizers → translates into one health.
- **Pollution and Contamination** in environment can affect both human and animal health.
- **Ecosystem Health** supports diverse species, which can prevent the spread of certain diseases by maintaining ecological balances.
- **Climate Change** affects the distribution and behaviour of disease vectors such as mosquitoes → lead to spread of diseases like malaria and dengue fever.
- **Habitat Disruption** forces animals into closer contact with humans, increasing the risk of zoonotic disease transmission.
- **Disease Regulation**- Diverse ecosystems can help regulate the spread of infectious diseases by maintaining natural predators and ecological balances.
- **Resource Efficiency**- Coordinated efforts can optimize the use of resources and expertise, improving overall health outcomes.

## Indian Initiatives Aligned With One Health Concept

- **Standing Committee on Zoonoses, 2006**: Purpose of this committee was to provide the Union and the State governments guidance and recommendations on challenges related to zoonoses.
- **Consortium on One Health, 2021** launched by Department of Biotechnology.
  - It brings together 27 organisations from several ministries and plans.
  - Focus on assessing burden of five transboundary animal diseases and 10 select zoonotic diseases.
- **One Health pilot project, 2022**- launched by Department of Animal Husbandry and Dairy (DAHD) + in partnership with Bill & Melinda Gates Foundation and the Confederation of Indian Industry from Karnataka and Uttarakhand.
  - It intends to strengthen intersectoral collaborations through capacity building → for improving livestock health, human health, wildlife health and environmental health.

→ National One Health Mission- is currently under consideration to be spearheaded by the Office of the Principal Scientific Advisor.

- The idea behind this mission is to coordinate, support and integrate all existing One Health initiatives in the country.

## Challenges In Implementing One Health Approach In Practice

- Siloed approach with separate disease surveillance programs pertaining to infections in plants, animals and humans.
- Lack of communication and adequate data sharing, limiting the opportunities for detecting zoonotic.
- Inadequate Funding
- limited practical guidance and understanding on how to foster and sustain cross-sector collaborations.
- limited awareness among common people limiting their cooperation and active engagement.
- Lack of trained professionals and verterinarians.

### What is the concept of 'One Health'

**Definition:** Worldwide strategy for interdisciplinary collaboration in healthcare.
**Focus:** Human-animal-environment interface, including zoonotic diseases.
**International Adoption:** FAO, WHO, OIE recognition.
**National Context:** Part of India's National Mission on Biodiversity and Human Well-Being.

### Importance of One Health

**Interconnectedness:** Zoonotic diseases, environmental pressures, food security, antimicrobial resistance.
**Pandemic Preparedness:** Vital for combating outbreaks like Covid-19.
**Factors Driving Zoonotic Diseases:** Land-use changes, climate change, human-animal contact, travel, trade.

ENVIRONMENTAL HEALTH
ONE HEALTH
HUMAN HEALTH
ANIMAL HEALTH

### Outcomes of One Health Approach

**Education and Training:** Enhances interdisciplinary programs.
**Information Sharing:** Facilitates disease detection, diagnosis, research.
**Disease Prevention:** Focus on infectious and chronic diseases.
**Therapeutic Advances:** Develops new therapies and treatments.

### National Mission on Biodiversity and Human Well-Being

**Government Initiative:** Launched by India.
**Objectives:** Explore biodiversity links to health, development, agriculture, livelihood.
**One Health Component:** Connects biodiversity and human health.
**Surveillance Systems:** Set up at emerging infectious disease hotspots.

### Conclusion:-

**Collaborative Approach:** Emphasizes collaboration among sectors.
**Solutions:** Addressing emerging diseases, food safety, antimicrobial resistance.
**Building a Better World:** Attention and investment from policymakers, researchers, and the public.

# ANTIMICROBIAL RESISTANCE

- About - Antimicrobial resistance (AMR) is essentially when germs learn to fight back against the drugs designed to kill them. This makes infections harder to treat, putting us at risk of more severe illness and even death.
  - Micro-organisms that develop antimicrobial resistance are referred to as "superbugs".

## Severeity of AMR

| India | World |
|---|---|
| • India becomes AMR capital of World.<br>• As per Health Ministry → between 2017 to 2022, AMR cases spiked more than 4.5 times.<br>• India is also world's largest consumer of antibiotics in terms of total volume.<br>• ICMR study found that E. coli bacteria, accounting for 33% of AMR cases in 2022. | • AMR has been declared as one of top 10 global public health threats by WHO.<br>• As per Lancet, AMR was responsible for 4.95 million deaths per year worldwide in 2019.<br>• AMR may cause a global annual GDP loss of $3.4 trillion by 2030.<br>• AMR may push 24 million people into extreme poverty. |

## Drivers/Causes of AMR

- Misuse and Overuse of Antimicrobials - As per Lancet Regional Health Southeast Asia, the total defined daily dose per day - assumed average maintenance dose per day in 2019 was 5,071 million (10.4 DDD/1,000/day).
  - Over the Counter Sale of Antibiotics in India without a prescription, leading to their inappropriate use.
- Lack of access to clean water, sanitation and hygiene (WASH) for both human and animals → allows for spread of pathogens, increasing reliance on antibiotics to treat infections.
  - ICMR study found that E. coli bacteria, accounting for 33% of AMR cases in 2022.
- Poor infection and disease prevention and control in health-care facilities can contribute to the spread of resistant bacteria between patients.
  - Disproportionate use of Colistin in Poultry and Veterinary to prevent and treat infections.

- Poor access to quality, affordable medicines, vaccines and diagnostics; As per National Health Accounts Estimates for India 2019-2020 it stands at 47.07%.
- Lack of awareness and knowledge → led to the consumption of antibiotics or not doing a full course of Medicine.
  - Cyberchondria → People abruptly stop their treatment because they have trusted internet medical information.
- Lack of enforcement of legislation: World Bank 2021 report → found that over 60% of low and middle income countries lack effective regulations on the sale and use of antibiotics in animals.

## Measures Taken to Prevent AMR

| India | World |
|---|---|
| • National Action Plan for AMR (2017-21) to reduce the impact of AMR through focusing on One Health Approach.<br>• AMR Surveillance Network- to generate evidence and capture trends and patterns of drug resistant infections in the country.<br>• Joint Indo-German collaboration for research on AMR.<br>• India agreed to join the International Centre for Anti-Microbial Resistance (ICARS)- research platform to tackle AMR in low and Low Middle-Income Countries as mission partner.<br>• The Drug Controller General of India (DCGI) has banned several inappropriate fixed dose combinations (FDCs).<br>  • DCGI also bans use of Colistin as growth promoter in animal feed in poultry.<br>• Delhi Declaration on AMR- An inter-ministerial consensus was signed at launch of NAP-AMR. pledging their whole-hearted support in AMR containment. | • WHO Global Action Plan on AMR to tackle microbial resistance, a major global health threat.<br>• Global Antimicrobial Resistance and Use Surveillance System (GLASS)- Standardized and decentralized collection, analysis and sharing of data on AMR and AMU at a national, regional and global level.<br>• Essential Medicines List category by WHO → ACCESS, WATCH RESERVE to address the abuse of antibiotics.<br>• Muscat Ministerial Manifesto on AMR → signed by health ministers from around the world in 2017. committing to take action to address growing threat of AMR. Its targets:<br>  • Reduction of total amount of antimicrobials from agrifood systems by atleast 30-50% by 2050.<br>  • Preserving critically important antimicrobials for human medicine and ending the use of medically important antimicrobials for growth promotions in animals). |

## Way Forward

- Preventive Measures:
  - Pharmaceutical companies- to upgrade manufacturing processes to reduce runoff.
  - Farmers- Avoid using chemicals like streptomycin, oxytetracycline, copper-based products.
  - Hospitals- should Consider on-site treatment of antimicrobial pollutants in wastewater.
  - One Health Approach- AMR requires a united multisectoral approach → brings together multiple sectors and stakeholders to work together to attain better public health outcomes.
  - 3C approach to R&D: Coordination Collaboration and Communication → is essential to ensure effective resource utilization and awareness among stakeholders about progress in development of new antibiotics.
- Improving WASH Services is key to address → Poor waste management and WASH services in metro cities driven outbreaks of infectious diseases, which spread through the fecal-oral route.

## GENERIC DRUG

- Generic Drugs/ Medicines- These are medications created to be same as an already marketed brand-name drug in dosage form, safety, strength, quality, composition & intended use. Thus these are Bioequivalence, i.e generic medicine works in the same way as branded medicine.
- These are comparatively much cheaper, since their manufacturer don't have to undertake extensive R&D & chemical trails for their development.
- India's Pharmaceutical industry is the 3rd largest in the world in terms of volume and 14th largest in terms of value.
- India is the largest provider of generic medicines globally, occupying a 20% share in global supply by volume.
- Economic Survey 2022-23 estimated India's domestic pharmaceutical market to touch $ 130 billion by 2030.

## Regulation of Generic Medicine in India

- Indian Medical Council (Professional Conduct, Etiquette and Ethics) Regulations, 2002 prescribes that every physician should prescribe drugs with generic names legibly to ensure that there is a rational prescription and use of drugs.
- National Medical Commission Act, 2019 → empowers State Medical Councils or Ethics and Medical Registration Board of Commission, to take disciplinary

action against a doctor for violation of provision of the aforesaid Regulations.

- Drugs Technical Advisory Board of India → allows pharmacies to tell generic medicines to patients even if the prescriptions specify branded versions.

| Reason for Promoting Generic Drugs | India's Initiative related to Generic Drugs |
|---|---|
| • Improving medicine affordability - is crucial in a country like India with the world's highest population.<br>• As per Economic Survey 2022-23 about 48.2% (2018-19) of total health expenditure in India is financed by household out-of-pocket expenditure.<br>  • Medicines constitute 20% to 60% of total healthcare expenditure.<br>• Expanding Generic medicine export market - Currently, India supplies over 50% of Africa's requirement for generics, 40% of generic demand in the USA and 25% of all medicines in the UK. | • Pradhan Mantri Bhartiya Janaushadhi Pariyojana, 2008 → PMBJ Kendras across country will produce quality generic drugs and implants accessible at affordable prices.<br>• National Health Mission → Assistance is provided for provision of essential generic drugs free of cost in public health facilities.<br>• Production Linked Incentive → Scheme for Promotion of Domestic Manufacturing of Critical Key Starting Materials (KSMs) Drug Intermediates and Active Pharmaceutical Ingredients (API). |

## Lacunae in Promoting Generic Drug in India.

- Regulatory Cholesterol - Variability in regulatory standards across states can create confusion and hinder uniform implementation → delay entry of generic drugs into market.
- Negative Perception Issues - among both healthcare providers and patients that generic drugs are of lower quality compared to branded drugs.
- ILLEGITIMATE Drugs - In 2018, Central Drug Standard Control Organization - Identified nearly 4.5% of all generic drugs circulated in the domestic market to be substandard.
- Promotional Activities - Branded drug companies often invest heavily in marketing and promotional activities, which generic drug manufacturers may not match.
- Inefficient supply chain management - can limit availability of generic drugs in certain regions, especially in rural areas.
- Patent Challenges - Patent laws and litigation can delay the entry of generic drugs into the market.
- Evergreening - Practices by pharmaceutical companies to extend the life of patents and delay the introduction of generics.

- Doctors Prescriptions - may prefer prescribing branded drugs due to perceived efficacy or relationships with pharmaceutical representatives.
- Import dependency for Key Starting Materials (KSMs)/Active pharmaceutical ingredients (API): Example - around 70-80% of the APIs are imported from China.

## Way Forward

- Clear Categorization by DCGI to differentiate between poor-quality drugs and counterfeit drugs to ensure targeted action.
  - Product Authentication through technologies like digital verification systems can help authenticate genuine drugs and combat counterfeiting.
  - Tamper-Resistant Packaging to defer the circulation of fake drugs.
- Implementing Track and Trace Technology to improve supply chain transparency and identify potential tampering.
- Patient Awareness Campaigns: Educating patients about benefits and quality of generic drugs can increase their acceptance.
  - Raising awareness about Pradhan Mantri Bhartiya Janaushadhi Pariyojana (PMBJP) Kendras.
- Balancing Access and Innovation - Through comprehensive regulatory framework.
- Securing Access to Essential Medicines by Granting compulsory licenses for essential drugs can ensure affordability and prevent monopolies that restrict access.
- Refining Production linked Incentive (PLI) schemes for pharmaceuticals can incentivize production of essential and affordable drugs.

# NEGLECTED TROPICAL DISEASE (NTDs)

- About - NTDs are a diverse group of infectious diseases that primarily affect improverised communities in developing regions.
  - NTDs are caused by various pathogens like viruses, bacteria and parasites.

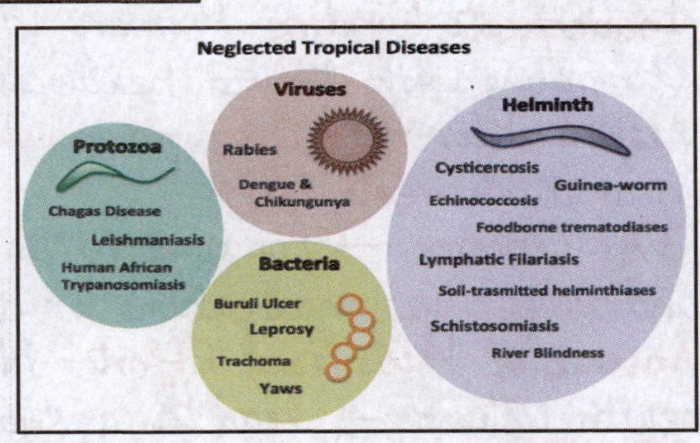


Status -

- India has the world's largest absolute burden of at least 10 major NTDs including dengue, lymphatic filariasis, leprosy, visceral leishmaniasis or Kala-azar and rabies.
- As per Global Report on NTD 2023 → 16 countries account for 80% of global NTD burden and 47 countries eliminated atleast one NTD.
- As per Global Report on Neglected Tropical Diseases 2024 →

- India was certified free of NTDs like dracunculiasis and yaws.
- India, has the highest disease burden, treating about 117 million fewer people for lymphatic filariasis and soil-transmitted helminthiasis in 2022 compared to 2021.
- 40.56% of India's population needed interventions against NTDs in 2022.
- Till December 2023, a total of 50 countries have successfully eliminated at least one NTD, making the halfway point towards the 2030 target of 100 countries.
- Iraq became the 50th country to eliminate at least one NTD.

## Impact of NTDs

- Affecting World's Poorest People- NTDs perpetuate a cycle of poor educational outcomes and limited professional opportunities + associated with stigma and social exclusion.
- On Women's Health- Diseases with cutaneous manifestations are disfiguring, particularly for women, because they delay health-seeking behaviour, diagnosis and treatment.
- On children's Health- Impair physical and cognitive development amongst children as infection leads to malnutrition, cognitive impairment, stunted growth, and treatment.
- Additional Strain on Health Care System- In developing countries → lead to catastrophic expenditures and reduce individual productivity.
- Increasing Disability - Adjusted life years → Conservative estimates indicate that NTDs contribute 19 million DALYs which represents about 1% of the global burden of disease.

## Hurdles in Tackling NTDs

- Inadequate Funding- Primary victims are low and middle-income countries → struggling with limited healthcare budgets → difficult to allocate sufficient resources for mass drug administration programs, research & development of new treatments.
- 3 A's Concerns → For some NTDs the issue lies with readily available, affordable and accessible medications or diagnostics.
- Absence of Prioritized Efforts- NTDs are overshadowed by more prominent health concerns → lead to a shortage of trained healthcare workers dedicated to NTDs control, inadequate surveillance systems to track disease burden.
- Prevalence of Social Stigma- NTDs like Leishmaniases can cause skin ulcers, visible disfigurement or disabilities leading to social stigma and discrimination due to fear of rejection or isolation → people stop treatment and create a cycle of trasmission.

## Measures Taken to Combat NTDs

| India | Global |
|---|---|
| • National Filaria Control Programme (NFCP) - 1955 → Reduce the burden of Lymphatic Filariasis.<br><br>• National Vector Borne Disease Control Programme (NVBDCP) - 2003 → Control and prevent vector-borne diseases like Lymphatic Filariasis, Kala-azar, Malaria, Dengue, Chikungunya and Japanese Encephalitis.<br>• Hathipaon Mukt Bharat Abhiyan - 2015 → To eliminate Lymphatic Filariasis transmission.<br>• Bangladesh India and Nepal jointly established a regional alliance to eliminate kala-azar, with assistance of WHO<br>• Mass Drug Administration (MDA) was launched in January 2023 to eliminate LF by 2027. | • WHO's NTD Roadmap → WHO current roadmap (2020-2030) outlines concrete actions to achieve a world free of NTDs by 2030.<br>• World NTD Day - Observed annually on 30th January → Raising awareness is vital in the fight against NTDs.<br>• Abu Dhabi Declaration on Eradication of Guinea Worm Disease.<br>• Kigali Declaration on NTDs renewed global commitment to control, eliminate or eradicate a variety of NTDs by 2030.<br>• Declaration of Second Global Ministerial Meeting on Neglected Tropical Diseases, London 2009 → helped in mobilizing resources and political will to address NTDs. |

Preventive Chemotherapy

WHO's five core Strategic interventions For NTDs

Innovative and intensified disease management.

Vector control

Veterinary public health.

Provision of safe water, sanitation and hygiene.

# TRADITIONAL KNOWLEDGE

- Traditional knowledge (TK)- is knowledge, know-how skills & practices that are developed, sustained & passed on from generation to generation within a community, often forming part of its cultural or spiritual identity.

India is rich in TK especially because of its rich biological diversity heritage. This TK is the foundation of cultural patrimony. The majority of indigenous & local communities are found in bio-rich and diverse regions.

Article 8(j) of Convention on Biological Diversity defines TK as the "awareness inventions and traditions of local & indigenous cultures worldwide." TK acquired from experience gained over the centuaries and adapted to the local culture & environment, is transmitted orally from generation to generations.

## Reasons to Protect TK

(1) Cultural Preservation & Identity.
(2) Economic Benefits (marketable potential)
(3) Promoting sustainable Practices (eg- Traditional Farming Methods)
(4) Preventing Misappropriation & Biopiracy.
(5) Healthcare & Medicinal Benefits (Unani, Ayurveda, Siddha)
(6) Scientific Validation & Research (medicinal properties of plants)
(7) Promoting Diversity & Respect for Indigenous Rights.

## Challenges to TK

(1) complex Documentation & Codification- (often passed orally through generations) & thus lack the kind of proof typically required in IPR cases)
(2) Complex legal & Regulatory Framework- (not well suited to protect TK)
(3) Biopiracy (commercial exploitation of TK without any fair compensation to the community from which it originates).
(eg- Neem Patent in USA - objection raised by India citing Traditional Neem Use.
Turmeric Patent in USA. objection raised by India citing centuries old usage of this Indian-Herb.
(4) Difficulties in Benefit-sharing.
(5) Inadequate Recognition & misunderstanding
(6) Transboundary Nature of TK.
(7) Fragmented legislation & Enforcement.

# Traditional Knowledge Digital library

- TKDL → a database of Indian traditional knowledge established in 2001, by council of Scientific and Industrial Research (CSIR) and Ministry of AYUSH.
  - It contains information related to Ayurveda, Unani, Siddha, Sowa Rigpa and Yoga in five international languages (English, German, French, Japanese and Spanish).
- Effective deterrent against bio-piracy- seeks to prevent misappropriation of country's traditional medicinal knowledge through patenting worldwide.

| | |
|---|---|
| Government | • Enhanced Transparency-through TKDL publicly available under an open-source license → allows for public scrutiny → fosters transparency in the government's approach to safeguarding traditional knowledge.<br>• Global leadership-Open access to TKDL can elevate India's standing on the world stage.<br>• Fostering Collaboration-Open-source licensing creates an environment conductive to international collaboration and partnerships. |
| Indigenous Communities and Traditional Healers | • Safeguarding Heritage-Preserving and promoting time-tested healin practices and knowledge passed down through generations within indigenous communities.<br>• Empowering Traditions-By making this knowledge openly accessible through TKDL, traditional healers and local communities receive well-deserved recognition for their invaluable contributions. |
| Pharmaceutic and Biotech | • Treasure Trove for Drug Discovery-TKDL serves as a repository of traditional knowledge for pharmaceutical companies.<br>• Safeguarding Innovation-Open access to TKDL empowers companies to make informed decisions during the research and development process. |
| Global Stakeholders | • Preventing Wrongful Patents-TKDL access to a vast database of traditional knowledge, it allows patent offices to verify and compare applications, preventing the accidental granting of patents that already exist as traditional knowledge. |

## Concerns Associated with TKDL

| | |
|---|---|
| Government | • Uncontrolled Dissemination- Unrestricted public access to TKDL → Exploitation of Valuable information by unethical actors for unauthorized commercial purposes.<br>• Intellectual Property Ambiguity- Open-accessibility may lead to misinterpretation or misuse of traditional knowledge outside its cultural context. |
| Pharmaceuticals Biotech Industries | • Reduced Commercialization- The potential for exclusive ownership and commercialization of research findings might be limited, impacting potential profits.<br>• Eroding Competitive Edge- Competitors can readily access the research, diminishing the initial advantage of the early developers. |
| Global Stakeholders | • Linguistic Inaccessibility- Despite the TKDL's commendable translation efforts, ensuring complete comprehension and utilization of the knowledge by all researchers may be hindered by persistent language barriers. |

## Achievements of TKDL

- Colgate-Palmolive's Nutmeg Mouthwash Patent Denied:
  - Colgate-Palmolive's attempt to patent a mouthwash containing nutmeg extract (Myristica fragans) was unsuccessful. The application, filed in 2010 and assigned number EP2689806. was rejected due to prior knowledge and existing use of nutmeg's in traditional Indian medicinal practices for oral health.
- TKDL preserves India's rich yoga heritage- by documenting over 1500 yoga postures (asanas) → preventing foreign entities from patenting these ancient practices. This initiative has already seen success in major countries like the USA, Japan and several European nations.
- India Protects Hair loss Remedy:
  - A UK company, Pangaea Laboratories, attempted to patent a hair loss formula in 2011. Their formula included curcumin, pine bark extract and green tea extracts as the key ingredients.
  - CSIR through TKDL demonstrated that these ingredients have been used for centuries in Indian medicine (Ayurveda and Unani) to treat hair loss.

# BIOTECHNOLOGY

**About:** According to Organisation for Economic Co-operation and Development (OECD), Biotechnology is application of science and technology to living organisms, as well as parts, products and models thereof, to alter living or non-living materials for the production of knowledge, goods and services.

- India ranks 12th largest biotechnology economy in the world and 3rd in Asia-Pacific and holds 2nd highest number of plants approved by the US Food and Drug Administration (USFDA).

## Status of Biotechnology in India

- India exports vaccines to more than 150 countries and is a prime destination for contract manufacturing and clinical trials.
- There are a total of 6,756 biotech startups in India in 2022.

| | |
|---|---|
| US$ 12 billion<br>India's Biotech Industry Revenue | 1 million<br>India's Biotech Work Force |
| 6000+<br>Biotech Companies in India. | 15500+<br>Biotech Graduates Every year. |

- India's bio-economy industry has grown from US$ 10 billion in 2015 to US$ 130 billion in 2024.
- The Indian biotechnology industry is likely to reach US$ 150 billion by 2025 and has the potential to reach US$ 270-300 billion by the year 2030.

### Type of Biotechnology

- Red Biotechnology- Biopharma a relates to medicine and veterinary products.
- White Biotechnology- Industrial Biotech a to design more energy efficient, low resource consuming products.
- Yellow Biotechnology- Biotech in the Food Industry.
- Grey Biotechnology- Environmental applications to maintain Biodiversity.
- Green Biotechnology- Emphasizes on Agriculture interests.
- Blue Biotechnology- based on use of marine resources.
- Violet Biotechnology- deals with law, ethical and philosophical issues of biotechnology.
- Dark Biotechnology- associated with bioterrorism and biological weapons.

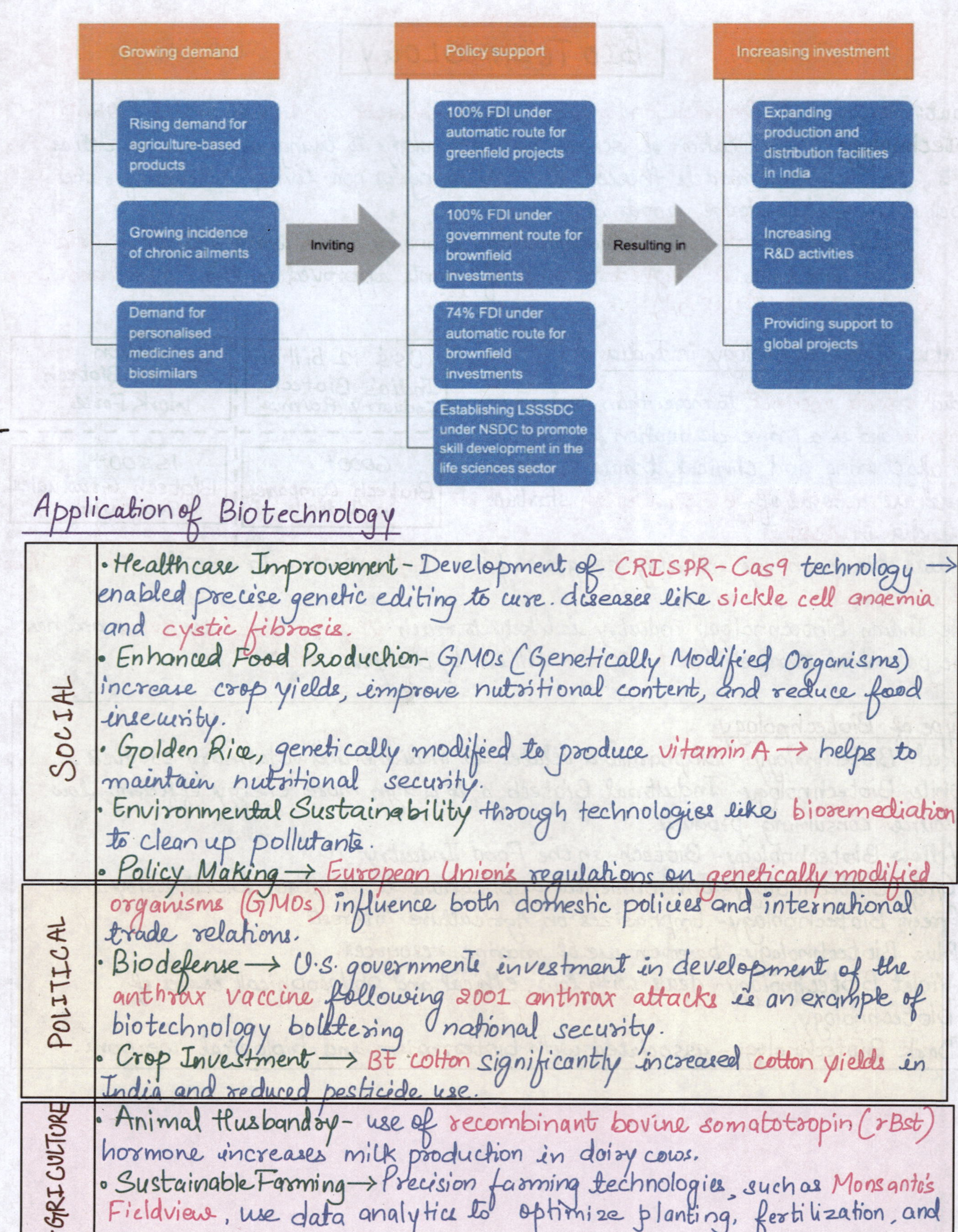


## Application of Biotechnology

| | |
|---|---|
| SOCIAL | • Healthcare Improvement - Development of CRISPR-Cas9 technology → enabled precise genetic editing to cure diseases like sickle cell anaemia and cystic fibrosis.<br>• Enhanced Food Production - GMOs (Genetically Modified Organisms) increase crop yields, improve nutritional content, and reduce food insecurity.<br>• Golden Rice, genetically modified to produce vitamin A → helps to maintain nutritional security.<br>• Environmental Sustainability through technologies like bioremediation to clean up pollutants. |
| POLITICAL | • Policy Making → European Union's regulations on genetically modified organisms (GMOs) influence both domestic policies and international trade relations.<br>• Biodefense → U.S. governments investment in development of the anthrax vaccine following 2001 anthrax attacks is an example of biotechnology bolstering national security.<br>• Crop Investment → Bt cotton significantly increased cotton yields in India and reduced pesticide use. |
| AGRICULTURE | • Animal Husbandry - use of recombinant bovine somatotropin (rBst) hormone increases milk production in dairy cows.<br>• Sustainable Farming → Precision farming technologies, such as Monsanto's Fieldview, use data analytics to optimize planting, fertilization, and |

| | |
|---|---|
| | irrigation.<br>• Enhancing Soil Fertility and Nutrient Management for Staple Crops by application of Microbial inoculants and biofertilizers.<br>• Blue biotechnology leverages power of marine organisms which include aquaculture (fish farming), development of transgenic cold-resistant fish varieties. |
| SECURITY | • Biodefense → Fighting against use of bioweapons like weaponised viruses by early detection and containment.<br>• Biosecurity and Biosafety → Development of secure protocols and containment systems for handling and storing hazardous biological materials. |
| LEGAL | • Forensic Biotechnology- Use of DNA profilling and DNA fingerprinting in investigation and prosecution of crimes. |
| ENVIRONMENT | • Pollution Control- Use of Pseudomonas putida, a genetically engineered bacterium, to degrade toluene and other pollutants in contaminated soil and water.<br>• Conservation - cloning of endangered species like - black-footed- ferret to preserve genetic diversity and prevent extinction.<br>• Sustainable Development- Production of bioplastics from corn starch, such as PLA (poly lactic acid) → offer biodegradable alternatives to traditional petroleum- based plastics.<br>• DNA barcoding- for species identification and conservation. |
| INDUSTRY | • Biomanufacturing- Production of bioethanol from corn and sugarcane → reduces import dependency on fossil fuels and lower greenhouse gas emission<br>• Process Improvement- Use of enzymes in laundry detergents, improves cleaning efficiency at lower temperatures, saving energy.<br>• Product Development- Creation of genetically engineered yeast strains for the production of artemisinin, an antimalarial drug. |
| BIOPHARMA | • Drug Discovery and Development- by identifying a specific protein involved in cancer cell growth using gene sequencing genomics proteomics.<br>• Recombinant Protein Production- Production of human insulin using genetically modified E. coli bacteria.<br>• Monoclonal Antibodies (MAbs)- Development of Herceptin → that targets a specific receptor on breast cancer cells. |

- Gene Therapy- Luxturna treatment for a rare form of inherited blindness, uses a modified virus to deliver a healthy copy of the RPE65 gene to retinal cells.
- Personalized Medicine- Genetic testing, biomarker analysis, and gnomic profilling, to tailor treatment-plans for individual patients, considering their unique genetic makeup and disease characteristics.
- Drug Delivery Systems- Developing liposomes tiny fat-based spheres, to encapsulate a drug and deliver it directly to tumor cells.
- Bioprocessing and Manufacturing- Engineering cells for higher yields, optimizing fermentation conditions, + refining purification processes to ensure efficient and cost-effective production of therapeutic products.

## Challenges Associated with Biotechnology

### SOCIAL

- GM crops- Engineered seeds widen the gap between small and big farmers.
- High cost of agriculture- Terminator technology locks farmers in, forcing them to buy new seeds each season.

### LEGAL

- Seed Royalty Battles- Monsanto's Bt cotton technology exemplifies a legal dispute in GMOs. Seed companies using this technology must pay royalties to Monsanto, raising concerns about seed ownership and access.
- Regulatory Hurdles- can delay the introduction of potentially life-saving products and technologies to the market.

### HEALTH.

- GM Food Safety for Humans- Ongoing scientific discussions about their long-term health effects raises concern over human health.
- Public Perception of Biotech- Public concerns regarding the safety and environmental impact of biotechnologies.

### ENVIRONMENT.

- Biotechnology and invasive Species- Minimise risks of genetically modified (GM) crops becoming invasive or polluting the gene pool of wild relatives.

- Biotech Waste Management- Implement responsible practices for handling laboratory waste and byproducts from biotechnological processes to reduce environmental impact and ensure safe disposal.
- Biosafety and Biosecurity- Prioritize robust biosafety measures and biosecurity protocols to prevent accidental release or potential risks associated with genetically modified organisms (GMOs).

## TECHNICAL

- Biotech breakthroughs require:
  - High-tech labs: Advanced equipment and facilities are crucial.
  - Fast access to supplies: Costly research materials need rapid delivery.

- Biotech manufacturing bottleneck:
- limited production capacity- Existing parks lack facilities for full-scale drug production.
- Service focus- Current emphasis is on diagnostics and research services, not drug manufacturing.

## IPR

- India's Talent Drain- Leading global biotech companies lure away India's top minds with lucrative offers, hindering research and development.
- Quality vs. Quantity in Research- The pressure to publish research papers in India incentivizes quantity over quality.
- Limited Innovation- Dominant public funding in Indian biotech research restricts applied innovation, as private sector involvement and academic collaboration are crucial for advancements.
- Intellectual Property Hurdles: Uncertainity around intellectual property rights, including patent protection and enforcement, discourages investment and hinders the transfer of valuable technologies.

SECTORAL ANALYSIS OF INDIA'S BIOTECHNOLOGY

## Advantages of India in tapping Biotechnology

### 1. Skilled human capital

- With a total population of 1.4 billion, 47% being under the age of 25, India has a large pool of young and skilled workforce.
- India has a large reservoir of scientific human resources including scientists and engineers.
- Biotechnology has emerged as a trending career option among the youth. According to a survey of Class 12th students in Delhi, Biotechnology was ranked as the preferred stream at No.4/5.

### 2. Infrastructure facilities

- 9 DBT-supported biotech parks and 60 BIRAC-supported bio-incubators.
- In the Interim Budget 2024-25, the Department of Biotechnology (DBT) was allotted Rs. 2,251.52 crore (US$ 271 million).
- Dr. Jitendra Singh inaugurates the Northeast's first International Biotech Conclave.
- In February 2023, Serum Institute of India announces centre of excellence in Hyderabad to tackle future pandemics.
- Dr. Jitendra Singh, inaugurated a new Biotechnology Centre for Northeast tribals in the remote area of Kimin (Arunachal Pradesh).
- In July 2023, 15 companies sign MoUs worth Rs. 2,000 crore (US$ 239.99 million), in a day, for investments in biotech sector.

**Source:** *Department of Biotechnology, FDI India*

ADVANTAGE INDIA

1 2 3 4

### 4. Epidemiological factors

- Patient pool expected to increase over 20% in the next 10 years, mainly due to rise in population.
- New diseases & lifestyle changes to boost demand for drugs and devices.

### 3. Policy support

- National Biopharma Mission is supporting 101 projects including more than 150 organizations and 30 MSMEs. It has increased employment opportunities and engaged 1,065 manpower including 304 scientists/ researchers.
- While 74% is permitted under automatic route for brownfield projects, 100% under government route is permitted for brownfield investments.
- DPIIT's launched Startup SEED fund scheme is inspired by BIRAC's BIG scheme and guided by BIRAC's MII cell interface.
- The National Biotechnology Development Strategy 2020-25, provides the government with a platform to strengthen skill development, resource and innovation converging into one strong ecosystem for knowledge sharing.

Opportunities in various segments

## Bio-Services

- India has potential for clinical trials due to a large and low-cost market.
- Clinical trials in India are regulated by the Central Drug Standard Control Organisation, which has reduced approval time to about 30-60 days, giving opportunity for market growth.
- The country also has the advantage of English-speaking researchers and required medical infrastructure to conduct medical research.

## Bioindustrials

- Biofuels and bioenergy are considered alternative resources and are gaining popularity in India.
- Rise in energy demand is leading to an increase in dependence on fossil fuel imports.
- As a result, companies can develop a strategy to reduce import dependence through biofuels and bioenergy.

## Biopharma

- The Indian biologics market is expected to register a CAGR of 22% from 2019 to 2025, to reach US$ 12 billion by 2025.
- Growth of biologics provides opportunity for biosimilars in the market.

## Bio-Agri

- India's Union budget 2021-22 stated the government's plan to enhance farm productivity and focus on food security.
- This increased the importance of bio-agriculture, which will enhance efficient food production.

## Bio-IT

- Biotechnology has immense growth potential in the Bio-IT segment, given the rising need for technology to transform data generated by R&D institutes, clinics, hospitals, etc., into a defined format.
- India's IT industry is witnessing substantial growth and has the requisite IT infrastructure to cater to the needs of the global Bio-IT industry.

# STEM CELL THERAPY

About Stem Cell- Stem cells are undifferentiated and unspecialised cells with the ability to evolve into differentiated and specialized cell types in the body, acting as a continuous repair system that replenishes other cells throughout an organism's lifespan.

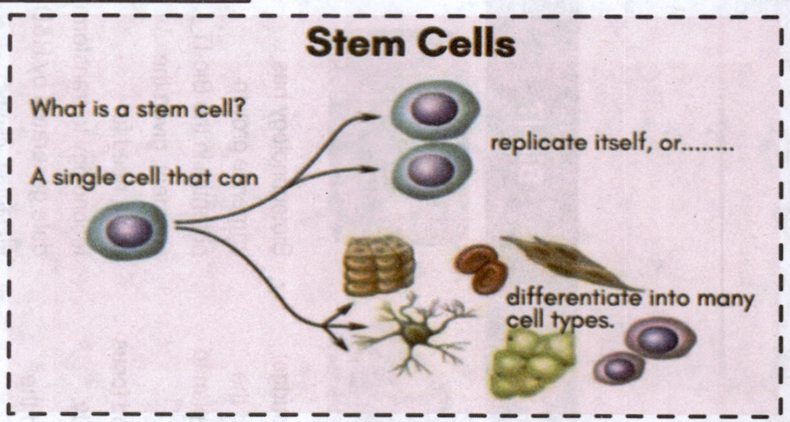


About Stem Cell- Stem cell therapy leverages the unique potential of stem cells to treat or prevent diseases.

- Stem cell Transplants used to treat diseases like Leukaemia, Lymphoma, Myeloma, Aplastic anemia, Sickle cell disease that do not respond to other treatments like chemotherapy and radiation therapy.

## Types of Stem Cell Therapy

- Autologous Stem Cell Transplant- Patients stem cells, taken from bone marrow or blood, are saved before a treatment that destroys blood cells. Post-treatment, these cells are re-infused into the patient to aid recovery.
- Allogeneic Stem Cell Transplant- Stem cells are donated from a matched donor's (sibling, parent, or unrelated person) bone marrow or blood and given to the patient.

### Status in India

- Stem cells and their derivatives fall under definition of 'Drug' as per the Drugs and Cosmetics Act 1940 and are categorized as 'Investigational New Drug (IND)' or 'Investigational New Entity (INE)' when used for clinical application.
- Regulated by National Guidlines for Stem Cell Research-2017: Only bone marrow/ hematopoietic SCT for blood disorders is permitted and use of stem cells all other conditions has to be done only under purview of clinical trials in compliance with National Guidlines for STEM CELL RESEARCH 2017.

## Advantages of Stem Cell Therapy

- Cellular Precision and Targeted Therapy- Focus on repairing or replacing only damaged cells → instead of chemotherapy which acts like a shotgun, hitting both healthy and cancerous cells.

- Ex- Thalassemia Leukaemia → by targeting abnormally rising WBC.

- Beacon of hope- It offers cure for diseases like Thalassemia, Alzheimer's and Parkinsons which were previously considered untretable or only manageable with lifelong therapies.
- Reduced Reliance on Organ Donation- It will address issues of limited donor availability and rejection risks.
- Pain Management and Improved Function- It reduces inflammation and modulates immune system, leading to pain relief and improved functionality in conditions affecting muscles, joints or nerves.
- Ex - Osteoarthritis → can be used by regenerating damaged cartilage in the knee, potentially reducing pain and improving joint mobility.
- Drug Development- Stem cells allow scientists to test new drugs for safety and effectiveness.
  - Ex- Heart cells from stem cells streamline drug testing for heart diseases, reducing animal testing.
- Regenerative Potential- It allows to replace damaged or diseased tissue, promoting regeneration where the body may struggle on its own.
  - Ex- Advancement in Stem Cell Therapy can be effectively utilized to treat Acid attack victims.

## Challenges Associated with Stem Cell Therapy

- Manufacturing and contamination issues- Especially pluripotent stem cells. which have the ability to form any type of cell in the body → If not manufactured correctly, there is a risk that they could develop into tumours.
- Limited understanding of stem cell biology- makes it difficult to develop effective stem cell therapies.
- Delivery of stem cells- to the right place in the body is another challenge, Stem cells need to be delivered to the damaged tissue in order to be effective.
- Upfront Cost- Stem cell therapy is very expensive due to costs of manufacturing stem cells and developing stem cell therapies.
- Ethical considerations- There are some ethical concerns surrounding stem cells and developing stem cell therapy.
  Ex- Use of embryonic stem cells is controversial.
- Gastrointestinal issues- Patients may experience diarrhea, nausea, vomiting or other digestive problems as a result of the transplant and accompanying treatments.

## Way Forward in Stem Cell Therapy

- Enhancing Oversight - A tiered regulatory framework → to establish clear guidlines for basic research, clinical trials, and product development based on the type of stem cell and the extent of manipulation involved.
- Empowering Patients - Informed consent in stem cell trials is paramount. Researchers must provide realistic and clear explanations of potential risks and benefits in language that participants can easily understand.
- Scientific Rigour - Stringent scientific measures are essential to guarantee the safety quality control of stem cell products for human use.

## CHIMERIC ANTIGEN RECEPTOR T-CELL THERAPY

About :- CAR-T cell Therapy is a type of immunotherapy that uses a patients own immune system to fight cancer.

- It has been approved for diseases like leukaemias, lymphomas and myeloma.
- It is referred to as 'living drugs' → since 2017, six CAR T-cell therapies have been approved by Food and Drug Administration (FDA).

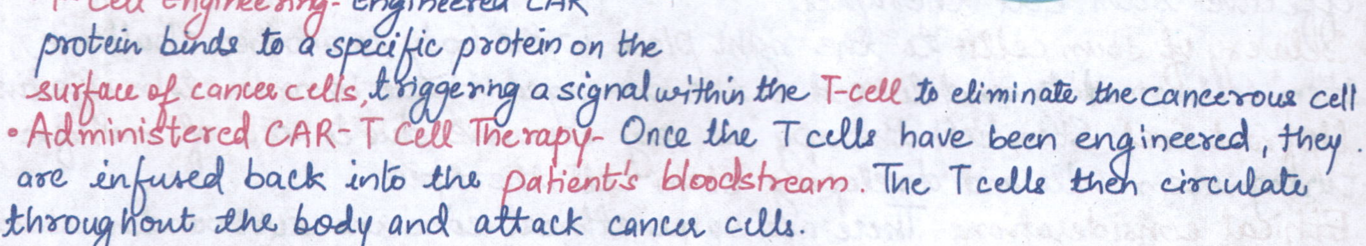


- T-Cell Collection - It involves extracting T-cells from a patient's blood and modifying them to possess a chimeric antigen receptor (CAR).
- T-Cell Engineering - Engineered CAR protein binds to a specific protein on the surface of cancer cells, triggering a signal within the T-cell to eliminate the cancerous cell
- Administered CAR-T Cell Therapy - Once the T cells have been engineered, they are infused back into the patient's bloodstream. The T cells then circulate throughout the body and attack cancer cells.

## Benefits Offered by CAR-T Cell Therapy

- New Hope for Advanced Cancers - CAR-T therapy offers a chance for complete remission in patients with advanced cancers who haven't responded to other treatments.
- Precise Strike - CAR-T therapy targets only cancer cells with a specific protein, leaving healthy cells unharmed. This precision can lead to better results with fewer side effects compared to traditional therapies.

- Impressive Results- CAR-T therapy has been particularly effective against certain blood cancers, like Leukaemia and Lymphoma achieving remission in patients who haven't benefitted from other treatments.
- One-Time Treatment- CAR-T therapy involves a single infusion of engineered T-cells that can provide lasting effects.
- Custom-Made Therapy- CAR-T therapy can be personalized for each patients by targeting the specific proteins on their cancer cells.

## Challenges Associated with CAR-T Cell Therapy

- Cytokine Release Syndrome is a systemic inflammatory response triggered by activation and proliferation of CAR-T cells in the body.
- Cytopenias - CAR-T cell treatment may lead to cytopenias → which includes anaemia, neutropenia and platelets (thrombocytopenia)
- It will increase the risk of infections, bleeding, and other complications.
- Immune Effector Cell- Associated Syndrome- ICANS encompasses a range of neurological symptoms associated with CAR-T-cell therapy, including confusion. aphasia and seizures.
- Tumour Lysis Syndrome (TLS)- Rapid destruction of cancer cells following CAR-T cell therapy can lead to release of intracellular contents into bloodstream. causing metabolic abnormalities such as hyperkalemia, hyperuricemia, and acute kidney injury.

## Way Forward

| Affordability | CRS Management |
|---|---|
| • Negotiate better deals with manufacturer<br>• Explore value-based pricing models (pay for results).<br>• Invest in streamlining production processes to reduce costs. | • Develop standard protocols for early detection and treatment.<br>• Train healthcare providers to identify and manage CRS effectively.<br>• Emphasize close monitoring and timely intervention |

| Minimising Cytopenias | Immune Effector Cell-Associated |
|---|---|
| • Implement supportive care to manage potential blood cell deficiencies.<br>• Optimize CAR T-cells dosage to balance effectiveness and side effects. | • Standardize. methods for assessing and managing ICANs symptoms.<br>• Conduct research to understand ICANs better and identify risk factors. |

# India's Genome Project

- About - It endeavors to sequence 10000 Indian human genomes and create a database.
  - It is inspired by the (international Human Genome Project) carried out by 20 national institutes with support from Department of Biotechnology.
  - A genome is a genetic material that provides instructions for development growth, and functioning of all living organisms, composed of DNA with a sequence of chemical bases that determines an organism's characteristics.

## Significance of Genome India Project

- Understanding Disease in India's rich genetically diverse population. GIP aims to sequence 10000 Indian genomes to create a database specific to Indian Population → to decode the nuances manifestation of disease and genetic diversity
- Precision Healthcare - By analyzing these genomes, GIP paves way for developing personalized medicine.
  - It allows for targeted interventions and therapies, leading to better healthcare outcomes.
- Drug Discovery - GIP can aid in discovering potential drug targets. By identifying disease-causing mutations, researchers can design drugs to counteract those specific mutations.
- Addressing Complex Diseases - It will focus on diseases like cancer, diabetes and neurological disorders which have a complex interplay between genes and environment.
- Rare Genetic Disorders - GIP will help to identify India's rare genetic disorders leading to earlier diagnosis, better genetic counseling.
- Predictive Diagnostics - It aims to develop markers that predict disease susceptibility based on an individual's genes.
- Pharmacogenomics - By understanding a person's genetic makeup → doctors can prescribe drugs with better efficacy and fewer side effects.

## Challenges Against Genome Project

- Representative Diversity - Sequencing 10000 genomes doesn't fully represent India's diverse population of over one billion, comprising around 4500 population groups.
- Complex Genetic Landscape - India's history of endogamy within castes preserves rare, potentially harmful genetic variants, complicating genetic analysis

• Limitations of Monogenic Disease Focus- Most diseases are not monogenic posing challenges in simplifying genetic research to establish direct disease links.
• Data accessibility - Ensuring widespread access to project findings beyond academia is a significant challenge.
• Ethical concerns - regarding sensitive genomic data sharing, data security and privacy.

## Way Forward

• Ensuring Ethical Conduct: GIP must prioritize ethical considerations → Robust safeguards are crucial to guarantee that project adheres to the highest ethical standards.
  • It includes protecting individual privacy and upholding human rights throughout the research process.
• Balancing Speed and Caution- While GIP holds immense potential for advancements in biotechnology, agriculture and healthcare in India, a balanced approach is necessary.
  • It should prioritize both speed in scientific discovery and caution in handling sensitive genetic data.
  • Addressing privacy concerns, preventing data misuse, and upholding medical ethics are essential for responsible research.

## PYQs Corner
*(Write the Answer and Get Free Evaluation)*

1. What are the research and developmental achievements in applied biotechnology? How will these achievements help to uplift the poorer sections of the society? [250 Words] [15 Marks] [2021]
2. How can biotechnology help to improve the living standards of farmers? [250 Words] [15 marks][2019]
3. How is the Government of India protecting traditional knowledge of medicine from patenting by pharmaceutical companies? [250 Words] [15 marks] [2019]
4. Why is there so much activity in the field of biotechnology in our country? How has this activity benefited the field of bio pharma? [250 Words] [15 marks] [2018]
5. Stem cell therapy is gaining popularity in India to treat a wide variety of medical conditions including leukaemia, Thalassemia, damaged cornea and several burns. Describe briefly what stem cell therapy is and what advantages it has over other treatments? [150 Words] [10 Marks] [2017]
6. India's Traditional Knowledge Digital Library (TKDL) which has a database containing formatted information on more than 2 million medicinal formulations is proving a powerful weapon in country's fight against erroneous patents. Discuss the pro and cons of making the data base available publicly available under open-source licensing. [200 Words] [12.5 Marks] [2015]
7. Can overuse and free availability of antibiotics without Doctor's prescription, be contributors to the emergence of drug-resistant diseases in India? What are the available mechanisms for monitoring and control? Critically discuss the various issues involved. [200 Words] [12.5 Marks][2014]

CHAPTER 21

# NUCLEAR ENERGY

## ENERGY MIX

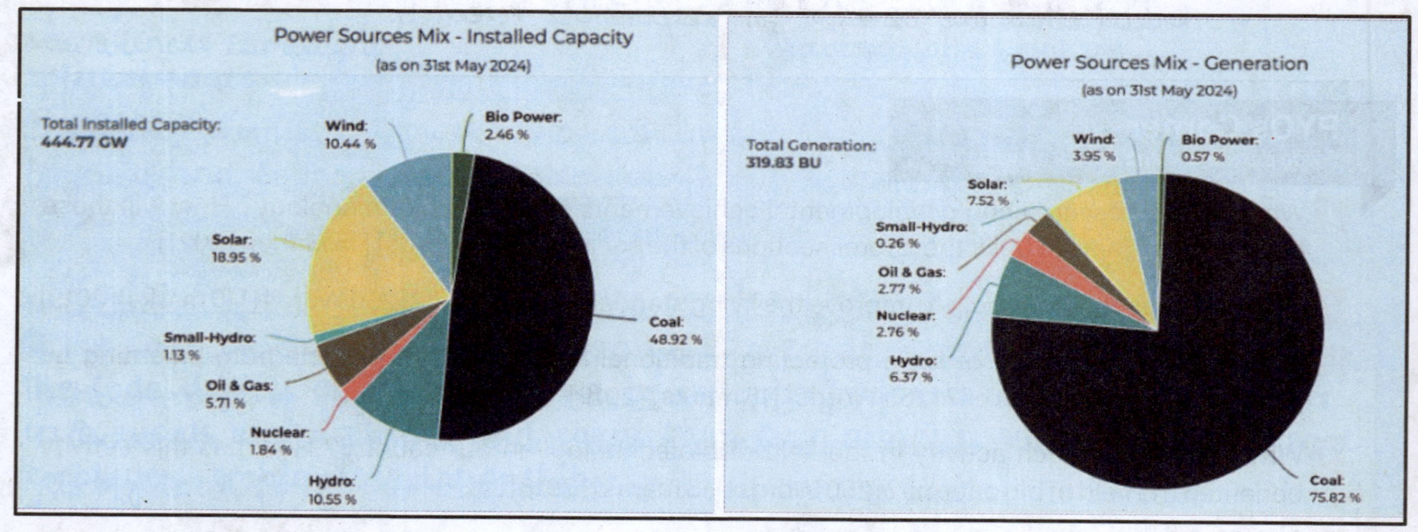


- Fossil fuels is the primary source of power (>50%).
- Renewable energy contributes more than 40% to the total installed power capacity.

India presented the following five nectar elements (Panchamrit) of India's climate action at COP 26:

1. Reach 500 GW non-fossil energy capacity by 2030.
2. 50% of its energy requirements from renewable energy by 2030.
3. Reduction of total projected carbon emissions by one billion tonnes from now to 2030.
4. Reduction of carbon intensity of an economy by 45% by 2030 over 2005 levels.
5. Net zero emissions target by 2070.

# NUCLEAR ENERGY

- Energy related from the Nucleus (core) of an atom.

Compact Nucleus of an atom has tremendous amount of energy & the nucleus is held together by a "strong Force". This nucleus of atom undergoes changed either through nuclear fission or fusion & in turn releases tremendous amount of energy.

- Nuclear Fuel is utilised to generate heat - which is then utilized to generate electrical power.

Nuclear Fuel —Heat→ Steam Generation —Pressure steam→ Mechanical Energy —Turbines Rotate→ Electrical Energy

- Double-Edged Sword
  - → May be the cheapest, Greenest & Safest source
  - → Responsible for worst Disasters known to Mankind (eg- chernobyl, Atom Bombs (Japan))

| | Nuclear Fission | Nuclear Fusion |
|---|---|---|
| Definition: | splitting of large nuclei into smaller ones. | Joining of smaller nuclei together to give larger atom. |
| Natural occurence | Doesnot normally occur in nature. | Fusion consistently occurs in stars such as SUN. |
| Energy Requirements | Little energy required to split atoms in fission reaction. | Extremely high energy required to bring two or more protons close enough that nuclear forces, overcome their electrostatic repulsion. |
| Energy Released | Million times greater than that released in Chemical Reactions, but lower than Fusion Reaction. | Three to four times greater energy released than the energy released by fission. |
| Conditions Required | 1. Critical Mass of Substance<br>2. High-speed Neutrons. | 1. High-Density.<br>2. High-Temperature. |
| By products | Many highly radioactive particles (More waste) | Few Radioactive particles produced (less radioactive waste). |
| Fuel | Uranium-235, Plutonium-239.<br>1. Nuclear Power Plants<br>2. Atom Bomb. | $H_2$ isotopes (Deuterium, Tritium)<br>1. China's Artificial Sun.<br>2. ITER (International Thermonuclear Experimental Reactor).<br>3. $H_2$- Bomb. |

# DISTRIBUTION OF ATOMIC MINERALS

India has huge reserves of Atomic minerals. Uranium & Thorium are the main atomic minerals to which may be added i.e. Beryllium, Lithium & Zirconium.

## → Uranium

Uranium is a silvery-gray metallic radioactive chemical element.

- It is only naturally formed in supernova explosions.
- Worldwide Distribution : About 2/3rd of world's production of Uranium from mines is from Kazakhstan, Canada & Australia. In 2022, Kazakhstan produced the largest share of Uranium from mines (43% of world's supply), followed by Canada (15%) & Namibia (11%).
- Distribution in India : Uranium deposits occur in Singhbhum & Hazaribagh districts of Jharkhand, Gaya district of Bihar, & in the sedimentary rocks in Saharanpur district of UP. But the largest source of Uranium comprise the Monazite sands.
  - Monazite sands occur on East & West coasts and in some places in Bihar. But largest concentration of monazite sands is on the Kerala coast.
  - Some U deposits are found in copper mines of Udaipur, Rajasthan.
  - India produces about 2% of World's Uranium.

URANIUM DEPOSITS IN INDIA

Major Uranium Deposits

Rohil
North Delhi Fold Belt
**Vein Type**

Domiasiat, Wahkyn
Mahadeks
**Sandstone type**

Jaduguda, Narwapahar
Singhbhum Shear Zone
**Vein Type**

Gogi
Bhima Basin
**Vein Type**

Lambapur, Chitrial
N Cuddapah Basin
**Unconformity related**

Tummalapalle
S Cuddapah Basin
**Stratabound**

- Uranium Deposits
- A.M.D. Headquarters & SCR Hqrs.
- Regional Headquarters
- Sectional Headquarters

→ Thorium

- Thorium-232 is the most stable isotope of Thorium & accounts for nearly all natural thorium.
- Thorium is several times more abundant in Earth's crust than all isotopes of Uranium combined and Thorium-232 is several hundred times more abundant than U-235.
- India & Australia are believed to possess more than half of world's Thorium reserves.
- Main reserve include Monazite beach sands in Kerala. Found in Andhra Pradesh (largest producer), TN, Odisha, Kerala and WB.

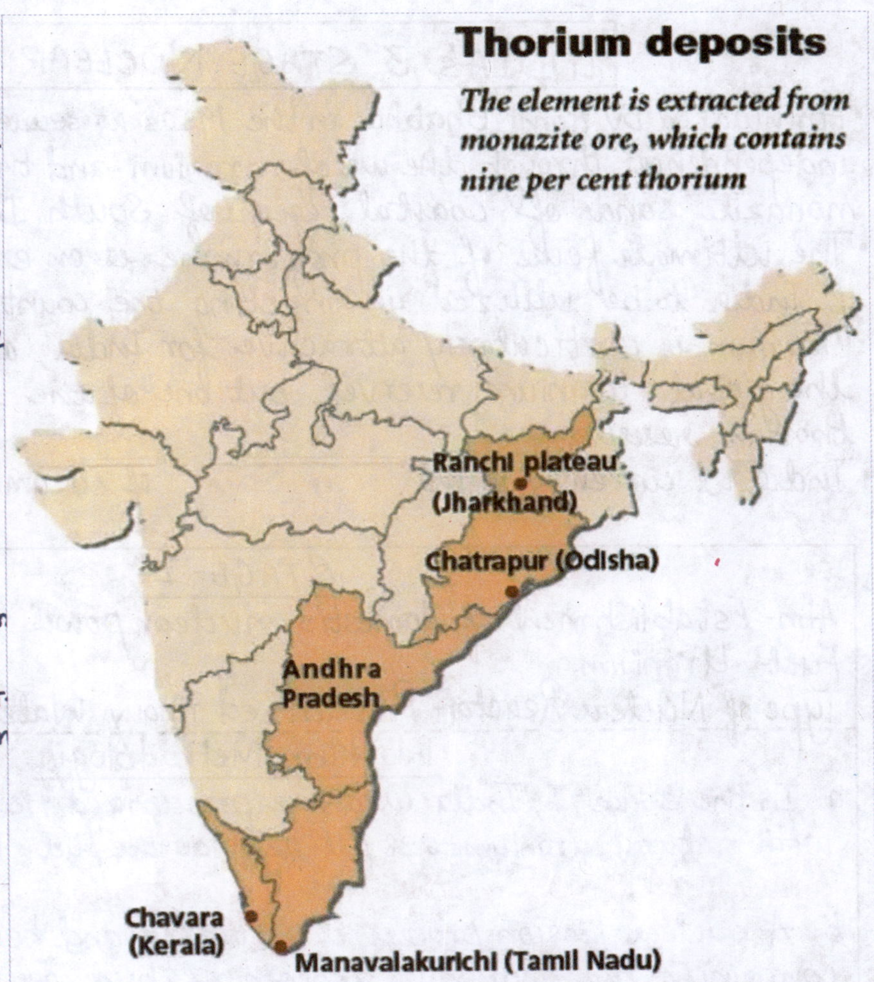


→ Operational Nuclear Reactors.

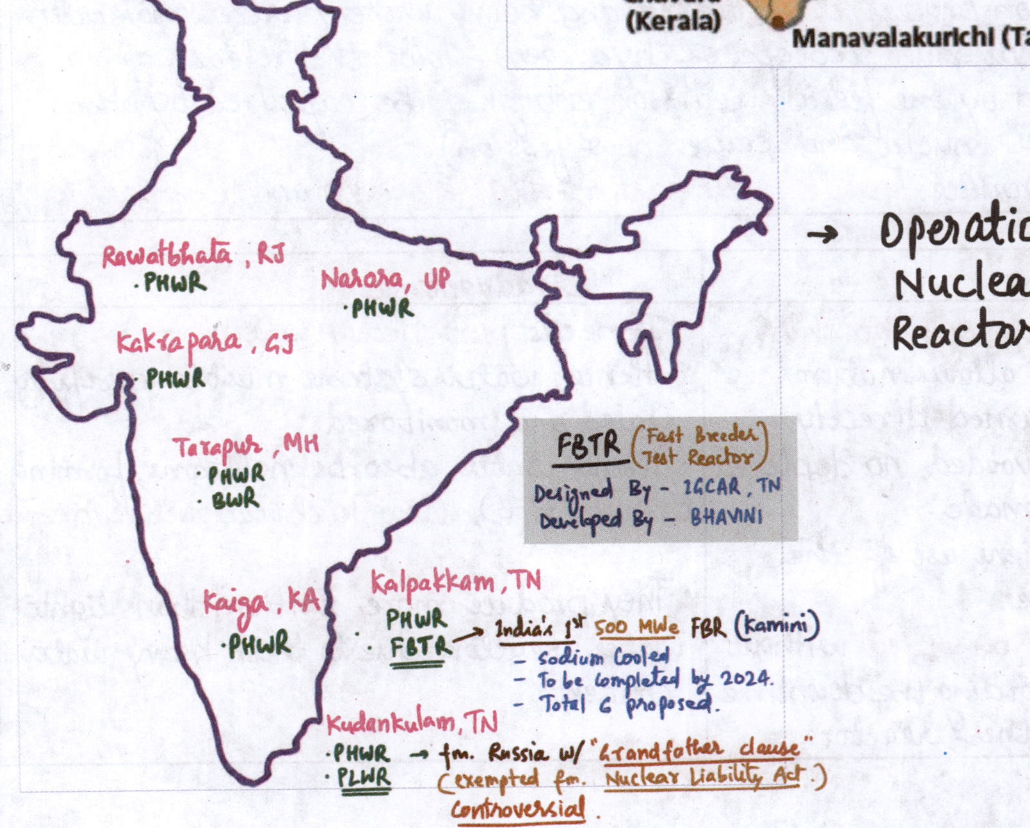

# INDIA'S 3 STAGE NUCLEAR PROGRAMME

- Formulated by Homi Bhabha in the 1950s to secure the country's long term energy independence, through the use of uranium and thorium reserves found in the monazite sands of coastal regions of South India.
- The ultimate focus of the programme is on enabling the thorium reserves of India to be utilized in meeting the country's energy requirements.
- Thorium is particularly attractive for India, as it has only around 1-2% of the global uranium reserves, but one of the largest shares of global thorium reserves.
- India is currently in the Second stage of its ambitious nuclear program.

## STAGE-I

Aim- Establishment of domestic nuclear power industry.
Fuel- Uranium.
Type of Nuclear Reactor- Pressurized Heavy Water Reactors (PHWRs).

### Working Methodology

a. In the stage-I, India used the pressurized Heavy Water Reactors (PHWRs) with natural uranium-238 (U-238) as the fuel. The U-238 contained minuscule amounts of U-235, as the fissile material.
b. A nuclear fission process is initiated and heavy water (water molecules containing the deuterium isotope of hydrogen) slows the release of neutrons released by one fission reaction enough to be captured by other U-238 and U-235 nuclei and cause new fission).
c. The reactions produce fissile Plutonium-239 (Pu-239) and energy.

| Advantages | Disadvantages |
|---|---|
| • There is no need for enrichment.<br>• As heavy water allows natural uranium to be burned directly.<br>• As enrichment is avoided, no depleted uranium tails are made.<br>• This allows efficient use of the uranium resource.<br>• The reactor can be refuelled without shutting it down, avoiding the downtime required by most other reactors. | - It needs pure heavy water.<br>• Hence, water systems must be carefully sealed and monitored.<br>• Heavy water absorbs neutrons, forming tritium (H-3), a low-level radioactive hazard.<br>• They produce more tritium than light-water reactors due to their heavy water content. |

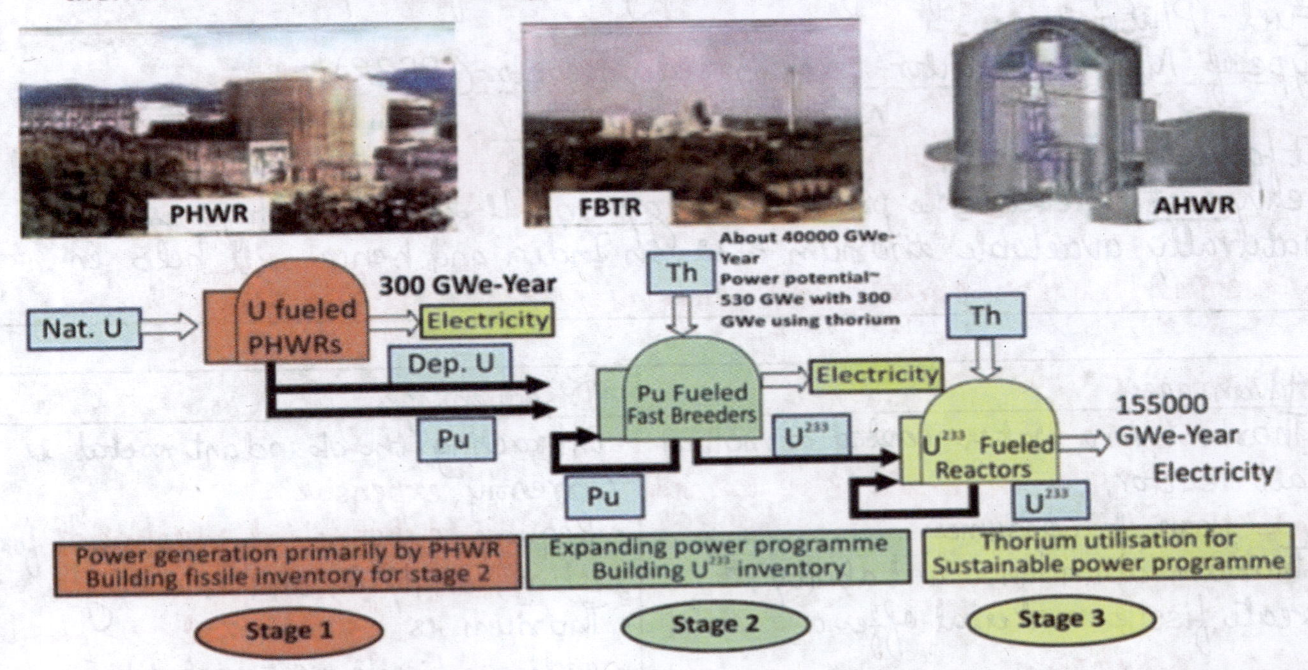


## STAGE-II

Aim- Development of self-sustaining nuclear fuel cycle.

Fuel- Plutonium.

Type of Nuclear Reactor- Fast Breeder Reactor (PFBR).

### Working Methodology

Only U-235 can sustain a chain fissile reaction. However, it is consumed fully in stage I. Hence, Stage II aims at using the fissile Plutonium-239 (Pu-239) produced as the end product of stage I with U-238 to produce energy, U-233 and more Pu-239. By the end of the second stage of the cycle, the reactor produces more fissile material than it consumes. Hence, it is called a 'Breeder' reactor. In these, 'fast breeder' reactor, the neutrons aren't slowed.

| Advantages | Disadvantages |
|---|---|
| • Safe and efficient.<br>• Green energy source because waste from the first stage nuclear program is reprocessed and used as fuel in FBR.<br>• Capability of efficient utilization of uranium. | - FBRs are cooled by liquid sodium, which reacts explosively with both air and water.<br>  • As a result, even a minor leak of sodium coolant can start a fire.<br>• FBRs containment dome is not as strong as in other reactors. |

## STAGE-III

- Aim- Development of self-sustaining nuclear fuel cycle.
- Fuel- Plutonium.
- Type of Nuclear Reactor- Fast Breeder Reactor (PFBR).

### Working Methodology

It focuses on combining Pu-239 with thorium-232 (Th-232) in advanced heavy water reactors to produce energy and U-233 This stage uses the naturally available thorium-232 in India and hence will help in achieving nuclear energy self-sufficiency.

| Advantages | Disadvantages. |
|---|---|
| • Thorium, in a water-cooled or molten salt reactor, can generate more uranium-233 than it consumes.<br>• Thorium abundance and ability to create fissile material offer a lasting energy solution.<br>• Thorium reactors may be greener, yielding less long-lived nuclear waste than uranium reactors.<br>• Thorium fuels are deemed proliferation resistant, unlike uranium fuels as they don't produce plutonium. | • Extracting the abundant metal is currently expensive.<br>• Require substantial investments for testing, analysis, and licensing.<br>• Thorium is 'fertile' and non-fissile, needing a fissile materéal like recycled plutonium for a chain reaction.<br>• High temperatures are essential due to the elevated melting point of thorium oxide for high-density production.<br>• Large amounts of Uranium-232 in irradiated thorium fuels can lead to substantial gamma-ray emissions. |

## Advantages of India's 3-Stage Nuclear Programme

1. Energy Sovereignty- Fossil-based energy sources is the primary energy but India imports a significant part of its fossil fuels (coal and gas) for energy generation, which raise economic and strategic vulnerabilities.
2. Decarbonisation of power sector- Thermal power plants have high carbon footprint as they contribute heavily to global warming, climate change and air pollution.
3. Step towards the achievement of India's COP-26 Goals and net-zero emission target by 2070.
4. limitations attached with other renewable energy sources - Solar energy is land intensive, wind energy requires energy storage systems.

- Also, they require imported technologies and matereals such as photovoltaic cells. batteries and storage equipment.
- Indigenous nuclear reactors have reduced dependency in critical imports.

5. Cheaper to Operate- Nuclear power plants are cheaper to operate than coal or gas plants, despite the cost of managing radioactive fuel and disposal.
   - According to estimates, nuclear plants cost only 33-50% of a coal plants and 20-25% of a gas combined-cycle plant.
6. Nuclear energy provide reliable and continuous base load power, unlike solar and wind energy, which are intermittent and dependent on weather conditions.
7. Resource Base- India has vast thorium reserves (monazite sands of coastal regions) which could be exploited using a thermal breeder reactor.
8. Creation of jobs and foster innovation, leading to economic growth.
9. Geographical Influence- India's nuclear program enhances its geo-political stature by fostering strategic partnerships and technological collaborations with leading global powers.

## Challenges before India's Nuclear Energy

1. Limited domestic resources of uranium- has forced the country to import a significant portion of its uranium requirements from the country like Canada, Russia, Kazakhstan, Uzbekistan etc.
2. Civil liability for Nuclear Damage Act (2010) in India has been a contentious issue
   - Foreign companies find it excessive, potentially making them liable for significant compensation in case of an accident.
   - Despite signing nuclear deals with various countries, foreign presence remains minimal, with Russia's Kudankulam project being an exception.
3. Limited private sector participation- especially in the area of operational control and fuel management that affects innovation and efficiency.
4. Technical Challenges- The development of nuclear power plants involve complex technical challenges, including the design and construction of reactors, the management of nuclear waste, and the maintenance of nuclear safety standards.
5. Land Acquisition- leading to delays in projects such as Kudankulam (Tamil Nadu) and Kovvada (Andhra Pradesh).
6. Environmental Impact- Nuclear power plants require cooling water, which affects aquatic ecosystems. Additionally, mining uranium can lead to habitat disruption and pollution.
7. Negative public perception- due to historical accidents and misconceptions about radiation safety can hinder nuclear energy adoption.

8. Regulatory Barriers- The regulatory framework for the development of nuclear power in India is complex and has been criticised for being slow and bureaucratic, leading to delays in the implementation of projects.

9. Nuclear power plants are capital intensive and recent nuclear builds have suffered major cost overruns.

10. Geological constraints- Identifying suitable sites for nuclear builds can be challenging due to geological factors like seismic activity and water availability.

11. Decommissioning Challenges- Properly decommissioning nuclear facilities is costly and time-consuming.

12. Safe disposal of radioactive materials remains a concern. India has not developed a comprehensive and long-term plan for managing and disposing of its nuclear waste.

## Futuristic measures to increase the share of Nuclear Energy

1. Indigenous Small Modular Reactors (SMRs) must be built at coal plant sites which would be retiring in the coming decades.
   SMRs offer the advantages of being safe, economical, compact and adaptable.
2. Expansion of indigenous PHWR reactors- The Indigenous 700 MWe PHWR, must be expanded in fleet mode to add to the installed nuclear power capacity in India.
3. Push to the Stage-3 of Nuclear Power Program to utilise the existing thorium energy potential in the country.
4. Development of Nuclear Fusion technology which is safer than nuclear fission.
5. Augmentation of safety of nuclear facilities- There must be constant updation of safety skills of nuclear operators.
6. Public Awareness- Further, masses must be comprehensively sensitised about the functioning of nuclear power plants using highly intellectual individuals having mass appeal.
   Forex- Dr APJ Abdul Kalam sensitizing the masses before the establishment of the Kudankulam nuclear power plant.
7. Ensuring Regulatory Autonomy- The AERB, India's nuclear regulatory body, must be provided functional autonomy by removing its reporting from the Department of Atomic Energy (DAE).

## PYQs Corner

*(Write the Answer and Get Free Evaluation)*

1. With growing energy needs should India keep on expanding its nuclear energy programme? Discuss the facts and fears associated with nuclear energy. [250 Words] [15 marks] [2018]
2. Give an account of the growth and development of nuclear science and technology in India. What is the advantage of fast breeder reactor programme in India? [250 Words] [15 marks] [2017]